COLLINS

EUROTUNNEL

Weekend Guide

Published in 1994 by
HarperCollins*Cartographic*
A Division of HarperCollins*Publishers*

EUROTUNNEL OFFICIAL GUIDE

C O N T

ENTS

museums, festival information . . . with some useful addresses for accommodation and eating out. Finally, six suggested themed routes.

MAP SHOWING RECOMMENDED ATTRACTIONS IN NORTHERN EUROPE AND SOUTH-EAST ENGLAND

Festivals, sites of outstanding natural beauty, noteworthy towns, museums, works of art, etc *(inside back cover)*

Picture captions:
Opposite, from left to right:
Pressure equalisation gallery; Cap Blanc-Nez (Pas-de-Calais); Scotney Castle (Kent); Rubens, Descent from the Cross (detail), Palais des beaux-arts, Lille

Authors

Philippe Demoulin

Pascaline Dron

Marie-Hélène Lavallée

Martine Le Blan

Monique Teneur-Van Daele

Contributors

Marie Vanesse: design

Martine Riboux: research and editorial assistance

Etudes et cartographie (Lille): maps and diagrams

Acknowledgements

Eurotunnel

Crédit du Nord
(Lille-Rouen)

ENGLISH EDITION

Stephanie Hammond: Translation, adaptation and co-ordination

Aardvark Editorial (Suffolk): Origination, proof reading and editorial assistance

Published in 1994 by
HarperCollins *Cartographic*
A Division of HarperCollins *Publishers*
77–85 Fulham Palace Road
London W6 8JB

© HarperCollins *Publishers*
and Casterman SA 1994

British Library Cataloguing in Publication Data

A catalogue record for this book is available from the British Library

Printed in Belgium

ISBN 0 0044 8164

Anglo-French relations in the making

"The Straits of Dover prevent the cordial joining of hands of two peoples who have so much in common. We shall drive a railway across it." These words of visionary Jules Verne go back some one hundred and fifty years.

Over the course of Anglo-French history some twenty-five different projects have sought to bring this vision to life.

Through the chronological countdown that follows, the reader can discover the people and the projects that have confronted the challenge, and how, little by little, they have overcome all the obstacles.

Opposite:
Colonel Beaumont's tunnel (19th century)

7

MAN AND THE SEA

"There the ocean hurls itself with mighty force upon the land, two times in every twenty-four hours, covering a huge area that one knows not whether to call land or sea. There the miserable inhabitants live on hillocks or man-made structures raised above the level of high tide. To see them at high tide you would call them seafarers, but at low-tide they look as if they might have been shipwrecked, cooking their food over mud (or peat), that wind rather than the sun has dried." Pliny the Elder, *A Natural History*.

The Roman conquest of the shores of the North Sea was a laborious affair, not least because the Belgians drew support and reinforcements from the people of south-eastern England. To push his victory home, Caesar crossed the Channel. Portus Itius (Calais) had become an important transit port during this period, since overland travel was difficult and dangerous. Conquest of the British Isles was seen as vital to ensuring continued Roman domination of the North Sea. In the year 40 AD, Caligula attempted a landing, but this was abandoned, though not before a lighthouse had been built at Gesoriacum (Boulogne). Three years later, Claude entrusted the command of 40,000 men gathered in the port to Aulus Plautius. This time the Britons were defeated and the invasion successful.

From the third century onwards, in the face of the Roman Empire's decline, marauding Frisians and Saxons roved the North Sea and Channel, attacking with increasing impunity. Around the fifth century, after the final withdrawal of Roman troops from the region, Angles, Jutes and Saxons gradually settled in England. The first Jutes arrived in Kent in 499 AD, followed by the Saxons (East Saxony: *Essex*, South Saxony: *Sussex*, West-Saxony: *Wessex*). The Britons joined forces with the earlier arrivals to fight against the Picts, but they had to retreat and take refuge in the mountains and in Armorique (present-day Brittany). Around the year 600 AD, the consolidation of Germanic kingdoms around the North Sea earned it the name *Oceanus germanicus*.

Principal tribes around the Channel and North Sea at the time of Roman colonisation

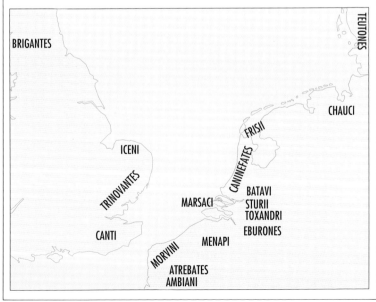

8,000 YEARS AGO . . .

Around 8000 BC, the part of France known as the Pas-de-Calais and which had previously been joined to England, became separated from it when the North Sea and the Channel merged into one: what was to be 'Britain' became an island, divided from the rest of the European continent by a 22-mile stretch of deep water; time passed and physical separation was reinforced by a developing separateness of outlook of the island's inhabitants. So much so that the French historian Michelet began a discourse at the Collège de France: "England is an island, and now you know as much about its history as I do . . ."!

Around 50 BC, Caesar made two landings in 'Britain' (the part of Britain we now call England); Celtic civilisation succumbed to the heavy imprint of Rome. Over a period of some four hundred years, this most distant of Rome's 'provinces' adopted Roman models of public administration, transportation and town planning.

4th century AD The Saxons came to England, then the Angles. The Anglo-Saxon identity was forged.

1066 William the Conqueror, 750 boats and 12,000 men, among them 6,000 horsemen, landed on the English shore at Pevensey in September 1066, and thus began a long period in Anglo-French relations when French princes ruled England and English kings ruled parts of France. But William the Conqueror's was the last invasion that England suffered, though the Spanish, Napoleon, and Hitler too, were all to try in time.

1337 Beginning of the One Hundred Years' War

17th century Large numbers of Huguenots fled France and came to England following the Revocation of the Edict of Nantes, which had afforded protection to non-Catholics. (These would be followed in 1789 by Royalists fleeing the French Revolution and, in 1940, by members of the French Resistance.) Alone among the European nations England adopted a system of parliamentary monarchy, limiting the power of the State and giving priority to the liberty of the individual. With maritime superiority combined with a strong economy, England was seen at this time to have outstripped her European neighbours: "L'Angleterre invente la machine au moment où la France invente la démocratie". (François Bédarida)

• **1694** Foundation of the Bank of England.

1750 Nicolas Desmaret prepared a report for the Academy of Amiens on the 'rupture of the isthmus', the physical separation of England from France that had created the Calais strait, and went on to propose a re-linking of the countries, by means of a tunnel, dyke or bridge.

1751 Nicolas Desmaret published a book entitled *Le Moyen d'améliorer la traversée de la Manche* (Ways to improve the crossing of the Channel).

CIVILISATION AROUND THE NORTH SEA AND THE CHANNEL

The Vikings

The advent of the 'men of the North' added a further page to the European history book: Norman and Viking bands roamed the seaboards, penetrating the interior by river and thence mounting commando attacks. Towards the end of the first millenium these invaders settled on the continental shore and, in fact, contributed to William's victory at Hastings. After 1066, the hitherto large-scale movement of peoples around Western Europe came to an end.

Western Europe is converted to Christianity

The civilising features that the Romans left behind were not lost, in large part thanks to the Christianity established among the Celts and Gauls. The first people to spread this religion further were demobilised Roman soldiers, among them a man named Victricus. He became Bishop of Rouen and converted the Morins and the Menapiens from the end of the sixth century onwards. Still further to the west, Christianity percolated through to those western parts of the British Isles where ancient Britons had scattered and taken refuge after the Anglo-Saxon invasions. Here, in the fifth century, a Celtic preacher called Pelaius was accused of heresy and challenged by Saint Germain for denying the concept of original sin. One of Saint Germain's followers, Saint Patrick, was to take Christianity to Ireland.

On the continent, Christianity spread rapidly through the Merovingian states (the first Frankish dynasty) of northern France, through the work of bishops and the political conversion of Clovis. A century after the arrival of the Saxons, Saint Augustine was made Bishop of Canterbury by Pope Gregory. Victricus' work in France was resumed by Lul, an Irishman, in Thérouanne (Pas-de-Calais), and in Flanders by Saint Armand. Little by little, the North Sea became Christian, and ever greater numbers of clergy gathered in monasteries to participate in the material life of the North Sea states. Tournai became the flourishing Merovingian capital.

Dykes and polders

Under the influence first of the monasteries and then of secular and civic institutions, men organised themselves into groups for the construction and maintenance of dykes, polders and drainage canals: activities first practised by the Frisians who created polders equipped with irrigation systems. An early refinement (known as the *wateringue*) consisted of a circular canal dug round reclaimed land, with sluice-gates for evacuating water at low tide. Around 1400 man- and animal-powered pumps improved water extraction rates. These were followed by windmills, first fixed-sail, then free-sail, oriented to wind direction and driving, first millwheels, and later and more efficiently, Archimedes' screws. Then came the steam-engine. The reclamation of the Haarlemmermeer (7,000 acres) was completed in twelve years (1852) with three pumping stations, compared with the sixty windmills that would previously have been necessary. As far back as 1667 the Dutch had talked about closing off the Zuiderzee, a task actually completed in 1932! Work to close up the Escaut/Meuse/Rhine delta reduced the sea frontage from 1,000 miles to 500 miles. After the 1953 tragedy (which claimed 1,835 victims), the Delta Plan was initiated (*see page 204*).

Far from the Mediterranean basin, where civilisations had flourished since ancient times, a new focus of civilisation was taking root at the beginning of the Middle Ages on the shores of the North Sea and the Channel. This was to be the maritime springboard to later colonial ambition, with its ultimate major achievement in founding the New World. Fishing and commerce contributed to the might and wealth of the seaboard cities and nations. During the course of the last hundred years, practically the entire coastline has been built upon or in some other way tamed by man.

Organisation of the economy

With ethnic stabilisation around the North Sea came social and civic organisation within a political and military feudal hierarchy. Maritime activity, essential to both everyday prosperity and military security, gave rise to the first supranational grouping, the Hanseatic League, linking ports from the Baltic to England and from Norway to France.

WILLIAM THE CONQUEROR

William the Conqueror, also known to the French as *Guillaume le Bâtard* (William the Bastard), was born in Falaise in the *département* of Calvados in 1027, died in Rouen in 1087, but was, of course, King of England from 1066 until his death.

He was, in fact, the last of England's invaders, following after the Vikings and the armies of Julius Caesar. After him, English shores were to remain inviolable, to Napoleon and Hitler's machinations alike. Having imposed order in Normandy, where he founded numerous churches (most notably the Abbey of Saint-Etienne at Caen in 1064), he asserted his right to the English throne in opposition to King Harold (who had been crowned on 6 January 1066). At the head of an army of 50,000 men and a superbly equipped fleet, William landed in England on 29 September 1066 and defeated Harold at Hastings on 14 October.

Henceforth, he became known as William the Conqueror. He was crowned on 25 December and established firm rule over the English, through a strictly applied feudal hierarchy. His respect for local customs earnt him the obedience of his new subjects.

Across the Channel, his wife, Mathilda of Flanders, daughter of Count Baudouin V, governed Normandy. But, when quarrels arose between him and his son Robert Courteheuse, William decided to split the Anglo-Norman kingdom between his two sons: Robert Courteheuse, the elder son, received Normandy, while the younger, William Rufus, received England.

The prospect of a single state incorporating territory either side of the Channel was thus for ever laid to rest by the deeds of William the Conqueror. By contrast, future English noblemen would govern French regions or cities . . . indeed, right into the nineteenth century, when Wellington was created mayor of Pau in the Pyrenees in 1825!

Before the Battle of Hastings, William the Conqueror sits down to eat with his barons. Embroidery by Queen Mathilda (late 11th century)

1777 Philippe le Hire, geometrician to Louis XIV, calculated the breadth of the Straits of Dover at 21,360 fathoms (25 miles).

1785 First airborne crossing of the Straits of Dover by balloonists Blanchard and Jeffries, a few months after an attempt by Pilâtre de Rosier.

1802 A new tunnel project was conceived by mining engineer Albert Mathieu and provided for a tunnel with a paved road lit by oil lamps along its entire length. The tunnel was to be built on the Varne sandbank with the aid of an artificial island, whence the journey would be completed by mail-coach. The first map of the geography of the north French coast was drawn up by Charles-François Beautemps-Beaupré, bringing attention to the similarity

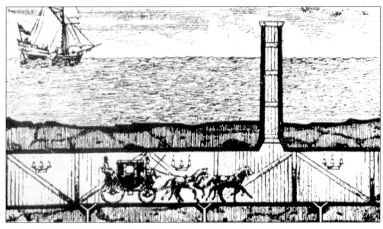

Detail of one of the early proposals: a carriage crosses the Channel in under five hours, in a candle-lit tunnel ventilated by a gigantic chimney

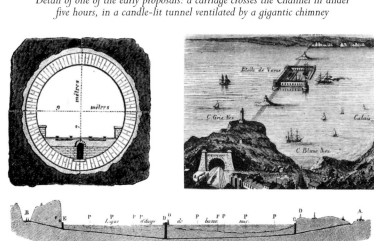

Tunnel under the Thames built by Brunel between 1825 and 1843, today used by the London Underground: the first tunnel to be drilled under water using the 'shield drill' method

BELOW: Thomé de Gamond, père du tunnel. ABOVE: One of his projects (1859) – section under the Channel (centre); section of a tunnel (left); and tunnel project with underwater station (right)

Hubert Clerget's Channel tunnel, based on Thomé de Gamond's design ideas, le Journal illustré, *1875*

between English and French coastal soils. The dream of a tunnel began to take shape.

1804   Cornish mining engineer Richard Trevithick unveiled the first road and rail steam-engine. The first metal bridges had already been built, one over the River Severn (1779), and two over the River Seine, the Pont d'Austerlitz (1804) and the Pont des Arts. Mining engineering was increasing its knowledge and sophistication, due in large part to experience gained in English coal mining.

1816   The first steamboat crossing of the Channel.

1825   A tunnel being dug under the River Thames was abandoned when river water flooded into some of the galleries.

1833   The French engineer Thomé de Gamond produced six designs, including both tunnel and bridge alternatives, for improved links between France and England. He was to become the French *père du tunnel,* ultimately favouring the idea of an under-sea tunnel, and his was the first properly scientific proposal put before Napoléon III; by 1857 Thomé de Gamond was looking for English support for his ideas. Official reticence ("You expect us to contribute to a scheme whose sole objective is to shorten the already insufficient distance between us?") was tempered by discreet support from Queen Victoria's husband, Prince Albert. In the years that followed, the tunnel project suffered through difficulties in Anglo-French relations; yet it was kept alive and relevant by increasing international rail links and the new maritime companies (in particular the General Maritime Company, created in 1855 by the Pereire brothers). Telegraphy, too, was shortening the distances between continents, the first under-sea telegraphic cable being laid between Calais and Dover, and followed, first in 1860, by a cable linking England to the United States of America and, in 1870, by one linking France to Algeria. The same period witnessed substantial success in the boring of mountain tunnels . . . the 8-mile-long Fréjus tunnel, begun in 1857, was completed in 1871, thanks to accelerated progress made possible by the steam drill (previously drills advanced at no more than 60cm a day): "A fantastic achievement, previously only dreamt of, and now seeming to be such a simple thing, as is so often the case with human endeavour". (Charles de Rémuzat, Minister for Foreign Affairs, at the inauguration of the Fréjus tunnel)

1860 Conclusion of a commercial accord between Great Britain and France agreeing to a 10-year period of reduction of levies payable on British manufactured goods (textiles) and French silk, fruit and wine. This treaty heralded little less than a revolution in European commercial relations: it gave rise to numerous further treaties between European countries and lead, in turn, to a complete overhaul of customs duties, that proved an immense stimulus to international business. This new situation inevitably fostered improved communications between countries and was, therefore, good news for the Anglo-French tunnel project. In England all these changes enjoyed the strong support of the Chancellor of the Exchequer, Gladstone; and in France were promoted by Michel Chevalier, founding father of the Anglo-French commercial treaty and founder of the first French tunnel company. In his book *Des Intérêts matériels de la France*, Chevalier maintained "the northern route is the Paris–London route. When we can reduce the gap between these capitals to 14 hours and 20 francs, then Europe and European policy will be quite altered".

"WAIT AND SEE"

Inauguration of the Suez Canal, 17 August 1869, Darjou sketch

1867 Thomé de Gamond presented his tunnel design to the public at the opening of the *Exposition universelle* (Paris 1866), with the support of Napoléon III. An Anglo-French committee was set up to obtain feasibility reports from four engineers – among them Thomé de Gamond. Numerous public figures from both countries lent support to the proposed undertaking whose estimated cost was 50 million francs. In the event, however, both sides agreed to postpone a decision on the project, concurring that the time was

Shaft entrance near Shakespeare Cliff

not ripe. In 1872 the British Foreign Office re-affirmed the policy of delaying a decision pending further investigations.

1872 Creation of the Channel Tunnel Company Limited, followed by agreement in principle by the British government to a concession for an under-sea railway, while providing for neither support nor financial guarantees from the government. In 1873 the French government set up an official enquiry in the Pas-de-Calais region, as a preliminary to tunnel boring. Thus the way was cleared in both countries for the new company to make a start: two deep holes were sunk, one at Calais and one at Dover, and trial tunnels bored beneath the sea. The work was financed by the French Northern Railway, *La compagnie des chemins de fer du Nord*, by the Rothschild brothers and by a British committee which contributed £30,000, rather than the £80,000 that had been expected.

1873–1876 Preliminary construction work and formalities were impeded by the decease of Thomé de Gamond. On the English side of the Channel, Disraeli succeeded Gladstone and popular support for the tunnel continued, although the military were concerned about security. Basic differences of perspective emerged between the English (political viewpoint) and the French (technical aspects of the project).

• **2 August 1875** Simultaneous passage of a bill to clear the way for the signing of a protocol:

"When the engineers of two countries meet for the first time in the middle of the Dover Strait, beneath a sea bloodied by so many previous combats, the handshake of friendship which they exchange will do more to assure the true alliance of the two groups than can any instrument of diplomacy." (Krantz, French *député*) Simultaneously, the tunnel's technical feasibility was confirmed when investigations of the Straits' rock strata indicated that the Channel had been formed by 'subsidence without rupture'.

The construction site at Sangatte 1882

1880   At Sangatte in the Pas-de-Calais region drilling into the chalk bed reached a depth of 88 metres. A drill which was the forerunner of the modern tunneller was able to cut at the rate of 11 metres a day.

1880–1884 Political instabilities either side of the Channel: Disraeli and Gladstone took turns at Downing Street and, in France, spectacular Prussian defeat of Napoléon III at Sedan provoked a popular uprising in Paris and the downfall of the Second Empire. Financial difficulties further hindered progress. In 1881 *The Times* published an alarmist front-page article on the defence implications of the tunnel, maintaining that it would become England's military Achilles' heel. Following publication of this article, control of the tunnel project was taken over by the British military. Wolseley, moreover, was violently opposed to the scheme. He questioned France's motives and enumerated the risks that England would be laying herself open to, particularly with regard to her 'freedom and sovereignty', 'merely that men and women might come and go between England and France without feeling sea-sick'!

• **1882** A new entry appeared in *The Oxford Dictionary* for the word 'unemployed'. More than a thousand people signed a petition called 'The Nineteenth Century', exposing the dangers which the tunnel represented for England. In the same period an intense press campaign gave high profile to the anti-tunnel lobby:

"The tunnel could be for England what the wooden horse was for Troy." *Manchester Examiner and Times*

"The Channel tunnel could have important consequences on the political and social institutions of this country." *Leeds Mercury*

"Will the advantages of the tunnel outweigh the cost to the nation of the increased taxes necessary to guarantee the security of the country?" *The Scotsman*

The tunnel became the scapegoat for all England's problems, targeted by one and all, press, caricaturists and leading members of the British ruling class, as harbinger of a plethora of future ills. The constructors, meanwhile, paid scant heed to the arguments and pressed on with the drills, encouraged by the frequent visits of 'celebrities', who seemed not the least bit perturbed or concerned as they descended to the furthest reaches of the excavations, to view passages and tunnels in the making.

• **1883** France awaited an unambiguous statement on the tunnel project from the British before drilling continued. Victor Hugo lent warm support to the project: "My dear fellow English and French countrymen, for we are but one people, a time will come when differences of race will no longer matter, when all frontiers will fall".

1895 Discovery of the radio aerial enabling signals to be transmitted by wireless over a distance of several miles. Digging of the 62-mile-long Kiel Canal to join the Baltic to the North Sea. In Greece, the Corinthian Canal had taken ten years to build (1883–1893), while work on the Panama Canal was halted in 1890 due to lack of funds.

1898 Preliminary phase of the construction of the Paris underground railway system: underground lines were laid, overcoming problems associated with marshy terrain and crossing the River Seine.

1901 Queen Victoria died, ending a reign of sixty-three years.

1906 The Chambers of Commerce of London and Paris tried to revive the tunnel project. Director of the *Société française du tunnel sous-*

Queen Victoria, Winterhalter (1842)   *Airplane crossing of the Dover Straits*

Some Gallic welcome for magnificent Willows and his flying machine! Hardly touched down on French soil and the tax man already after him!

Sir Winston Churchill

marin rekindled interest with a suggestion for a horseshoe-shape viaduct to link the rail tunnel to the mainland. Aimed at reassuring the military, it failed to persuade the Anglo-French authorities.

1908   Henry Ford went into production with the first mass-produced motor-car.

1912   Stainless steel was discovered. Several significant engineering projects were completed in the pre-war period:

- Panama Canal (3 August 1914)
- the Rove to Marseilles tunnel, 4½ miles long and the longest in the world, linking Marseilles to the Etang de Berres.

The threat of war gave a new edge to the tunnel debate. In the event of a Franco-German war, the tunnel was thought likely to play an important role in the fight against a French defeat or a German blockade of England.

1914   First Lord of the Admiralty Winston Churchill insisted on one pre-condition only: that he be able to immobilise the tunnel in the event of its two extremities falling into enemy hands.

1916   The horror of the First World War did not quite snuff out all enthusiasm for the tunnel. "The terrible fight against our common enemy has brought France and England closer together than ever, so that the heart of the English nation beats to the same rhythm as the hearts of the people of France. Mistrust and fear have gone for good, and the way is open for new talks on the tunnel." *L'Echo de France*

1919 25 August marked the official opening of the Paris–London air route, with flights taking between 2 and 4 hours. Ferry crossings grew in number. Engineering science provided the know-how to construct the world's highest bridge (321 metres) over Arkansas in 1919; followed ten years later by the world's longest bridge, the 1,280-metre-long Golden Gate Bridge in San Francisco. Accomplishments abounded in the European countries: Italy constructed the Milan–Varèse autoroute (85 km) in 1924. After the war and as part of a policy to strengthen the Anglo-French alliance, Lloyd George hailed the construction of the tunnel as a means " to hasten the arrival of British troops" in future time of war. For the first time London took the initiative in pushing for a construction programme, notably supported by Winston Churchill, Minister of War. Difficulties and resistance nonetheless persisted, highlighted by this declaration from the same Winston Churchill: "For an offensive war we want the tunnel. For a defensive one, we don't".

1921 Creation of a French Committee for the Channel Tunnel, chaired by Paul Cambon, former ambassador to London and with Field-Marshal Foch as its honorary president.

1923 Britain confirmed that its government's finances were insufficient to fund the construction project. Substantial mistrust of the French persisted among the majority of British political leaders.

1923–1928 The project was put on ice in the face of financial difficulties on either side of the Channel.

> • **1928** A series of storms paralysed Channel traffic: "Each new storm reinforces the arguments for the Channel tunnel." *Daily Mail*

1930 The Peacock Report, prepared at the request of the British government, struggled against the anti-tunnel lobby, in particular Hankey and Crawford: "I am a xenophobe; I regard France as the source of corrupt and corrupting influences". The reaction in France was immediate, and press articles conveyed the over-riding disappointment: "The tunnel has been buried without public debate, an execution behind closed doors". Popular English rejection was confirmed by a vote against the tunnel in the House of Commons, though this was a vote against the Government, since 172 Members of Parliament voted in favour of the tunnel (including numerous members of the Government itself), against 179 MPs who voted against.

1930–1940 The French engineer André Basdevant put forward the first plan for a road tunnel under the Channel. His plans provided for two circular tunnels 8 metres in diameter, with linking passages between them every kilometre. The Group for Study & Co-ordination of Underground Planning proposed a combined tunnel with a road suitable for motor vehicles overlaying a railway. During the thirties the tunnel construction site at Sangatte (Pas-de-Calais) was broken up and the extraction shafts abandoned.

• **1936** The Popular Front came to power in France.

1939–45 The Second World War. The fall of France came early in spite of support from Britain. With France occupied, England stood alone against Germany. In London on 18 June 1940 General de Gaulle made his famous call to the people of France to resist and not capitulate to the enemy. Through all the difficulties of the war years Anglo-French solidarity grew. Emerging victorious from the conflict, England was described as "morally enriched, financially and materially weakened". (André Maurois)

1951 Formation of the CECA (Economic Community of Coal and Steel) which included France, West Germany, Italy, Belgium, the Netherlands and Luxembourg. Plans for a European Defence Community (CED) did not materialise.

1958 The Channel Tunnel Company was revived; the shaft and tunnel at Sangatte were recommissioned; and as drilling got under way again some 70 metres beneath the sea, investigations confirmed the conclusions made by engineers back in 1880. Experts recommended a two-way railway tunnel and the go-ahead was signalled for 1960. General de Gaulle's visit to London the same year served to re-affirm French resolve and British Prime Minister Harold Macmillan declared "the military objections are no longer pertinent".

1960 Britain expected to become a member of the Common Market. Channel traffic had increased to 370,000 vehicles per year. In Paris, Louis Armand, member of the French Institute and supporter of the tunnel option for a Channel crossing, opposed the view of Jules Moch: a graduate of the élite *Ecole polytechnique*,

Georges Pompidou, Harold Wilson and Charles de Gaulle, 27 January 1969

Ayacliff (1974): the tunnel shaft entrance after work is halted. "No Channel Tunnel"

an engineer and former Minister of the Interior, Moch favoured the bridge option. A French 'society for channel bridge research' was founded on 27 December, in large part due to the efforts of the constructor of the Tancarville bridge over the Seine near to Le Havre.

1964 A joint Anglo-French commission decided in favour of a rail tunnel. Expert appraisement of the drilling re-confirmed the feasibility of the project.

1967 Both governments published invitations to tender in the international press, for a construction contract to be undertaken by a private company and managed by a Franco-British public body.

1971 The British parliament approved the principle of membership of the Common Market.

1972 The tunnel was still not 'in the bag': Leo Erlanger, President of the *Société du Tunnel* for more than thirty years, averred that "it was still impossible to say with any degree of certainty that the tunnel would go ahead".

1973 On 17 November, President Pompidou and Prime Minister Edward Heath were joint signatories to an agreement to build the tunnel.

1974 As the oil crisis shook the Western world, political upheaval moved in opposite directions in England and France: right-wing Giscard d'Estaing succeeded centrist Georges Pompidou, while in

England Harold Wilson replaced Edward Heath. Communications between the two new leaders did little to help the tunnel project. At the year end, the British Minister of the Environment announced the decision to abandon — for financial reasons — construction of the Dover–London expressway that was to have linked tunnel and capital. The decision revived French disquiet and confirmed doubts expressed in 1972 by Leo Erlanger.

1975 On 20 January, after ten years of research and two years of construction work, the project was abandoned by the British. "Great Britain is an island and intends to remain one" was the sober comment of *Le Monde* newspaper. While in London the *Daily*

Thatcher and Mitterand sign the accord at Lille Town Hall (20 January 1986)

Telegraph concluded: "It's a good thing". With an economy weakened by the oil crisis (22% inflation), Britain deferred plans for the tunnel, pending successful exploitation of her North Sea oil and membership — on the best possible conditions — of the Common Market. The tunnel, and its forecast one thousand million franc budget, was "sacrificed on the altar of austerity".

"WE SHALL DIG A TUNNEL!"

1979 Margaret Thatcher formed her first government.

1981 François Mitterand became President of France, the first to have risen through the ranks of the left, half a century after Léon Blum's Socialist presidency of the Popular Front government. At the Anglo-French summit of 10 and 11 September, relations between the two countries looked very promising, as delegates talked about a relaunch of the *serpent de mer,* as the French called the Channel tunnel.

1982 On 18 June, ministers responsible for transport in both countries announced the launch of the tunnel project in a joint communiqué. Discussions continued for a further three years.

Sangatte (1987): drilling

1985 On 31 October, in line with normal procedure for a project of this kind, five alternative proposals were presented to the appropriate ministers. They opted for what appeared the most sensible solution, for Eurotunnel, consisting of two tunnels complemented by a service tunnel. Environmentally sound yet employing tried and tested techniques, this proposal also demanded an expenditure (£5 billion) that was far inferior to that of its competitor proposals.

PROPOSALS A-PLENTY

The notional merits of an Anglo-Continental liaison may have been recognised as far back as the eighteenth century but, as to the manner and means of the physical link, this question gave rise to a succession of proposals and counter-proposals from north and south of the Channel. Of the plethora of ideas, some of them, it must be said, pretty far-fetched, less than a dozen of the more 'plausible' alternatives are given below (listed according to their siting, from beneath the seabed upwards):

• A tunnel drilled through the sub-stratum beneath the seabed, the proposal recognising dependence on: an unbroken geological stratum; rock impermeable to seepage and of sufficient thickness and density to preclude the risk of collapse or subsidence.

• A submerged tunnel resting on the sea-bed and consisting of a series of prefabricated airtight chambers linked by watertight joints.

• A floating tunnel constructed in the same way as the submerged tunnel, but floating underwater, with anchoring to the seabed to prevent drift.

• A floating bridge with a superstructure resting on solidly-fixed pontoons and with gates to allow for the free circulation of ships in the Channel.

• A dyke similar to those of the Netherlands, with swing and lever bridges creating shipping fairways.

• A dyke complete with tidal power station.

• Two parallel dykes enclosing a calm-water canal linking the river navigation systems of the two countries.

• A bridge across the deepest part of the Channel linking a jetty extending into the sea from either coast.

• A tunnel linking two jetties.

• A bridge spanning the sea from coast to coast.

• A bridge-tunnel hybrid project consisting of two bridges linked in the middle by a tunnel constructed below the level of a shipping canal.

Drawings of Channel Tunnel (1857 and 1873) and Channel Bridge (1961)

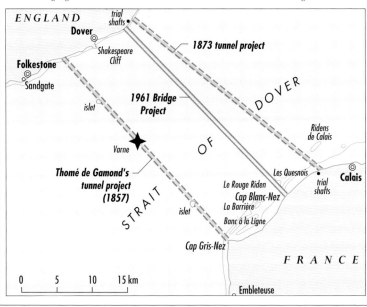

1986 On 20 January, at Lille in northern France, the tunnel project was given the official go-ahead by an announcement from both governments. Signing of the Franco-British accord followed quickly at Canterbury in Kent in February. This accord specified the conditions for construction and operation of a tunnel by private concessionnaires, to be exclusively funded by private enterprise with no government guarantee. Complementary road links were projected for the year 2000. Tariffs were to be freely fixed by the operating companies and the tunnel ready by 1993. Construction work began, financed by a consortium of 40 banks: £4 billion was added to a start-up capital of £50 million and a private loan of £200 million.

1987 The European Bank announced its participation in the tunnel, as well as in the new high-speed TGV-Nord rail service in northern France. Work got under way, materials were purchased. The tunnel was becoming a reality!

The French construction site at night

On **6 March** the sinking of the Channel ferry the *Herald of Free Enterprise* in Zeebrugge harbour caused the loss of 135 lives. This sad event served to reinforce support for the tunnel. The Tunnel Bill was passed by both Houses of Parliament and given the Royal seal of approval. In France, the 'decree for the declaration of a public utility' was signed by the French government and the President of the Republic 'promulgated the laws necessary to its ratification and concession'. With all political obstacles removed, the work pressed on apace: 20 metres were drilled! The tunnel site became a popular venue for politicians and journalists on both sides of the Channel.

A new European era dawned!

"The construction project of the century" *and* a practical guide to the Tunnel

At the dawn of the third millenium, no obstacles remain: neither political (both countries have approved appropriate treaties) nor financial (in spite of inevitable budget overruns, Eurotunnel has attracted tremendous small shareholding investment). The 22-mile-long building site beneath the sea has finally become the Tunnel.

Also contained in this chapter, all you need to know about the underground life of the Tunnel, its safety systems, how to reach it from national road networks and where to get information on timetables and prices.

Opposite: The service tunnel

Beneath land and sea

The Tunnel is 30 miles long in total, approximately 22 of these being under the sea; if you add together the combined lengths of the two traffic tunnels for passengers and freight, and the third service and maintenance tunnel, the total length comes to 90 miles. The passenger and freight traffic rail tunnels have a diameter of 7.6 metres, while the service tunnel is a smaller 4.8 metres in diameter. On the French side the Tunnel cuts deep into the rock south-west of Calais, following the bed of blue chalk that made boring relatively easy. Beneath the Channel, too, the stable contours of the seabed presented neither rupture nor fold to complicate the work of the tunnel-boring machines. Persistent difficulties encountered with the under-sea drilling on the French side did require a shift of the planned under-sea meeting point from halfway across the Channel to a point nearer the French coast. Geological research was undertaken by the *Bureau de recherches géologiques et minières* (BRGM) in France, and in Britain by Mott, Hay and Anderson, their joint surveys culminating in a precise three-dimensional analysis of the seabed.

Air, water, electricity and communications

The Tunnel's air-conditioning and ventilation systems consist of powerful ventilators variously situated at Sangatte and Shakespeare Cliff. Drainage conduits are included in the service tunnel in case of seepage. The Tunnel's electrical installations include back-up generators in case of power supply deficits, with cable networks for signalling, telephones, public address systems, fibre optics and fire-fighting water conduits.

Tunnel-boring machines

Two types of boring machines were used in the Tunnel: on the English side a dry-rock boring machine, on the French side a machine designed for tunnelling through water-bearing rock. After the experimental start-up period a boring rate of fifty metres per day was established.

Section of Channel seabed

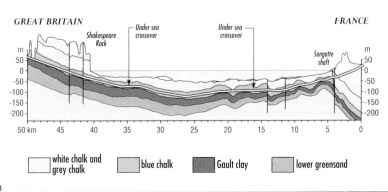

The construction schedule

Expected to take seven years (the Eurotunnel concession is for 55 years, including the construction period), boring was actually completed in less than three. Admittedly, the magnitude of the financial burden associated with the research and construction period encouraged Eurotunnel to keep this non-commercial phase to a minimum. Eleven tunnel-boring machines worked continuously in the different tunnels, drilling night and day, 365 days a year, with simultaneous evacuation of spoil material and installation of pre-cast concrete tunnel lining sections.

Access shafts

In France, the Tunnel construction site was accessed by a huge 56-metre diameter shaft situated at Sangatte, from which the three

French tunnel-boring machine

tunnels extend seawards and inland. This was the point of entry for workforce, tunnel linings and (in dismantled form) tunnel-boring machines alike; equally it was the spoils extraction point. In England, the old Shakespeare Cliff site of the aborted 1881 and 1974 tunnel attempts was re-opened as the main Tunnel construction site. Contrary to Sangatte, space here was at a premium, calling for an oblique 300-metre descent, with a second shaft and small 11-metre diameter tunnel for workforce access. These three access points then converged in assembly and manoeuvring bays that were entirely underground.

The tunnels

Undoubted stars of the project were the enormous tunnel-boring machines which first hollowed out the tunnel and then positioned tunnel lining sections, these already being part-equipped with the services' infrastructure. The little transversal linking tunnels had, by contrast, to be hand-drilled, given their small dimensions and difficulty of access. This operation was accomplished with small excavators mounted on caterpillar tractors, with articulated arms to manipulate a series of cutting heads – like some monster dentist! The big tunnel-boring machines, on the other hand, consisted of a cylindrical shield corresponding to the diameter of the tunnel (around 9 metres), 13 metres in length and weighing around 1,200 tonnes; but these also included spoil evacuation and tunnel lining installation

*Shakespeare Cliff:
construction area by night*

*French access shaft showing
rail and service tunnel entrances*

systems. A 7cm metallic casing held rock in place while the tunnel lining sections were positioned and secured. A technical 'train' followed the boring machine to ensure efficient two-way flow of spoils and tunnel linings, and then laid on power, air, ventilation . . . The cutting head at the front of the tunnnel-boring machine turned slowly, making no more than 2 to 4 revolutions per minute. The teeth of the tungsten carbide cutting wheel shattered the rock into small pieces, while a spiral extractor continuously carried away the spoils from the cutting head. On the French side, where water seepage sometimes occured as the tunnel-boring machines progressed, cement had to be injected into the rock prior to positioning of the tunnel linings. The operation of these boring machines is obviously no easy task. The nature of the rock, exterior pressure, viscosity or 'stickiness' of the spoil material, accurate tunnel lining placement, displacement of the tunnel-boring machine itself: all of these factors have a bearing on mode of operation . . . Teams of some 20 to 30 men worked shifts round-the-clock manning these veritable underground factory units.

Tunnel-boring machine at work in rail tunnel

EUROTUNNEL SHAREHOLDINGS

On 31 January 1993, the Eurotunnel shareholding was predominantly European (95%) with a (not surprising) Franco-British majority holding.

A further preponderance of French shares (66%) may be explained by the fundamental difference in French and British perspectives: on the one hand, the French love-affair with large-scale public building projects, contrasting with legendary British reserve, traditionally favouring private business initiatives. Add to this a good deal of British reticence over the Tunnel project arising from the years 1986–87, reflecting anxiety at the prospective loss of island status and physical integration with continental Europe.

In spite of this, Eurotunnel has enjoyed considerable success so far. When shares were first offered to the public in 1987, there were 120,000 shareholders. By 31 January 1994 – even in the face of legitimate concerns over work in progress, the delay in opening the Tunnel to traffic and inevitable budget overruns – there were already 500,000 shareholders.

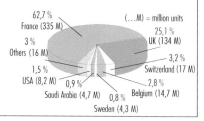

(...M) = million units

62,7 % France (335 M)
25,1 % UK (134 M)
3 % Others (16 M)
3,2 % Switzerland (17 M)
1,5 % USA (8,2 M)
0,9 % Saudi Arabia (4,7 M)
2,8 % Belgium (14,7 M)
0,8 % Sweden (4,3 M)

Precision being of course vital, the machines were computer-controlled at all times via a network of computer stations every 187 metres. This was the first time that tunnel-boring machines had been used on such a large scale, following trials in Japan for the construction of the *TGV Atlantique* and Lyons and Lille underground railway systems. The British used tunnel-boring machines made in the UK, the French machines were of American/Japanese manufacture. As quickly as the drilling progressed, so the cut-away rock was faced with its lining section, a curved, reinforced concrete, watertight segment. Nearly

Boring machine emerging from Tunnel at Castle Hill

Tunnel lining sections at Tunnel entrance

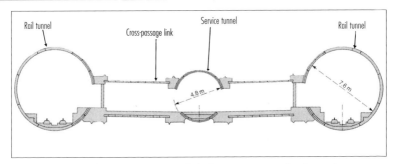

Section showing cross-passage links between service and rail tunnels

720,000 of these precision-made sections with watertight connection joints make up the interior of the Tunnel. Finally, came the problem of disposing of some 8 million cubic metres of excavated material. This was handled differently on either side of the Channel. In France the spoils were taken by train to the Sangatte access shaft, where they were mixed with water, ground into a sort of slurry, and pumped to the surface at Fonds-Pignon. In England, the drier extracted material was delivered by conveyor belt to the Shakespeare Cliff site at the rate of 2,400 tons an hour, and then transported by lorry to five sea lagoons formed by artificial dykes, to eventually create an 115-acre polder.

French spoil material handling area

Additional installations

The project site also included: special workshops for the assembly of the tunnel-boring machines, two large (200 x 20 metres) 'crossover' caverns (to allow a train to cross to the other track in exceptional circumstances), plus five pumping and drainage stations. Above-ground tunnel lining fabrication units produced nearly 450 sections per day on the French side, nearly 700 daily in England. These steel-reinforced sections were made of exceptionally high quality concrete, subjected to vigorous vibration for air bubble dispersement, and hand finished to ensure watertightness. The special micro-silicon-free composition of this concrete offers twice the strength of traditional concrete. The Sangatte fabrication unit was fortunate in being supplied with concrete from the nearby Dannes factory made from two different sands and locally excavated aggregates. The English tunnel lining unit on the Isle of Grain was supplied by boat from the Glennsanda quarry in Scotland.

Tunnel lining depot

The Tunnel terminals

Entry to the Tunnel is via Channel terminals at Coquelle in France and Cheriton in Great Britain. Cars, coaches and lorries using the Tunnel check in and board trains at these two points. These, too, are the embarkation points for the high-speed passenger services linking London with Paris, Brussels and, indeed, the rest of Europe. As well as arrival and departure platforms, the site includes shops, toll booths, Customs checks, car parks, hotels and restaurants. At Coquelles the terminal extends over an area of some 1200 acres of reclaimed land, while at Folkestone the terminal is squeezed into a 400-acre strip between the hillside and encroaching town.

Section of a rail tunnel

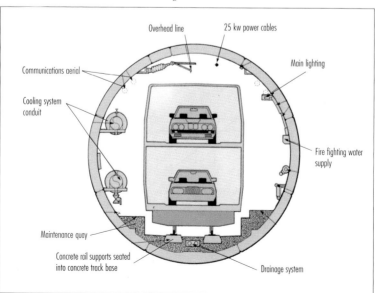

Overhead line

25 kw power cables

Communications aerial

Main lighting

Cooling system conduit

Fire fighting water supply

Maintenance quay

Concrete rail supports seated into concrete track base

Drainage system

WHO OR WHAT IS EUROTUNNEL?

Eurotunnel is a private Anglo-French consortium composed of a French and a British holding company, Eurotunnel SA and Eurotunnel plc, and two operating companies – The Channel Tunnel Group Ltd and France Manche SA. The group has a 55-year concession (expires in 2042) and has undertaken the design, financing, construction and operation of the Channel Tunnel and its transport systems. Eurotunnel is quoted on the Paris Bourse, the London Stock Exchange and the Brussels Bourse. Ten big English and French construction companies within the trans-Channel consortium are ultimately responsible for design, construction and operation of the project on behalf of Eurotunnel.

FURTHER INFORMATION

Eurotunnel Great Britain
Victoria Plaza
111 Buckingham Palace Road
London SW1W 0ST

Tel: 071-834 7575
Fax: 071-821 5242

Eurotunnel France
112 avenue Kléber
BP 116
75770 Paris Cedex 16

Tel: 44.05.62.00
Fax: 44.05.62.94
Minitel: 3615 Eurotunnel

Eurotunnel Exhibition Centre
Saint Martin's Plain
Folkestone
Kent CT19 4QD

Tel: 0303 270111
Fax: 0303 270211

Centre d'information Eurotunnel
BP 46
62231 Coquelles (Calais)

Tel: 21.00.69.00
Fax: 21.35.89.89

Coquelles Terminal

Folkestone Terminal

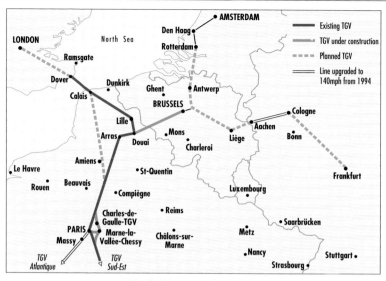

North-European TGV network

Services provided by Eurotunnel

The Tunnel links the railway terminal at Folkestone with the Sangatte (Calais) terminal. There are two one-way tunnels for rail traffic and a third service tunnel running between the first two, all three bored 25–45 metres beneath the seabed. Tunnel traffic will consist of the following:

- passenger trains travelling direct from major European stations with high speed train links
- direct freight trains
- passenger shuttles carrying cars and coaches
- freight shuttles carrying commercial vehicles.

Direct passenger trains

High speed trains operated by national railway companies will provide one or more trains per hour, daily, between Paris (Gare du Nord) or Brussels and London (Waterloo). Intermediary stations will be built at Fréthun (Pas-de-Calais), Lille (Nord) and Ashford (Kent). Close to 40 trains will be in service in both directions, night and day. Until new lines are completed in the UK and between Lille and Brussels, journey times for London–Paris and London–Brussels links will be 3 hours and 3 hours 10 minutes respectively. The travel time between London and Brussels is set to be cut to 2 hours 40 minutes with the opening of the high speed line between

Eurostar: TGV high speed Europe

Freight shuttles

Lille and Brussels some time after 1995. High speed lines around Paris are due to open some time in 1995 to link up the Atlantic TGV service, Charles-de-Gaulle airport and Eurodisney with the London–Paris line.

Modernisation of the line between London and Folkestone by British Rail, expected to be completed by 2000, will reduce journey times even further to 2 hours 30 minutes, London–Paris, and 2 hours 10 minutes for the London–Brussels link. Special trains have been supplied to the different national rail companies in order to ensure a perfect service between the European capitals of Brussels, Paris and London. These will be able to travel at 180mph on parts of the French line, but more slowly on the existing Belgian, French and British lines. Work currently in progress between Waterloo and Folkestone will eventually allow speeds of up to 100mph on the London–Folkestone line.

Loading platforms at Coquelles

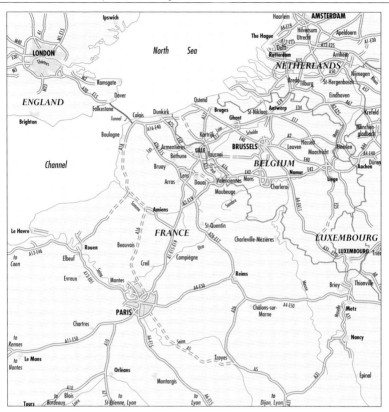

European motorway network

Direct freight services

The rail network will link a number of regional cargo depots in the UK to the commercial and industrial heartlands of continental Europe. The Tunnel is expected to handle around 50 freight trains a day, leading to a growth in UK/European trade, as well as to a reduction in pollution given the environmental superiority of rail over road traffic. The current volume of freight traffic, 7 million tonnes a year, is expected to grow to 10 million tonnes. British Rail, SNCB (Belgian Rail) and SNCF (French Rail) have undertaken to modernise their rolling stock, equipping themselves with smaller-wheeled wagons designed to carry the latest European types of freight box and standardised container. The standardisation of rail gauge at both ends of the Tunnel will mean that changing trains will no longer be necessary. In order to offset variations in the size of different types of wagon (height and width), Eurotunnel's shuttle is larger than the other European trains, and this explains its operation solely between the Folkestone and Sangatte terminals. At the same time, only trains that can function within the constraints of the BR network can be used on the direct passenger and freight services.

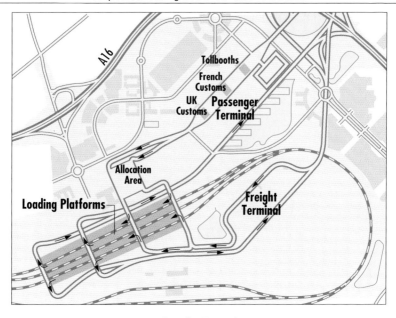

Coquelles Terminal

Cars and coaches

Car and coach drivers drive on to the terminals' access roads straight from either motorway or main road and with no need to pre-book. They will board the shuttles having first passed through a toll booth. The journey will take approximately 35 minutes, during which time, with a few exceptions, passengers remain in their vehicles. The same procedure applies to motor-cyclists, with the exception that they are requested to leave their motorcycles in a special section of the shuttle and to travel in passenger compartments. There

are also special measures for cyclists and their bicycles. Double-decker shuttles will carry vehicles up to 1.85m high; other vehicles, including coaches, travel on single-decker shuttles. Shuttle carriages are linked in groups or half-trains; sliding doors and blinds separate the carriages during the journey. Drivers drive on to the shuttle from the side and position their vehicles as directed. At the end of the crossing, vehicles exit from the front of each of the

Freight shuttle cab interior

train sections on to platforms alongside. Boarding and leaving the trains is facilitated by the internal ramps. There are toilets in every third carriage. Coaches using the Tunnel must be equipped with toilets and other facilities. At the end of the crossing, vehicles exit the shuttle through the terminal and then drive directly on to a road linked to the motorway network. Customs controls will take place at the point of departure. For the first few years, car and coach shuttles will leave every 15 minutes at peak periods, and every 20 minutes at other times. Journey times, including boarding and disembarking, should range between 50 and 80 minutes.

Commercial vehicles
Unlike other travellers, HGV drivers do not stay with their vehicles on the shuttle. They travel in a separate, air-conditioned carriage, where they can relax and refresh themselves. Commercial vehicles and passenger cars are segregated on arrival at the toll booths, and, thereafter, follow separate customs and boarding procedures. The commercial vehicle shuttles run every 20 minutes at peak times and hourly through the night, with plans to increase to one every 15 minutes at peak times by 1996. Total travel time, including embarkation and disembarkation procedures, is expected to be around 1 hour 20 minutes.

Services in the Tunnel
The Tunnel is equipped with a lighting system designed to meet all safety, maintenance and user needs. Lighting is operated either from the main control centres or from various points along the Tunnel, to ensure that it will never be in darkness. Fire hazards, such as overheated train axles, can be detected by fire-safety systems installed along the length of the Tunnel.

View of control cabin

Ventilation
There are ventilation turbines at either end of the Tunnel. Air passes to both rail tunnels from the service tunnel via the communicating galleries. There is an independent back-up system for emergencies. These systems are all controlled from a central control room.

Cooling the Tunnel
To counteract the heat produced by the trains, a cooling system passes refrigerated water (produced by turbines at either end) along steel canals running alongside the rail track. Additionally, passenger and freight shuttles are air-conditioned.

Water drainage and pumping

Pumping stations in the underwater section of the Tunnel remove any seepage water, water that may run off rolling stock, and water left after cleaning operations or resulting from exceptional circumstances such as fire-fighting.

The terminals

The terminals at Folkestone and Sangatte link the Tunnel to the road and motorway networks of the UK, France and, hence, the whole of Europe. The terminals provide simple, well-signposted access, with toll booths and customs points as well as restaurants, shops, conveniences and service stations. Shuttles are serviced at the terminals. The control tower for Tunnel traffic also operates here. At normal times, the Eurotunnel line is controlled from the Folkestone terminal.

Control and communication systems

All communications, including radio links with train drivers and on-board personnel, are passed from the control centre. Other personnel are equipped with portable radios allowing them to communicate from anywhere in the tunnels. There are emergency phones in every cross-passage, sub-station and pumping station. These lines remain open even in the event of a total power failure.

Signalling

Signalling is operated directly from the control centre to the shuttle driver's cabin. Should a driver not react to a signal, the system will slow the train down or bring it to a halt (automatic train safety) as is already the practice on other railway trains. The line is divided into automatic signalling zones in order to maintain safe separation of trains. The signalling system is geared for one train every 2½ minutes.

How the tunnels operate

Each tunnel works in a single direction. Under normal working conditions, trains run on the left in the direction France–Great Britain in the south tunnel; in the other direction they use the north tunnel. Crossover caverns, linking the tunnels together (at either end and under the Channel), allow trains to cross from one line to the other for maintenance or in the event of an accident.

The service tunnel

Positioned between the rail tunnels, the service tunnel provides them with air and a means of access for maintenance purposes. Power cables and water pipes pass from the service tunnel, which could also serve as a refuge and evacuation point in the event of an emergency. The lateral galleries linking the tunnels would allow passengers to leave an immobilised train and reach the service tunnel, although trains would, in nearly every case, be able to complete the crossing and leave the Tunnel.

Personnel training

Eurotunnel personnel follow practical and theoretical courses, as well as on-going training and development throughout their careers, in order to maximise their technical competence. Regular practice drills ensure safety awareness.

Safety

Total user confidence in the Tunnel's safety systems is assured. Trains travelling in different directions use different tunnels so that head-on collision is impossible. In the event of fire, shuttles and shuttle doors are fire-resistant for 30 minutes, a period far superior to that needed in practice evacuations of the Tunnel. Fire would be contained by fire-fighting gas following transfer of passengers to another shuttle compartment. In the case of electrical failure, an immobilised shuttle could be pulled or pushed by another train – all shuttle trains being equipped front and rear with electric locomotive engines (Brown-Boveri and Bush Engineering 7,600hp). In the exceptionally unlikely event of simultaneous power failure in both tunnels, stand-by diesel locomotives, positioned at either end of the Tunnel, would be used.

Safety inside the shuttle

At least eight crew members are on duty for each train crossing, six of these keeping a constant check on safety measures and regulations. Passengers are given precise instructions on safety and emergency procedures on boarding. Drivers are in direct contact with the control tower at all times. A closed-circuit TV surveillance system operates throughout the shuttle. Drivers and train 'captains' can speak to passengers through the on-board public-address system. Last but not least, basic passenger guidelines are clearly displayed in each carriage.

Fire safety measures

The risk of fire at the heart of the Eurotunnel network is reduced to a minimum by a combination of fire-safety systems including:

- a carriage drainage system to eliminate any accumulation of fuel
- a carriage fire-detection system
- equipment to tackle fires should they start: hand-held fire extinguishers and automatic foam jets; halon gas, should the first two methods prove ineffective; and water pipes in the service tunnel, plus fire-fighting teams.

In an emergency, passengers would be protected during removal to another carriage by the closure of fire-resistant doors. Similarly, sections of the train can be disconnected to allow passengers easy exit from a carriage. Evacuation can also be effected via the service tunnel (protected by fire-resistant doors) to reach another train or the train used in the service tunnel.

Protection against rabies

British law does not permit Eurotunnel to allow animals susceptible to rabies infection to travel through the Tunnel. Pets cannot, therefore, be brought into Britain – as is the case with ferries, planes and ships.

Hazardous freight

Certain hazardous cargoes cannot be transported through the Tunnel:

- gases and liquid fuels
- oil products and other highly volatile or inflammable products
- nuclear waste
- highly corrosive or dangerous chemicals.

The toll at Coquelles

Tariffs and timetables

Advice on tariffs and timetables can be obtained from the following information centres:

- **Customer Service Centre – UK**
  Customer Service Centre
  Cheriton Park, St Martin's Plain
  Folkestone, Kent CT19 4QD, England
  Tel: 0303 271100
  Fax: 0303 272690

- **Service Relations Clients – France**
  BP 69, 62231 Coquelles
  Tel: (01033) 21.00.61.00
  Fax: (01033) 21.00.60.92

- **Paris**
  Maison de la Grande-Bretagne
  19 rue des Mathurins, 75009 Paris, France
  Tel: (33) 21.00.61.00
  Fax: (33) 21.00.60.92

- **Amsterdam**
  Leidseplein 31b, 1017 PS, Amsterdam, Nederland
  Tel: (31) 20 420 33 33
  Fax: (31) 20 420 10 29

- **Brussels**
  56 Boulevard de l'Impératrice, 1000 Brussels, Belgium
  Tel: (32) 2 512 79 99
  Fax: (32) 2 512 07 87

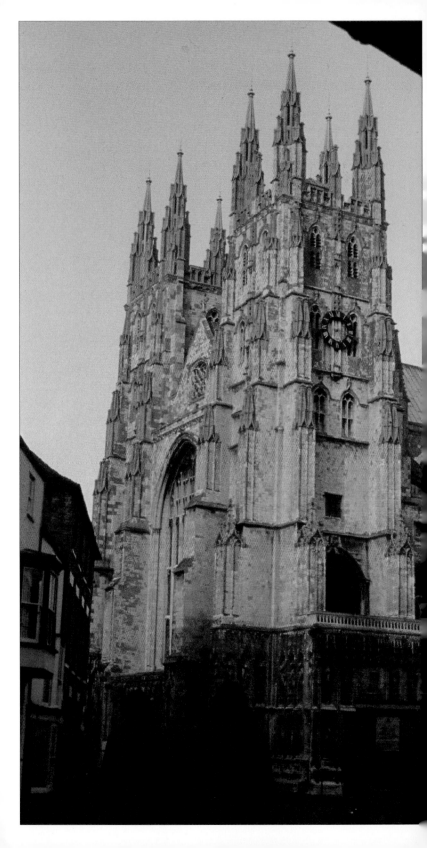

Touring
South-East England

Opposite: the
Cathedral,
Canterbury
(Kent)

*The four counties of Kent, Surrey,
East Sussex and West Sussex are
rather like a huge sandwich: two
slabs of hill, the North and South
Downs, enclosing the woodland
and farmland of the Weald . . .
just beyond the hungry grasp of
London's suburban sprawl.*

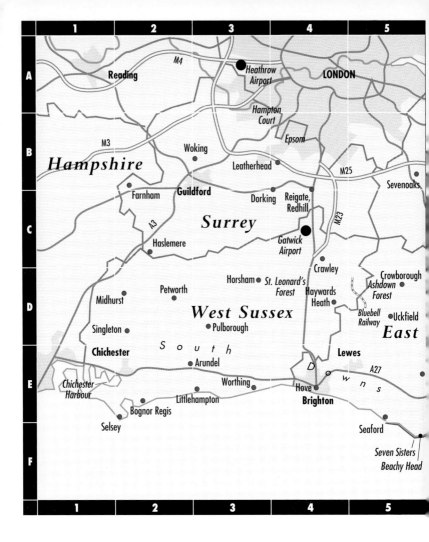

Birth of a separate identity

Higher sea-levels caused by increasing temperature after the last Ice Age gave rise to a body of water that separated the most westerly confines of the peninsula, not yet called Europe, from the rest, a stretch of water, little more than an inlet – or 'sleeve' of its French name *La Manche*. Though of negligible importance in planetary terms, this geophysical phenomenon had a considerable impact on *homo sapiens*, at the time one of the planet's frailest creatures, with a far from certain future.

As for the Celtic invasion of Europe – the replacement or assimilation of indigenous populations by invaders who came from the east through Germany – we are still not in possession of all the facts. But we may reasonably deduce that the obstacle presented by the new sea contributed to the island's underpopulation – and it did not catch up demographically, until the nineteenth century. What we can be more certain of is that both landscape and people either side of the sea were to remain pretty much as and where they were, from this time forth.

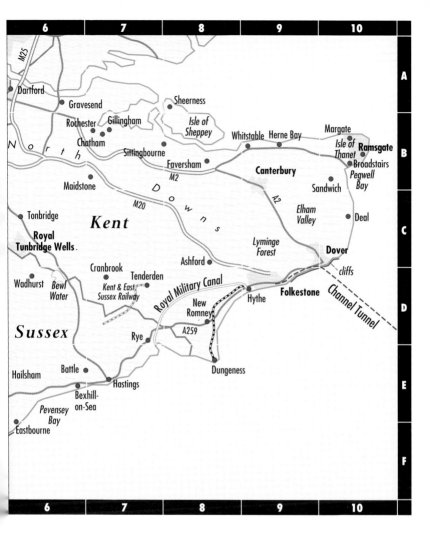

Julius Caesar, who was much given to invasion, made no exception when it came to England. He established the authority of Rome by the sword, in England as in France and Belgium before it. Three centuries of peace followed, making an impression on the landscape, if less in the hearts and minds of men.

When the Roman Empire withdrew, several Germanic tribes came to divide the spoils; the Jutes took Kent, Angles and Saxons took Sussex and Wessex. These tribes, with counterparts on the continent, constituted highly aggressive, highly competitive groupings, with no national focus. Before any idea of nationalism could emerge, it was necessary for one tribe to dominate all the others to establish a central power base. The Saxons had barely settled camp when, as has often happened in the course of history, a rogue tribe sneaked in by the back door and took them by surprise! These were the Danes and their intervention might very nearly have succeeded in Danish domination . . . But, in the event, the Normans, another Nordic race lately settled north of the *Ile de France* in France, upstaged them.

The birth of a British national identity is often dated from the Norman invasion . . . which might seem paradoxical given that the Normans were French. The French language may (if only of recent date) have been the language of the court, but William's troops would almost certainly have talked a kind of Viking.

But why should the birth of an identity be considered to date from this particular invasion? Essentially, because this invasion was the last invasion. It may have been justified by contentious judicial argument (Edward the Confessor's designation of William as heir was never firmly established) and preceded by earlier 'acquisitions' (the Normans and their clergy already possessed territory on the English side of the Channel). But this was the last time that the island was invaded. Then, following the failure of her continental policy and a series of defeats suffered in the Hundred Years' War, England adopted a staunchly isolationist stance for the next 500 years. The island identity was immutably fixed.

Next, the colonial expansion that might have opened Great Britain to the world, in fact transformed large tranches of the world into British dependencies. This made sense in economic terms – some would say the exploitation of wealth was the *raison d'être* of colonialism. Yet it made rather less sense in cultural terms. The cultural wealth of the colonies had little impact on Britain, until relatively recently.

Ironically, France, over the centuries, has often been cast in the role of 'island' in an increasingly British universe . . . perceived as a place from which danger might spring. Which explains the heavy fortification of the south-east of England, Great Britain's potential Achilles' heel. From the League of Cinque Ports to the runways from which Spitfires took off in the glorious Battle of Britain, from the Martello towers – named after the Corsican engineer who built them in the rock of his native island (and which, in their new setting, were to repel Napoleon, himself born on Corsica) – to the many castles erected by a succession of sovereigns, all have shaped, and many still shape, the landscape of the south-east.

At Rochester, Lewes and Hastings, Norman castles in varying stages of decay or restoration still keep watch. Henry VIII built castles at Deal and Walmer; at Dover a fort was added during the time of Napoleon. Yet most are Roman, having stood the test of 2,000 years of changing fortune and history. And few really saw enemy fire. Or if they did, this was from within the island, from the soldiers of Simon de Montfort or Henry III, from members of the Houses of York or Lancaster, from Parliamentarians and Royalists . . . disembowelling here, razing to the ground there.

The coast near Dover

Compared with northern France, the landscape of south-east England is untamed. British iron-ore mining and forest clearance for charcoal came to an end at the close of the seventeenth century, when forests were able to grow back where the land was not under cultivation; or if not forest, low growing moorland re-established itself on the sides of the Downs. This is the landscape that provides the perfect backdrop to the quintessentially English garden; gardens whose designs are much more closely allied to nature than their French counterparts – and with more emphasis on the individual plants themselves.

All of which serves to make this part of England particularly appealing to French visitors, few of whom – particularly those closest to south-east England – have yet discovered its secrets. It is very likely that the Tunnel will play an important part in remedying the situation.

Kent

The county of Kent has a thousand-year history and largely conforms to the boundaries of the Jute kingdom of the same name founded in the fifth century. Its major attributes include seaside resorts, strong links with the Continent (which will increase with the opening of the Tunnel), proximity to London (many of its population are commuters) and its agriculture.

The title 'Garden of England' is a celebration of Kent's orchards and hop-fields, as well as its exceptional number of ornamental gardens, parks and nurseries. Kent also has some of Britain's most beautiful castles – Knole, Leeds, Hever – a cathedral of world renown at Canterbury, and a plethora of unique villages, inns and pubs, making it a very attractive holiday destination. Distances given are from Folkestone.

ASHFORD
C-8 · 14 miles

Tourist information
18 The Churchyard
Ashford TN23 1QG
Tel: 0233 629165

Hotels
Eastwell Manor ★★★★
Boughton Aluph (4 miles north)
Ashford TN25 4HR
Tel: 0233 635751
Croft Hotel ★★★
Canterbury Road
Ashford TN25 4DU
Tel: 0233 622140

Restaurants
Chimneys
London Way
Godington Park, Ashford
Tel: 0233 636871
Downtown Diner
Park Street, Ashford
Tel: 0233 624276

Entertainment
The Stour Centre
Tannery Lane, Ashford
Tel: 0233 639996

Festivals
European Week, early July.
Music Festival at Wye, summer.

Situated at a rail and road intersection that renders Ashford vulnerable to the usual ennui of traffic and urban sprawl, the town is nevertheless worthy of a second look, and for two reasons: first, it stands in some magnificent countryside and, second, Ashford itself also boasts several fine Georgian streets set around **St Mary's church**. This was built during the 14th and 15th centuries and, with its four-bell tower, is a fine example of late perpendicular Gothic.

In the hop-fields all around are the steep roofs of the oast houses and farms; and in every village, focus and hub of community life, the village pub. Visit the village of **Great Chart** (and The Wooden Horse pub), situated a couple of miles west of Ashford, with its 15th-century church; or take tea at **Willesborough Windmill**, 2 miles to the south-west (Saturdays and Sundays, 2–5pm April to October. Tel: 0233 637029). Two miles to the west is **Godinton Park and House**, a Jacobean manor with fine wood panelling, set amidst beautiful, mixed gardens: open to visitors by arrangement. Tel: 0233 620773. Further to the west again lies the hamlet of **Smarden**, where **The Bell** makes a tranquil country stop for the road-weary (details in Country Pubs route, p108).

CANTERBURY
B-9 · 20 miles

Tourist information
34 St Margaret's Street
Canterbury CT1 2TG
Tel: 0227 766567

Hotels
County Hotel ★★★★
High Street
Canterbury CT1 2RX
Tel: 0227 766266
Pilgrims Hotel ★★★
18 The Friars
Canterbury CT1 2AS
Tel: 0227 465531
Falstaff Hotel ★★★
St Dunstan's Street
Canterbury CT2 8AF
Tel: 0227 462138
Oriel Lodge ★★
3 Queen's Avenue
Canterbury CT2 8AY
Tel: 0227 462845
Yorke Lodge ★★
50 London Road
Canterbury CT2 8LF
Tel: 0227 451243
Canterbury Youth Hostel ★
54 New Dover Road
Canterbury CT1 3DT
Tel: 0227 462911

Restaurants
Marlowe's Restaurant
55 St Peter's Street
Canterbury
Tel: 0227 462194
Pilgrim's Restaurant
18 The Friars, Canterbury
Tel: 0227 464531
Sweenies Eating House
8 Butchery Lane, Canterbury
Tel: 0227 453148

Entertainment
The Marlowe Theatre
The Friars, Canterbury CT1 2AS
Tel: 0227 767246

Gulbenkian Theatre
University of Kent, Giles Lane
Canterbury CT2 7NB
Tel: 0227 769075

Festivals
Carnival, June.
Mystery Plays, July/August.
Canterbury Festival, October.

When, in 45 AD, the Emperor Claudius decided to assert control over those territories that Caesar had (perhaps over-hastily) identified as already conquered, the machinery of the great Roman army swung into action: a swift and bloody campaign was followed by the construction of fortified garrisons to maintain a lasting peace – which indeed then followed. One such garrison town, built in the 2nd century AD on the road that linked the Channel ports to London, was called *Durovernum*, now Canterbury. When Saxons established their capital there in 560 AD, they renamed it *Cantwarabyrig* (camp of the men of Kent). One of their kings, Ethelbert, married a Christian princess called Bertha, and it was his conversion, followed by a wholesale conversion of his subjects, that led to Saint Augustine's eventual establishment of a monastery here in 598.

Around 1070, the Normans erected an impressive cathedral, built on the site of an earlier church destroyed by the Danes. Increasing clerical and secular antagonisms in Europe, and in England a quarrel between Church and State under Henry II, culminated in the infamous murder of the Archbishop of Canterbury, Thomas à Becket, whose body was found in the north-west transept of the cathedral. His canonisation, less than two years after his death, transformed Canterbury into one of the most important places of English pilgrimage. For four centuries mystics, charlatans, inquisitive travellers and simple believers, all streamed to his shrine, bringing wealth to the town as they did so. Many of the stories of these plurisecular pilgrims are to be found in Geoffrey Chaucer's famous *Canterbury Tales*.

Canterbury Cathedral: the nave

Henry VIII, whose wrangles with Rome are well known, was responsible for the destruction of monasteries and religious property throughout England; Beckett's shrine was to suffer further desecration at the hands of Oliver Cromwell's men. Canterbury nevertheless remained the seat of the country's principal religious authority, namely the Anglican church – second only in authority to monarchy.

Christopher Marlowe was born in Canterbury in 1564, during the reign of Queen Elizabeth I; a poet and playwright who shared Shakespeare's year of birth, but who, unlike him, died a young man of only 29.

The centre of Canterbury has hardly changed over the years; extensive damage incurred during the Second World War has done little to alter the town's character, thanks to an extensive restoration programme.

Canterbury is reached from the Tunnel via Dover. Alternatively, take exit 11 off the motorway towards Stanford), and then take the B2068: in

addition to following the old Roman route from Lympne, you will also enjoy the considerable charms of the Kentish countryside (in particular Elham Valley to the east and Lyminge Forest to the west).

As you come into the town the old Norman castle dungeon is a little disappointing. Leave your car there and follow the path that runs along the ramparts or, alternatively, go via Castle Street, St Margaret's Street and Mercery Lane to the cathedral. In Burgate Street the magnificent **Christchurch Gate**, a Tudor gateway built between 1504 and 1521, forms the entrance to the Cathedral Close.

Built between 1067 and 1503, the **Cathedral** itself is a harmonious blend of Norman and perpendicular Gothic style. The sense of solemnity and repose of the exterior, the quiet of the great cloister, the mystery of the crypt and the superb examples of craftsmanship of the nave – the work of mason Henry Yevele, the stained glass of the west and north-west transepts and those of Trinity Chapel, the Norman capitals of

51

the crypt pillars and the extraordinary gold wrought work of the Black Prince's tomb and alabaster sculpture of Henry IV – all these conspire to make this building one of the masterpieces of British architecture and craftsmanship, and an essential part of any visit to Kent.

• **Canterbury Cathedral**, open Monday to Saturday 8.45am to 7pm (5pm in winter) and Sundays 12.30–2.30pm and 4.30–5.30pm. Tel: 0227 762862.

East of the cathedral you can see the ruins of the **Abbey of Saint Augustine** and, on the little rise adjacent, the church of **Saint Martin**, England's oldest parish church, dating from Roman times and one that witnessed the baptism of Ethelbert.

Opposite, and running along one of the arms of the River Stour which crosses the town, are the **Weavers' Houses**, a collection of Tudor houses. From here, take a pleasant boat ride upstream to a 14th-century hospice, **Poor Priests' Hospital**, now the home of **Canterbury Heritage**, the town's history museum (Monday to Saturday 10.30am–5pm. Tel: 0227 452747).

Then further to the west, on the other arm of the Stour, is **West Gate**, the only gate to the old town to have retained its original 14th-century identity. It houses an interesting museum and affords a magnificent view from the top.

In Butchery Lane, not far from the cathedral, is the new **Roman Museum**. Situated close to the main shopping area, this has been conceived around the most recent archaeological discoveries, including the mosaic floor of a Roman house (Monday to Saturday 10.30am –5pm; from June to October, Sundays too 1.30–5pm. Tel: 0227 452747).

The **Canterbury Tales Museum** offers something a little different. Through an audiovisual reconstruction of the setting of Chaucer's tales, the visitor is immersed in all the colour, religious fervour and excitement of the medieval pilgrimage (St Margaret's Street, open daily 9.30am–5.30pm. Tel: 0227 454888).

There is an interesting permanent exhibition at the **Royal Museum** at 18 High Street, together with occasional temporary exhibitions.

Canterbury makes a good base from which to explore the lovely surrounding countryside and the villages responsible for the particular flavour of the region: **Upper Hardres** and **Petham** (4 miles south); **Patrixbourne** (1 mile southwest) with a Norman church surrounded by Tudor-look houses, actually built in the 19th century; **Harbledown** and its Norman church (half a mile to the east); **Littlebourne** with its fine thatched barn (3 miles east); **Wickhambreaux** (4 miles west); and not forgetting **Chilham** (4 miles south-west). Here, in the pretty White Horse pub, enjoy a meal in traditional surroundings before embarking on a visit of **Chilham Castle gardens**, designed by Capability Brown (April to October 11am–5pm. Tel: 0227 730319, see Gardens route, p104). Two miles to the south-west, **Howletts Wild Animal Park** at Bekesbourne offers a safari amid gorillas, tigers and many other species. This is where John Aspinall, high-profile guru of the new zoo, began his zoological career.

CRANBROOK
D-7 • 32 miles

Tourist information
Vestry Hall, Stone Street
Cranbrook TN17 3ED
Tel: 0580 712538

Hotels
Tolehurst Barn **
Cranbrook Road
Cranbrook TN17 2BP
Tel: 0580 714385
Star and Eagle Hotel **
High Street
Cranbrook TN17 2EU
Tel: 0580 713555

Restaurants
Cranes Restaurant
2 Waterloo Road, Cranbrook
Tel: 0580 712396
Rankins Restaurant
The Square, Sissinghurst

Cranbrook
Tel: 0580 713964
The Windmill Inn
Waterloo Road, Cranbrook
Tel: 0580 713119

This prosperous little town continues a manufacturing tradition established in the 17th century. Pretty 15th- and 16th-century houses line the High Street and its church of **St Dunstan** is constructed of local sandstone. Pride of place in the town is given to the **Union Mill**. Recently restored, this once more grinds the good grain of the Kent Weald, the area of wooded hills that extends between the North and South Downs (open Saturdays, Easter to end October as well as Sundays during July and August, 2.30–5pm. Tel: 0580 712256).

Of the forest that covered much of the Weald in the Middle Ages, only Ashdown Forest (East Sussex), St Leonard's Forest (West Sussex) and Bedgebury Forest, 2 miles south-west of Cranbrook, remain today. Part of the latter constitutes the **National Pinetum**, an impressive collection of conifers from all over the world. In a park of many acres set around a lake and two streams (at Goudhurst, tel: 0580 211044, open daily 10am–8pm or nightfall). West of the forest on the road to **Bewl Water** (south-east England's most extensive stretch of freshwater offering every possible watersport) is **Combwell Priory**, where visitors can see special medieval events and spectacles (tournaments, archery contests, battle re-enactments . . . Tel: 0580 87754) throughout the summer.

In quite another vein, more disciplined and certainly much more 'English', the gardens of **Sissinghurst** can be visited from Cranbrook (1 mile northeast). These are a must for any foreign visitor keen to get to grips with the underlying character of the British: imagination and tenacity, qualities shared by great gardeners and great conquerors alike! A series of little gardens-within-a-garden, extending over five acres and created by Vita Sackville-West in the 1930s (more information in Gardens route, p104). A short distance from Sissinghurst on the Biddenden road, **The Three Chimneys** pub offers liquid refreshment and meals too, in a setting as pleasant as it is welcoming (further details in Country Pubs route, p108).

Iden Croft Herbs at Staplehurst (5 miles north-west) is one of England's biggest herb gardens. Every sort of oregano and thyme resistant to the British climate is here, sold both as plants in the garden and dried in sachets in the shop (Monday to Saturday 9am–5pm and, from 1 March to 30 September, Sundays as well, 11am–5pm. Tel: 0580 891432).

At Rolvenden (9 miles south-west), the **C M Booth Collection of Historic Vehicles** is one of Britain's most impressive motor-car museums, with a unique collection of Morgans (63–67 High Street, Rolvenden TN17 4LP. Tel: 0580 241234. Open Monday to Saturday 10am–6pm).

DARTFORD

A-6 · 55 miles

Tourist information
The Clocktower, Suffolk Road
Dartford DA1 1EJ
Tel: 0322 343243

Hotels
Royal Victoria and Bull Hotel **★★**
1 High Street
Dartford DA1 1DU
Tel: 0322 224415

Restaurants
Bridewell
46 Lowfield Street, Dartford
Tel: 0322 284849
Chefs Restaurant
15 Lowfield Street, Dartford
Tel: 0322 221120

Entertainment
The Orchard Theatre
Home Gardens, Dartford
Tel: 0322 220000
Fairfield Leisure Centre
Lowfield Street, Dartford
Tel: 0322 224400

Cranbrook: Sissinghurst Gardens

Festivals
Dartford Festival, end July.

Dartford could not be called a tourist town. Moreover it has paid the double price of industrialisation followed by recent, brutal recession; yet much of it still looks quite trim and, in fact, it is a good example of successful suburban planning. The **Dartford Borough Museum** in the town centre has an interesting collection of Roman remains, as well as a few magnificent examples of Saxon art, including a 5th-century glass vase.

• **Dartford Borough Museum,** Market Street, Dartford. Tel: 0322 343556. Open 12.30–5.30pm, Saturday 9am–5pm. Closed Wednesday and Sunday.

Of course, Dartford's most remarkable structure is the **Elizabeth II Bridge**, Europe's longest suspended bridge, which became operational in 1991. This carries the southbound traffic from the M25, while northbound traffic uses the Dartford river tunnel under the Thames. There is an excellent view of the new bridge, the River Thames and the county of Essex from the suburb of **Stone**, north of the town.

Dartford is also the town where Mick Jagger was born – though it may be a little early to organise pilgrimages just yet . . . Coming from the coast, it is on the way to Cambridge, for those who would avoid London, and is a neighbour of **Greenwich**, known throughout the world for its **Observatory**, yet deserving still greater acclaim for its architecture – masterpieces by Inigo Jones and Christopher Wren.

There are some fine Norman churches, including **Holy Trinity** in Dartford itself and **Darenth's** 10th-century nave.

A mile east of Dartford, **Stone Lodge Farm Park** is an activity farm with all the usual treats for children: rare animal breeds, agricultural museum, milking sessions (March to October daily 10am–5pm. Tel: 0322 343456).

Stone Lodge is also the home of the amazing **North Downs Steam Railway Museum**, where steam locomotives, diesels and carriages of the Kent of bygone days are on display (weekends February to December 11am–5pm. Tel: 0634 861878).

Fantaseas Water Park is Britain's largest aqua-park (daily 10.30am–10.30pm. Tel: 0322 288811).

DEAL

C-10 · 16½ miles

Tourist information
Town Hall, High Street
Deal CT14 6BB
Tel: 0304 369576

Hotels
Royal Hotel ***
Beach Street
Deal CT14 6JD
Tel: 0304 375555

Clarendon Hotel **
Beach Street, Deal
Tel: 0304 374748

Restaurants
The Crown Inn (pub)
The Street, Finglesham
Tel: 0304 612555

Dunkerley's Restaurant
19 Beach Street, Deal
Tel: 0304 375016

Star of India
13 King Street, Deal
Tel: 0304 380490

Festivals
Summer Music Festival,
August.

This little seaside resort prides itself on its quiet avenues and Georgian seafront. It has not played a great part in British history, in spite of its castle. In the face of a threatened invasion from François I, **Deal Castle** was built between 1538 and 1540 by Henry VIII, in the shape of the Tudor rose (further information in Defence Structures route, p112).

Timeball Tower, situated on the seafront, houses one of the world's longest surviving ball-clock mechanisms. The Tower has recently been converted into a clock and telegraphy museum (Tel: 0304 360897).

Inside the town hall in the High Street, the **Victoriana Museum** has a fine collection of paintings, furniture and jewellery (Tel: 0304 380546).

Less than a mile to the south is **Walmer**. This coastal town has a **Castle** in many respects similar to Deal Castle, though in much better condition (April to September 10am–6pm, October to December and March, Monday/Tuesday 10am –4pm, *see* Defence Structures route, p112). The castle is the residence of the Governor of the Cinque Ports – the league of south-eastern coastal towns set up to supply the king with ships in time of war. Originally consisting of Dover, Hastings, Hythe, Sandwich and Romney, the Cinque Ports were of real strategic importance, but the title of governor has long since been reduced to a courtesy title, its former status having passed away with some of the greatest defenders of the realm to have held the post: Wellington (the most illustrious of these), whose apartments are open to the public, and Churchill. The castle gardens are equally worth a visit.

DOVER

C-10 · 8 miles

Tourist information
Townwall Street
Dover CT16 1JR
Tel: 0304 205108

Hotels
Dover Moat House Hotel ***
Townwall Street
Dover CT16 1SZ
Tel: 0304 203270

Wallett's Court ***
West Cliffe, St Margaret's at Cliffe CT15 6EW
Tel: 0304 852424

White Cliffs Hotel ***
Waterloo Crescent, Marine Parade, Dover CT17 9BP
Tel: 0304 203633

Number One Guest House *
1 Castle Street
Dover CT16 1QH
Tel: 0304 202007

St Brelade's Guest House *
80/ 82 Buckland Avenue
Dover CT16 2NW
Tel: 0304 206126

Dover Youth Hostel *
Charlton House
306 London Road
Dover CT17 0SY
Tel: 0304 201314

Restaurants
Cliffe Tavern
St Margaret's at Cliffe
Dover CT15 6AT
Tel: 0304 852749

Beefeater Restaurant
The Plough
Folkestone Road, Dover
Tel: 0304 213340

Deal Castle: Henry VIII's French deterrent

Blakes Restaurant
52 Castle Street, Dover
Tel: 0304 202194

Festivals
Dover Festival, May.
Dover Carnival, July.

With a rich and glorious past, Dover has always been the first British line of defence against would-be invaders; today it serves as gateway to the British Isles for many continental visitors. The destruction wrought by the last war, combined with planning policies that have had more to do with practicality than aesthetics, as well as complications inherent in the difficult site, have not resulted in the town wearing a very welcoming smile to would-be overnight guests in the past. However, recent and new awareness, in part allied to the building of the Tunnel and the town's commercial potential, given its position, has coaxed planners into a more aesthetically aware approach. Stricter planning regulations combined with discreet monitoring of the town's hotels and restaurants is likely to produce results in the long term but, meanwhile, impressive efforts have already been made to maximise existing assets. **Dover Castle**, one of the best preserved and finest examples of a medieval fortress in Europe, has undergone extensive restoration, opening to the public not only the castle itself but also the Roman lighthouse, the Norman ramparts and the medieval tunnels (**Hellfire Corner**). These were the tunnels in which the 1940 evacuation of Dunkirk was masterminded and kept such a good secret (further information in Defence Structures route, p112).

• **Dover Castle.** Open daily April to September 10am–6pm and October to March 10am–4pm. Tel: 0304 201628.

There is no shortage of tourist-oriented enterprise. The **Dover Museum** (Market Square, tel: 0304 201628) may be strictly local in its scale and appeal, but this is not the case elsewhere. The **Old Town Gaol**

has been turned into a museum of places of incarceration; at the **Roman Painted House**, the Roman occupation is depicted via a descriptive commentary of a Roman villa, while the Middle Ages are brought to life at the **Maison Dieu**, where pilgrims would stop overnight on their way to Canterbury from 1203 onwards. Finally, thanks to the best in modern audiovisual technology and excellent acting skills, the **White Cliffs Experience** offers a 2,000-year tour of history. The town reveals a formidable determination to sell itself to the consumer-traveller. And what's more, these fairly high-risk ventures look set for great success. These attractions, the imposing cliffs that visitors can scale at **Grand Shaft** (a flight of steps cut into the chalk), the view of France on a clear day and all the delights of the surrounding countryside, make Dover one of the two or three best stops on any tour of Kent.

• **Old Town Gaol**, Biggin Street, Dover CT16 1DQ. Summer open daily 10am–5pm, likewise in winter excluding Mondays and Tuesdays. Tel: 0304 242766.

• **Roman Painted House,** New Street, Dover CT17 9AJ. Tel: 0304 203279. Open April to October, Tuesday to Sunday 10am–5pm.

• **The White Cliffs Experience,** Market Square, Dover CT16 1PB. Tel: 0304 214566. Open April to October, 10am–5pm and in winter 10am–3pm.

Crabbe Corn Mill, a mile north of Dover town centre on the little River Dour, is the largest watermill in south-east England. It was built in 1812 to grind the corn that could not be brought from Europe because of Napoleon's blockade. Restored to working order with audiovisual presentation and tea room.

• **Crabbe Corn Mill**, Lower Road, Dover CT17 OUY. Tel: 0303 823292. Open daily except Tuesday, April to November 10am (noon on Sunday)–5pm.

St Margaret at Cliffe is a pretty little place at the end of the cliff walk north-east of the town. Lovely views of France on the way. And beneath you, **St Margaret's Bay**, one of the best and quietest beaches around, accessed down the steep path.

The Pines Garden (Beach Road, St Margaret's Bay, Dover CT15 6DZ. Tel: 0304 852764) is a magnificent garden set around a little lake (open daily 10am–5pm).

Tourist information
13 Preston Street
Faversham ME13 8NS
Tel: 0795 534542

Hotels
Sea View Hotel ★★★
Broadway, Sheerness
Tel: 0795 662003
Preston Lea ★★
Canterbury Road
Faversham ME13 8XA
Tel: 0795 535266
The White Horse Inn ★★
The Street
Boughton ME13 9AX
Tel: 0227 751343
Frith Farm House ★★
Otterden ME13 0DD
Tel: 0795 890701

Restaurants
Reads Restaurant
Mummery Court House
Painters Forstal, Faversham
Tel: 0795 535344
Shelleys
1 Market Place, Faversham
Tel: 0795 531570

Festivals
Spring Blossom Festival, Brodgale, May.
Sheerness Show, August.

Long a busy port, **Faversham** suffered the same fate as many another important harbour, gradually silting up to become landlocked. Permanently fixed in the garb of its more prosperous past, Faversham has been content to look back with a fond nostalgia, rather than to seek change. Added to this picturesque architectural inheritance, the loveliness of her immediate surroundings definitely makes Faversham worth a visit.

55

The Guildhall – built at the beginning of the 19th century on top of an earlier structure which constitutes the present building's base – is a wonderful achievement in architectural equilibrium, set off to perfection by the handsome Tudor and Stuart façades which surround it to form the market-place. A few steps away, **Abbey Street**, of even earlier provenance, is definitely not to be missed.

The **Fleur de Lis Heritage Centre** presents a fascinating audiovisual montage of 1,000 years of the town's past.

• **Fleur De Lis Heritage Centre**, Preston Street, Faversham ME13 8NS. Open daily 10am–4pm, except Sundays October to May. Tel: 0795 534542.

St Mary's, the most beautiful of the town's churches, has a cycle of 14th-century paintings representing the life of Christ.

Beer-making, long established in the town, is important to the local economy. **Shepherd Neame Brewery**, Kent's largest independent brewery, offers tours and beer sampling.

• **Shepherd Neame Ltd**, 17 Courty Street, Faversham ME13 7AX. Tel: 0795 532206. Tours by arrangement.

A Kent orchard . . .

Places of particular interest to visit from Faversham – other than Canterbury, detailed above and only 11 miles to the east – include **Mount Ephraim Gardens** (further details in Gardens route, p104) and **Belmont Mansion** (further details in Castles and Country Houses route, p106).

But there's much, much more too, time and itinerary allowing.

Doddington Place (5 miles south-west), a large garden with 100-year-old trees and a planting scheme specially designed to produce maximum colour and bloom at summer's end (open Sundays May and every Wednesday Easter to September, or by arrangement. Tel: 079586 385). Just half a mile away to the east at Newnham is **The George** pub/restaurant, an excellent village inn (details in Country Pubs route, p108).

Farming World at Nash Court (2 miles south-east) is lovely for children. It is an educational farm laid out to maximise observation and enjoyment for the very young (May to October 9.30am–5.30pm and November to April 10am–4 pm. Tel: 0227 751224). Something a little out of the ordinary, and particularly delightful in the spring or autumn, is **Brogdale Horticultural Trust**, a living memorial to the fruit tree, where

visitors can stroll through acre after acre of orchard (Easter to Christmas, Wednesday to Sunday and public holidays 10am–5 pm).

West of Faversham is **Davington Priory**, dissolved during Henry VIII's reign. The former abbey church was restored in the 19th century and is now in use again as a place of worship. The remaining convent buildings have been converted into a manor house, now the home of Bob Geldof.

Five miles from Faversham is the paper manufacturing town of **Sittingbourne**. The **Dolphin Sailing Barge Museum** displays and restores the sailing boats which once transported the town's merchandise up and down the Medway (Tel: 0795 424132).

Sittingbourne is also the point of departure for the **Sittingbourne and Kemsley Light Railway**, a narrow-gauge railway open for steam locomotive rides every weekend April to October, as well as Tuesdays and Wednesdays in August (Tel: 0795 424899).

To the north of Faversham lies the **Isle of Sheppey**, linked to the rest of Kent by a road and rail bridge built in 1959. Its major town is **Sheerness**, a small port and pretty seaside resort whose beaches have been awarded

the blue flag for cleanliness. Car ferries leave Sheerness for Vlissingen.

Minster, near Sheerness, has a very beautiful church, once part of a monastery. Here is the tomb of Sir Robert Shurland, a medieval knight told by a witch that he would be killed by his horse, Grey Dolphin. It is said that he accordingly killed the horse, leaving its carcass on the beach. Much later, the knight was walking along the shore when he snared his foot in the horse's cranium and died of the ensuing poisoning!

FOLKESTONE
D-9 · 1/2 mile

Tourist information
Harbour Street
Folkestone CT20 1QN
Tel: 0303 258594

Hotels
Clifton Hotel ★★★
The Leas, Clifton Gardens
Folkestone CT20 2EB
Tel: 0303 851231
Langhorne Garden Hotel ★★
10–12 Langhorne Gardens
Folkestone CT20 2EA
Tel: 0303 257233
Banque Hotel ★★
4 Castle Hill Avenue
Folkestone CT20 2QT
Tel: 0303 253797
Wards Hotel ★★
39 Earls Avenue
Folkestone CT20 5HB
Tel: 0303 245166

Restaurants
British Lion (pub)
10 The Bayle
Folkestone
Tel: 0303 251478

Copperfields
3a West Terrace, Folkestone
Tel: 0303 249900
Paul's Restaurant
2a Bouverie Road West
Folkestone
Tel: 0303 259697

Entertainment
The Leas Cliff Hall
(concerts, theatre, spectacles, music hall)
The Leas, Folkestone
Tel: 0303 253193
The Leas Club
(bar with regular concerts Thursday and Sunday)
The Leas, Folkestone
Tel: 0303 245062

Festivals
Folkestone Carnival, August.
Festival of English Literature, October.

Dover's twin town but without the historic inheritance of her more illustrious sister, Folkestone has always suffered from the comparison. In 1842 it was no more than a little fishing port when the South-Eastern Railway Company decided to route the London–Dover line through Folkestone, and its impressive brick viaduct can still be seen. The choice of Folkestone as the Tunnel entry point, arising primarily out of technical expediency, is likely to have considerable impact on the town's future development.

Folkestone is not without its attractions. After the opening of the railway, it became a popular seaside resort and today still boasts wide avenues of elegant Victorian houses. **The Leas** is a mile-and-a-half-long walk across the cliffs, accessed by a funicular from the beach (built in 1885), and finishing at its eastern end at the interesting church of **St Mary and St Eanswythe** with its surround of attractive period houses.

The **Martello Tower** (East Cliff, at East Wear Bay) was part of a line of similar defences constructed in case of Napoleonic invasion, but today houses exhibits of the flora, fauna and geology of the adjacent **Warren Nature Reserve** (Easter to September 10.30am–5.30pm. Tel: 0303 850388).

Visitors to Folkestone should not miss the **Eurotunnel Exhibition Centre**, at Cheriton (first exit, no 12, off M20 to London). As well as providing technical background to the Tunnel (model tunnel-boring machine, geological sections, etc) and an account of the history leading to this 'first European-scale, joint venture' plus descriptions of the transport system itself (model trains, etc), there is also a map of the transport network of Europe: ultimate illustration of the Tunnel's *raison d'être*! The map makes the point that, given Great Britain's political and economic integration with Europe, her continued physical separation is inappropriate.

• **Eurotunnel Exhibition Centre**, St Martin's Plain, Cheriton High Street, Folkestone CT19 4QD. Tel: 0303 270547. Open 10am–6pm (5pm in winter).

Just two miles west along the coast from Folkestone, is **Sandgate**, and **Sandgate Castle**. Presenting a less war-

Folkestone: the Tunnel terminal

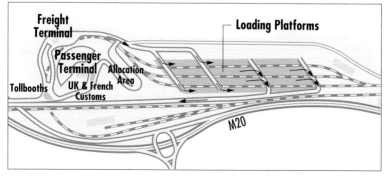

like exterior is **Spade House**, former home of H G Wells, author of *War of the Worlds*.

On the A260 towards Canterbury is **Hawkinge**, a little town whose flying club houses the **Battle of Britain Museum**. Here are displays of items from the air battle which perhaps decided the outcome of the Second World War, engines, flying instruments, photographs, explanatory maps, and every sort of flying memorabilia (Easter to October 10am–5pm, *see* Defence Structures route, p112).

Continue a mile or so further west along the road and you come to the paradise of the farming vale of Elham Valley. **Parsonage Farm Rural Heritage Centre** at North Elham is an activity farm offering town-dwellers an insight into the working life of a farm and its animals, both domestic and rare breeds (Easter to October, Tuesday to Sunday 10.30am–5pm. Tel: 0303 840766).

Elham Valley Vineyards at Breach, near Barham, is a charmingly situated vineyard.

HERNE BAY & WHITSTABLE
B-9 • 27 miles

Tourist information
12 William Street
Herne Bay CT6 5EJ
Tel: 0227 361911
and
The Horsebridge
Whitstable CT5 1BU
Tel: 0227 275482

Hotels
Wyndridge ★★★
Wraik Hill, Whitstable CT5 3BY
Tel: 0227 263506
Marine Hotel ★★
Marine Parade, Tankerton
Whitstable
Tel: 0227 272672
St George ★
Western Esplanade, Herne Bay
Tel: 0227 233776

Restaurants
Pearsons (pub)
Sea Wall, Whitstable
Tel: 0227 272005
Beau Rivage
101 Tankerton Road, Whitstable
Tel: 0227 272056

Riggins Restaurant
6 East Street, Herne Bay
Tel: 0227 361880

Festivals
Oyster Festival, July to August in Whitstable.

Herne Bay and Whitstable, less well known perhaps than Ramsgate and Margate, manage – perhaps for this very reason – to retain a certain air of the past; a time when visitors might have come here for champagne and oysters rather than today's ubiquitous tea and scones!

At **Herne Bay**, turn-of-the-century houses look across the promenade out to sea, growing more handsome with every passing year.

A little further inland the old village of **Herne** is ringed around by its harbour extension, its chief pride and joy being a completely restored 18th-century windmill (**Herne Windmill**, Easter to end September, Sundays and public holidays 2pm–5pm. Tel: 0227 361326).

Alternatively, make an interesting excursion 3 miles east along the coast to a Saxon church standing amid the ruins of the Roman fort of *Regulbium* – today's **Reculver** (April to end September, Monday to Saturday 9.30am–6.30pm, and Sunday 2–6.30pm, *see* Defence Structures route, p112).

Whitstable, whose July–August oyster festival includes lots of special events, is a small, modern town. A scattering of fishermen's houses and boats now converted into houseboats make for a pleasant saunter around the harbour.

Whitstable Museum and Gallery is a celebration of both the Royal Native Oyster – the local variety – and of its habitual or occasional predators, fishermen, oyster-growers and tourists.

Chuffa Trains Railmania Museum salutes another human pastime that is as old as the hills, namely playing with models. Here, of course, the models in question are miniature trains, all the more enjoyable for affording such a harmless leisure pursuit. Plenty of space

for the children to enjoy themselves, though of course everyone knows this is really one for the adults! (Monday to Saturday 10am–5pm, 3pm low season. Tel: 0227 277339.)

HYTHE
D-9 • 2½ miles

Tourist information
Prospect Road Car Park
Hythe CT21 5NH
Tel: 0303 267799

Hotels
Imperial Hotel ★★★★
Princes Parade
Hythe CT21 6AE
Tel: 0303 267441
Stade Court ★★★
West Parade, Hythe CT21 6DT
Tel: 0303 268263

Restaurants
Four Winds Restaurant
West Parade, Hythe
Tel: 0303 266409
The Red Lion (pub)
Red Lion Square, Hythe
Tel: 0303 266686

Entertainment
Jam's Café (nightclub)
Marine Parade and South Road
Hythe
Tel: 0303 263838

Festivals
Hythe Venetian Fete, August bi-annually.

Hythe was one of the Cinque Port towns. Originally five coastal towns, later more, which grouped together to sign a commercial-military treaty with the sovereign, to equip and supply men for a fixed number of ships whenever these should be needed, in exchange for relative independence from the crown. The history of the Cinque Port League established in the Middle Ages is told in the local museum, **Hythe Local History Room**, at Hythe Library.

The **Church of St Leonard** which dominates the town has a fine 13th-century choir. Best known for its crypt containing hundreds of human skulls, dating from the Middle Ages but whose history is otherwise unknown.

When the port of Hythe silted up, it might well have lost all strategic importance, had it not been for its position at one end of the **Royal Military Canal**, which separates the old town from the beach. Dug between 1804 and 1806, the canal goes all the way to Rye, East Sussex (see Defence Structures route, p112).

Hythe is also the home of the famous **Romney, Hythe and Dymchurch Railway**, 'the smallest real train', which since 1927 has linked the town to Dungeness more than 12 miles away. From Easter to October, a constant flow of accurately modelled, one-third-actual-size locomotives and carriages take visitors on rides along the coast (Tel: 0679 62353).

Close to Hythe, at **Saltwood**, the 14th-century castle once belonged to the archbishops of Canterbury.

Further along the B2067, the little town of **Lympne** grew up around the Roman fort of *Portus Lemanis*. This was demolished during the Norman period and the materials used to build a church and the foundations of a castle, the latter being modified in the 14th century. **Lympne Castle**, now magnificently restored, has excellent views from its gardens over **Romney Marsh**, a tract of extremely fertile land reclaimed from the sea (Easter to end September – best to book, see Defence Structures route, p112).

A little further along the B2067, you come to **Port Lympne Zoo Park and House**, one of John Aspinall's two zoos. The house is an unusual design on several levels, the gardens, especially in the spring, are splendid, and the zoo's 150 acres are home to dozens of species, including gorillas, elephants, tigers . . . (open in summer 10am–7pm and winter 10am–5pm. Tel: 0303 264647).

MAIDSTONE
B-7 · 34 miles

Tourist information
The Gatehouse
Old Palace Gardens, Mill Street
Maidstone ME15 6YE
Tel: 0622 673581

Hotels
Grangemoor Hotel ★★★
4 St Michael's Road
Maidstone ME16 8 BS
Tel: 0622 677623
Tudor Park Hotel ★★★
Ashford Road
Bearsted ME14 4NQ
Tel: 0622 734334
Dog & Bear Hotel ★★
The Square
Lenham ME17 2PG
Tel: 0622 858219
Willington Court ★★
Willington Street
Maidstone ME15 8JW
Tel: 0622 738885
Roslin Villa ★
11 St Michael's Road
Maidstone ME16 8BS
Tel: 0622 758301

Restaurants
Ringlestone Inn
Between Harrietsham and Wormshill
Maidstone ME17 1AX
Tel: 0622 859900
Sir Thomas Wyatt Beefeater
London Road, Maidstone
Tel: 0622 752515
Cobblestones Restaurant
Lees Road, Yalding, Maidstone

Tel: 0622 814326
The Royal Orchid
106 Week Street, Maidstone
Tel: 0622 756285

Entertainment
Hazlitt Theatre
Earl Street, Maidstone
Tel: 0622 758611

Festivals
Leeds Castle Easter Egg Hunt, Easter.
Kent County Show, July.
Carnival, end July.
Beer and Hop festival, Museum of Kent Life, early September.

Kent's major town, a manufacturing centre (textiles, paper and brewing industries), standing in the heart of a farming region (hops, some vines), Maidstone is above all else a shopping centre. Home to the head offices of many wholesale and retail outlets, with many of the better known names to be found in or near the **High Street**, it is a display case of the region's prosperity.

There was no town here in Norman times, but the archbishops of Canterbury chose the site for a palace on the banks of the River Medway. A period of relative prosperity followed,

Maidstone: a timbered house typical of the Weald and home to the famous Tyrwhitt-Drake Museum of Carriages

Leeds Castle: dramatic architecture in a stunning setting

increasing when the town decided to free itself from the ecclesiastic yoke in 1459.

The **archiepiscopal palace** is open to visitors and dates from the 14th century. Completely restored, it includes a restaurant and gift shop (free entry), and an excellent **Heritage Centre** local history museum – where an entrance fee is payable (open daily 10.30am–5.30pm. Tel: 0622 663006).

As well as visiting the old town near the river and the magnificent Gothic church of **All Saints** (built around 1390), leave enough time if you can for the carriage museum, the town museum and the **Museum of Kent Life**, three very interesting further attractions.

• **Tyrwhitt-Drake Museum of Carriages**, Mill Street, Maidstone ME15 6YE. Tel: 0622 754497. Open Monday to Saturday 10.30am–5.30pm.

• **Maidstone Museum and Art Gallery**, St Faith's Street, Maidstone ME14 1 LH. Tel: 0622 756405. Open daily 10.30am–5.30pm, except Sunday 2–5pm.

• **Museum of Kent Life**, Lock Lane, Sandling ME14 3AU. Tel: 0622 763936. Open Easter to October 10.30am–5.30pm.

Close by is **Hollingbourne** (4 miles to the east), nestling at the foot of the North Downs, and famous for its Saxon church and Tudor manor (**Eyhorne Manor**).

Aylesford (3 miles northwest), though reached via a lacework of motorways and industrial wasteland, presents a pretty picture on arrival: a 14th-century bridge, Tudor houses and, rising above these, the tower of the Carmelite monastery, called **The Friars**, in late Norman style. Hounded from England by Henry VIII – along with all the other religious orders – Carmelites re-settled here in 1949 (Tel: 0622 790796).

The windows of **Boughton Monchelsea Place**, an Elizabethan manor house in Kent stone, afford visitors a wonderful view over the gardens and the Weald beyond. (Open Sundays and public holidays, Easter to end October, and Wednesday in summer 2.15–6pm. Tel: 0622 765400).

Leeds Castle, 4 miles east of Maidstone is, in the eyes of many, Britain's most beautiful castle. It would certainly not look out of place in a fairytale, set picturesquely astride two islets in the lake of a 600-acre park (further information in Castles and Country Houses route, p106).

To the west are two farms open to visitors. One is **Nepicar Farm**, concentrating on animal rearing (Borough Green, tel: 0732 883040, open mid March to December, 11am–5pm). The other is the very popular **Whitbread Hop Farm**, with enough to do to fill a whole day (hop museum, children's zoo, birds of prey flying displays, children's play area).

• **Whitbread Hop Farm,** Beltring, Paddock Wood. Tel: 0622 872630. Open all year 10am–6pm (4pm in winter).

NEW ROMNEY
D-8 • 11 miles

Tourist information
2 Littlestone Road
New Romney TN28 8PL
Tel: 0679 64044

Hotels
Broadacre Hotel ★★
North Street, New Romney
TN28 8DR
Tel: 0679 62381
Cotswold Lodge Hotel ★★
Coast Road, Littlestone
Tel: 0679 63646

Restaurants
Blue Dolphins
Dymchurch Road, New Romney
Tel: 0679 63224
Brian's Bistro
Dymchurch Road, New Romney
Tel: 0679/ 62138

Festivals
Dymchurch Day of Syn, August.
New Romney Vintage Rally, summer.
Phillipine Festival, Brookland, summer.

Bibliography
Paul Theroux, *The Kingdom by the Sea*, Hamish Hamilton.

Fortune deals as capriciously with towns as with men: little villages have become flourishing capitals, great cities blessed by earlier gods are today sunk into oblivion.

New Romney suffered the latter fate. Launched into history by increased cross-Channel trade and her position at the mouth of the Rother, little wonder that New Romney became the principal town of the League of Cinque Ports, the prime military force and rampart of the island kingdom.

That is, until the day came, in 1287, when the storm raged with such ferocity, when the rain swelled the Rother to such an extent, that the terrain through which the river passed on its last few miles to the sea was broken up and the river, forgetting about New Romney, flowed on instead to Rye. It is difficult now to imagine that ships once cast anchor a stone's throw from the church of St Nicholas.

The biggest station of the famous Romney, Hythe and Dymchurch railway (whose miniature trains still delight the young at heart), New Romney is situated behind a series of unexceptional seaside resorts, their bungalows lining the coast up to Dungeness, where the RSPB reserve is open daily except Tuesday 9am–9pm (or sunset).

• **RSPB Nature Reserve**, Boulderwall Farm, Dungeness Road, Lydd TN29 9PN. Tel: 0679 20588.

Romney Marsh, a couple of miles inland, was once an ancient marsh, now drained. Today, the celebrated salt-meadow sheep graze here, much like their French counter-parts on Mont-Saint-Michel.

"From the dawdling open car, where I sat with my feet up, in the cool empty light that slowed everything it touched this spring evening, I saw sheep and horses, wheat fields with breezes swimming through them and small houses built close to the ground. At Dymchurch there were yellow fields, one of the pleasures of May in England, the brightest crop: a whole field brimful of vivid buttery rape flowers."

Paul Theroux

RAMSGATE, MARGATE & BROADSTAIRS

B-10 · 27 miles

Tourist information
The Argyle Centre, Queen Street, Ramsgate CT11 9EE
Tel: 0843 591086
and
Pierremont Hall, 6B High Street
Broadstairs CT10 1LH
Tel: 0843 862242
and
22 High Street
Margate CT9 1DS
Tel: 0843 220241

Hotels
Bridge Hotel ★★★
13–15 St Mildred Road
Westgate CT8 8RE

Tel: 0843 831023
Ivyside Hotel ★★★
25 Sea Road
Westgate CT8 8SB
Tel: 0843 831082
The Bay Tree Hotel ★★
12 Eastern Esplanade
Broadstairs CT10 1DR
Tel: 0843 862502
Goodwin View Hotel ★
19 Wellington Crescent
Ramsgate CT11 8JD
Tel: 0843 591419
Broadstairs Youth Hostel
Thistle Lodge, 3 Osborne Road
Broadstairs CT10 2AD.
Tel: 0843 604121

Restaurants
Beau's Restaurant
8 Charlotte Street, Broadstairs
Tel: 0843 862711
The Bistro
4 Hawley Square, Margate
Tel: 0843 224347
The Four Lanterns
6 Market Place, Margate
Tel: 0843 / 293034
Harbour View Restaurant
42–44 Harbour Street
Ramsgate
Tel: 0843 595341

Entertainment
Granville Theatre
Victoria Parade, Ramsgate
Tel: 0843 591750
Winter Gardens Theatre
Fort Crescent, Margate
Tel: 0843 865726
Pavilion Theatre
Broadstairs
Tel: 0843 865726

Festivals
Dickens Festival at Broadstairs, June.
Folklore Week, Broadstairs.

The Isle of Thanet is the most easterly part of the county of Kent. It has, of course, long since ceased to be an island. Named after a Carthigian god-dess, Thanet appears entirely dedicated to tourism.

But, in fact, it offers a very varied menu. The Broadstairs of Dickens, so beloved of him that he holidayed here year after year (leaving more than a few traces, like **Bleak House** – aptly named, up on the cliff domin-ating the beautiful golden sands below), this Broadstairs is entirely different from Margate, Cliftonville, Westgate and

Birchington. These are family resorts, whose peace and quiet is interrupted only once a year on May Day weekend, when neo-mods and neo-skinheads with a nostalgia for violence come to cross swords with one another in memory of the more glorious battles of the 1960s!

And then, Ramsgate . . . happy to trade on the cachet of its regally named Royal Harbour.

With so much to choose from, where to begin? At **Broad-stairs,** the **Dickens House Museum** (2 Victoria Parade, Broadstairs CT10 1QS. Tel: 0843 862853) will be of par-ticular interest to anyone already familiar with the life and novels of the great author (Easter to mid October, *see* Writers route, p110).

Crampton Tower Museum, named after the transport engineer of the same name, has model displays of old buses and trams (High Street, Broadstairs. Tel: 0843 862078. Open Easter to end September, Monday, Tuesday, Thursday and Friday 2.30–5pm).

At **Margate**, a restored 19th-century windmill, **Draper's Windmill** (Tel: 0843 291696), a medieval barn formerly ad-joining a church (**Salmestone Grange**, Nash Road, Margate. Tel: 0843 226909) and a mag-nificent flower garden (**Quex House**, Park Lane, Birchington. Tel: 0843 842168, open Satur-day afternoon July to October) all vie for the attention of visitors.

At **Ramsgate**, the **Maritime Museum** beautifully illustrates Thanet's stormy relationship with the sea (open 9.30am–4.30pm, Monday to Friday and Saturday and Sunday after-noons in summer. Tel: 0843 587765).

At **Pegwell Bay**, you can see a reconstruction of a Danish *drakkar*, the ships that landed in their dozens along the English coast around the year 1000 AD, in search of a new home in a (relatively) clement climate.

Four miles west of Ramsgate is **Minster's** Norman church and convent. On the way back, why not visit the **Spitfire Memorial**

Pavilion at Manston, full of Battle of Britain miscellanea (*see* Defence Structures route, p112).

ROCHESTER. CHATHAM AND GILLINGHAM

B-7 · 41 miles

Tourist information
Eastgate Cottage, High Street
Rochester ME1 1EW
Tel: 0634 843666

Hotels
Bridgewood Manor Hotel ★★★★
Maidstone Road
Chatham ME5 9AX
Tel: 0634 201333
Gordon Hotel ★★★
91 High Street
Rochester ME1 1LX
Tel: 0634 842656
Royal Victoria & Bull Hotel
16–18 High Street,
Rochester ME1 1PX
Tel: 0634 846266

Restaurants
Golden Crown
26 High Street, Chatham
Tel: 0634 846248
The Castle
151 High Street, Rochester
Tel: 0634 342812

Entertainment
Medway Little Theatre
256 High Street, Rochester
Tel: 0634 379425

Festivals
Rochester Sweeps Festival,
1 May.
Rochester Dickens Festival,
June.
Norman Festival, Rochester,
August.
Christmas with Dickens,
Rochester.

Bibliography
The Mystery of Edwin Drood, by
Charles Dickens

The towns of Rochester and Chatham, long since merged into one, together with neighbouring Gillingham, all look seaward, though they are, in fact, a little way from the mouth of the Medway. Their position may have limited the development of deep-draft maritime trade but has, by contrast, served to assure the military importance of the three towns, admirably protected by their geography. The Navy is still here, though admittedly today it is more the preserve of leisure boats.

Rochester was the last fortified town before London on the road from Kent. The Romans built *Durobrivae* here, imitated some eight centuries later by William the Conqueror, and it is his castle, plus a dungeon added in the 13th century, that tourists can visit today (gardens and good views).

• **Rochester Castle.** Open 1 October to 31 March, Tuesday to Sunday 10am–4pm and 1 April to 30 September, daily 10am–6pm. Tel: 0634 402276.

The **Cathedral**, largely Norman, is worth an in-depth visit, not so much for the excellent craftsmanship – though some of the tombs, in particular, are beautifully ornamented – but more to take in the wonderful medieval atmosphere of the place. The porch, nave and crypt are of particular interest. The buildings around the cathedral are all of a fairly respectable age, sufficient at least to have known the young Dickens (who lived at Chatham between the ages of 2 and 12). **Eastgate House** among them figures in many Dickensian episodes, so it is no surprise to find the **Dickens Centre** here, with a series of animated tableaux to transport visitors back to the world of the great novelist (*see* Writers route, p110).

• **The Dickens Centre**, High Street, Rochester ME1 1EW. Tel: 0634 844176. Open daily 10am–5pm.

Also in the High Street, the **Guildhall** is a fine 17th-century building and home to the local history museum (open daily 10am–5.30pm. Tel: 0634 848717).

Across the Medway Bridge is **Strood**, less interesting except for its Knights of the Templar manor house. Then, on the same west bank, but a little further downstream, is **Upnor Castle**, a fortress dating from Elizabethan times (*see* Defence Structures route, p112).

Chatham, east of Rochester, owes its prosperity to the arsenal that Henry VIII decided to establish here. **Chatham Dockyard's** 120 acres have been converted into a huge – and very popular – maritime

Rochester: The Dickens Centre

One of the many oast houses whose characteristic silhouettes punctuate the Kent countryside

museum illustrating the ship-building process and maritime transport management (October to March, Wednesdays and weekends 10am–4.30pm and April to September, Wednesday to Sunday 10am–6pm, *see* Defence Structures route, p112). From May to October, the *Kingswear Castle* paddle-steamer plies passengers up and down the Medway from Chatham dock (Tel: 0634 827648).

Fort Amherst, dating from the Napoleonic era, is still a garrison but is open to the public (further details in Defence Structures route, p112).

Gillingham, further east, is a modern town, worth visiting for its harbour and the interesting **Royal Engineers Museum**, which traces the rich history of the British Empire through a retrospective of the Royal Engineers Regiment.

• **Royal Engineers Museum**, Prince Arthur Road, Gillingham ME4 4UG. Tel: 0634 406397. Open all year 11.30am–5pm weekends, 10am–5pm weekdays.

SANDWICH
B-10 · 20 miles

Tourist information
The Guildhall, Cattle Market
Sandwich CT13 9AH
Tel: 0304 613565

Hotels
The Bell Hotel ★★★★
The Quay, Sandwich GT13 9EF
Tel: 0304 613388

Restaurants
Admiral Owen (pub)
8 High Street, Sandwich
Tel: 0304 612261
16th-Century Tea House
9 Cattle Market, Sandwich
Tel: 0304 612392
Scarecrow Restaurant
The Quay, Sandwich
Tel: 0304 617492

After sand and silt brought misfortune to Hythe, **Sandwich** became the most important of the Cinque Ports (already owing its local importance to Richborough's silting up at the end of the Roman period). But alas for Sandwich, the same fate was, in turn, to befall her. Alas for her, yet not for her visitors, for today her appearance and atmosphere is much as it would have been in the Middle Ages. Of the old town, two gates remain, **Barbican Gate** and **Fishers Gate**; three churches, which share the parish's church-goers, **St Peter's**, **St Mary's** and **St Clement's**; while old houses grace most of her winding and picturesque streets.

A couple of miles north of Sandwich are the ruins of the Roman fort of *Rutupiae* (**Richborough Castle**, *see* Defence Structures route, p112). Little may remain of the Roman

structure, but what does confirms how strategically important this former port was to the Romans.

West of Sandwich, on the A25, is the charming village of **Wingham**, and off Rusham Road is **Wingham Bird Park** (open November to February weekends 10am–5pm and March to October daily 10am–6pm).

Turning off to the south from Wingham, you will soon see signs for **Goodnestone Park**, beloved of Jane Austen (further details in Gardens route, p104).

SEVENOAKS
B-5 · 52 miles

Tourist information
Buckhurst Lane
Sevenoaks TN13 1LQ
Tel: 0732 450305

Hotels
Moorings Hotel ★★★
97 Hitchen Hatch Lane
Sevenoaks TN13 3BE
Tel: 0732 452589
Royal Oak ★★★
Upper High Street
Sevenoaks TN13 1HY
Tel: 0732 451109
Donnington Manor ★★★
London Road
Dunton Green TN13 2TD
Tel: 0732 462681
Sevenoaks Park Hotel ★★
Seal Hollow Road, Sevenoaks
Tel: 0732 454245

Sevenoaks: Great Comp Garden

Restaurants
Blighs
135 High Street, Sevenoaks
Tel: 1732 454092
The Chequers (pub)
High Street, Sevenoaks
Tel: 1732 454377

As well as being attractive in its own right, this town at the foot of Knole house (with a museum in the library in Buckhurst Lane, Tel: 1732 452384) makes another excellent touring base.

Knole (in grounds extending to some 1,000 acres) is the main and nearest attraction in the truly lovely countryside around Sevenoaks. It was built by an archbishop of Canterbury, confiscated by Henry VIII, then held in feoff by the Sackville family, from the time that Elizabeth I made a present of it to her cousin until the last member of the family bequeathed it to the National Trust (further details in Castles and Country Houses route, p106).

Two miles south of Knole is **Riverhill House**, a charming house standing in an equally charming garden. In spring and early summer, flowering azaleas and rhododendrons make a breathtaking show (open Sundays and public holidays April–June or by arrangement. Tel: 1732 458802).

Going west from Sevenoaks, the committed tourist can take in

Emmetts Garden, Chartwell and Squerryes Court.

Emmetts is a superb, medium-sized garden on a hill, with wonderful views (further details in Gardens route, p104).

Chartwell also has fine gardens and is a beautiful and beautifully-kept house in the best English country house tradition. It was also, of course, the home of Winston Churchill, and this, as well as the setting, makes it a very enjoyable place to visit (further information in Writers route, p110).

At **Squerryes Court**, the gardens are different, rather more formal than is usual for an English garden, but with an enchantment all their own. The manor house was built in 1681 and contains an interesting collection of paintings, porcelain, furniture and tapestries (at Westerham. Tel: 0959 562345. Open April to end September, Wednesday, Saturday, Sunday and public holidays, 2–6pm or by arrangement).

East of Sevenoaks, other treats are in store. Visit **Ightham Mote** (**The Plough** pub at Ivy Hatch 5 miles away serves food as exceptional as the surroundings, further details in Country Pubs route, p108). Or **Great Comp Garden** (near Borough Green, 8 miles away) is worth the detour.

Ightham Mote medieval manor house, surrounded by a moat, is a cultural and aesthetic feast (further details in Castles and Country Houses route, p104).

Great Comp comes into its own in the month of May . . . early summer daydreaming and reverie, as well as tea, the latter has to be booked in advance (further details in Gardens route, p104).

TENTERDEN
D-7 · 26 miles

Tourist information
Town Hall, High Street
Tenterden TN30 6AN
Tel: 0580 763572

Hotels
Little Silver Country ****
Ashford Road, St Michael's
Tenterden TN30 6SP
Tel: 0233 850321
White Lion Hotel ***
High Street
Tenterden TN30 6BD
Tel: 0580 765077

Restaurants
Cinque Ports Restaurant
52–56 High Street, Tenterden
Tel: 0580 762060
Tudor Rose Restaurant
29 High Street, Tenterden
Tel: 0580 763381

Tenterden is a very quiet and very pretty old town. The broad High Street with Georgian and Victorian houses, beautiful lawns and ancient trees for shade, is exquisite, dominated by the bell-tower of the Gothic church of **St Mildred**.

Tenterden is the starting point of the famous **Kent and East Sussex Railway**, whose veteran steam locomotives still provide a rail link to Northiam (**Great Dixter Garden** and **Bodiam Castle**, *see under* Rye and Battle, Sussex), passing en route through the magnificent countryside of the Rother valley (Tel: 0580 765155).

In the road leading to the station is the **Tenterden and District Museum** (Tel: 0580 763350). Worth a visit.

In the surrounding area, besides visiting **Sissinghurst Garden** (*see under* Cranbrook), take time to turn off the beaten track for wonderfully soothing views over the cultivated countryside.

On the approach to Biddenden (to the north), there is an excellent vineyard open to the public (**Biddenden Vineyards**, Little Whatmans, Biddenden TN27 8DH. Tel: 0580 291726).

Wittersham, to the south, reached via the B2082, is dominated by **Stocks Mill Windmill** built in 1781, from which you can enjoy an excellent view, as well as the little **Millwright's Museum**, open June to September Sunday and public holidays. Tel: 0797 270537.

To the west is the little town of **Woodchurch**: streets of thatched cottages, and the home of the **South of England Rare Breeds Centre** (open 10.30am–5.30pm all year. Tel: 0233 861493), an animal breeding and rearing unit specialising in south-east England breeds.

TONBRIDGE
C-6 · 49 miles

Tourist information
Tonbridge Castle, Castle Street
Tonbridge TN9 1BG
Tel: 0732 770929

Penshurst Place: the path to the Tudor garden

Hotels
Rose and Crown Hotel ★★★
125 High Street
Tonbridge TN9 1DD
Tel: 0732 357966
Goldhill Mill ★★★
Golden Green
Tonbridge TN11 0AB
Tel: 0732 851626
The Chaser Inn
Stumble Hill
Shipbourne TN11 9PE
Tel: 0732 910360

Restaurants
The Cock House (pub)
Hildenborough, Tonbridge
Tel: 0732 833232

Tonbridge, by virtue of its key position on the River Medway, was already an important town in medieval times.

On a little rise overlooking the river, first Saxons, then Normans, built a fortified castle. Though now a ruin, this archetypal feudal castle is still impressive; without too much difficulty, the visitor can visualize how 12th-century life might have been played out within its walls (open Monday to Saturday 9am–5pm; Sundays and public holidays 10.30am–5pm. Tel: 0732 770929).

Lots of unusual old houses line the streets immediately adjacent to the castle. But the best of Tonbridge is to be found on its outskirts. The ideal starting point for so many other excursions, Tonbridge is a must for anyone visiting Kent.

A couple of miles to the north, the village of **Hollanden** is very proud of two things: a special farm where children delight at more than 40 different rare breeds; and, to balance their education, a reconstruction of an Iron Age village (open Easter to end September 10.30am–5pm. Tel: 0732 833858).

Then, to the west, two stunning villages and a fairytale castle vie for the attention of visitors – emphasising (if emphasis were needed) that one day is nowhere near enough to explore the Tonbridge region.

The village of **Penshurst** has a wealth of medieval, Tudor and Stuart houses, 12th- and 13th-century churches and, just over a mile away, the quintessential country pub, **The Spotted Dog**. Take time for a game of darts, or, weather permitting, gaze out upon the lovely countryside from the vantage point of the pub garden (further details in Country Pubs route, p108).

But Penshurst is also known for the rather good white wine produced at **Penshurst Vineyards** (a few examples of exotic wildlife to amuse the children while adults sample the wine . . . open all year 10am–5pm. Tel: 0892 870255); and, finally, **Penshurst Place**, a splendid country house with fine furniture and a toy museum, set in a Tudor garden and offering an impressive array of activities for children (open daily Easter to end September 11am–6pm. Tel: 0892 870307).

The village of **Chiddingstone**, a little further to the west, is so exceptional that it has been conveyed in its entirety to the National Trust. Its 16th- and 17th-century streets, as well as the adjacent neo-Gothic castle, hold much to delight and interest. **The Castle** pub is perhaps top of the list, with delicious food, good English beer and excellent local wine.

Hever Castle was in a very poor state when American multi-millionaire William Waldorf Astor took it on and began to restore it. Though very close now in appearance to the original

Penshurst Place: seductive in its sobriety

fortified Tudor manor house, the odd unconscious touch of Hollywood kitsch might make the visitor expect to bump into Ava Gardner or Rita Hayworth, rather than Anne Boleyn, who was born here. Anne, of course, made the mistake of bumping into Henry VIII who seriously curtailed her life 'performance'. The castle gardens are intriguing too (further details in Castles and Country Houses route, p106).

East of Tonbridge, the working life of this essentially agricultural region is presented at **Badsell Park Farm** (April to November 10am–5.30pm. Tel: 0892 832549).

TUNBRIDGE WELLS
C-6 · 44 miles

Tourist information
The Old Fish Market
Tunbridge Wells TN2 5TN
Tel: 0892 515675

Hotels
Swan Hotel ***
The Pantiles
Tunbridge Wells TN2 5TD
Tel: 0892 541450
Periquito Hotel ***
84 Mount Ephraim
Tunbridge Wells TN4 8BU
Tel: 0892 542911
Kingswood Hotel ***
Pembury Road
Tunbridge Wells TN2 3QS
Tel: 0892 535736
Spa Hotel ***
8 Tonbridge Road
Tunbridge Wells

Tel: 0892 528757
Danehurst **
41 Lower Green Road
Rusthall TN4 8TW
Tel: 0892 527739
Vale Royal Hotel *
54/57 London Road
Tunbridge Wells TN1 1DS
Tel: 0892 525580

Restaurants
Cheevers
56 High Street
Tunbridge Wells
Tel: 0892 545324
La Galoche
The Common, Tunbridge Wells
Tel: 0892 526823
Boatright Calverley
Crescent Road
Tunbridge Wells
Tel: 8092 526455

Festivals
Georgian Festivities, Tunbridge Wells, first fortnight August.
Finchcocks Festival, September to mid October.

Tunbridge Wells, or to give it its nomenclature bestowed by H M King Edward VII, Royal Tunbridge Wells, situated on the Kent/Sussex borders, is ideally placed to serve the visitor to south-east England.

It has been a fashionable spa for more than 200 years, with a rare, if not unique, example of a 17th-century street in the short walk bordered by shops known as **The Pantiles**.

Hever Castle: one of England's most popular attractions

Just behind The Pantiles, the **Corn Exchange**, which began life in 1802 as a theatre, has an exhibition 'A Day at the Wells', depicting the life of 18th-century Tunbridge Wells.

• **A Day at the Wells**. April to October 10am–5pm, 4pm in winter. Tel: 0892 546545.

Tunbridge Wells Museum and Art Gallery offers a fairly lively mix of exhibits (Mount Pleasant Road, open Monday to Saturday 9.30am–5pm. Tel: 0892 526121).

In 1828, Decimus Burton was chosen to design the first phase of the new town of **Calverley**. The beautiful proportions of the first phase of building were not, in the event, ever followed by further building, and Burton's handsome crescent of houses is encompassed within present-day Tunbridge.

Four miles to the south-west of Tunbridge is **Groombridge Place Gardens**, a magical encapsulation of the two opposite poles of garden design: on the one hand the 'natural' garden, melting in turn into enchanted forest; on the other, the formal garden, conforming to a set of established, formal design rules. Groombridge Place was used for the setting of the Peter Greenaway film, *The Draughtsman's Contract* (open April and May, Saturdays, Sundays and public holidays 2–6pm; June to September daily except Thursday and Friday 2–6pm, and for the first two weekends in October. Tel: 0892 863999).

In the village of Groombridge, **The Crown** pub makes for a very relaxing stop. A little turning off the other side of the road leads to Groombridge Place.

Other places of interest around Tunbridge Wells (in addition to those described under Tonbridge) are to be found at **Lamberhurst**. You might pass this village by with never a second glance, were it not, first, for **The Brown Trout**, a pub/restaurant offering meals of an exceptionally high standard (further details in Country Pubs route, p108), and second,

for its toy museum (**Lamberhurst Toy & Model Museum**, open 10am–6pm. Tel: 0892 890711).

South of Lamberhurst, **Lamberhurst Vineyard** has lots of wines to sample (Monday to Saturday 9am–6pm, Sundays 10am–5pm. Tel: 0892 890286).

Scotney Castle Garden is one of Britain's most romantic gardens. In late spring, when everything is burgeoning, a riot of intense colour encircles the moat of this ruined castle (further details in Gardens route, p104).

Finchcocks is a Georgian manor situated between Lamberhurst and Goudhurst. It has a pretty garden and an impressive collection of old tools and implements. (Open Easter to end September, Sundays 2–6pm, and in August, Wednesday to Sunday 2–6pm. Tel: 0580 211702.)

On the road back to Tunbridge Wells, a further two gardens beckon: **Marle Place Gardens** and **Owl House Gardens**.

The first of these, near **Brenchley**, offers a variety of garden landscapes (open 1 April to 31 October 10am–5.30pm. Tel: 0892 722304), and the second, on the A21 just a mile from **Lamberhurst**, has over 15 acres of romantic azalea and rhododendron walk (open daily 11am–6pm. Tel: 0892 890230).

Scotney Castle: romantic idyll

Sussex

Recently divided into two counties whose principal towns, Chichester (West Sussex) and Lewes (East Sussex), vie with one another in their claims of prettiest and most historic, Sussex nevertheless remains one county in terms of the character of its countryside and population.

The coast from Hastings to Selsey, including the large, historically, culturally and economically important towns of Eastbourne, Brighton and Worthing, can get rather busy in the summer. But inland, or out of season, the region's rich historical inheritance and rolling countryside offer the visitor more than adequate rewards.

Sussex is crossed from the south-east to the north-west by the hills of the South Downs. Where these go down to the sea near Eastbourne, they have been dramatically eroded to form Beachy Head and the Seven Sisters; while, inland, grass-topped chalk hills enfold countless little villages.

To the north, Ashdown Forest hides different treasures: thatched cottages, timber-framed buildings, huge and elegant houses set in sumptuous gardens . . .

ARUNDEL

E-2 • 89½ miles

Tourist information
61 High Street
Arundel, West Sussex
Tel: 0903 882268

Hotels
Amberley Castle ★★★
Amberley BN18 9ND
Tel: 0798 831992
Norfolk Arms Hotel ★★★
High Street, Arundel BN18 9AD
Tel: 0903 882101
Arundel House ★★
11 High Street
Arundel BN18 9AD
Tel: 0903 882136
The Swan Hotel ★
High Street
Arundel BN18 9AG
Tel: 0903 882314

Restaurants
Belinda's 16th Century Restaurant
13 Tarrant Street, Arundel
Tel: 0903 882977
Castle Tandoori Restaurant
3 Mill Lane, Arundel
Tel: 0903 882140

Festivals
Flower Festival, early June.
Arundel Festival, end August.

Arundel is famous for its castle, undeniably impressive in its medieval garb – even though antiquarians will know that much of what they see is late 19th century. In fact, some kind of bastion or fort has existed here since the very earliest times. Standing on the River Arun at the intersection of main county thoroughfares, Arundel has always been strategically important. The first real castle was erected by the Normans. In the 17th century, the town decided to support the king in the Civil War (1642–46); the castle was bombarded by the Parliamentarians, who installed a canon in a nearby church tower for the purpose. The century that fol-

lowed was not a very propitious one for the town, and the castle had to wait until 1890 for a restoration programme that would return it to something approximating its former glory. Today, visitors will be particularly impressed by the view from the dungeon, as well as by the castle's fine collection of paintings, its library, the ornate tombs of the Fitzalan Chapel and the splendid grounds.

• **Arundel Castle**. Easter to end October, Sunday to Friday (see Defence Structures route, p112).

Arundel town centre is old and very pretty, though with no one building of particular note, except perhaps the neo-Gothic Roman Catholic church. Built in 1870 by John Hansom, it was the butt of much contemporary criticism, but today many consider it to have a certain distinctive grace and finesse. Another, much older church you might like to visit is the church of **St Nicholas**, built in 1380.

Swan Lake in **Great Arundel Park**, to the north of the town, is very popular for boating (boat hire available). Another favourite

Bignor Roman Villa: mosaics

Arundel Castle: aerial view

is **The Wildfowl & Wetlands Centre**, a 75-acre pond and reed-bed reserve for many dozens of wildfowl species (Mill Road, open daily 9.30am–5.30pm, 4.30pm in winter. Tel: 0903 883355).

Less than 2 miles north-east of Arundel, on the River Arun, is the village of **Burpham**, a favourite with walkers. Its church of **St Mary the Virgin** dates in large part from the Norman period, but the village's greatest appeal lies in its views over Arundel, with the added attraction of a chance to take a break, or even an excellent meal, at the **George & Dragon** pub (more information in Country Pubs route, p108).

Then to the north, the four villages of **Amberley**, **Bignor**, **Bury** and **Houghton** offer the dual delight of a lovely day's walk combined with a good slice of history.

Houghton is a lovely little village whose main street runs down to the River Arun. Cross the river and you climb to Amberley, passing the **Amberley Chalk Pits Museum**, an open-air industrial museum in a former chalk quarry (open April to October, Wednesday to Sunday 10am–5pm. Tel: 0798

831831). This is also the embarkation point for the **Arun Valley Railway** that takes passengers through pretty countryside, either up to Pulborough or down towards Arundel and Littlehampton.

The village of Amberley, a mile to the north of the station, has two particular points of interest for the tourist – the church of **St Michael** and the **Castle** – but it is the wonderfully unhurried air of the village, perhaps one of Sussex's loveliest, that leaves the more lasting impression . . . In the church, several 13th-century frescoes bear witness to the skills and talents of medieval artists.

North of the village, **Amberley Wild Brooks** marshes are home to a wide variety of wild animals; while to the east lies the ostentation and considerable art collection of **Parham House**, with the additional lure of superb gardens and grounds (more information in Castles and Country Houses route, p106).

A little ferry boat over the Arun used to connect to Bury. There is talk of re-instating this during the summer months, and this would certainly cut out quite

a detour for the walker. **Bury** is another pretty village and it is not difficult to see why John Galsworthy (author of *The Forsyte Saga*) chose to spend his last years here (*see* Writers route, p110).

Two miles from Bury, after the village of West Burton, lies **Bignor**, best known for the fabulous mosaics discovered in the ruins of a Roman villa (open 1 March to 31 October, 10am –5pm, 6pm in summer. Tel: 0798 7259).

Finally **Slindon**, east of Arundel, is almost entirely National Trust-owned; very pretty, lovely old houses, craft shops . . . definitely worth a visit.

BATTLE
E-6 · 37 miles

Tourist information
88 High Street
Battle TN33 0AQ
Tel: 0424 773721

Hotels
Powdermills Hotel ★★★
Powdermill Lane
Battle TN33 0SP
Tel: 0424 775511
George Hotel ★★
23 High Street, Battle
Tel: 0424 764466

Restaurants

La Vieille Auberge
27 High Street
Battle TN33 0EA
Tel: 0424 764015

Merrieweathers Bistro
High Street, Battle
Tel: 0424 775566

Gateway Restaurant
78 High Street, Battle
Tel: 0424 772856

The King's Head (pub)
Whatlington Road, Battle
Tel: 0424 772317

William of Normandy, to give him his earlier appellation, made a lot of promises in anticipation of success at Hastings – or more properly, Battle: he promised his troops choice pickings in conquered England, while the Church expected to take over several of the Jute jurisdictions. It is said that, when the big day came, he promised to found an abbey on the battle site, and that this promise was responsible for his victory! The outcome of the battle was, of course, more likely a consequence of the weariness of Harold's troops, who had hurried south after defeating the Danes in the north; the erection of the abbey being a later gesture to mark the historic invasion. Or, even more pragmatically, to mark the spiritual, as well as physical, control of conqueror upon the conquered. Whichever explanation is the true one, the original abbey (of which only a few foundations remain) was of immense economic importance during the medieval and early Renaissance period. It gave rise to a large town which, in turn, became the venue for the region's biggest market.

When Henry VIII later suppressed the religious orders in England, the abbey building passed from one owner to another before slowly falling into disrepair. By contrast, the town grew and continued to increase in size until the 18th century. Present-day Battle is a beautiful town with a wealth of lovely old houses. In the High Street, at **Buckley's Yesterday's World**, an impressive series of historic tableaux conjures up the past for

adults and children alike (open 10am–6pm. Tel: 0424 775378). Of the abbey itself, little remains. Just a few walls, plus a 14th-century façade and a carefully restored 19th-century building that houses a school.

But it is the countryside around, better suited to sheep-rearing than soldiering (though the two activities may well have 'rubbed shoulders'), which is the real draw. To the north lie several villages of delightful brick and timber houses, such as **Robertsbridge** or, even better, **Brightling**. Here, landed classical architecture combines with architectural folly in buildings conceived by the British Museum architect Robert Smirk for one Jack Fuller, a highly successful, if eccentric, patron of the arts.

Three miles to the north of Brightling is **Burwash**, another pretty town made prosperous in earlier times by the iron trade. Rudyard Kipling chose to spend his last years here, between 1902 and 1936. **Bateman's**, a house built in 1634 for a well-to-do forge owner, has numerous mementos of Kipling, the youngest Nobel literature prize-winner in 1907 (until Camus, in 1957), a marvellous garden and a watermill. The mill still occasionally grinds corn as in days past (further details in Writers route, p110).

East of Burwash, towards the county boundary, are two other places of interest – **Haremere Hall and gardens** (Tel: 0580 819245) and **Bodiam Castle**, just a hop, skip and a jump from the old **Kent & East Sussex Railway** line, which takes passengers through some wonderful countryside to Tenterden.

Bodiam Castle is an exceptional example of the medieval castle, with walls still almost entirely intact (more information in Defence Structures route, p112).

Tourist information
De La Warr Pavilion
Bexhill-on-Sea TN40 1DP
Tel: 0424 212023

Hotels
Cooden Resort Hotel ★★★
Cooden Beach
Bexhill-on-Sea TN39 4TT
Tel: 0424 842281

Granville Hotel ★★★
Sea Road
Bexhill-on-Sea TN40 1EE
Tel: 0424 215437

Restaurants
Sutcliffe Catering
De La Warr Pavilion
Bexhill-on-Sea
Tel: 0424 212023

Stocks Restaurant
Devonshire Road
Bexhill-on-Sea
Tel: 0424 211188

Today's sedate seaside resort is a far cry from the Bexhill of the 1900s – when the town was one of a scandalous few to permit mixed bathing! The pleasant beach is nowadays the town's main draw.

Old Bexhill is largely Victorian (with just the occasional trace of Norman, Saxon . . . even Neolithic) and is grouped around **St Peter's**, a church that has been rebuilt many times over the centuries.

The **De La Warr Pavilion** (named after a leading local family), on the seafront, offers a wide variety of cultural and entertainment events. The same family is responsible for **Egerton Park Gardens**.

The **Costume Museum** (in Manor Gardens) presents an interesting history of clothes from 1700 to the present day (Tel: 0424 210045).

A couple of miles from Bexhill is **Norman's Bay**, witness to William's ships, vassals and soldiers on their way to Hastings to change the course of British history.

BOGNOR REGIS
E-2 · 95 miles

Tourist information
Belmont Street, Bognor Regis
Tel: 0243 823140

Hotels
Royal Hotel ★★★
The Esplanade
Bognor Regis PO21 1SZ
Tel: 0243 864665
Beachcroft Hotel ★★★
Clyde Road
Felpham PO22 7AH
Tel: 0243 827142
Bracken Lodge Guest House ★★
43 Church Street
Littlehampton BN17 5PU
Tel: 0903 723174
Regency Hotel ★
85 South Terrace, Littlehampton
Tel: 0903 717707
Lansdowne Hotel ★
55–57 West Street
Bognor Regis
Tel: 0243 865552

Restaurants
Murrell Arms
Yapton Road, Barnham
Tel: 0243 55332

Festivals
International Clown Convention

The two seaside resorts of Bognor Regis and Littlehampton are perhaps not the obvious choice for the holidaymaker on tour – their beaches are good but often crowded in summer. Both towns have, in their time, aroused the interest of would-be conquerors.

Bognor was founded in the 18th century, winning the appellation of Regis from George V who convalesced here during the summer of 1929.

Rainbow's End Family Adventure Park in Hotham Park in the centre (Tel: 0243 825255) and **Butlin's South Coast World** (Tel: 0243 822445) both offer good family entertainment.

For those who like their entertainment more 'natural', long walks around **Pagham Harbour**, west of Bognor, afford glimpses of countless species of sea-birds.

The road towards Littlehampton runs alongside the excellent **Climping** beach, very unspoilt and virtually deserted outside main holiday periods. The

Preston Manor and gardens

village itself, set back a little, consists of one house-lined street leading to **St Mary's**, surely one of the finest 13th-century Norman village churches still standing.

The town of **Littlehampton** grew prosperous during the Middle Ages through trade with the Duchy of Normandy. Today, there is little evidence of former wealth and it is largely dependent on tourism. Fishing trips operate from the port, either sea-fishing or river trips on the Arun. Alternatively, you can hire a canoe and paddle yourself up to **Arundel**.

Or you may like to see for yourself just how environmentally friendly Body Shop products are on an interesting factory visit.

• **The Body Shop Tour**, Watersmead, Littlehampton BN17 6LS. Tel: 0903 731500. Open Monday to Friday, first guided tour at 10.20am, last at 3.20pm, by reservation in advance only.

BRIGHTON & HOVE
E-4 · 70 miles

Tourist information
10 Bartholomew Square
Brighton BN1 1JS
Tel: 0273 323755

Hotels
The Imperial Hotel ★★★
First Avenue, Hove BN3 2GU
Tel: 0273 777320
Granville ★★
125 King's Road
Brighton BN1 2FA
Tel: 0273 326302
Ascott House Hotel ★★
21 New Steine
Brighton BN2 1PD
Tel: 0273 688085
Imperial Hotel ★★
First Avenue
Hove BN3 2GU
Tel: 0273 777320
Queensbury Hotel ★
58 Regency Square
Brighton BN1 2GB
Tel: 0273 325558
Brighton Youth Hostel
London Road
Brighton BN1 8YD
Tel: 0273 556196

Restaurants

Stubbs
14 Ship Street, Brighton
Tel: 0273 204005

Cripes
7 Victoria Road, Brighton
Tel: 0273 327878

Hamilton's Brasserie
First Avenue, Hove BN3 2GU
Tel: 0273 777320

Entertainment

The Dome, New Road
Brighton BN1 1UG
Tel: 0273 674357

Festivals

Brighton Festival, May.

The towns of Brighton and Hove, whose boundaries merged long ago, have now formally linked destinies. Hove is not without attractions for the tourist – the beaches are superb – but Brighton, by virtue of its prestigious past, holds more interest.

The small fishing village of *Brighthelmstone* (later shortened to Brighton) owed its sudden expansion in the middle of the 18th century to the arrival of a young doctor, author of an article which revolutionised contemporary British society and literally invented seaside tourism. His thesis on the use of sea water for glandular disease, advocated the virtues of sea water both for bathing and drinking!

Brighton today is a large town, making an important contribution to the regional economy. The Prince Regent, the future George IV, made the town *the* fashionable resort when he came here in 1782. He was responsible for some impressive building projects, the most famous of course being the **Royal Pavilion**, John Nash's stunning oriental pastiche.

Brighton's handsome Regency architectural inheritance, interspaced with the little alleyways known as **The Lanes** (that had criss-crossed the hill since the Middle Ages), may call to mind Nice or Barcelona for the European visitor. And this is an impression reinforced by the **Marina**, Europe's biggest yacht basin, where serious sailors and dinghy owners alike sport the sort of tans not normally associated with the chalk-faced south-east coast of England.

Among all the buildings from the Regency period up to the Victorian period – **Arundel and Chichester Terraces**, **Bedford Square** and **Royal Crescent** with its churches of **St Peter** and **St Bartholomew** – the Royal Pavilion is very definitely the one not to miss. Its opulence is breathtaking, its exoticism almost shocking. And inside, the Victorian furniture has now been replaced by copies of the original furniture from, or inspired by, the Far East.

- **Royal Pavilion**, Old Steine, Brighton BN2 1TB. Tel: 0273 603005. Open 10am–5pm (6pm in summer).

Brighton has two museums, both interesting in very different ways. The **Booth Museum of Natural History** has a fine display of the flora and fauna of the region (194 Dyke Road, Brighton BN1 5AA. Tel: 0273 552586).

Brighton Museum and Art Gallery has a large collection of decorative art, ethnography and paintings – ancient and modern (Church Street, Brighton BN1 1UE. Tel: 0273 603005).

At the **Sea-Life Centre,** children will delight in discovering some of the wealth of marine life normally hidden from view beneath the waves.

- **Sea-Life Centre**, Marine Parade, Brighton BN2 1TB. Open 10am.

Brighton Pier

A little way from the town centre is **Preston Manor**, in the park of the same name, a beautifully furnished Georgian residence illustrating the domestic life of the 18th century (Tel: 0273 603005. *See* Castles and Country Houses route, p106).

CHICHESTER
E-2 · 100 miles

Tourist information
29A South Street, Chichester
Tel: 0243 775888

Hotels
Goodwood Park Hotel ★★★★
Goodwood PO18 0QB
Tel: 0243 775537
The Millstream Hotel & Restaurant ★★★★
Bosham PO18 8HL
Tel: 0243 573234
The Dolphin and Anchor ★★★
West Street
Chichester PO19 1QE
Tel: 0243 785121
Bedford Hotel ★
Southgate
Chichester PO19 1DP
Tel: 0243 533175
Hotpins ★
Bosham PO18 8HL
Tel: 0243 572644

Entertainment
Chichester Theatre, Festival season, May to September.

Festivals
Chichester Festival, July.

Chichester is a beautiful city that has continued to enjoy good fortune through the vicissitudes of a thousand years of history. Founded by the Romans in the first century AD, the Normans built what is perhaps their most magnificent cathedral here, in a city which reached its zenith in the Georgian period, as present-day Chichester confirms.

The town-centre layout in the form of a cross was inherited from the original Roman town, but more extensive evidence of Roman occupation is found at **Fishbourne** on the town's western edge.

Fishbourne Roman Palace is unquestionably England's finest example of Roman secular building, dating from the end of the first century AD. One

Pallant House

wing of the palace is open to the public. The interesting new museum covering the ruins includes archaeological finds, comprehensive information on the site and some especially lovely mosaics from the former palace floor. A reconstruction of a Roman garden adjoins the museum (*see* Gardens route, p104). Partly destroyed by fire at the end of the third century, the old palace was a source of building material for Saxon Chichester.

• **Fishbourne Roman Palace**, Salthill Road, Fishbourne PO19 3QR. Tel: 0243 785859. Open 14 February to 16 December 10am–5pm.

Chichester soared to new status and wealth with the coming of the Normans and the construction of the cathedral. **The Cathedral Church of the Holy Trinity**, in West Street, was built at the beginning of the 12th century. The spire, visible at some distance out to sea, fell into the nave in 1861, but was replaced with one identical to the original.

Inside, the cathedral decorations are eclectic: in the south aisle, two carved 12th-century memorial stones; in the south transept, a 14th-century window; between the choir and the nave, a 15th-century screen (the Arundel Screen), together with the 1966 John Piper tapestry series, Graham Sutherland's *Noli Me Tangere* and a Chagall stained glass window.

The south nave leads into the cloister which, in turn, gives on to **Bishop's Palace Garden**, and thence into South Street via Canon Lane. A short walk up South Street brings you to **West Pallant** and to a part of town completely rebuilt after the Civil War (according to planning and design concepts that were far ahead of their time).

Wine merchant Henry Peckham had **Pallant House** built on the corner of East and North Pallants in 1712 and, from the vantage point of a little tower, he could see his ships returning from Spain or Portugal, laden with their precious cargoes. Pallant House is now home to an interesting **Museum of Modern Art** (open Tuesday to Saturday 10am–5.30pm. Tel: 0243 774557).

North Pallant crosses East Street and continues into St Martin's Street which runs alongside **St Mary's Hospital**, dating from the 15th century and today a hospice.

A little further on is Priory Park where the **Guildhall Museum** is accommodated in the church of the former (12th-century) convent. The building is impressive but the museum itself a bit disparate. The 16th-century **Market Cross** building in the centre is beautiful. During the Napoleonic wars, Chichester's fortunes were much enhanced by its situation in the bosom of a farming region that kept England's larders stocked against possible blockade. The latter part of the 19th century was a less propitious period for the city, but today it prospers anew, due in part to government departments whose offices are in the town.

The name **Chichester Harbour** relates not to a harbour as such but to all the little inlets and bays that lie between Selsey and the Hampshire border. This is a very popular weekend haunt of sailing and bird-spotting enthusiasts.

From **Fishbourne**, you can walk along the shore to **Itchenor**, where a ferry boat will take you to lovely **Chelsea Harbour** (information from 9 Crawley Road, Chichester PO19 1UZ. Tel: 0234 786418). Alternatively, you can go by car through the villages of Apuldram and Birdham. **Apuldram** is home to a specialist rose grower; **Birdham** has a hawk centre, so both make for a pleasant few hours' distraction.

• **Apuldrum Roses**, Apuldrum Lane, Dell Quay, Apuldrum PO20 7EF. Tel: 0243 785769. Monday to Saturday 9am–5pm and Sundays 10.30am–4.30pm.

• **The Sussex Falconry Centre**, Locksacre, Wopham Lane, Birdham PO20 7BS. Tel: 0243 512472. Open Tuesday to Sunday 9.30am–5pm. Flying demonstrations in fair weather only.

Bosham, tucked away in its own little cove, is one of the county's most charming villages. It has a Saxon manor house and church.

East of Chichester are the ruins of the former glory that was **Halnaker House**. Halnaker village still has some pretty old houses.

Boxgrove Priory is an altogether extraordinary piece of architecture, jewel in the crown of the many monasteries that once flourished in England.

Tangmere military airport, in the neighbouring village, played a major part in the defence of England during the Second World War. Indeed, it was from here that Spitfires took off to save the free world. A visit to the **Military Aviation Museum** (more information in Defence Structures route, p112) is a very moving experience.

Further to the north, **Goodwood House and Park** counts among the 'places not to be missed' in Sussex. Begun in 1720, the manor was extensively remodelled by James Wyatt, the greatest English architect of his time (more information in Castles and Country Houses route, p106). Goodwood is, of course, also known for its racecourse, and a few hundred yards from the course on the Chichester–Petworth road, the **Anglesey Arms** offers comfort and a fine selection of French wines (further information in Country Pubs route, p108).

North of Goodwood, the countryside of the Downs rolls into a delightful patchwork of arable fields, meadows and, here and there, the remains of the forest that once covered the entire region.

Charlton was, for a long time, a popular hunt venue and, at **Singleton**, the pub still known as **The Fox Goes Free** is a reminder of past disapproval of the aristocracy's crueler pursuits.

Singleton is also the home of a big open-air museum, **The Weald and Downland Museum**, an excellent information resource on the life of the county. Exhibits include examples of the region's varied building styles: houses, farms and mills, together with craft demonstrations and animal breeds, all serving to illustrate both differences and similarities between Sussex and its opposite numbers across the Channel, particularly Normandy.

West Dean is another pretty village known for its sumptuous gardens (more information in Gardens route, p104).

CROWBOROUGH
D-5 · 51 miles

Hotels
Winston Manor Hotel **
Beacon Road
Crowborough TN6 1AD
Tel: 0892 652772

Restaurants
The Friendly Eight
High Street, Crowborough

Tel: 0892 665102

Bibliography
Winnie the Pooh, by A A Milne.

Crowborough owes its present prosperity to two quite separate factors. First, iron forging, which began to decline during the second half of the 17th century; second, its proximity to the capital, which established it as an early favourite among the privileged classes, whose numbers increased as transport facilities improved. Today, the greatest appeal of this unexceptional town, largely populated by commuters, lies in its views (Sussex's highest town at about 900 feet). Lovely countryside is only minutes away: richly cultivated hills liberally dotted with pretty villages, and untamed woodland, part of a forest that once covered the entire region.

The biggest acreage of wood is **Ashdown Forest**, offering the widest variety of woodland scenery. Preservation of parts of this once great Saxon forest is due to its earlier use as a hunting venue for the great of the kingdom. Numerous paths criss-cross the forest and one that follows the former railway line (2 miles to the north) will take you past **Hartfield** (famous for its association with A A Milne's *Winnie the Pooh*), or perhaps to its pub, **The Anchor**. Take a moment for something to eat, or sample a pint of Flowers Original, reflecting as you do that Sherlock Holmes, or at least his creator Sir Arthur Conan Doyle (who spent his last years here), may have put his pint pot down in just the same spot. And as he settled himself, perhaps just like you, remarked 'What more could a man ask?' (*see* Writers route, p110).

EASTBOURNE
E-6 · 50 miles

Tourist information
3 Cornfield Terrace
Eastbourne BN21 4QL
Tel: 0323 411400

Hotels
Cavendish ***
40 Grand Parade

Eastbourne BN21 4DH
Tel: 0323 410222
Congress Hotel **
31–41 Carlisle Road
Eastbourne BN21 4JS
Tel: 0323 732118
West Rocks Hotel **
Grand Parade
Eastbourne BN21 4DL
Tel: 0323 725217
Oban Hotel **
King Edward's Parade
Eastbourne BN21 4DX
Tel: 0323 731581
Edelweiss Hotel *
10–12 Elms Avenue
Eastbourne BN21 3DN
Tel: 0323 732071

Restaurants
Arlington Arms
Seaside, Eastbourne
Tel: 0323 724365
Qualisea
9 Pevensey Road, Eastbourne
Tel: 0323 725203

Festivals
International Folk Festival.

On the evidence of archaeological finds, there would appear to have been some kind of settlement at Eastbourne since earliest times. Yet not till the middle of the last century did the town really start to grow, when a collection of landowners thought that the coming railway would transform it into a fashionable bathing resort. The open layout of the town, dating from this period, comprises all the features that draw its many retired visitors here in the summer months: a magnificent garden-lined promenade, Victorian hotels, handsome houses,

flowers in profusion throughout the summer, lovely old monuments, plus a few not too vigorous leisure activities, there for the taking, or for passing over in preference to a deckchair and a good book.

The Butterfly Centre is a huge greenhouse housing some 500 species of Lepidoptera, gathering honey from exotic flowers whose colours rival the butterflies' own (open daily 26 March to 30 October 10am–6pm. Tel: 0323 645522).

The church of **St Mary**, about half a mile east of the beaches in the old town, has an unusual sandstone tower. Two defence towers have been carefully restored. The **Redoubt** is today a museum with exhibits on coastal defence and the history of the Royal Sussex Regiment, founded in 1701 (*see* Defence Structures route, p112).

Eastbourne has three attractions for younger visitors. There's the **How we lived then** exhibition, depicting shops across five centuries (open daily 10am–5.30pm. Tel: 0323 737143). **Treasure Island** and **Fort Fun** offer children hours of more traditional seaside fun (both on Royal Parade, the former open April to October 10am–6pm, tel: 0323 411077; the latter open year round 10am–6pm, tel: 0323 642833).

To the west of Eastbourne, the Sussex coast rises up to embrace the end of the South Downs, with sweeps of high cliff providing dramatic walks at **Beachy Head** and **Seven**

Sisters (open-topped excursion buses run in summer). There are excellent views across the Channel from the cliffs, though these are treacherous in some places because of their relatively crumbly chalk structure.

A little way inland is **East Dean**, on the edge of Friston Forest. This is lovely in the autumn, whether just to enjoy the colours and lap up the atmosphere, or for mushroom hunting.

Still at East Dean, you can visit the **Seven Sisters Sheep Centre**, a trial breeding centre with more than 40 different species. Children and adults will all enjoy the milking sessions, the cheese-making, the shearing and, of course, the lambs (**Birling Manor House**, mid March to mid September open daily 2–5pm and by prior arrangement. Tel: 0323 423302).

To the east are the **Pevensey Marshes**. This fertile tract of cultivated land was the domain of the sea in medieval times. Then, the sea even lapped the walls of **Pevensey Castle** built on the site of an earlier Roman fort. Indeed, this castle was, for more than 1,000 years, one of the major obstacles to a French invasion of the British Isles (more information in Defence Structures route, p112).

Pevensey Castle

Michelham Priory

HAILSHAM
E-5 · 52 miles

Tourist information
The Library, Western Road
Hailsham BN27 3DN
Tel: 0323 840604

Hotels
Manor Farm **
Ripe (5 miles towards Lewes)
Tel: 0323 811425
*The Old Forge Hotel and
Restaurant*
Magham Down, Hailsham
Tel: 0323 842893

Restaurants
Sundial
Herstmonceux BN27 4LA
Tel: 0323 832217
*Waldernheat Country
Restaurant*
A271 Harebeating, Hailsham
Tel: 0323 840143
The Red Lion (pub)
Magham Down, Hailsham
Tel: 0323 840079

Seven miles inland from Eastbourne is Hailsham. Though not in itself particularly noteworthy, you may like to visit nearby **Michelham Priory** and **Herstmonceux Castle**, two of the most interesting places in the region.

A few hundred yards from the village of **Upper Dicker** (**The Plough** pub is highly recommended), with its church rebuilt in Norman style in the 19th century, stands **Michelham Priory**, an Augustinian priory up to the time of the Dissolution. Built of large square stones, surrounded by a moat, and standing in some 8 acres of garden, the priory looks very much the part of the fortified farm that it, in fact, was during the 17th and 18th centuries. Visitors can visit the old forge and the watermill, still in working order.

• **Michelham Priory**. Open 25 March to 31 October 11am–5.30pm. Tel: 0323 844224.

Herstmonceux Castle was one of England's first brick buildings (first half of the 15th century). Said to be haunted by a musical ghost, the Herstmonceux Drummer, it may equally be haunted by discontented astrophysicians: the Royal Observatory was moved here from Greenwich because of too much pollution in the capital, only to be moved on again to Cambridge to be nearer the necessary intellectual grey matter!

Of the several villages around that offer good walks, choose **Chiddingly**, to the north-west, at the intersection of two long-distance footpaths – the **Vanguard Way** and **Weald Way**. Chiddingly church spire can be seen for miles around and there are two Tudor houses to see: **Chiddingly Place**, now a ruin except for the fine timber barn, and **Stonehill House**, magnificently restored.

The **Six Bells** pub makes a lovely break on your journey, with simple and inexpensive food (more information in Country Pubs route, p108).

At **Gun Hill**, just east of Chiddingly, **The Gun** offers pleasant rooms in a delightful setting at very reasonable prices (*see* Country Pubs route, p108). What more could you ask for? Malcolm Lowry might have replied 'a bottle of tequila'. Except that this author of *Under the Volcano* (more information in Writers route, p110) ended his days not in Cuernavaca, Mexico, but at **Ripe**, a tiny village nearby which boasts a remarkable perpendicular church and the unusual **Old Cottage**, worth visiting for its wood carvings.

HASTINGS AND ST LEONARD'S-ON-SEA
E-7 · 33 miles

Tourist information
4 Robertson Terrace
Hastings TN34 1EZ
Tel: 0424 718888

Hotels
Royal Victoria Hotel ***
Marina, St Leonard's-on-sea
TN38 0BD
Tel: 0424 445544
Cinque Ports Hotel ***
Summerfields
Hastings TN34 1ET
Tel: 0424 439222
Eagle House Hotel **
12 Pevensey Road
St Leonard's-on-Sea TN38 0JZ
Tel: 0424 430535
Bryn-y-Mor **
12 Godwin Road
Hastings TN35 5JR
Tel: 0424 722744

Restaurants
Orange Tree Restaurant
4 Claremont, Hastings
Tel: 0424 429910
Harbour Restaurant
1 East Beach Street
Old Town, Hastings
Tel: 0424 425558

Hastings and St Leonard's make up a single seaside resort. St Leonard's, appealing more to families, is not as well known as its big sister.

Famous throughout the world as the site of a battle that actually took place just over 7 miles further inland at Battle, Hastings has other features that justify its renown: its particular atmosphere and authentic blend of sea air and the scent of dunes and breakwaters; or an autumn sun piercing through storm clouds to light the houses below . . . as if in warning 'The sea is high, fishermen, take care that the driftwood on the beach after the storm is not from your boat'. Neither the colourful little boats heaved up on the beach beneath the high cliff, nor the little wooden huts where the fishermen hang their nets have changed in over a century.

The **Norman castle**, in a very poor state of repair, is often used to stage historical reconstructions of the battle. It is open to the public (*see* Defence Structures route, p112).

Large numbers of visitors come to investigate the town's two museums, one ethnographical and zoological, the other on local history.

• **Hastings Museum & Art Gallery**, Cambridge Road, Hastings TN34 1ET. Tel: 0424 721202. Open Monday to Saturday 10am–5pm and Sunday 3–5pm.

• **Hastings Museum of Local History**, Town Hall, High Street, Hastings TN34 3EW. Tel: 0424 721209.

In addition to the local history museum, the **Town Hall** also has a 75-yard-long Bayeux-style tapestry that recounts English history since 1066.

Children are well catered for in this family-orientated tourist town. There is the **Museum of the Sea** and **A Smuggler's Adventure** and the **Shipwreck Heritage Exhibition**. Smugglers and looters of shipwrecks may not rank high in public esteem, yet their history is a long and exciting one, with the power to fire imaginations both young and old.

• **A Smuggler's Adventure**, St Clement's Caves, West Hill, Hastings TN34 3HY. Tel: 0424 422964.

• **Shipwreck Heritage Centre,** Rock-a-Nore Road, Hastings TN34 3DW. Tel: 0424 437452.

Fairlight, to the east of Hastings, is a friendly little village endowed with marvellous views of the surrounding area, particularly the 740-acre **Hastings Country Park**.

HAYWARDS HEATH
D-4 • 71 miles

Hotels
The Birch Hotel ★★★
Lewes Road
Haywards Heath RH17 7SF
Tel: 0444 451565

Hickstead Resort Hotel ★★
Jobs Lane, Bolney RH17 5PA
Tel: 0444 248023

Restaurants
Borde Hill Restaurant
Balcombe Road
Haywards Heath
Tel: 0444 441102
Avins Bridge
College Road, Ardingly
Tel: 0444 892393

There's really not much to see at Haywards Heath. This commuter town's rapid expansion at the beginning of the century put paid to any meagre tourist resources it might once have had. By contrast, the area immediately surrounding the town is so richly populated with wonderful gardens as to suggest that the locality's soil has some unique, magic ingredient.

Borde Hill Garden is the quintessential English garden, where colours and forms are balanced and blended to such perfection that identification of individual plants is very secondary in importance (further information in Gardens route, p104).

Further north, just outside the old village of **Ardingly**, lie the 150 acres of **Wakehurst Place Gardens**. These belong to the Royal Botanic Society at Kew,

Borde Hill Garden

and are planted with rare plants and exotic trees, surrounding an imposing Elizabethan manor house (more information in Gardens route, p104).

To the west, near **Handcross**, is a third exceptional garden, **Nymans Garden**, with species gathered from all over the world and displayed here with flair and passion in 40 acres (more information in Gardens route, p104).

Nearby, yet another superb garden, known as **High Beeches Garden**, has sweeps of flowers beneath the trees and wild meadow flowers, both a sheer delight (Handcross, Tel: 0444 400589). Open daily except Wednesday and Saturday 12 April to 26 June and 4 September to 30 October 1–5pm).

HORSHAM
D-3 · 76 miles

Hotels

South Lodge Hotel ★★★★
Brighton Road
Lower Beeding RH13 6PS
Tel: 0403 891711

Random House Hotel ★★★
Stone Street
Slinfold RH13 7QX
Tel: 0403 790558

Ciswood House Hotel ★★★
Sandygate Lane
Lower Beeding RH13 6NF
Tel: 0403 891216

Restaurants

The Old Barn
Worthing Road (A24)
Dial Post, Horsham
Tel: 0403 710000

Dog and Bacon
North Parade, Horsham
Tel: 0403 252176

Green Dragon
Bishopric, Horsham
Tel: 0403 252286

Festivals

Horsham Festival, July.

In past times Horsham was considered inaccessible, in winter at least, when the clay soil of the Weald turned the roads to rivers of mud, and cattle had to be taken to the sandier terrain of St Leonard's Forest. When the railway came to Horsham, unlike many another town, it managed to avoid over-rapid expansion, and was careful to preserve some of the older streets, the **Causeway** and the **Carfax**, for example, and the more gracious buildings, such as **Causeway House**, the **Town Hall**, **Manor House** and **Park House**. Horsham is, nevertheless, primarily a residential and shopping centre.

But, not far from the town, treats are in store . . . **Slinfold**, for example, is a charming little village to the north-west on the Chichester to London Roman road. A little way along, you come to the hamlet of **Rowhook**, where the **Chequers** pub has excellent and very varied food at hard-to-believe prices (further details in Country Pubs route, p108).

Then south-east a few hundred yards from **Lower Beeding**, the gardens of **Leonardslee** are a year-round delight of dazzling blooms extending over 250 acres. Kashmir's least accessible valleys have not greater natural beauty than these sumptuous gardens set around six lakes (more information in Gardens route, p104).

A couple of miles from Leonardslee, the hamlet of **Nuthurst** lies in the heart of lovely countryside, and its pub, **The Black Horse**, is worthy of particular mention (more information in Country Pubs route, p108).

A castle was built at **Shipley**, 6 miles south of Horsham, in the early Norman period. The town enjoyed a strategic position on the River Adur and **Knepp Castle** helped keep peace in the region. Though today only a ruin, an evocative atmosphere pervades . . . John Nash designed the new Knepp castle, which was built in 1809 but is not open to the public.

The village church of **St Mary the Virgin** was built by the Knights Templar in the 12th century, a fine example of Norman architecture.

King's Land, formerly owned by author Hilaire Belloc, has a windmill built in 1879, recently restored to working order.

Leonardslee Gardens

LEWES

E-5 · 63 miles

Tourist information

187 High Street
Lewes BN7 2DE
Tel: 0273 483448

Hotels

Shelley's Hotel ***
The High Street
Lewes BN7 1XS
Tel: 0273 472361

Barn House **
Rodmell (3 miles south)
Tel: 0273 477865

Bull Hotel *
2 High Street, Ditchling
Tel: 07918 3147

Crown Hotel *
191 High Street
Lewes BN7 2NA
Tel: 0273 480670

Telscombe Youth Hostel
Bank Cottages
Telscombe BN7 3HZ
Tel: 0273 556196

Restaurants

Leonie's
197 High Street, Lewes
Tel: 0273 473235

The Gardener's Arms (pub)
46 Cliffe High Street, Lewes
Tel: 0273 474808

Festivals

Guy Fawkes Night,
5 November.

Capital of East Sussex, Lewes' fiercely independent spirit has often been put to the test during the course of its stormy history. When William the Conqueror ceded the 'Rape' of Lewes to his faithful servant Guillaume de Warenne, he built a castle and an abbey here. (A rape was one of six administrative districts into which Sussex was divided, the reference being to the fencing off of land with a rope.) Both added to the status and wealth of the town.

When Henry VIII closed the abbey and later Cromwell burnt the castle, Lewes sunk unsurprisingly into a period of decline. But, in the 18th century, the agricultural wealth of the surrounding countryside brought new prosperity. Today, the town owes its economic vigour to tourism and service industries.

Only the dungeon and a few walls of the castle still stand, but are impressive for all that, and the view from the top of the dungeon is exceptional.

• **Lewes Castle**, 169 High Street, Lewes BN7 1YE. Monday to Saturday 10am–5.30pm, Sunday 11am–5.30pm (*see* Defence Structures route, p112).

In the town centre, visit **Bull House** where Thomas Paine, supporter of American Independence and the French Revolution, once lived; **Anne of Cleves' House**; and the **Sussex Folk Museum**, with a Tudor garden (52 Southover High Street, Lewes BN7 1JA. Tel: 0273 474610. Open 1 April to 31 October Monday to Saturday 10am–5.30pm).

Discover some of the nearby villages, too: **Ditchling**, for example, 8 miles north-west, has period houses around a 12th-century church built in stone imported from Normandy. The village borders **Ditchling Common**, extending to some 200 acres and, from 800-feet-high **Ditchling Beacon,** you can enjoy wonderful views not just of the countryside, but even of the sea, on a clear day.

Kingston, nearly two miles west of the town on the Newhaven road, is not particularly picturesque but worth the detour for its pub, **The Juggs** (more information in Country Pubs route, p108).

A little further along the Newhaven road at **Rodmell** is **Monks House**, long-time home of the extraordinary Virginia Woolf (further information in Writers route, p110).

South-east of Lewes, the village of **West Firle** (often

Anne of Cleves' House

called simply Firle since there is no East Firle), at the foot of the South Downs, offers an ideal watering place at the pub/inn **The Ram**, before embarking on a visit to **Firle Place** or a visit to **Glyndebourne**, or just a walk in the hills (further information in Country Pubs route, p108).

Firle Place is a Tudor manor with several Georgian modifications. Its collection of paintings, furniture and porcelain makes it one of Sussex's top museums and an essential port of call for anyone with an interest in these items (open Easter to end September, Wednesday, Thursday, Sunday and public holidays, see Castles and Country Houses route, p106.)

A mile from Firle is **Charleston Farmhouse**, formerly the residence of Vanessa and Clive Bell and Duncan Grant who, along with Virginia Woolf, were some of the most famous members of the Bloomsbury Group. Their decoration of the manor has been preserved, together with writing memorabilia (see Writers route, p110). **Charleston Gardens** are among some of the most beautiful in Sussex (open 2 April to 30 October Wednesday to Saturday 10am–4.30pm. Tel: 0323 811265).

Another village full of interesting things to see is **Glynde**, with its magnificent neo-Palladian church and Elizabethan manor, **Glynde Place**, housing a fine collection of paintings and bronzes. A mile or two to the north is **Glyndebourne**, elegant host, since 1934, to the world's most fashionable opera festival.

MIDHURST
D-2 • 97 miles

Hotels
Spread Eagle ***
South Street
Midhurst GU29 9NH
Tel: 0730 816911
The Angel Hotel ***
North Street
Midhurst GU29 9DN
Tel: 0730 812421
Park House Hotel ***
Bepton GU29 0JB
Tel: 0730 812880

Restaurants
The Swan
Lion Street, Midhurst
Tel: 0730 812853
The Wheatsheaf (pub)
Wool Lane
Rombolds Hill, Midhurst
Tel: 0730 813450

Midhurst is a lovely town. Although it has grown considerably in recent times, the centre still has some original streets and houses. **Market Hall**, built in 1552, **Elizabeth House**, a magnificent timbered house, and **Knockhundred Row** which houses the public library, are three good examples of local architecture.

Within gunshot range of the town, the ruins of **Cowdray**, an extraordinary Tudor palace, stand in 750 acres of parkland. In summer, polo is played here.

South Harting, a small village some half a dozen miles to the west of Midhurst, enjoys a privileged position on the edge of the Downs bordering Hampshire. The churches of **St Mary** and **St Gabriel** are worthy of close inspection. Then, driving back towards Midhurst, less than a mile away is the pretty village of **Elsted**, with very good food on offer at the **Elsted Inn** (more information in Country Pubs route, p108).

PETWORTH
D-2 • 90 miles

Hotels
Roundabout Hotel ***
Monilmead Lane
West Chiltington RH20 2PF
Tel: 0798 813838
White Horse Inn **
The Street, Sutton RH20 1PS
Tel: 0798 43432
Chequers *
Church Place, Pulborough
Tel: 0798 22486

Restaurants
Three Moles (pub)
Selham, Petworth
Tel: 0798 875303
The Barn Owls
London Road,
Coldwaltham, Pulborough
Tel: 0798 872498

Petworth House is a magnificent French-style château offering an oasis of calm and shade next to the small town of the same name; a place to ponder on the historical role of houses such as this one, owned by the Percy family, Earls of Northumberland.

Set in 1,000 acres of parkland, Petworth House offers the visitor delightful walks with the added bonus of deer that will

Rodmell

feed from the hand (more information in Castles and Country Houses route, p106).

Tillington hamlet, west of the park, has some very pretty houses. The A283 from Petworth to Bramber, then Shoreham, takes in the villages of **Byworth**, **Fittleworth**, then **Stopham** and **Pulborough**. The first two have only their inherent charm to lure the visitor, but the third, with a not unimpressive Norman church, has the additional pull of the **White Hart** pub (more information in Country Pubs route, p108), as well as a fine medieval stone bridge dating from 1423.

Pulborough has a perpendicular Gothic church and, at the entrance to the nature reserve at the edge of town, a little museum informs visitors on the region's ecosystem.

• **Pulborough Brooks Nature Reserve**, Wiggonholt, Pulborough RH20 2EL. Tel: 0798 875851. Open daily 10am–5pm.

RYE
D-7 · 21 miles

Tourist information
The Heritage Centre
Strand Quay, Rye TN31 7AY
Tel: 0797 226696

Hotels
Flackley Ash Hotel ★★★
Peasmarsh TN31 6YH
Tel: 0797 230651
Jeake's House ★★
Mermaid Street, Rye TN31 7ET
Tel: 0797 222828
The Top of the Hill ★★
Rye Hill, Rye TN31 7NH
Tel: 0797 223284
Playden Cottage ★★
Military Road, Rye TN31 7NY
Tel: 0797 222234
Aviemore ★
28–30 Fishmarket Road
Rye TN31 7LP
Tel: 0797 223052
Little Orchard House ★
West Street, Rye
Tel: 0797 223831

Restaurants
Mermaid Inn
Mermaid Street, Rye
Tel: 0797 223065
The Ferryman
12–14 Rye Road, Rye
Tel: 0797 223140

Festivals
Medieval Weekend, August.
Rye Festival, September.

To wander through this medieval fishing town is a delight. One is struck both by the charm of the old town, as well as evidence of a way of life resolutely unchanged over the centuries. The tortuous inclines of this smugglers' town may get fairly busy in the summer months, but don't let this deter you from the pleasure of the ascent to the very top . . . along the famous **Mermaid Street**, with its beautiful old half-timbered houses, red-roofed or, alternatively, green with moss.

Rye was yet another victim of the gradual invasion of sand suffered by so many of the Channel ports, and for which seafaring communities had no remedy in past centuries. A member of the League of Cinque Ports, a market town, the home of sailors and fishermen and principal outlet for iron and wool going to the continent, Rye's prosperity was once envied by many in the Middle Ages. There were spates of repeated French plundering of the town. Yet France was also a commercial partner and, as such, also involved in the town's long-term prosperity.

Then came decline, the decline that fixed the old town in its present 16th-century appearance – to the benefit and enjoyment of its Tunnel-age visitors.

Visitors who are not content to just soak up the atmosphere could do worse than try the **Mermaid Inn** – pub, hotel, restaurant and former smugglers' haunt. The décor has changed little over the centuries:

Rye

16th-century paintings on the walls, an open fireplace where once whole tree trunks would burn, and the pistol rack – where the local rogues would leave their still-loaded pistols, while engaging in endless hands of cards as they waited for the bad weather that would hide both the moon and their nefarious activities. You may not see Errol Flynn, Captain Blood or Gentleman Jim come swaggering through the door, but you might easily imagine a pirate or two among the strong-featured, weathered faces around you.

St Mary's church, built between the 12th and 14th centuries, is strong evidence of the town's past splendour.

Lamb House, former home of Henry James (*see* Writers route, p110), is a large Georgian residence and a pleasure to visit, as is the town's museum in the more severe architecture of Ypres Tower, built in 1249.

• **Town Museum**, Gungarden, Rye TN31 7NH. Tel: 0797 226728. Open 1 April to 1 November 10.30am–5.30pm.

A new son et lumière show tells the town's history through the ages at the **Heritage Centre**, Strand Quay (open daily Easter to end October 10am–5pm and only at weekends for the rest of the year. Tel: 0797 226696).

Winchelsea, a mile and a half away, was once Rye's sister town. The town was extended and enlarged in the form of a cross in the 13th century, when it began trading wine with the French Guyenne and Bordeaux regions. But her good fortune was short-lived, following a series of violent storms that returned the town to obscurity when the port silted up in the 16th century. A few clues can be seen of her brief prosperity in the one street surviving from this era and the tombs of wealthy merchants in **St Thomas'** churchyard. Three of the four old town gates are still in evidence, their solidity a reminder of past French interest in the one-time wealth of the town.

Northiam, 10 miles to the north, is a delightful village with exceptionally well-preserved Renaissance houses.

The gardens at **Great Dixter**, less than a mile away, surround the house of the same name. This dates from the 15th century and was superbly restored by Sir Edwin Lutyens. The gardens are kept by Christopher Lloyd, a well-known writer on the art of gardening (further information in Gardens route, p104).

SEAFORD
E-5 · 58 miles

Tourist information
Station Approach
Seaford BN25 2AR
Tel: 0323 897426

Hotels
Deans Place Hotel ***
Alfriston, Polegate, BN26 5TN
Tel: 0323 870248
Avondale Hotel *
5 Avondale Road, Seaford
Tel: 0323 890008
Alfriston Youth Hostel
Frog Firle, Polegate BN26 5TT
Tel: 0323 870423
Traslyn Hotel **
Pelham Road, Seaford
Tel: 0323 892312

Restaurants
Schmitts
Dane Road, Seaford
Tel: 0323 892771
Regency Restaurant
High Street, Seaford
Tel: 0323 895206

Less industrialised than Newhaven and with more character than Peacehaven, the seaside town of Seaford manages to retain a certain charm, in spite of an apparent lack of forethought, from both environmental and aesthetic standpoints, during its period of greatest growth. A few 18th-century streets remain, the odd Georgian building or two . . . barely enough to put it on the tourist map – were it not for the prospect of good walking offered by the town's immediate surroundings. To the east of the town, at **Seaford Head**, 450-feet cliffs plunge into the sea. A cliff-top path leads through a nature reserve to **Cuckmere Haven**, at the mouth of the River Cuckmere.

At the little hamlet of **Exceat**, you can visit the **Living World Centre** and the **Seven Sisters**, also accessible from Eastbourne. The Seven Sisters (in fact, there are *eight* particularly impressive cliffs) constitute some of the most beautiful coastal scenery in England.

• **The Living World**, Exceat, Seaford BN25 4AD. Tel:0323 870100. Open daily mid March to October 10am–5pm and weekends during the rest of the year.

Alfriston, to the north of Exceat, is a fine town that has withstood the ravages of time exceptionally well. Beautiful **St Andrew's** church is known as the Cathedral of the Downs.

Clergy House is a beautifully restored 14th-century house worth a visit as much for itself as for the small **Museum of Traditional Weald Life** that it houses (open daily 1 April to 31 October 10.30am–5pm. Tel: 0323 870001).

The Heritage Centre includes a museum of village history and a reconstruction of a forge.

• **Alfriston Heritage Centre** and **Blacksmith's Museum**, The Old Forge, Sloe Lane, Alfriston BN26 5UP. Tel: 0323 870303. Open 1 April to 31 October 11am–5pm.

To the north of the village, just off the A27, **Drussila's Zoo Park** is by far the best kept and nicest of small zoos in the south-east (open daily 10am–5pm, 4pm in winter. Tel: 0323 870234).

Alciston is a village to the north of Alfriston. Known mainly for its magnificent medieval barn and exceptional views, though equally deserving of recognition is its wonderful pub, **The Rose Cottage**: tranquil surroundings and gorgeous food (further information in Country Pubs route, p108).

UCKFIELD

D-5 · 61 miles

Hotels

Buxted Park Country House ★★★★
Buxted Park, Buxted TN22 4AY
Tel: 0825 732711
Maiden's Heart Hotel ★★
91 High Street, Uckfield
Tel: 0825 762019
Hooke Hall Hotel ★★
246 High Street, Uckfield
Tel: 0825 762019

Restaurants

The Chalk and Cheese (pub)
117 High Street, Uckfield
Tel: 0825 761366

Once again, it is not the sprinkling of 18th-century houses around the **Holy Cross** church – elegant though these are – that will draw you to this town, much expanded in recent years. The countryside, however, will. Low, wooded hills shelter tiny villages of traditional houses huddled around a church and a pub and, here and there, crafts to see and buy that are special to this part of England.

Nutley is one such village – on the A22 a few miles north of Uckfield – with a church and pub both worth a visit, but with the added bonus of a windmill now restored to full working order. **Nutley Windmill** can be reached by a track that runs along the edge of famous **Ashdown Forest**. Not far from here, at **Heron's Ghyll** on the A26, is **Barnsgate Manor Vineyard and Wine Museum**, with attractions for the children, too.

To the west of Uckfield, **Fletching** is perhaps the most delightful of all the region's villages. The church is interesting for several reasons, particularly because it is the burial place of Edward Gibbon, author of the classic *History of the decline and fall of the Roman Empire.*

The Griffin pub/restaurant/hotel provides gourmets with a reason to lick their lips, travellers with rest, Epicurians with excellent beer and lovers of gardens a chance to catch their breath before going on to **Sheffield Park Garden** (further information in Country Pubs route, p108).

Sheffield Park Garden is an enchanting place. Its contours and plantations are the work of Capability Brown and cover 125 acres, including five lakes. The manor, built by James Wyatt in 1779, can be admired from the grounds but is not open to the public (further information in Gardens route, p104).

The park is also the departure point for the famous **Bluebell Railway**, a Victorian railway line with fully-restored trains and stations. The trains go to Horsted Keynes in West

Sussex (open daily 22 May to 30 September and at weekends for the rest of the year. Tel: 0825 722370).

Heaven Farm Country Tours and Museum, at Furners Green to the north of Sheffield Park, provides an instructive and enjoyable visit; a former farm, open weekends 2.30pm–6pm 20 March to 24 October. Tel: 0825 790226.

South of Uckfield, **Bentley Wildfowl Centre** is a wildfowl reserve set around numerous lakes, interesting for adults and children alike (open mid March to end October 10.30am–4.30pm and winter weekends. Tel: 0825 840573).

WADHURST

D-6 · 43 miles

Hotels

Dale Hill Hotel
Dale Hill, Ticehurst TN5 7DQ
Tel: 0580 200212

Restaurants

The Greyhound (pub)
St James's Square, Wadhurst
Tel: 0892 783224

Wadhurst is a lovely little town. It suffered terribly during the war from its position under the flight path of German bombers, and V1 and V2 rockets en route to London. It did not succumb however, but drew on the resources of a prosperous past. It was one of the first and the last Sussex towns to forge iron. It still has a scattering of fine old houses: **Churchgate House** near the cemetery, **Cousley Wood** and **Welland House** are good examples.

Mayfield, to the south-west, is another lovely village with many of the half-timbered houses typical of the Weald in its main street. The **Infant Jesus Convent** was built on the ruins of a palace belonging to the archbishops of Canterbury; Archbishop Islip's grand hall is today a chapel. The perpendicular parish church is ornately decorated inside and out.

South-east of Wadhurst, on the B2099 which runs past Bewl Water reservoir, **Ticehurst** has an unusual church and an excellent pub. **St Mary's** dates from the 14th century, whereas **The Bull** opened something under a century later (further information in Country Pubs route, p108).

A short distance to the south of Ticehurst, **Pashley Manor** has magnificent 17th-century gardens, including waterfalls, a moat, lakes and ponds (open April to October, Tuesday, Wednesday, Thursday and Saturday, 11am–5pm. Tel: 0580 200692).

Two miles from Ticehurst on the B2087, **Flimwell Bird Park** is a 99-acre ornithological park, lovely for walks in unspoilt surroundings (open daily April to end September 10.30am–5.30pm. Tel: 0580 87202).

Fishing is still important to the region

WORTHING
E-3 · 81 miles

Tourist information
Town Hall
Chapel Road, Worthing
Tel: 0903 210022

Hotels
Windsor House Hotel ★★★
14–20 Windsor Road
Worthing BN11 2LX
Tel: 0903 239655
Chatsworth Hotel ★★★
Steyne
Worthing BN11 3DU
Tel: 0903 236103
Cavendish Hotel ★★
115–116 Marine Parade
Worthing BN11 3QG
Tel: 0903 236767
Castle Hotel ★
The Street, Bramber
Tel: 0903 812102
Nash Hotel ★
Horsham Road, Steyning
Tel: 0903 814988

Restaurants
Captain's Table
339 Goring Road, Worthing
Tel: 0903 246100
Connaught Corner House
32 Marine Parade, Worthing
Tel: 0903 210084
Plaza Restaurant
5–6 Rowlands Road, Worthing
Tel: 0903 236053
Steers Restaurant
Marine Parade, Worthing
Tel: 0903 232982

Entertainment
Pavilion Theatre
Maine Parade, Worthing
Tel: 0903 820500

Worthing grows a bit bigger every year, which is hardly surprising given the popularity of its beaches with both British and foreign holidaymakers. This was not always the case. A long time ago, the little village of Worthing may have had a Norman church, but in its early days the only source of income was mackerel fishing; not until a system of irrigation dykes drained tracts of land did it emerge from obscurity, freed from the risk of flood.

Then, the advent of sea-bathing and visiting royalty put the town squarely on the map as a fashionable resort. New housing and new hotels sprang up. But, despite a surprisingly mild climate and vastly improved facilities, the rich and famous – in a typical display of ingratitude – gradually drifted away. Thankfully, this loss in revenue was in part compensated for by high-income crop cultivation, made possible by Worthing's exceptional sunshine levels. The 19th century started well for Worthing, and then . . . the rest is history. Industrial expansion brought paid annual holidays, which in turn brought families to the seaside, giving impetus to a complete remodelling of the town. The exemplary story of West Sussex's most densely populated town is described in **Worthing Museum and Art Gallery** (Chapel Road, Worthing BN11 1HP. Open 10am–6pm, 5pm in winter. Tel: 0903 204229).

Nearby is **Goring-by-Sea**. The reproduction of the Sistine Chapel's 'English Martyrs' in Goring's catholic church has a certain kitsch appeal, whilst perhaps not a masterpiece. The local Michelangelo is called Gary Bevans and his replica is two-thirds original size (open 10am–6pm, 4pm in winter. Tel: 0903 242624).

Just out of town, **Highdown Chalk Gardens** present a stunning collection of plants, shrubs and trees (open year round Monday to Friday 10am–4.30pm and in summer, weekends too, 6–8pm. Tel: 0903 239999).

North of Highdown, visit the typical Downs village of **Clapham** with its pretty 13th-century church of **St Mary**.

Due north of Worthing, Findon's **St John the Baptist** church is worth investigation; while **Findon Place** prides itself on its sheep fair, an extraordinary assembly of more than 20,000 animals and nearly as many curious human beings.

At **Sompting**, along the River Adur, the church of **St Mary** boasts the only Rhenish crown or four-turreted spire in England. **Lancing College's** neo-Gothic chapel is still more impressive.

North of the College is **Coombes**, barely big enough to be called a hamlet even, but home to a 1,200-acre farm where members of the public can see (and participate in) the full range of farming activities (open daily March to mid April 9am–6pm or by arrangement. Tel: 0273 452028).

Shoreham-by-Sea, at the mouth of the River Adur, has a magnificent Norman church, **St Mary's**, which dates from the 12th century, when Shoreham was one of England's premier ports, a role it was denied when the harbour became sand-locked. Happily, a sustained programme of dyke building was able to reverse this process at the end of the 18th century. Today, Shoreham is a medium-size but extremely busy industrial port. Along the railway line that used to connect Shoreham to Guildford, a long-distance path has been created, called the **Downs Link**, and constitutes a good walk of several days' duration.

Some 5 miles north of Worthing, the charming town of **Steyning** spreads out along the River Adur, many of its original buildings carefully preserved; these include the Norman church of **St Andrew** which rewards close inspection. Steyning is not far from the once strategically important town of **Bramber**. The ruins of **Bramber Castle**, built by Guillaume de Braose, faithful lieutenant to William the Conqueror, are just a stone's throw from the Norman church of **St Nicholas**. In the main street, **St Mary's House** is a magnificent timbered building with trompe-l'oeil motifs and believed to have been an inn used by pilgrims on their way to Canterbury.

Surrey

Often discounted as too close to London's sprawl and inclined to snobbery, the pretty county of Surrey has, in fact, a great deal to offer.
Some of England's most beautiful, if – not just by chance – most formal gardens (Wisley, Painshill, Claremont) and some of her finest houses (Polesden Lacey and Loseley House) present a different perspective.

DORKING
B-4 · 73 miles

Hotels
Bookham Grange Hotel ★★★
Little Bookham Common
Bookham (Leatherhead)
KT23 3HS
Tel: 0372 452742
Burford Bridge Hotel ★★
Box Hill, Dorking RH5 6BX
Tel: 0306 884561

Restaurants
White Horse
High Street, Dorking
Tel: 0306 881138
Lord Howard Bar
& Restaurant
Forest Road, Effingham
Junction, Leatherhead
Tel: 0483 282572

Entertainment
Thorndike Theatre
Church Street, Leatherhead
Tel: 0372 377677

Dorking is a pleasant town. At the crossroads of Stone Street – the Roman road from London to Chichester – and the medieval Pilgrims' Way joining London to Canterbury, Dorking has everything to recommend it to the tourist: old houses line many of its streets, it has a magnificent 19th-century church with gleaming spire, a good selection of pubs and restaurants; and last, but definitely not least, the surrounding countryside offers peace and quiet and a variety of leisure pursuits.

Four miles north-west of the town is **Polesden Lacey**, the magnificent mansion built by Thomas Cubitt, one of the Regency period's greatest architects. Its collections of paintings, tapestries and furniture are of world renown (more information in Castles and Country Houses route, p106).

A little further on, at **Leatherhead**, visitors can enjoy, by contrast, resolutely contemporary works of art at the **Fire and Iron Gallery**, where temporary exhibitions of metal sculptures, drawn from the four corners of the globe, often surprise and provoke. A stimulating experience.

• **Fire & Iron Gallery**, Rowhurst Forge, Oxshott Road, Leatherhead KT22 OEN. Tel: 0372 375148.

At **Fetcham**, less than a mile from the forge, is Bocketts Farm Park model farm, a good example of the genre, with rare breeds, educational displays, etc. Children will want to go back a second time.

• **Bocketts Farm Park**, Young Street, Fetcham KT22 9DA. Tel: 0372 363764.

Denbies Wine, on the northern edge of Dorking, is England's biggest wine producer. Its 350 acres include vineyards, museum, cellars, garden, children's play area and, last but not least, wine tasting.

• **Denbies Wine Estate**, London Road, Dorking RH5 6AA. Tel: 0306 876616.

South of Dorking, **Leith Hill** is the south-east's highest point, while **Newdigate** has a very pleasant pub, the **Surrey Oaks** (more information in Country Pubs route, p108).

FARNHAM
B-2 · 96 miles

Tourist information
Vernon House
28 West Street
Farnham GU9 7DR
Tel: 0252 715109

Hotels
The Bush Hotel ★★★
The Borough
Farnham GU97NN
Tel: 0252 715237
Bishop's Table Hotel ★★
27 West Sreet
Farnham GU9 7DR
Tel: 0252 710222
The Mariners Hotel ★★
Millbridge, Frensham GU10 3DJ
Tel: 0251 252050
Frensham Pond Hotel ★
Churt, Farnham GU10 2 QB
Tel: 0252 795161

Restaurants
The Bishop's Table
27 West Street, Farnham
Tel: 0252 710222
Fox and Pelican (pub)
Headley Road, Hindhead
Tel: 0428 604757

At Surrey's most westerly point, Farnham is a quiet town boasting a few fine Georgian streets. It is dominated by the castle of the bishops of Winchester, built by Normans in the 12th century. The **Bishops' Residence** is open Wednesdays only 2–4pm, but the best bit of the castle – **the dungeon** – is open daily 10am–6pm between 1 April and 30 September, and affords an excellent view over the surrounding countryside.

At **Holt**, south-west of Farnham, **Birdworld and**

Underwaterworld is a new-style zoo specialising in aquatic birds and animals. Penguins, flamingoes, ostriches, parrots, etc. compete for interest with tropical fish (open year round 9.30am–6pm, 5pm in March and October, 3.30pm in winter. Tel: 0420 22140).

Manor Farm Craft Centre, on the Guildford road, includes displays of craft techniques, ancient and modern (open Tuesday to Saturday 11am–5pm and Sunday 1–5pm. Tel: 0252 783333).

GUILDFORD
B-3 • 87 miles

Tourist information
The Undercroft
72 High Street
Guildford GU1 3HE
Tel: 0483 444007

Hotels
Forte Crest Hotel ★★★★
Egerton Road
Guildford GU2 5XZ
Tel: 0483 574444

Lythe Hill Hotel ★★★
Petworth Road
Haslemere GU27 3BQ
Tel: 0428 651251
Bramley Grange Hotel ★★
Bramley, Guildford GU5 0BL
Tel: 0483 893434
Thatchers Resort Hotel ★★
Epsom Road
East Arsley KT24 6TB
Tel: 0483 284291

Restaurants
Amalfi Pizza House
135 Swan Lane, Guildford
Tel: 0483 506306
Toby's
1 The Shambles, Guildford
Tel: 0483 302190

Surrey's major town has invested heavily in tourist initiatives in recent years. Its policy to provide the tourist with the very best information will reap its own rewards in the future, and at the same time makes Surrey a fine ambassador for the whole of the country. The **High Street** climbs from the (navigable) River Wey up to **Civic Hall** and, once at the top, **Castle Street** to the right leads to the castle; or alternatively, **Quarry Street** leads to **St Mary's** church.

Of the castle, built on a man-made hill ablaze with flowers in summer, little more than the 13th-century dungeon remains (open April to end September 10.30am–6pm). St Mary's church, Saxon in origin if Norman in appearance, stands next to the 17th-century home of the **Guildford Museum**. The latter's charming collection includes archaeological finds and craft artefacts, as well as items associated with another neighbour, Lewis Caroll, who lived in **The Chestnuts** a little further up the street (further information in Writers route, p110). Walk up the High Street and admire a number of old timbered buildings, among them the fully restored Tudor guildhall, **Guildford House** (no 155) and the **Town Hall** which dates from the 17th century. A little further on is the fine Renaissance brick building of **Archbishop Habbot Hospital** and, beyond, the impressive façade of the **Royal Grammar School** public school.

Polesden Lacey

Across the river, the Anglican cathedral stands on **Stag Hill**. Consecrated in 1961, it began life on the drawing board in 1936 – as its architectural style perhaps suggests.

The **University of Surrey** campus, which starts just the other side of the cathedral, has rooms to let in the summer months (Tel: 0483 509243).

The River Wey is navigable between **Farncombe**, south of the town, and **St Catherine's Lock**, the first lock going north. This mini-cruise is good fun. The boats leave from **Millbrook**, almost opposite the acclaimed **Yvonne Arnaud Theatre** building.

• **Guildford Boat House River Trip**, Millbrook, Guildford GU1 3XJ. Tel: 0483 504494. Open Easter to end October.

South of the town is **Loseley House**, a richly decorated Elizabethan manor in a magnificent park which abuts an excellent model farm (more information in Castles and Country Houses route, p106).

Further south again, at **Hascombe** near Godalming, the **Winkworth Arboretum** is more park than garden. Go there in the spring to enjoy the azaleas and bluebells in bloom beneath century-old trees; and, as you turn a corner here and there, the views of ponds glimpsed through the trees will turn all your worries on their heads! (Open daily 9am–6pm. Tel: 0483 208477.)

North along the A3 towards London, via Richmond and Wimbledon, four further attractions beckon. **Burpham Court Farm Park**, on the outskirts of Guildford, is a 100-acre home for 'at risk' farm animals, whether rare breeds or animals that are sick and need special care. Open daily 10am–6pm .

• **Burpham Court Farm Park**, Clay Lane, Jacobs Well, Guildford GU4 7NA. Tel: 0483 576089. Open daily 10am–6pm.

At **Wisley,** the famous **Royal Horticultural Society Garden** extends over 375 acres (more information in Gardens route, p104).

Pains Hill Park is a garden created in the 18th century at **Cobham**, a little further along the A3 . . . not very big, but cleverly conceived to encompass both garden design and horticultural technique and innovation within its 20 acres.

• **Painshill Park**, Portsmouth Road, Cobham KT11 1JE. Tel: 0932 868113. Open 10 April to 16 October Sundays 11am–6pm.

Further north, just before you get into London, **Claremont Landscape Garden** is one of the last surviving new-wave English gardens influenced by French design. Architects Vanbrugh and Bridgeman's masterpiece is on a par with the greatest French classic

Wisley Garden

Winkworth Arboretum

gardens (more information in Gardens route, p104).

Finally, **Clandon Park** and **Hatchlands Park**, to the north-east along the A246: the first of these is a magnificent park surrounding a Palladian manor house, whose marble hall, room furnishings and art collections more than justify a detour.

• **Clandon Park**, West Clandon, Guildford GU4 7RQ. Tel: 0483 222482.

Hatchlands Park stands in a garden designed by the famous Gertrude Jekyll. The brick-built manor house is itself very striking, and the Adam-style interior décor makes a superb showcase for a magnificent collection of furniture and musical instruments.

• **Hatchlands Park**, East Clandon, Guildford GU4 7RT. Tel: 0483 222482. Open Tuesday to Thursday 10am–5pm.

REIGATE AND REDHILL

B-4 · 67½ miles

Hotels

Nutfield Priory ★★★
Nutfield, Redhill RH1 4EN
Tel: 0737 822066

Bridge House Hotel ★★★
Reigate Hill, Reigate RH2 9RP
Tel: 0737 246801
Cranleigh Hotel ★★
West Street, Reigate RH2 9BL
Tel: 0737 223417
The Mill House ★★
Brighton Road
Redhill RH1 5TB
Tel: 0737 767277

Restaurants
The Home Cottage
Redstone Hill, Redhill
Tel: 0737 762771
The Garland (pub)
5 Brighton Road, Redhill
Tel: 0737 760377

Entertainment
The Harlequin Theatre
Warwick Quadrant, Redhill
Tel: 0737 773721

These twin towns at the foot of the North Downs have very different pasts but today are both commuter towns.

Reigate began life as an Anglo-Saxon village called Cherchefelle, whose stature increased with the building of a Norman fortified castle (of which only a few walls remain). In the 12th-century church you can see the tomb of Lord Admiral Howard of Effingham, victor over the previously invincible Armada.

The area around the town hall (called **Market House** and built in 1708) and the church holds most to interest the visitor. Notice, in particular, **Reigate Priory**, which is not a priory but a beautiful 18th-century house in magnificent grounds. There is a museum here:

• **Reigate Priory Museum**, Bell Street, Reigate. Tel: 0737 245065. Open Friday and Saturday 2–4.30pm and by arrangement.

Redhill is a relatively modern town. Established in 1841 on the new London–Brighton railway line, it is still an important rail junction.

Between Redhill and Reigate, the **Cobham Bus Public Transport Museum** has buses from 1930 to the present day. Children will appreciate the fire-fighting museum, with all of the Surrey brigade's equipment on display.

• **Fire Brigade of Surrey Prevention Trust Museum**, Croydon Road, Reigate. Tel: 0737 221759.

A mile west of the town, via the A25 on Reigate Heath, is the only known church mill. **Windmill Church** is a 400-year-old windmill standing on a hill (also a golf course) from which you can enjoy a lovely view over the Weald.

• **The Windmill Church**, Reigate Heath, Reigate. Tel: 0737 221100. Open daily 9am–5pm. Services every third Sunday of the month at 3pm.

Near **Bletchingley**, south-east of the town, the sails of **Outwood Windmill**, built in 1665, turn alongside an agricultural museum (Tel: 0342 843458).

Finally, not far away, towards **Godstone**, a children's rural museum has recently opened, with adventure playground and pets' corner – **Godstone Farm Park** (open 10am–6pm. Tel: 0883 742546).

Gardens route

There are too many British gardens to get to know in a single lifetime. Even discounting the many exceptional private gardens only open by special arrangement, and those gardens which are a part of even more celebrated houses (details in Castles and Country Houses route), there are literally dozens to visit in Kent, Sussex and Surrey alone. So, how to narrow down the choice?

Every epoque and garden style is represented . . . Chichester's famous Fishbourne Roman Palace Garden comes close to being anecdotal, 'Capability' Brown's work at Sheffield Park approaches the sublime.

There are gardens where colour and form are the major preoccupations, others where species rarity is the draw, while others still seek to illustrate particular gardening concepts, aimed first at the intellect and only second at the senses.

Three elements combine to make Great Britain, in general, and its south-east coast in particular, a garden lovers' paradise: the endeavours of exceptionally creative gardeners; an ideal climate – frequent rain with moderate winds and temperatures – and, most important, a gardening tradition stretching back over several centuries. We are told that future generations will spend less of their time at work and more in leisure pursuits; we envy them the extra time they will have, both to explore and enjoy these horticultural masterpieces and, suitably inspired, to create their own gardening set pieces. Perhaps like Voltaire's hapless voyager, Candide, they too will find consolation from the ills of the world in a garden.

Leonardslee Gardens

Sheffield Park Gardens

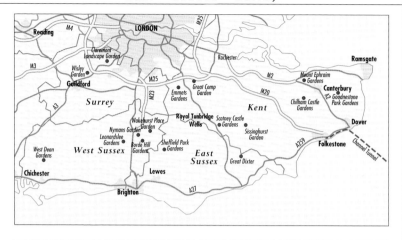

RECOMMENDED GARDENS

KENT

Chilham Castle Gardens
Chilham, Canterbury CT4 8DB
Tel: 0227 730319
Gardens: 3 April–6 October,
daily 11am–5pm. Castle only
by prior arrangement.

Emmets Gardens
Ide Hill
Sevenoaks TN14 6AY
Tel: 0732 750367
April–end October, Wed-
nesday to Sunday, 1–6pm.

Goodnestone Park Gardens
Wingham, Canterbury CT3 1PL
Tel: 0304 840107
Gardens: 28 March–28
October, daily except Tuesday
and Saturday, 11am–5pm,
manor house by prior
arrangement only.

Great Comp Garden
Comp Lane
Borough Green
Sevenoaks TN15 8QS
Tel: 0732 882669
1 April–31 October, daily
11am–6pm, or by prior
arrangement.

Mount Ephraim Gardens
Hernhill
Faversham ME13 9TX
Tel: 0227 751496
18 April–end September, daily
2–6pm.

Scotney Castle Gardens
Lamberhurst
Tunbridge Wells TN3 8JN
Tel: 0892 890651
2 April–end October,
Wednesday to Friday
11am–6pm (or dusk), 2–6pm
at weekends.

Sissinghurst Garden
Sissinghurst
Cranbrook TN17 2AB
Tel: 0580 712850
April–15 October, Tuesday to
Friday 1–6.30pm and
10am–5.30pm weekends.

EAST SUSSEX

Great Dixter
Northiam TN31 6PH
Tel: 0797 253160
1 April–10 October, daily
except Monday 2–5pm.

Sheffield Park Garden
Uckfield TN22 3QX
Tel: 0825 790655
April–7 November, Tuesday to
Saturday 11am–6pm and
Sunday 2–6pm (or dusk).

WEST SUSSEX

Borde Hill Garden
Haywards Heath RH16 1XP
Tel: 0444 450326
9 April–31 October, daily
10am–6pm.

Fishbourne Roman Palace Garden
Salthill Road
Fishbourne PO19 3QR
Tel: 0243 785859
14 February–16 December,
daily 10am–5pm.

Leonardslee Gardens
Lower Beeding
Horsham RH13 6PP
Tel: 0403 891212

1 April–31 October, daily
10am–6pm.

Nymans Garden
Handcross
Haywards Heath RH17 6EB
Tel: 0444 400321
1 April–end October, daily
except Monday and Friday
11am–7pm (or sunset).

Wakehurst Place Gardens
Ardingly
Haywards Heath RH17 6TN
Tel: 0444 892701
Daily 10am–4pm in winter,
10am–7pm in summer.

West Dean Gardens
West Dean
Chichester PO18 0QZ
Tel: 0243 811303
1 March–31 October, daily
11am–6pm.

SURREY

Claremont Landscape Garden
Old Portsmouth Road
Esher KT10 9JG
Tel: 0372 469421
April–end October, Monday to
Friday 10am–6pm and week-
ends 10am–7pm. November–
end March, daily (except
Monday) 10am–5pm (or
sunset).

Wisley Garden
Wisley, Woking GU23 6QB
Tel: 0483 224234
Monday to Saturday
10am–7pm (or dusk).

Castles and Country Houses route

In former times, castles and fortresses were built along the entire length of the south coast as a safeguard against possible invasion from the other side of the Channel – *see* Defence Structures route.

But further inland and in more recent times, other buildings were to shape the landscape, themselves shaped in turn by history and changing architectural development.

The Saxons were to see most of their buildings destroyed during the period of Norman invasion, which is why Leeds Castle (*see below*) prides itself on its 19th-century provenance – though it has undergone many modifications in the intervening centuries.

The post-Conquest Anglo-Norman style is to be found in only a handful of castles (restored, albeit often rather poorly, in the 19th century), and in vast numbers of small country churches. The principal characteristics of these buildings are Norman arches and a certain robustness of style, favouring rectangular ground plans and materials that were often imported from Normandy. Hever Castle provides an interesting interpretation of this influence on secular building style, while Ightham Mote is a more consistent Norman model.

Next came Gothic, influenced by international Gothic (ie, French) to create English Gothic style, frequently found in monasteries – though many of these were destroyed following the schism with Rome – as well as in the great cathedrals. This comparatively plain Gothic was in time to incorporate ornamentation similar to the continental Flamboyant Gothic, to become the English Decorated style, before further refinements evolved into the masterly Perpendicular. Country house architecture, meanwhile, began to be more concerned with increased flexibility of layout and interior comfort (as at Knole).

The Tudor reigns of Henry VIII and Elizabeth I witnessed formidable economic growth, which was marked by the building of great houses as statements of power and status. The Tudor arch, brick façades interrupted by many windows, terraced roofs topped with forests of chimneys, turret-flanked entrances: these were all marks of status – as can be seen at Firle Place in East Sussex (much of the manor house was restored in the 18th century).

Goodwood House

RECOMMENDED CASTLES

KENT

Belmont Mansion
Throwley
Faversham ME13 0HH
Tel: 0795 890202
3 April–25 September,
Saturday, Sunday and Bank
Holiday Mondays, 2–5pm.

Hever Castle
Hever
Edenbridge TN8 7NG
Tel: 0732 865224
15 March–beginning
November, daily noon–6pm.

Ightham Mote
Ivy Hatch
Sevenoaks TN15 0NT
Tel: 0732 810378
April–October, noon (11am
Sunday)–5pm. Closed
Tuesday and Saturday.

Knole
Sevenoaks TN15 0RP
Tel: 0732 450608
April–October, Wednesday to
Sunday, 11am (2pm
Thursday)–5pm.

Leeds Castle
Leeds
Maidstone ME17 1PL
Tel: 0622 765400
All year 11am–5pm (4pm
November–15 March).

EAST SUSSEX

Firle Place
Firle BN8 6LP
Tel: 0273 858335
Easter–end September,
Wednesday, Thursday and
Sunday 2–5pm.

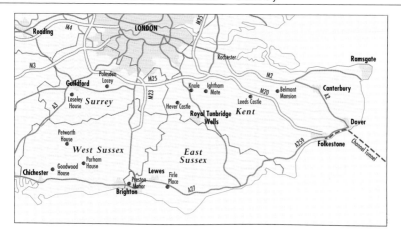

By the end of Elizabeth's reign, the strongest architectural influences were coming from Flanders, and Loseley and Parham are two magnificent examples of the Flemish style. The first great parks also date from this period.

Next, Baroque – interpreted much more rigidly in Britain than in the Latin countries – inspired grandiose designs of houses and churches alike and, in the wake of Christopher Wren, Hawksmoor, Archer and Gibbs, gave rise to some impressive churches and country houses.

Architects in the first half of the 18th century reacted to Baroque with a return to Classicism, skilfully combining simplicity of form with elaborate decoration. The voyage to Greece or Rome to seek inspiration from original models became de rigueur for every aspiring architect. Similar inspiration from the Ancients, derived via Poussin's landscapes, contributed to William Kent and 'Capability' Brown's magnificent gardens (as at Petworth).

From the second half of the 18th century up to 1914, Britain's formidable economic expansion made her the richest nation of the globe, with such a healthy economy that momentous events like the American War of Independence, the Napoleonic wars and colonial unrest did little to dent her confident prosperity.

The early part of this period produced a wealth of fine houses: Belmont Mansion, designed by the great Samuel Wyatt, and Goodwood House are both excellent examples.

The Regency period ushered in a further new wave of architectural vigour. Polesden Lacey or John Nash's extraordinary Royal Pavilion at Brighton are two obvious examples.

AND COUNTRY HOUSES

Preston Manor
Preston Park
Brighton BN1 6SD
Tel: 0273 779108
All year, Tuesday to Saturday
11am (Sunday 2pm)–5pm.

WEST SUSSEX

Goodwood House
Goodwood
Chichester PO18 0PX
Tel: 0243 774107
May–September, most
Sundays and Mondays
2–5pm, best to phone.

Parham House
Pulborough RH20 4HS
Tel: 0903 744888
Easter to first Sunday in
October, Wednesday,
Thursday and Sunday:
Gardens 1–6pm, House
2–6pm.

Petworth House
Petworth GU28 0AE
Tel: 0798 342207
Gardens 8am–sunset, House
April–October, 1–5.30pm.
Closed Monday (except Bank
Holidays) and Friday.

SURREY

Loseley House
Loseley Park
Guildford GU3 1HS
Tel: 0483 304440
2 June–2 October,
Wednesday to Saturday:
Gardens and Restaurant
11am–5pm, House 2–5pm.

Polesden Lacey
Great Bookham
Leatherhead RH5 6BD
Tel: 0372 458203
Daily 11am–5pm.

Country Pubs route

The French may be deserting their bars – traditionally the place for setting the world to rights, denouncing politicians of every persuasion and, latterly, politics itself – but the connection between the British pub and political ideology has always been less marked. Excepting the effects of the recession, their popularity remains unchanged.

Some may have become more sophisticated. Many offer a much wider selection of better presented food than previously. But the essential attractions remain the same: good beer, the chance for a game of darts or dominoes, cribbage or pool (some, sadly, have succumbed to the modern scourge of video games and juke-boxes), and a robustness of décor and atmosphere that reflects their often considerable age.

Among the dozens of excellent pubs of the south-east, some of the country pubs are particularly attractive. Tucked away in pretty villages, they may take a bit of finding but will never disappoint.

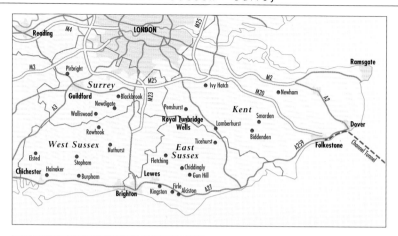

COUNTRY PUBS

KENT

Biddenden
The Three Chimneys
About a mile west of the village on the A262 near Sissinghurst.
Tel: 0580 291472.

Ivy Hatch
(north of Tonbridge)
The Plough
Coach Road
Tel: 0732 810268

Lamberhurst
The Brown Trout
South of the village near Scotney Castle.
Tel: 0892 890312

Newham (near Faversham)
The George
44 The Street
Follow signs from A2.

Penshurst
(near Chiddingstone)
The Spotted Dog
Smarts Hill
¾ mile on the left off B2188
Tel: 0892 870253

Smarden
The Bell
Just outside the village.
Tel: 0233 77283

EAST SUSSEX

Alciston
The Rose Cottage
Follow signs from A27 Polegate–Lewes road.
Tel: 0323 870377

Chiddingly
The Six Bells
Signs from A22 Uckfield–Hailsham road.
Tel: 0825 872227

Firle
The Ram
Signs from A27 Lewes–Polegate road.
Tel: 0273 858222

Fletching
The Griffin
Signs from A272 west of Uckfield.
Tel: 0825 722890

Gun Hill
The Gun
A22 north-west of Hailsham (after junction with A269, turn north at the Happy Eater).
Tel: 0825 872361.

Kingston (near Lewes)
The Juggs
Tel: 0273 472523

Ticehurst
The Bull
Tel: 0580 200886

WEST SUSSEX

Burpham
The George & Dragon
Signs from A27, 1 mile east of Arundel.
Tel: 0903 883131

Elsted
The Elsted Inn
Just outside the village.
Tel: 0730 813662

Halnaker (near Chichester)
The Anglesey Arms
On the A285 Chichester–Petworth road.
Tel: 0243 773474

Nuthurst
The Black Horse
In the centre of the village, via the A281.
Tel: 0403 891272

Rowhook
The Chequers
Village signed from A29.
Tel: 0403 790480

Stopham
The White Hart
Just outside the village.
Tel: 0798 873321

SURREY

Blackbrook (near Dorking)
The Plough
Tel: 0306 88603

Newdigate (near Dorking)
The Surrey Oaks
Parkgate Road
A24 south of Dorking, then right towards Beare Green. Drive through the village then first fork left.
Tel: 0306 77200.

Pirbright
The Royal Oak
Aldershot Road.
On the A324 south of the village.
Tel: 0483 232466.

Walliswood
The Scarlett Arms
Tel: 0306 79243

Writers route

The writer is a curious creature, at once fiercely engaged with capturing the way of the world yet equally engaged in shutting it out, often indifferent to accolade yet seeking a kind of immortality.

The impulses that drove men and women of letters to this part of England – some of her greatest literary names – were the impulses of writers everywhere. Away from the pressures of the capital, Dickens (who was born here) and Kipling (who spent his last days here) found a common refuge.

Having discovered these captives of the literary Muse through their work, revel in the exploration of the places and objects that framed their lives and writing.

Charleston Farmhouse

Bateman's

WRITERS OF THE SOUTH-EAST

KENT

Broadstairs
(Dickens, *Bleak House*)
At important milestones in his life, Dickens came to Kent for his holidays. It was a house set high up on the cliff overlooking Broadstairs which was his model for *Bleak House*, written between 1851 and 1853.
• **Dickens House Museum**
2 Victoria Parade, Broadstairs
Tel: 0843 862853. 2.30–5.30pm, Easter to mid Oct.

Canterbury
(Chaucer and Marlowe)
Separated in time by 200 years, two of the greatest contributors to English literature were both born in Canterbury.

Chartwell (Churchill)
Winner of the 1953 Nobel Prize for Literature, Churchill ended his days in this magnificent house.
Tel: 0732 866368. April to October, 11am–5.30pm.

Chatham (Dickens)
Though born near Portsmouth, Dickens spent his early youth at Chatham, near Rochester. After a full and accomplished life, he came to spend his last days in a country house at Godshill, close to the area where he had been brought up.
• **The Dickens Centre**, Eastgate House, High Street, Rochester. Tel: 0634 844176. 10am–5pm.

Goodnestone Park
(Jane Austen)
A magnificent 16-acre garden and romantic manor house, haunted by the memory of the great novelist.
Wingham CT3 1PL. Tel: 0304 840107. 28 March to 28 Oct.

Sheerness-on-Sea
(Uwe Johnson)
It was here, far from the Pomerania of his birth, that the

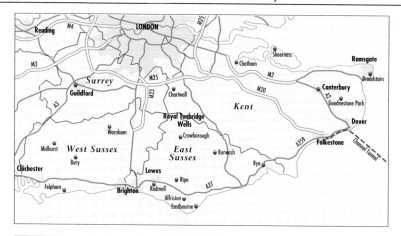

writer (considered by many to be the best post-war German author – with Thomas Bernhardt) chose to end his days. Novels that dealt with a divided Germany still retain their force today.

EAST SUSSEX

Burwash (Kipling, Bateman's)
Born in Bombay in 1865, Kipling withdrew to this magnificent 17th-century house in 1902, where he received the Nobel Prize in 1907. He died there in 1936. Tel: 0435 882302. 1 April to end October, 11am–5pm.

Charleston (Vanessa Bell, Charleston Farm)
Furnished and decorated throughout by the members of the Bloomsbury Group, this farm, a mile out of Alfriston, is encircled by an enchanting garden. J M Keynes wrote *The economic consequences of peace* here in 1919. Tel: 0323 811265. 2 April to 30 October, 10am–6pm.

Crowborough
(Arthur Conan Doyle)
Though Scottish by birth, the creator of Sherlock Holmes spent his last years here, where he developed a passion for spiritualism.

Eastbourne (George Orwell, Cyril Connolly, Lewis Carroll)
The first two were at secondary school in Eastbourne

during the First World War. Thirty years earlier they could have bumped into Lewis Carroll, alias Reverend Dodgson, who holidayed in the town.

Ripe
(near Lewes, Malcolm Lowry)
The author of *Beneath the Volcano* acquired cult writer status, so it is surprising to find that the house where he died has not been turned into a museum. For the time being, visitors must content themselves with re-reading their favourite pages of the novel down at the local pub, where he was surely a customer.

Rodmell
(Virginia Woolf, Monk's House)
Virginia and her husband Leonard lived here, first intermittently then all the time, during the 20 years preceding her tragic death. The victim of serious psychiatric problems following a period of depression, she drowned herself in the River Ouse.

Rye
(Henry James, Lamb House)
Henry James lived in beautiful Lamb House until his death in 1916. Most of the era's intellectuals came to visit him here: H G Wells, Joseph Conrad, Ford Maddox Ford ... The house is open to the public on certain days during the spring and summer. Tel: 0797 223763.

WEST SUSSEX

Bury (John Galsworthy)
The author of *The Forsyte Saga* (Nobel Prize 1932) who was born in Coombe, Surrey, spent the last years of his life here. Fundamentally social at the start, his preoccupations embraced environmental issues later in life, for which Bury was the ideal setting.

Felpham (Blake)
Visionary and romantic poet, William Blake composed his most famous poem, *Jerusalem* at Felpham.

Midhurst (H G Wells)
Born in Bromley, Kent, in 1866, Herbert George was a pupil and then teacher in this little town's secondary school.

Warnham (Shelley)
Born at Field Place, Warnham in 1792, Shelley spent his early youth here. Memories of the archetypal romantic poet still linger.

SURREY

Guildford (Lewis Carroll)
The creator of Alice lived at The Chestnuts for most of his life, a little house just a stone's throw from the town museum now partly dedicated to Carroll.
• **Guildford Museum**
Quarry Street.
Tel: 0483 444750. Monday to Saturday, 11am–5pm.

Defence Structures route

'The insularity imposed by geography upon the inhabitants of Great Britain could have resulted in obsessional paranoia. Being surrounded is never easy, especially when it is by the vastness of the deep. Add to this the often hostile gaze of the French from across the water, and one may begin to understand, if not entirely forgive, past British attitudes.' (anonymous French perspective on the British)

But enough of national stereotyping. If this guide has any function beyond enumerating the attractions on offer in south-east England and northern France, it is to point out that these two regions separated by a few miles of salt water have, in fact, much more in common than is popularly ad- mitted. That being said, France and England have had very different histories over the past 1,000 years, which may explain a difference of national outlook. Scarcely a town in northern France (or indeed Belgium) has escaped involvement in battle, or being used as a bargaining tool, or has not changed hands during the last millenium, while south-east England has known no aggression since 1066, save that of civil strife (revolt of the barons, Wars of the Roses, the Civil War).

This period of non-violation by outside forces testifies to the effectiveness of the great fortresses that line Britain's south-east coast.

Bodiam Castle

DEFENCE STRUCTURES OPEN TO THE PUBLIC

ROMAN FORTRESSES

Reculver (Kent)
Ruins of the fort of *Regulbium*, on the coast 3 miles from Herne Bay.
Tel: 0227 366444.

Richborough (Kent)
Ruins of the fort of *Rutupiae*, 2 miles inland north of Sandwich.
Tel: 0304 612013.

Pevensey (Sussex)
Walls of the fortress of *Anderida* (4th century) surrounding the Norman castle.

Chichester (Sussex)
The layout of present-day Chichester still reflects the original Roman plan enclosing a fortress.

SAXON STRONGHOLDS

Dover Castle (Kent)
Although unquestionably Norman in style and only very recently restored (1958), Dover Castle is reputed to have been founded by King Harold. *See* p113 for visiting details.

NORMAN CASTLES

Pevensey Castle (Sussex)
Begun by William the Conqueror, but utilising Roman outer walls, 5 miles from Eastbourne.
10am–6pm (4pm and closed Monday 1 October to 31 March).
Tel: 0323 762604

Lewes Castle (Sussex)
Ruins of Guillaume de Warenne's castle (William the Conqueror's lieutenant).
Tel: 0273 486290.

Arundel Castle (Sussex)
Dating from the early Norman occupation and entirely restored in the 19th century, this castle offers outstanding views and houses the Fitzalan Chapel. 11am–5pm.
Tel: 0903 882173

Hastings Castle (Sussex)
Ruins of the castle built by William the Conqueror immediately after the battle of Hastings. 10am–5.30pm, April to October and 11am–4pm November to March.
Tel: 0424 442122.

Dover Castle (Kent)
One of Europe's most impressive medieval fortresses, mostly Norman. 10am–6pm (4pm 1 October to 31 March). Tel: 0304 201628.

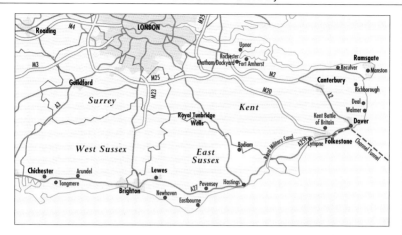

Lympne Castle (Kent)
Small castle built around 1360 in Norman-Gothic style. Beautiful gardens. 6 miles from Folkestone. Easter to end September, 10.30am–6pm. Tel: 0303 267571.

Bodiam Castle (Sussex)
Beautiful moated castle built in 1385. Daily 10am–6pm, closed Monday in winter. Tel: 0580 830436.

TUDOR AND STUART CASTLES AND FORTRESSES

Deal Castle (Kent)
Formidable fortress built by Henry VIII, with 119 canons aimed at France. 10am–6pm (4pm and closed Monday from October to 31 March). Tel: 0304 372762.

Walmer Castle (Kent)
In the shape of the Tudor rose, this castle was built by Henry VIII as protection against invasion from François I. 10am–6pm, April to September. Tel: 0304 364288

Upnor Castle (Kent)
Built in 1559 to protect Elizabeth I's navy anchored at Chatham. 10am–6pm April to end September. Tel: 0634 718742.

18TH CENTURY

Chatham Dockyard (Kent)
In the 18th century Chatham Naval Dockyard built dozens of warships of every size. The 100-acre dockyard has been given a face-lift and now includes a range of exhibits and permanent attractions. Tel: 0634 812551.

Fort Amherst
(Rochester, Kent)
One of the most beautiful fortresses built to counter Napoleonic ambition, with 875 yards of underground passages and 18 acres of redoubts and bastions equipped with dozens of canons to greet the Emperor!

Royal Military Canal
This extraordinary construction, a 16-mile-long canal built as a second line of defence against possible French invasion, is today put to good use for water sports and tourist activities.

Eastbourne Redoubt Fortress (Sussex)
One of the famous Martello towers, now a war museum. 17 April to 5 November, 9.30am–5.30pm. Tel: 0323 410300.

19TH CENTURY

Newhaven Fort (Sussex)
Victorian fort built in 1862 by Lord Palmerston to complete the country's defences. 27 March to 2 October, 10.30am–6pm. Tel: 0273 517622.

20TH CENTURY

Dover Castle (Kent)
Comprehensively restored before the Second World War, the castle served as British HQ, co-ordinating continental troop movements, including the embarkation of 340,000 allied soldiers from Dunkirk in 1940.

Minster-in-Thanet (Kent)
The Spitfire Memorial Pavilion on the RAF airfield at Manston recounts the glorious Battle of Britain.
Tel: 0843 823351.

Kent Battle of Britain Museum
At Hawkinge airfield, a vivid account of the different phases of the terrible battle waged in English skies between Spitfires and Messerschmitts.
Tel: 0303 893140.

Tangmere Military Aviation Museum (Sussex)
Historic airfield where visitors can follow the events of the air battle. Photographs and maps, aeroplanes, simulated Spitfire flights and various other attractions.
1 February to 30 November 10am–5.30pm.
Tel: 0243 775223.

Discovering Northern France: the Nord, Pas-de-Calais and Somme *départements*

The three French départements *of the Nord, the Somme and the Pas-de-Calais await the visitor at the French exit to the Tunnel, and indeed are the most likely to attract the attention of the weekend visitor.*

Past centuries of commerce, warfare and co-operative endeavour mean that these départements *are already familiar to many of their British neighbours. While for other Europeans, this part of France will be a pleasant surprise, rich in both architectural and artistic heritage, in countryside as varied as it is little known.*

Opposite:
Saint-Valery
chapel,
Saint-Valery-
sur-Somme

The Tunnel delivers visitors to a part of France steeped in history and abounding in memorials to her past. It was here, very probably at Boulogne, that Caesar assembled his legions in readiness for the invasion of England; here, too, the English armies would have landed at the beginning of the Hundred Years' War, taking Calais which remained in English hands for two centuries. A few miles on, between Guînes and Ardres, François I, King of France, met Henry VIII, King of England, at the Field of the Cloth of Gold, in 1520, surrounded by the splendour and opulence of the courts of both countries. At Boulogne too, Napoleon made futile preparations for an invasion of the British Isles. And here, where occupied French soil came closest to England, Hitler, duped by British Intelligence, waited in vain for a British landing, having already installed an enormous canon that could fire missiles across the Channel, as well as take-off pads for the V2, even more formidable than the V1 but soon knocked out by the RAF.

Fortunately, there were those who came across the Channel without bellicose intent: over the centuries travellers departed from this part of France for Dover and Folkestone; and in the other direction, engineers – chief players of the drama that was the Industrial Revolution – writers, like Byron and Dickens, and voyagers attracted by the different cultures of continental Europe as well as by the mild climate of the Mediterranean. Just 3km from the Tunnel exit, Blériot took off for the cliffs of Dover in his (some would say toy) aeroplane, on 25 July 1909.

From the time of the very first imaginings of a fixed cross-Channel link in the mid-eighteenth century, this was always the proposed point of departure for a bridge or a tunnel. Here, where the Straits of Dover are at their narrowest, the same sedimentary rock and geological structures are found on either side of the strait, set down prior to the relatively recent collapse of the isthmus that once separated the Channel from the North Sea.

Here, the Eurotunnel shuttle from England delivers you to the threshold of three distinct regional destinations.

To the north, the coastal plain spreads out towards Dunkirk, the scene in 1940 of large-scale Anglo-French losses at the hands of the German army. Here, French towns are justifiably proud of belfries that symbolise their liberation from occupying forces. Town squares, like Lille, Arras and Saint-Omer, all bear witness to civic pride, with their complement of handsome town halls, market halls and rows of fine, Gothic or baroque gabled houses. And whether this urban scape is preserved or the result of rebuilding after the destruction of two wars, it is a feature of charming northern towns in Belgium and France alike, of Bruges, Ghent and Arras; a testimony to their former wealth and merchant enterprise.

As you come out of the Tunnel, the motorway to the south-east takes you past Saint Omer, Béthune and Arras, on to the plateaux of the Parisian Basin. The road passes the slag heaps which are now the sole reminders of an activity that once brought wealth to the north; then further on, where silt has covered the underlying chalk, wide-skyed country opens out into the sugar-beet belt. It is hard to imagine that this prosperous, orderly-looking countryside once witnessed the unimaginable slaughter of the First World War, yet the seas of burial stones and crosses in the cemeteries do not allow the visitor to forget the sacrifices of English 'tommy' and French *poilu* alike (Vimy cemetery). The Pas-de-Calais has some exceptional urban architecture, particularly at Arras where three town squares attract the visitor's attention. Here, in this 13th-century capital of the Artois, the first French plays were penned, *le jeu de Saint Nicolas* by Jean Bodel and *le jeu de la feuillée* by Adam de la Halle. Here, too, were woven the finest tapestries, which in time transformed the name of the town into the Italian word for tapestry, *arazzo*.

Driving south along the coast, you come to Boulogne, to the Picardy coast and to Normandy. The region around Boulogne, known as the *Boulonnais*, is mixed woodland and pasture, high green hills and hedged, fertile grassland. Further along the coast the resorts of Le Touquet and Hardelot hide the most beautiful of their villas behind a wide cordon of dunes. These towns have welcomed visitors from England and the Paris region for more than a century, while the inlets of the Canche and Authie rivers, often folded in mist, have long been the favoured haunts of wildfowlers. Coming directly from Normandy and heading north, Montgomery liberated this region in 1944 before reaching Lille, Belgium and the Netherlands. From the coast at the *Baie de Somme*, the site of a wonderful bird reserve, you can see the Gothic spire of Amiens cathedral; then futher east, the land ravaged by the First World War battlefields and the *Historial* at Péronnes.

Getting information and making bookings in France

TOURIST INFORMATION:

Tourist information offices may be called:

- syndicat d'initiative
- office de tourisme
- maison de tourisme

TELEPHONE:
☎

All French telephone numbers have 8 digits (preceded by an extra [1] for Paris), with no preceding STD code equivalent.

If calling from the UK, use international code 01033 and the 8 (or 9) digits of the French telephone number.

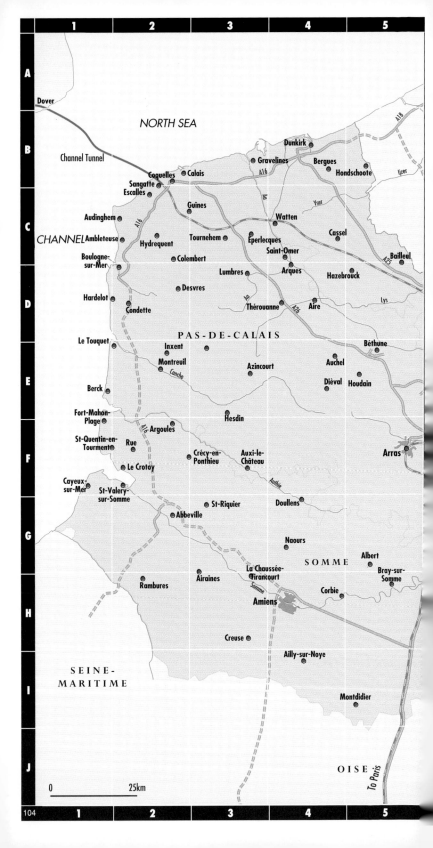

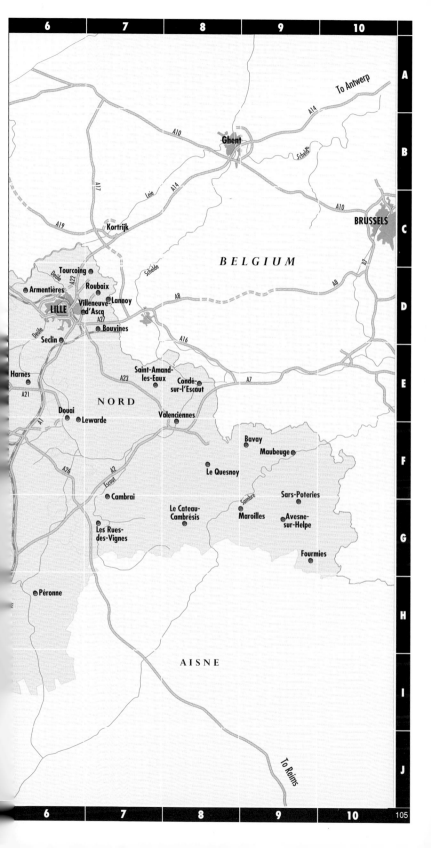

Nord, Pas-de-Calais and Somme

In this, the first part of your discovery of northern Europe, you will find descriptions of both the countryside and the cultural inheritance of the three départements which are nearest to the French Tunnel exit as well as practical information: the Pas-de-Calais, home to the French Tunnel terminal at Coquelles; the Somme to the south and the Nord to the north-east. Three départements with much to offer the weekend visitor: monuments, museums, old towns, beautiful churches, or perhaps that rather special hotel or restaurant . . . Distances shown are in kilometres from Calais.

ABBEVILLE
80100 · G-2 · 111 km

Tourist information
1 place Amiral-Courbet
Tel: 22.24.27.92

Hotels
Hôtel de France **
19 rue du Pilori
Tel: 22.24.00.42

The belfry, Abbeville

Le Relais Vauban **
4 boulevard Vauban
Tel: 22.31.30.35

Restaurants
Auberge de la Corne
32 chaussée au Bois
Tel: 22.24.03.65
Au Châteaubriant
3 rue des Lingers
Tel: 22.24.08.23
L'Escale en Picardie
15 rue des Teinturiers
Tel: 22.24.21.51

In the 12th century, Abbeville was the French kingdom's only North Sea port. It was at Abbeville that Louis XIII dedicated the realm of France to the Virgin Mary. The town prospered, especially with the establishment in 1665 of oar and cloth manufacturing, and in the 19th century the town competed economically with Amiens. In 1914, after centuries of hostility between France and England, the town became the head-quarters of the British army. Abbeville's saddest day was 20 May 1940 when German bombers reduced the town centre to rubble and killed 2,500 of its inhabitants.

St Vulfran is the archetypal Flamboyant Gothic church with its magnificently ornate façade and beautiful Renaissance doors. This building has held many a voyager spellbound, "to see Saint-Vulfran before the setting sun has left its towers is reason enough to cherish our past" (Victor Hugo). It is currently undergoing restoration.

• Guided tours organised from the tourist office (headsets for English, German and Dutch visitors).

The **Boucher-de-Perthes museum** has wide-ranging exhibits: in the archaeology room are artefacts found in the 19th century in the Somme by Boucher de Perthes, known to the French as *père de la pré-histoire* (father of pre-history).

He found knapped flints, indicating the presence of antediluvian man, in strata beneath the interglacial alluvia of the Somme's lower terraces. The museum also has medieval sculptures, a collection of paintings including a *Sainte Thérèse* attributed to Ribera, a child's head from Frans Hals' studio, five female portraits attributed to Nicolas de Largillière, a *Lisseuse* attributed to Fragonnard, as well as paintings by local artist Choquet. Last but not least, a bust by Camille Claudel, Vron earthenware and a stuffed bird collection.

• **Musée Boucher-de-Perthe** 24 rue Gontier Patin. Tel: 22.24.08.49. Open 2 May to 30 September and during school holidays daily, except Tuesdays, 2–6pm; 1 October to 30 April, Wednesday, Saturday and Sunday 2–6pm.

The château de Bagatelle was built in brick and stone by Dutchman Abraham Van Robais during the 17th century. He came to Abbeville in 1665 to set up a cloth manufacturing business. The château stands in a very beautiful formal French garden and 25 acres of landscaped grounds. Inside the château are elegant furniture and painted wood carvings.

• **Château de Bagatelle** 133 route de Paris. Tel: (1) 47.53.91.19/22.24.02.69. Open first weekend in July to first weekend in September daily, except Tuesday, 2–6pm and by arrangement. Guided tours in French and English.

AILLY-SUR-NOYE
80250 • I-4 • 176 km

Restaurant
Auberge du Val-de-Noye
Plan d'eau
Tel: 22.41.12.75

Standing on the Somme canal at a spot where archaeological finds testify to the earlier presence of prehistoric man is Ailly-sur-Noye, which every year stages an impressive summer spectacle, *Terre de Picardie, rivière du temps*. This takes place on an 8-acre lake and

involves 1,800 costumed actors and 25 local horsemen.

• **Son et lumière d'Ailly-sur-Noye** 1 rue Docteur-Binant. Tel: 22.41.06.90.

AIRAINES
80270 • G-3 • 132 km

L'église du Prieuré or priory church is the oldest religious building in the *département* and is a good illustration of the transition from Norman- to Gothic-style monastic building. It has a fine 11th-century font decorated with sculpted figures and stages art exhibitions (Vasarely, Rouault, Manessie . . .) and concerts are organised in the summer.

• **Le Prieuré** Tel: 22.29.45.05. Open May, June and September, Saturday, Sunday and public holidays, 2.30–6pm; July and August daily 2.30–6pm.

AIRE-SUR-LA-LYS
62120 • D-4 • 61 km

Tourist information
Le Bailliage, grand-place
Tel: 21.39.65.66

Horseriding
Centre équestre du fort Gassion
Tel: 21.95.60.88

Hotels
Hostellerie des trois Mousquetaires ★★★★
Château du Fort de la Redoute
Tel: 21.39.00.11
Europ'Hôtel ★★
14 grand-Place
Tel: 21.39.04.32

Aire-sur-la-Lys enjoyed a certain degree of prosperity during the Spanish occupation of the 16th and 17th centuries. After the Treaties of Utrecht in 1713, Aire-sur-la-Lys was declared French, and subsequently became a centre for textile manufacture as well as becoming a busy religious centre with collegiate church, hospital, various religious communities and a Jesuit college. The military engineer, Vauban, later made it a strategically important fortified town. The collegiate church of Saint-Pierre, **collégiale Saint-Pierre**, is a huge building in

Flamboyant Gothic style, constructed alternately of brick and stone. The *hôtel de ville*, or town hall, and the clocktower stand on the *grand-place*. Built between 1717 and 1721, the town hall is typical of the grandiose architecture of the Louis XIV era. Its pediment depicts the heraldic arms of the town. The clocktower carillon plays a variety of familiar tunes on the quarter hour. The **baillage**, near the *hôtel de ville* is an elegant Flemish Renaissance building, constructed around 1600 as a guardroom but now the tourist information office; guided tours of the town (in English) leave at 1.30pm.

AMBLETEUSE
62164 • C-2 • 30 km

Tourist information
38 rue de Lille
Tel: 21.32.64.79

Ambleteuse has a colourful past and a **fortress** built by Vauban, standing on a rocky promontary looking out to sea. Its interesting 17th-century artillery tower houses a little museum on the geology, archaeology and history of the coastal region (open March to November, Sunday and public holidays 3–7pm; July and August, Saturday, Sunday and Monday 3–7pm, tel: 20.54.61.54). Ambleteuse's **museum of the Second World War** has displays of weapons and uniforms and contemporary film footage (1 April–15 October daily 9.30am–7pm; low season, weekends and public holidays, tel: 21.87.33.01).

AMIENS
80000 • H-4 • 149 km

Tourist information
12 rue du Chapeau-de-Violettes
Tel: 22.91.79.28

Hotels
Le Carlton ★★★
42 route de Noyon
Tel: 22.97.72.22
Le Prieuré ★★
17 rue Porion
Tel: 22.92.27.67
Le Postillon ★★★
17–19 place au Feurre

Amiens: the hortillonnages

Tel: 22.91.46.17
Grand Hôtel de l'Univers ***
2 rue de Noyon
Tel: 22.91.52.51
Alsace-Lorraine **
18 rue de la Morlière
Tel: 22.91.35.71

Restaurants
Le Petit Chef
8 rue Jean-Catelas
Tel: 22.92.24.23
Les Cultivateurs
17 rue Jean-Jaurès
Tel: 22.91.37.05
Le Vivier
593 route de Rouen
Tel: 22.89.12.21

Nearby
L'Aubergcade
78 route nationale
Dury-les-Amiens (7km)
Tel: 22.89.51.41

Amiens is the Somme *département*'s only sizeable town with 135,000 inhabitants. Damage sustained during two world wars gave rise to the rebuilding of complete sections of the town. The town appears to be built on water, so criss-crossed is it with canals, rivers and the *hortillonages* of the lower town and its typical vegetable markets. By contrast with this provincial aspect, the town also boasts some notable buildings: the cathedral, the futuristic *maison de culture* (cultural/leisure centre founded by André Malraux), the Perret tower . . . Visionary writer Jules Verne chose to live in Amiens after writing *Twenty thousand leagues under the sea*, at Le Crotoy. Fervently attached to the town, he described it in a short story *Une ville idéale: Amiens en l'an 2000* (The ideal

town: Amiens in the year 2000). The **Jules Verne Centre** draws thousands of visitors each year (2 rue Charles Dubois. Open Tuesday to Saturday 9.30am–noon and 2–6pm, tel: 22.45.37.84 and 22.95.30.32). Jules Verne's grave is in the 45-acre Madeleine park-cemetery, one of the loveliest cemeteries in France (*rue Saint-Maurice*).

The **Notre-Dame cathedral** is the ultimate Gothic edifice, the "*église ogivale par excellence*" according to Viollet-le-Duc and, in 1982, the cathedral was added to Unesco's 'international heritage' list. The cathedral interior is beautifully lit, and the exceptional furnishings and carvings include the oak choir-stalls made between 1508 and 1522 and ornamented with 4,000 figures; there are colourful 15th- and 16th-century sculptures depicting the Gospel and the lives of the saints, 13th-century recumbent figures in bronze . . .

• **Cathédrale d'Amiens,** open 1 October to 31 March 8.30am–noon and 2–5pm; in season, 8.30am–6pm. Guided tours organised by the tourist office.

The cathedral Treasury safeguards precious objects and documents including the famous reliquary known as the *chef Saint-Jean* and its magnificent crystal, and a 12th-century shrine with relics of Saint Firmin, Amiens' first bishop. (1 rue Dormont. Tel: 22.92.77.29. Open 3 April to 3 October daily, except Sunday morning and mornings of religious festivals, 10am–noon and 2–6pm.) The *son et*

lumière spectacle which tells the story of the cathedral's construction in five tableaux, is performed between 15 April and 16 October on Tuesday, Thursday, Friday and Saturday (in French, English and German). Reservations at the tourist office.

Le Musée de Picardie is housed in a building that typifies the architecture of the Napoleonic era. The museum includes 15th-century pictures of the Puy-Notre-Dame community, unique examples of primitive Picardian art; there is also medieval and Renaissance furniture, sculptures, religious artefacts; a wide-ranging selection of 15th- to 19th-century paintings: Picardian, Flemish and Italian primitive paintings; paintings from the Spanish, Italian, Flemish and Dutch Schools (Franz Hals), work by the French artists Fragonnard, Boucher, Chardin, Courbet, Corot, Rousseau . . .), and paintings by contemporary artists. Close by, in the **hôtel de Berny**, the museum of local art and regional history has collections of Louis XV and Louis XVI furniture, wood carvings, decorative wall panels . . . ceramics and glassware (18th to 20th century) and 17th- and 18th-century tapestries. Visiting times as for *musée de Picardie*.

• **Musée de Picardie** 48 rue de la République. Tel: 22.91.36.44. Open daily, except Monday, 10am–12.30pm and 2–6pm.

Between the cathedral and the hôtel de Berny the **Galerie du Vitrail** is housed in a late 16th-century house built over 13th-century cellars. Three floors display stained glass, religious and secular, from the 13th century to the present day.

• **Galérie du Vitrail** 40 rue Victor Hugo. Tel: 22.91.81.18. Open daily, except Sunday, at 3pm and by arrangement.

The district around the cathedral is known as *Saint-Leu*, and its streets of craft shops and stalls, cafés and restaurants have an attractive atmosphere. In the 19th century there was a floating market here, and veg-

The cathedral at Amiens

etables were brought by rowing boat from the nearby *hortillonnages*. This once marshy area has undergone drainage and reclamation programmes to become one of the region's most unusual spots. Parcels of land cut up by the waterway network have supported vegetable and flower gardens to supply the local markets for centuries. Weeping willows, alders, reeds and all kinds of river flora give the locality its distinctive personality. In the gardens are little wooden cabins and bridges, and pretty, flat-bottomed boats allow passage up and down and round this garden-on-water. Fish, ducks, birds, the buzz of insects and water flowers complete the unlikely town-centre idyll (floating market Thursday and Saturday mornings, *quai Parmentier*).

• **Les hortillonnages** 54 boulevard Beauvillé. Tel: 22.92.12.18. **Boat trips**: 1 April to 31 October daily at 3pm, weekends and public holidays 2–6pm.

ARGOULES
80120 • F-2 • 85 km

Hotel
Auberge du Gros-Tilleul ★★
place du Château
Tel: 22.29.91.00

Close to the Tunnel terminal at Coquelles, the lovely **Abbaye de Valloires** and its gardens await those newly emerged from the Tunnel. The origins of this monastery go back to the 12th-century monks of the Cîteaux order, and their patron, Guy II de Ponthieu. Monks settled in the Authie valley in 1158 and lived and prospered there until late in the 13th century. The fabric of the monastery suffered the effects of both the Hundred Years' War and the Thirty Years' War, but it was rebuilt in the 18th century by Prior Don Comeau and the bishop of Amiens. Inside its decoration is the work of Austrian sculptor Pfaff de Pfaffenhofen. The monks were driven from the monastery during the Revolution but, happily, the buil-

ding was spared the destruction of the Terror. Converted into an orphanage for the offspring of landworkers at the end of the 19th century, it was accorded historic monument status and used as a holiday centre for children. Today it is divided into two parts: one a reception centre for children of families in difficulties, the other, guest rooms for visitors.

Passing through the great gateway, the visitor enters a huge horseshoe-shaped area. To the left, a 16th-century round dovecote; furthest from view, a long stone-and-brick building spanning almost the entire width of the courtyard (20 feet). Inside this building, the great hall is hung with portraits of the monastery's 18th-century benefactors; and from here the visitor can pass into the cloister: bounded by buildings on all four sides, a sombre space with ribbed vaulting and encircled by a garden. A former wine store has been converted into a refectory while on the first floor the monks' cells now serve as rooms for paying guests. The chapel building, in local stone, is a model of sobriety; a 50-yard-long façade overlooks the tombs of monks who died here in the 19th century; there is also a little slate-roofed bell-tower. But once inside, the interior presents an altogether different aspect. Everywhere is ornamentation and elaborate detail: the organ, the monks' stalls, the statues and bas-reliefs of the transept, the marble altar and the magnificent wrought-iron work choir screen.

Since 1985, and with the support of nurseryman Jean-Louis Cousin and a local growers' collective, landscape designer Gilles Clément has been establishing a garden and plant collection faithful to the monastery genre. Aiming both to provide a reference collection of plants, and to supply saplings and seeds from the garden's own stock, it extends over 18 acres; the central section on the west side of the abbey adheres strictly to the traditional model; here are old roses, medicinal plants, herbs and vegetables, grown in

Arras: view of the grand-place

the 5-yard-square layout of the Cistercians.

• **Abbaye de Valloires**. Tel: 22.29.62.33. Open 1 April to 11 November daily 10am–noon and 2–6pm, guided visits hourly. Accommodation on site. Gardens only 1 April to 30 November daily 10am–6pm, 1 June to 31 August, 10am–8pm. Further information tel: 22.23.53.55.

manufacture. Textiles have been a part of the town's life since the 11th century. Armentières suffered great damage during the First World War and was largely rebuilt afterwards. This is the home of the *Lady of Amentières*, of popular war-time song fame.

The **hôtel de ville** was rebuilt in Flemish style by architect Louis Cordonnier in 1925. Its stained glass panels depict local events and activities. The **church of Saint-Vaast** (1929) was also the work of Cordonnier, rebuilt in neo-Gothic style with a 265-feet-high tower. Inside, there is a Van Dyck School Descent from the Cross, a painting of Jesus' crowning with thorns attributed to Valentin de Bourgone and a Rubens copy, *la Stigmatisation de Saint François d'Assise*.

In a bend in the river are lovely gardens leading to the **Pré du Hem** where Cordonnier's covered market can be found. The **musée de la bière** beerbrewing museum is installed in the former Motte-Cordonnier brewery. It is undergoing renovation, but when completed will portray the beer-making process through a display of the tools of its trade: microscopes, filter chambers, vats, pumps, Flemish-style drinking bars . . .

On the site of two former farms, a new leisure park has facilities for wide-ranging water activities.

• **Base du Pré-du-Hem** avenue Marc-Sangnier. Tel: 20.77.43.99. Open 12 April to 30 September daily 9.30am–8pm.

ARMENTIÈRES
59 • D-6 • 96 km

Tourist information
33 rue de Lille
Tel: 20.44.18.19

Hotels
Albert Ier **
28 rue Robert-Schuman
Tel: 20.77.31.02
Joly **
12 rue Kennedy
Tel: 20.77.00.94

Standing beside the River Lys, Amentières is a town whose name is synonymous with cloth

Arras: recumbent figure of Guillaume Lefranchois, 1446

ARQUES

62510 · D-4 · 46 km

Hotel
La Grande Sainte Catherine **
51 rue Adrien-Denvers
Tel: 21.38.03.73

Restaurant
Au Rocher de Cancale
27 rue Adrien-Daniers
Tel: 21.98.145.31

Arques is known throughout the world for its glass and crystal manufacture. The town itself is pleasantly endowed with lakes (**Arques sailing**, tel: 21.35.42.06), rivers, canals, and the nearby forest. The office for the Audomarois regional nature park is here, with information for ramblers and guided visits to points of interest.

• **Parc naturel régional Audomarois** Le Grand-Vannage.
Tel: 21.98.62.98.

The **church of Notre-Dame-de-Grâce**, built in 1530 in Flamboyant Gothic style, has a wooden statue dating from the 13th century. The **castle** (*le bastion Condette*) and its fortifications were remodelled by Vauban. Arques' most unusual feature is perhaps the **Fontinettes boat-lift**, built in 1888 to allow boats to make a 43-feet ascent from one water level to another. This testimony to earlier industrialisation is now restored and open to visitors (model exhibition and film on nearby boat).

• **Ascenseur à bateaux des Fontinettes** rue Denis-Papin.
Tel: 21.98.43.01. Open daily 15 June to 15 September 3–6.30pm; 1 April to 15 June and 15 September to 31 October, Saturday, Sunday and public holidays 3–6.30pm.

ARRAS

62000 · F-5 · 112 km

Tourist information
Hôtel de ville
place des Héros
Tel: 21.51.26.95

Golf d'Arras (18-hole)
Anzin-Saint-Aubin
Tel: 21.50.24.24

Hotels
Le Moderne ****
1 bd Faidherbe
Tel: 21.23.39.57
L'Univers **
3 place de la Croix-Rouge
Tel: 21.71.34.01
Astoria-Carnot **
10–12 place Maréchal-Foch
Tel: 21.71.098.14
Le Diamant **
5 place des Héros
Tel: 21.71.23.23

Restaurants
La Faisanderie
45 grand-place
Tel: 21.48.20.76
Le Victor Hugo
11 place Victor-Hugo
Tel: 21.71.84.00

The town of Arras has produced cloth for many centuries, and its name became synonymous with tapestry (Shakespeare's Hamlet murdered Polonius 'behind an Arras').

The best way to get to know Arras is to visit its squares. Already celebrated in the 12th century as meeting places for flourishing international trade, these squares have been the subject, since 1574, of a protection order forbidding construction other than in stone, and requiring owners to comply to a particular style. Thanks to this foresight, Arras today offers the imposing perspective of 155 identical façades (17th and 18th century) which make up the **place des Héros** (*petite-place* of the town hall and its tower), **la rue de la Taillerie** (where cloth was once cut, or *taillé*), and **la grande-place**, where the town's oldest house (1460) is easily identified by its Gothic style and stepped gable-ends (called in French, *à pas de moineaux*, 'like sparrows' footsteps'). Numerous arcades are a distinctive feature of the squares.

The **tower** and **town hall** were meticulously rebuilt and restored between 1924 and 1932; the first floor of the town hall displays four modern statues, by Jean Bodel, Adam de la Halle, Mahout d'Artois and Mathias d'Arras. In the banqueting room Hofbauer paintings (1932) depict – in Bruegelesque style –

Arras life at the turn of the 16th century. The tower is also open to the public (lift available), as well as the vaults beneath *la petite-place*.

The **Saint-Vaast palace and cathedral** (former Saint-Vaast abbey church) are neo-classical. Inside decoration is sparse; statues brought from the church of Sainte-Geneviève de Paris (Panthéon) decorate the lateral naves. In the chapel behind the altar is a *Vierge* by Corot (1830), a painted cupola by Maret and tombs of 19th-century Arras bishops. The Saint-Vaast palace houses a museum and various administrative offices. The 190-yard façade is an impressive example of architectural restraint. A gateway bearing the arms of Saint-Vaast, leads to the palace forecourt, a small cloister and the well courtyard. Guided walks are organised by the tourist office through the **Saint-Germain** district.

The fine arts museum, **musée de beaux arts**, is in the former Saint-Vaast monastery, a masterpiece of 18th-century monastic architecture. Its collections divide, essentially, into four categories: romano-gallic archaeology; medieval art; French, Flemish and Dutch (18th- and 19th-century) paintings and ceramics.

The most interesting collection is perhaps the funerary monuments: the burial stone of Bishop Frumauld (end 12th century), the woman's funerary mask, one of the masterpieces of 14th century sculpture, the recumbent figure of Guillaume Lefranchois (1446), quite stunning in its realism. For those who appreciate statuary there is the *Vierge à l'Enfant* from the Mont-Sainte-Marie monastery at Gosnay, sculpted in 1320 by Jean Pépin de Huy for the Comtesse Mahaut d'Artois. The tour of the ground floor draws to an end with the two altar-pieces painted by Jean Bellegambe for the Saint-Vaast monastery: *l'Adoration de l'Enfant* and *le Christ aux bourreaux*. Finally, a fragment of the great tapestry hanging depicting the legend of Saint Vaast, bears witness to the weaving skill that made Arras's reputation; unfortunately, few examples of this wool, silk and gold thread tapestry remain, making even more precious the museum's *Saint Vaast et l'ours*. The museum's first floor is devoted to paintings: 17th century French, different aspects of Flemish and Dutch 17th-century . . . Moving up to the second floor, there are several rooms of ceramics: varnished clays, Italian majolica, Arras and Tournai porcelain. The museum visit concludes with French 19th-century paintings, in particular landscape artists among whom the celebrated Dutilleux and Corot (*une Route près d'Arras*) inspired the creation of the Arras Landscape School.

• **Musée des beaux-arts** 22 rue Paul-Doumer. Tel: 21.71.26.43. Open 1 April to 15 October daily, except Tuesday, 10am–noon and 2–5pm (6pm Saturday and Sunday). Guided tours can be arranged.

AUCHEL
62260 • E-4 • 78 km

Coal mining began in 1853 and completely changed Auchel. After more than a hundred years of growth based on mining, the pits began to close in the period after the Second World War. A mining museum details this activity symbolic of northern France: 275 yards of underground tunnels, with working equipment (and demonstration coal-cutting) and audio-visual exhibit (20 mins), plus a display of early machinery, tools and fossils.

• **Musée de la mine** boulevard de la Paix. Tel: 21.52.66.10. Open Tuesday and Thursday, 9am–noon and by arrangement. (Near Auchel, at Bruay-la-Buissière, you can visit disused mine galleries at the mining 'ecomuseum', where there is also a *son et lumière* display about the mine from 1855 to 1979. Open daily 2–6pm and by arrangement. Tel: 21.62.25.45 and 21.53.52.33.

Bailleul: Jacob Savery II, la Place de Bailleul, *c1620*

AVESNES-SUR-HELPE
59440 • G-9 • 219 km

Tourist information
21 place Maréchal-Leclerc
Tel: 27.57.92.40

Hotel
La Pénitière ★★
route de Paris
Tel: 27.61.22.22

This picturesque little town, perched above the left bank of the River Helpe, is best explored from the *place Maréchal-Leclerc* in the centre. This is dominated by the square tower of **Saint-Nicolas collegiate church**, built in the 12th century, destroyed, then partly rebuilt in the 15th century and completed in the 16th. Her 200-feet-high bell-tower is thought to have been designed by one of Philippe II's Spanish architects. It has one of the loveliest peals of bells in northern France, produced by a total of forty-eight bells. Inside are 16th-century brick and stone ribbed arches. The key-stones of the arches in the nave bear the arms of Charles Quint (a two-headed eagle) and of the Croÿ family, Avesnes noblemen. The choir was replaced in the 17th century and the five-sided apse is lit by seven tall, narrow stained glass windows. Between the nave and the choir is a Transfiguration, after the style of Raphaël.

La place Maréchal-Leclerc, a rectangular square, is lined with old brick-built houses, their doors and windows framed in blue stone. **No 5** was formerly the corn hall, complete with a beautiful balcony and wrought-iron anchors. **No 30** has a 16th-century façade decorated with stone arches (this house dates from the Spanish occupation). If you walk along the little square **de la Madelaine**, you come to the east bastion of the interior redoubt of Vauban's 17th-century fortifications.

La mairie, the town hall, built in 1757, has a classic façade, complete with pediment and coat of arms; in front is an elegant, double flight of steps and pretty wrought-iron balustrade. The great salon, formerly used for entertainments, retains the balcony once used by musicians; in 1789 the common people of the bailiwick of Avesnes congregated here to elect representatives for the Revolutionary government.

The lovely old houses of **la rue d'Albret** make this a delightful part of town. The 18th-century **presbytery** was formerly the King's lieutenant's house.

AZINCOURT (Agincourt)
62310 • E-3 • 72 km

Tourist information
Tel: 21.04.41.12

The **history and folk museum** has audiovisual presentations in English and French, and a way-marked walk around the battlefield with viewing table (open May to September daily 10am–6pm, tel: 21.04.41.12). The **Azincourt Medieval Centre** stands on the famous battlefield where, according to the chronicles, 7,000 English soldiers led by Henry V defeated 40,000 French soldiers under Charles VI in 1415. There is an information centre, a video theatre and a restaurant. Also guided visits of the battlefield, battle reconstructions, a display of weapons, birds of prey display . . . daily 10am–9.30pm.

BAILLEUL
59270 • D-5 • 82 km

Tourist information
3 grand-place
Tel: 28.49.18.17

Hotels
Belle Hôtel ***
19 rue de Lille
Tel: 28.49.19.00
Auberge Le Seau *
Lieu dit le Seau
Tel: 28.48.62.00

"The fine silhouette of Bailleul's belfry dominates the Flanders plain. Since the Middle Ages a siren called Mélusine, in the form of a copper weather-vane, has looked down from the belfry. She symbolises charm and seduction, cruelty and danger; and in laying claim to this high-born, mythological figure, the citizens of Bailleul have asserted their own capacity to weather the dangers that the years have thrown up." (Laurent Guillaut)

Standing in the main square at the very centre of the town, the **hôtel de ville** and its belfry were rebuilt in neo-Flemish style: stone alternates with brick and slate. In the lower part of the belfry, an 18th-century Gothic room is constructed around an imposing sandstone pillar; the only part to have escaped shelling in 1918. At the front is an elegant bretèche (proclamation balcony) with wonderful views of the plain of La Lys and the monts de Flandre. The carillon has 35 bells.

• Open Easter to end September, Saturdays 10.15–11.00am and 3.15–4pm.

Behind the town hall, the rue du Musée leads to the **musée Benoît-De-Puydt**, a largely 15th- and 19th-century Flemish collection complemented by a good number of porcelains of Far Eastern provenance, as well as 19th- and 20th-century paintings from the Bailleul School. The museum also houses a large lace collection and has regular temporary exhibitions.

• **Musée Benoît-De-Puydt** rue du Musée. Tel: 28.49.18.17. Open daily, except Tuesday, 2–5pm.

Close by is the neo-Byzantine **church of Saint-Vaast**. Its numerous stained glass windows depict the town's history: Charles Quint; the Gueux des bois peasant revolt; the 1789 uprising; the First World War and, in the apse, episodes from the life of Saint Antoine.

In the place Pichon is the imposing façade of the **présidial de Flandre**. Built in stone on a foundation of Artois sandstone in typical 18th-century French style, this early law court is decorated with tall pillars and a sculpted pediment. The rings in the front wall were used as hitching posts for horses. Before the Revolution the présidial's jurisidiction extended throughout French Flanders; the building later became the palais de justice.

Bailleul has been home to an activity half art, half industry, since the 17th century, namely lace-making. After the Revolution, Bailleul simplified its Valenciennes lace to produce the charming and more quickly produced torchon lace. This reached a peak of popularity in the 19th century, when it was widely sold throughout France, in particular in the big Parisian shops. After the First World War, the institute Le Retour au foyer encouraged the continued production of lace at Bailleul, promoting lace-making competitions and giving rise to a new school of lace-making in 1928. Though often under threat in the past, this 'art-industry' continues to survive, and the lace-making school still takes in apprentices. On public holidays lace-makers

can often be seen wearing traditional costumes that include lovely head-dresses.

• **Ecole de dentellière**, Le Retour au foyer, rue du Collège. Tel: 28.41.25.72. Open daily, except Friday and Sunday, 9am–noon and 2–5pm.

BAVAY
59570 • F-4 • 197 km

Tourist information
8–10 rue Saint-Maur
Tel: 27.39.81.65

Hotel
Saint-Maur **
1 rue Saint-Maur
Tel: 27.66.90.33

Restaurant
Le Bourgogne
Porte Gommeries
Tel: 27.63.12.58

The Nerviens, who occupied the south of present-day Belgium, French Hainaut and Cambrésis, were unable to defeat the Romans following a series of unfortunate military alliances. Under the reign of Augustus, Bavay became the Nervien capital and centre of an important road network.

Today, the main square is dominated by the statue of Queen Brunehaut, and the hectagonal pedestal below bears the name of seven Roman roads which passed through Bavay (monument erected in 1872).

The classic architecture of the town hall (1734) backs on to the 17th-century square-towered, brick-and-stone belfry. Near the church, the Forum archaeological site and Roman-Gallic museum is one of France's major centres of archaeology.

• **Forum et musée archéologique** 2 rue de Gommeries. Tel: 27.63.13.95. Open daily, except Tuesday, 9am–noon and 2–5pm.

BERCK-SUR-MER
62600 • G-1 • 71 km

Tourist information
place de l'Entonnoir
Tel: 21.09.50.00

Agora
Esplanade de la mer
Tel: 21.09.01.81

Sailing Club
Les Sternes, Baie d'Authie
Tel: 21.09.50.00

Ecole de char à voile (sail-boarding)
Tel: 21.09.71.85

Hotels
La Banque **
43 rue de la Division Leclercq
Tel: 21.09.01.09
du Littoral **
36 av Marianne Toute Seule
Tel: 21.09.07.76
Le Neptune **
Esplanade Parmentier
Tel: 21.09.21.21

Restaurant
Auberge du Bois
149 av Guettier
Tel: 21.09.03.43

A seaside and spa since 1850, Berck has a beautiful sandy beach. A path through the dunes leads to a coastal conservation site (90-minute walk) with easy access for all – thanks to gentle inclines and solid ramps (for information tel: 21.32.13.74). The 130-feet-high lighthouse is open to the public (200 steps), its light visible 20 miles away. Berck is the venue of an important jazz and rock festival in July, *le festival de la Côte d'Opale* (information from tourist office).

Berck's municipal museum, opened in 1979, grew out of a collection of some hundred paintings by artists who had visited the spa town around 1900: Lepic, Tattegrain, Roussel, Chigot, Chambon, Trogoulet, Lavezzari . . . , all inspired by the Berck seascape and the special quality of the light of the Opal Coast. Popular art and tradition and archaeological exhibits complement original paintings; in particular those associated with the sea and sea life, and archaeological finds from the Celtic sanctuary at Compierre-sur-Authie. There are also deep-sea finds (from Canche, Authie and Ternoise).

• **Musée municipal** 60 rue de l'Impératrice. Tel: 21.84.07.80. Open daily, except Tuesday, 3–6pm.

BERGUES
59380 · B-4 · 50 km

Tourist information
Place de la République
Tel: 28.68.71.06

Hotel
au tonnelier **
4 rue du Mont-de-Piété
Tel: 28.68.70.05

Restaurant
au Cornet d'Or
26 rue Espagnole
Tel: 28.68.66.27

Bergues is distinguished by a moat and encircling ramparts, the best of their kind in northern France. A very colourful and lively market takes place here every Monday in the **place du Beffroi**, a reminder of the rich agricultural region in which the town is located. The Palm Sunday fair, *la Foire du dimanche des Rameaux*, with its origins going back to 1550, brings together farmers and growers from neighbouring towns.

In 1022, Baudoin the Beautiful Beard, founded a monastery here. The monks and the people of the area set about draining the marshlands and, as in other Flemish towns, began making cloth. Philippe le Hardi (1341–1404) laid the foundations of present-day Bergues; its fortifications were further improved by Philippe le Bon but, in 1558, the town was destroyed by the French. After a further series of battles, Bergues entered into the French fold, following the Treaty of Aix-la-Chapelle (1668), after which she enjoyed a long period of peace. Nevertheless, the prudent Louis XIV charged his military engineer, Vauban, with the task of equipping the town with robust fortifications.

Vauban reinforced the north defences, integrating the old walls and fortifying the *couronne Saint-Winoc*, a 5,800-yard enclosure completed in 1740. In 1940, French troops took refuge here during a German bombing offensive. In 1944, due particularly to its proximity to Dunkirk, the town suffered further war damage, and the belfry and church tower were both destroyed.

The town ramparts are among the finest and best preserved of their kind in northern France, and still surround three-quarters of the town. Entry to the town centre is via one of four original gateways: Hondschoote, Bierne, Cassel (archery nearby) and Dunkerque. The Cassel gate is the most majestic, bearing the emblem of the Sun King, Louis XIV, as well as a tribute to Vauban.

The main square is dominated by the **belfry**, rebuilt after the Second World War in a style and of materials inspired by the original belfry. The 50-bell (17th and 18th-century) carillon is well known. Carillon concerts are a regular feature of Monday mornings (11am). *Le Reuze Lied* plays hourly and *Mari complaisant* every half hour.
• Visits by arrangement with the keeper of the carillon, tel: 28.68.60.44.

Opposite the belfry is the **town hall**, rebuilt in 1872 with the blue marble of the original building (1666), and obelisks inspired by Antwerp town hall. To the right is a bust of poet Lamartine who represented the town at the Chamber of Deputies from 1833 to 1839.

At the end of the *rue des Annonciades*, the marble gateway once marked the entrance to the celebrated **Saint-Winoc monastery** (destroyed in the Revolution). Now only two towers remain of the great Benedictine monastery. A large part of the monastery library was saved, however, and this is now on view to the public at the town hall every first Saturday of the month, 3pm onwards: 12th- and 15th-century manuscripts, 6,980 12th–15th-century books. Paintings that once hung in the monastery are now in the Bergues museum or the Dunkirk museum of fine arts.

The *rue des Annonciades* leads to the main square, and this is dominated by the high tower of **Saint Martin church** (destroyed in 1940), which keeps alive the spirit of the Flemish *hallekerke* church. Two of the three naves were rebuilt, the ruins of the third stand open to the sky. To the south, a 16th-century gate still stands.

Near the church is the town's most beautiful public building, built between 1629 and 1633 by Wenceslas Coebergher, the **Mont-de-piété**. Built in Flemish Renaissance style with carved stonework reminiscent of Lille's *Vieille Bourse*, it has a series of broken pediments with garlands decorating the windowless gable-ends. Inside, the **musée municipal** has Italian and French paintings (Georges de la Tour), Flemish Brueghels, Verlinde drawings, and a large ornithological collection.

• **Musée municipal**, 1 rue du Mont-de-Piété. Tel: 28.68.13.30. Open daily, except Tuesday, 10am–noon and 2–5pm.

As you come out of the museum, the *rue du Mont-de-Piété* leads to the **Saint-Jean bridge** from which Bergues' oldest houses (1597) can be admired; built in the yellow brick called *de sable* or sand brick. A walk along the picturesque canals takes you past the Dunkerque gate and the Hondschoote gate, with its nearby early 17th-century guard-room.

The **Hondschoote gate** is the departure point for a one-hour walk of the ramparts.

BÉTHUNE

62400 • E-5 • 87 km

Tourist information
34 grand-place
Tel: 21.68.26.29

Beuvry lake
Tel: 21.65.17.37

Hotels
Bernard et de la Gare **
3 place de la Gare
Tel: 21.57.20.02
La Coupole **
30 grand-place
Tel: 20.57.35.01
de France **
26 rue de Treilles
Tel: 21.68.08.20
Le Vieux Beffroi **
48 grand-place
Tel: 21.68.15.00
Le Départ **
7 place de la Gare
Tel: 21.57.18.04

Nearby
La Chartreuse-du-Val-Saint-Esprit ***
1 rue de Fonquières
Gosnay (5km)
Tel: 21.62.80.00

Béthune's first church was built by Saint Vaast in the 6th century. The castle fortress of the seigneurs de Béthune, the brotherhood of the Arras monastery, was built here on a motte in the 13th century. The town that was established during the 12th century extended over 60 acres and had four gates: and it was this relatively small space which housed the majority of the town's population up until 1875 (4,000 inhabitants in the 12th century, 12,000 in the 14th, 7,000 in 1875). Béthune was a cloth-making town in the Middle Ages, trading with Flanders. Its medieval ramparts were improved by Louis XI, Charles Quint and Dupuy-Vauban. In the 19th century new industry came to supplement the principally agricultural economy and, at this time, the town figured in several literary works, most notably Alexandre Dumas' *Les Trois Mousquetaires* and Louis Aragon's *la Semaine sainte*. It suffered considerable damage in both the First and Second World Wars. Modern Béthune has a new river port and new industrial estates.

The **belfry** (open 15 April to 15 September, Sundays at 3pm) was built in local sandstone in the 14th century, next to the cloth and grain exchange (demolished 1664); high in the 110-feet tower are 36 bells, some of them from the town of Thérouanne (information on bell ringing from the town hall). The *rue des Charitables* leads to the *salle de la confrérie des Charitables*, meeting place of a guild established by blacksmiths Germon de Beuvry and Gauthier de Béthune, which still provides a free pallbearing service to the town; pallbearers wear a cape, two-pointed hat, ruffle and reveres and carry a cane decorated with a spray of boxwood.

The regional museum of ethnology, **musée d'ethnologie régionale**, grew from an amateur collection in the 70s with the aim of preserving a regional identity through an examination of the area's past, present and future. Close to 80,000 objects were assembled and chosen according both to aesthetic appeal and ability to reflect local life, beliefs and practices . . . some 50 themes emerged, among them cock-fighting, brewing, archery, water transport, mills, pigeon-fancying, chicory growing . . . There is also an archaeological collection. While improvements are being

The belfry at Béthune

Harbour view, Boulogne-sur-Mer

carried out, the museum is staging travelling exhibitions, concerts and conferences.

BOULOGNE-SUR-MER
62200 • D-2 • 32 km

Tourist information
quai de la Poste
forum Jean-Noël
Tel: 21.31.68.38

Casino
37 rue Félix-Adam
Tel: 21.83.88.00

Yacht Club boulonnais
166 boulevard Sainte-Beuve
Tel: 21.31.80.67

Sailboarding côte d'Opale
272 boulevard Sainte-Beuve
Tel: 21.83.25.48

Horseriding
Centre équestre du Boulonnais
route de Crémarest
La Capelle-lès-Boulogne
Tel: 21.83.32.38

Hotels
Le Métropole ★★★
51 rue Thiers
Tel: 21.31.54.30
de Londres ★★
22 place de France
Tel: 21.31.35.63
de Lorraine ★★
7 place de Lorraine
Tel: 21.31.34.78

Restaurants
La Matelote
80 boulevard Sainte-Beuve
Tel: 21.30.17.97
La Liégeoise
10 rue A Monsigny
Tel: 21.31.61.15

Nearby
Relais de la Brocante
près de l'église
Wimille (5km)
Tel: 21.83.19.31
Hostellerie de la Rivière
17 rue de la Gare
Pont-de-Briques (5km)
Tel: 21.32.22.81

The Nausicaa marine centre, rooted in Boulogne's maritime traditions, is both a source of public information and a professional experimental resource. It is the only one of its kind in Europe, comprising 3,000 square yards of exhibition dedicated to undersea life and man's management of the sea; plus the information centre comprising *médiathèque*, cinema and conference room, with restaurants and shops.

• **Nausicaa Centre national de la mer** boulevard Sainte-Beuve
Tel: 21.30.98.98.

The town's oldest building is the **belfry**; in the little entrance room is a stained glass window by Godefroi de Bouillon. Entrance is via the *hôtel de ville* (Monday to Friday, 8am–noon and 2–5pm; Saturday 2.30–5pm, tel: 21.80.51.55). Notice also Boulogne's 300,000 volume library accommodated in the cloisters.

Among other places to visit: the **basilica of Notre-Dame**, built in 1866 on the site of the former collegiate church. The crypt is home to a Roman temple (open daily, except Monday, 2–5pm). The **castle** was built in 1230 by Philippe Hurepel and remodelled in the 16th and 18th centuries. Works undertaken at the time of creating a new museum in the castle permitted the restoration of the castle to its 18th-century appearance. The museum comprises three sections: classic archaeology; ceramics and 17th- and 20th-century glassware; and non-European ethnography. There is also a fine collection of 19th-century paintings (Boilly, Corot, Boudin). A visit to the museum is thoroughly recommended. This medieval fortification is northern France's finest example of the type, and an excellent illustration of 13th–18th-century evolution in stronghold design.

• **Musée du château** rue Bernet.
Tel: 21.80.00.80. Open daily, except Tuesday, 10am–5pm.

The ramparts form a rectangle 450 yards by 350 yards; once a crenellated wall with glacis, redoubt and counterscarps, the wall has 17 towers (tours of ramparts and old town organised by tourist office).

Nausicaa marine centre

BOUVINES
59830 • D-7 • 125 km

Standing on the banks of the River Marque, Bouvines was first settled by the Gauls and became a hub of Roman-Gallic activity on the road the Romans built from Cassel to Tournai. Bouvines is best known for the celebrated battle which took place here on 27 July 1214 between the King of France, Philippe Auguste, and the grand coalition of Othon IV, Emperor of Germany, the English army under Salisbury and contingents from Flanders, Hainaut and Holland, led by Ferrand de Portugal. Bouvines played an important part in the creation of the French realm: "through the avoidance of dismemberment of the Royal territory which was the French state in embryo, and by assuring the supremacy of the Capétian dynasty, Bouvines is seen as a very important victory for France". (Georges Duby)

The neo-Gothic **church** (1880) was built on a promontary dominating the surrounding countryside. Inside, 21 Champigneulles stained glass windows trace the events of the famous battle.

From the main road, turn right towards the **château Deffontaines**; in the castle wall is the Saint-Pierre fountain where pilgrims with eye disorders came to seek the healing power of the water.

A little further on along the main road is an obelisk commemorating the battle.

On the battle site (east of the town, take the quarry road) is the **chapelle aux Arbres** erected in 1934 on the site of a wayside cross. This has been a site of worship for many centuries; legend recounts that the first chapel was built here in 1200 by the Count of Flanders. Of the battle site, "nothing has changed since 1214. Still there are ploughed fields, meadows. Not so much as a cottage to break the straight line of the plateau's horizon . . . Only in the middle of the plain, a little spinney and a chapel". (E M Lotthé)

BRAY-SUR-SOMME
80340 • H-5 • 176 km

Hotel
Les Etangs du Levant *
rue du 1ᵉʳ septembre
Tel: 22.76.00.90

Of Celtic origin, Bray-sur-Somme was fortified by Charlemagne, endured numerous sieges and was almost completely destroyed during the First World War. In the heart of the Somme marshland, Bray is surrounded by ponds and lakes, a paradise for birdlife and eel fishermen. From these ponds was once extracted the peat used for the stoves of modest Picardy households. A few kilometres away, at Froissy-Dompierre, is the home of the little Haute-Somme railway, *le petit train de la haute Somme*, built in 1916 to service the Somme front line. Today it affords a pleasant way of discovering the surrounding countryside.

• **Petit train de la Haute-Somme** Tel: 22.44.50.40. English spoken. Timetable: 1 May to 30 September, Sundays and public holidays, 2.15–6pm; 15 July to 5 September, Wednesday and Saturday, 3–4.30pm; Sunday and public holidays, 2.15–6pm; in August, Thursday, 3–4.30pm.

CALAIS
62100 • B-2

Tourist information ❶
12 boulevard Clemenceau
Tel: 21.96.62.40

Casino ❷
57 rue Royale
Tel: 21.34.64.18

Yacht-Club de Calais ❸
bassin ouest
Tel: 21.97.47.65

Hotels
Meurice ***
rue Edmond-Roche
Tel: 21.34.57.03
Pacary ***
av Maréchal-de-Lattre-de-T
Tel: 21.96.68.00

Bouvines: stained glass windows depicting the great battle

Georges V ***
36 rue Royale
Tel: 21.97.68.00
Bellevue **
23 place d'Armes
Tel: 21.34.53.75
Jacquard **
35 boulevard Jacquard
Tel: 21.97.98.98
Richelieu **
17 rue Richelieu
Tel: 21.34.61.60
Windsor **
2 rue Commandant-Bonnuiges
Tel: 21.34.59.40

Restaurants
Au Côte d'argent
1 digue Gaston-Berthe
Tel: 21.34.68.07
La Duchesse
44 rue du Duc-de-Guise
Tel: 21.97.59.69
Le Channel
3 boulevard de la Résistance
Tel: 21.34.42.30
Le Grand Bleu
8 rue J P Avron
Tel: 21.97.97.98

In the 14th century, English merchants were subjected to a series of raids from the inhabitants of Calais, earning the town a reputation for being a hotbed of piratical activity, and persuading Edward III to lay siege to It In 1346; this lasted for 11 months and ended in the episode immortalised by Rodin's sculpture: les Bourgeois de Calais. Calais became English and was to remain so for 210 years. Emptied of her own inhabitants, the town was repopulated with English subjects. A mint was created there and the port became an important trading post for the

Calais: belfry, seen from port

wool industry. The English enlarged the church of Notre-Dame, built the covered market and the hôtel des Etapes. When trading profits declined, the town became a military base run by a powerful group of governors, among them Warwick, the King-Maker. Around 1550, a series of manoeuvres enabled the Duc de Guise and the Seneschal of Boulogne, Monchy de Sénarpont, to win back Sangatte and then Calais, where the English capitulated on 7 January 1558. The victors expelled the English population and brought back the original inhabitants, selling land cheaply to the Huguenots. After a final Spanish occupation (1596–1598), Calais became definitively French following the Treaty of Vervins. Its fortifications were reinforced by Vauban and Richelieu, who planned to turn it into a powerful military port. When the French frontier moved further north, Calais lost its importance and port traffic diminished dramatically. During the revolutionary wars the sea off Calais was occupied by enemy ships and the town suffered terribly. The 19th century began well with the celebration of Louis XVIII's return at the time of the Restoration. Unusual circumstances brought looms to Calais in 1816, fraudulently imported from England. Textile factories sprang up in the very heart of the town. At the same time, commercial and passenger traffic through the port grew very rapidly and the town fortifications and glacis were destroyed to enlarge the port. During the First World War, Calais, just 60 miles from the Front, suf-

fered numerous bombardments. In 1940, French and English troops fought to maintain a stronghold on the sea front. When liberation finally came, nearly every house had been destroyed.

Today, Calais is one of the premier lace producers, with 25 lace-making companies and 2,000 employees. The local lace, Dentelle de Calais, can be seen in the fine arts and lace museum, **musée des beaux-arts et de la dentelle ❶**. This museum arose partly as a consequence of the large tourist draw of the nearby **Monument des Bourgeois de Calais**, home of Rodin's famous statue. Here, set around Rodin's models and designs are the works of the principal sculptors of the late 19th century: Bourdelle, Maillol, Poupelet, Carrier, Belleuse . . . and Carpeaux, native of Valenciennes. Twentieth-century sculptors are also represented by the work of Laurens, Fautrier, Zadkine, Germaine Richier, Antony Caro, John Lathan, Bill Woodrow, Picasso, Takis, Broodthaers . . . The museum ranks among the very best of its kind. Calais was the world centre for lace production in the 19th century, and the museum has some exceptional examples from Venice, Alençon, Valenciennes, Malines . . . The hand-made lace collections (15th- and 16th-century Italian and Flemish) and machine-made lace (Calais, Caudry, Lyon, Saint-Gall . . .) have been supplemented by lace-making tools and equipment, as well as made-up lace: 19th- and 20th-century undergarments and accessories, haute couture dresses using late 19th-century lace (Doucet, Poiret) and from the fifties (Patou, Chanel, Dior . . .). The museum's third point of interest is the display of sculptors' drawings (Rodin, Carpeaux, Gonzales), its 20th-century photographs (Warhol, Mercier, Mylaine) and its late 17th- and early 19th-century sketches by watercolourists: Bonington (whose father's work brought him to Calais), Louis Francia, Fielding, Callcott, Owen . . . con-

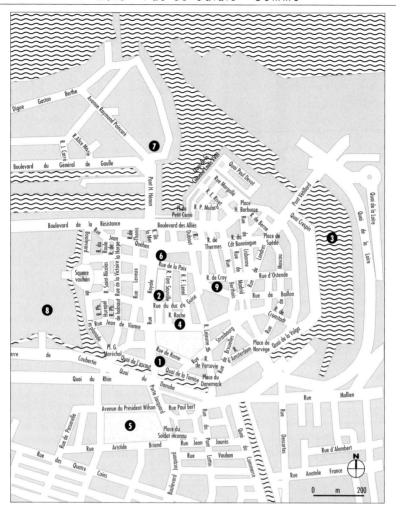

stituting one of the richest collections of British drawings and watercolours of any French provincial museum. Finally, arising out of a policy decision made in the 70s, the museum also has an exceptional collection of contemporary paintings . . . as well as Flemish and Dutch paintings, archaeological finds, the 'Marianne' collection and a model of the town.

• **Musée des beaux-arts et de la dentelle** 25 rue Richelieu. Tel: 21.42.62.00. Open daily, except Tuesday, 10am–noon and 2–5.30pm.

In an old blockhouse, the war museum, **musée de la Guerre** ❺, presents the life of Calais during the two World Wars (Parç Saint-Pierre: daily March to December

10am–4.15pm, tel: 21.34.21.57). A visit to the fortifications includes the **watch-tower** ❻ (late 13th century), the ❼ **Risbant fort**, the **Nieulay fort and the citadel** ❽ built by Richelieu and remodelled by Vauban (guided tours organised by the Society of the Friends of Old Calais, tel: 21.34.22.64). The **church of Notre-Dame** ❾ (visits arranged through the tourist office) is part 13th century; it was enlarged and completed during the English occupation, which explains its comparatively austere character, the only Tudor Gothic church in France. Flemish influence is, however, also evident in the use of shaped bricks and the absence of arches (except at the transept crossing).

CAMBRAI

59400 • G-7 • 179 km

Tourist information
48 rue de Noyon
Tel: 27.78.36.15

Hotels
Beatus ★★★
718 avenue de Paris
Tel: 27.81.45.70
Château de La Motte-Fénelon ★★★
allée Saint-Roch
Tel: 27.83.61.38
Ulys ★★★
67 route d'Arras
Tel: 27.83.83.25
Le Mouton blanc ★★★
33 rue d'Alsace-Lorraine
Tel: 27.81.30.16
La Chope ★★
17 rue des Docks
Tel: 27.81.36.78

The carillon, Cambrai

Restaurant
L'Escargot
10 rue du Général-de-Gaulle
Tel: 27.81.24.54

In the Roman period, Cambrai was an important settlement on the Amiens–Bavay route. The first recorded bishop was Saint Vaast of Arras, who died in 540 AD. Saint Géry, who died in 624, transferred the episcopal seat to Cambrai. These bishops, who bore the title *comtes de Cambrai,* became the sovereign lords of the town, and indeed minted their own coinage until 1580. A city wall was built by inhabitants in the 9th century as protection against the Normans. The **château de Selle** was built to the north-west of the town in the 13th century. The 25-feet-high ramparts are flanked by 50 towers and 7 gates. In 1477, the town was taken by Louis XI, followed in 1479 by the Burgundians. Charles Quint established a citadel on the *Mont des Boeufs* in 1543. In 1678, the town became French after the signing of the Treaties of Nim-

ègue, and Vauban and his engineers took this opportunity to consolidate the fortifications. In 1792, during the Revolution, the town endured the bloody tyranny of Lebon, who targeted Cambrai as a "town of priests, fanatics and aristocrats". Occupied in 1815 by the British, the town was to witness the dismantling of its fortress in 1892; some of the more notable towers and gates were saved (a wide boulevard was laid where the ramparts had been). During the 1914–1918 war, the Front was established to the west of the town; on 20 November 1917, a British offensive managed to pierce the famous Hindenburg Line and progress to the town gates. Cambrai was liberated in October 1918. During the Second World War, the town suffered numerous bombing raids.

Cambrai, the Baroque town of the North In *place Aristide-Briand*, rebuilt after the 1914–1918 war, stands the **hôtel de ville**, a huge classic building surmounted by a campanile framed by the two celebrated 16th-century wood and brass *Jacquemarts*, or Jack-of-the-

clocks, Martin and Martine, who strike the hour. In *rue Sadi-Carnot*, behind the *hôtel de ville* and to the left, is the house where French aviation pioneer **Blériot** was born, as indicated by a wall plaque.

Walking back up *rue Sadi-Carnot*, you may like to visit the **church of Saint-Géry**, constructed between 1698 and 1745, with classic façade dominated by a 250-ft spire. The decorated oak wood carving of the choir (1740) is ornamented with medallions representing the lives of saints; the pulpit is monumental, the work of Cambrai craftsmen; the beautiful 18th-century marble altar comes from Vaucelle Abbey. In the right arm of the transept is the headstone of the Baron d'Havrincourt (1642) and in the left, a *Mise au tombeau* painting by Rubens. Notice the oblique composition; the colour combination used by the painter renders the body of Christ luminous, prefiguring the resuscitated state of the body. The face of the Virgin is, by contrast, in cadaverous hue. The ambulatory has large Wamps canvasses (Flemish 18th century) and two beautiful 16th-century English alabasters. Beneath the organ is a rood-screen in red, black and white marble. The sacristy is lined with elegant 18th-century wood carving.

Opposite the church, and to the left, stands an octagonal brick-and-stone tower. Facing this, a beautiful triple-arcaded Renaissance portal (early 17th century) was once the entrance to the archbishop's palace – **palais Fénelon** – now occupied by the offices of the *sous-préfecture*. The little square of **place Fénelon** is home to a statue of the architect Villard de Honnecourt, designer of an earlier cathedral ('the marvel of the Low Countries') that once graced the site.

In the *rue Vaucelette* is the refuge of **Vaucelles Abbey**, with its 13th-century Gothic-style chapel. Notice the half-timbered house opposite which dates from 1626. *Rue de l'Epée* is home to the fine arts museum, **musée des beaux-arts**, which has just undergone extensive restoration. It is one of the major museums of northern France.

• **Musée des beaux-arts** 15 rue de l'Epée. Tel: 27.81.78.66. Open daily, except Tuesday, 10am–noon and 2–6pm.

The *rue de l'Epée* runs into the *rue du Grand-Séminaire*, which, in turn, leads to *place du Saint-Sépulcre*, the home of three delightful pieces of regional architecture. The former **collegiate church of Saint-Sépulcre, Notre-Dame**, was built as a cathedral following the Revolution. Inside, admire the five-bay nave; the two chapels which complete the transept are decorated with eight huge *trompe l'oeil* tint drawings, executed in 1760 by Martin Geeraerts. In the transept chapel is the Notre-Dame-de-Grace icon brought from Rome in 1440. The Fénelon tomb, re-interred in the cathedral in white marble sculpted by David d'Angers in 1826, is in the apse chapel. The sacristy is lined with pretty Louis XV wood panelling and decorated with a Geeraerts engraving.

Going back towards *place du Saint-Sépulcre*, on the left is the former chapel of the Jesuit College, **l'ancienne chapelle du collège des jésuites**, built at the end of the 17th century by Brother Jean Beergrandt, and one of the loveliest examples of Baroque art in Cambrai. The façade is in typical Flemish-style Baroque, in stone, decorated with a symmetrical arrangement of pilasters, bays and scrolls. The pediment, tall and lavishly decorated, depicts the Assumption at its centre.

On the corner of the *rue de Noyon* and *rue du Grand-Séminaire* is the **Maison espagnole**, home of the tourist office. It derives its unusual name from being under construction at the time of the Spanish occupation of Cambrai; the wood structure is in regional style. These types of building were once widespread throughout the towns of the North. The five caryatids that decorate the front date from restoration work carried out in 1897.

CASSEL
59670 • C-4 • 67 km

Tourist information
grand-place
BP10
Tel: 28.40.52.55

Hotel
Le Schoebecque *
32 rue Maréchal-Foch
Tel: 28.42.42.67

Restaurant
Le Petit-Bruxelles-en-Flandres
RN Sainte Marie Cappel
Tel: 28.42.44.64

The 575-feet-high **Mont Cassel** is one of northern France's highest points; here, seven Roman roads joined Cassel to the coast and neighbouring towns. A succession of invaders (Normans, Flemish, French, Spanish, English and German) tried to take this fortress and obvious vantage point. Its three most celebrated battles were:

1071: victory of the count of Flanders, Robert le Frison, over Philippe I, king of France.

1328: victory of Philippe IV de Valois over the peasant revolt led by Nicolas Zonnequin.

1677: victory of Philippe d'Orléans, brother of Louis XIV, over William of Orange and the king of Spain; following this battle Cassel and coastal Flanders became French (Treaties of Nimègue). During the 1914–18 war, Maréchal Foch and the British General Plumer directed the Battle of Flanders from here over the course of several months. Finally, British soldiers fought at the foot of the mount to slow down the German advance in 1940.

The best way to get to know Cassel is to wander through its cobbled streets, to climb its steep and picturesque alleyways; the *rampe alpine* takes you to the castle mound where the castle gate is all that remains of Louis XIV's fortifications.

Notre-Dame church, **l'église Notre-Dame**, built in 1290, suffered numerous assaults and fires before finally being restored in the 18th century. This *hallekerke* church has three naves, the central nave ending

in a flat wall at the eastern end. The base of the building and its oldest elements are built of iron-stone, while the flat wall of the central nave reveals three rows of herringbone brick between quarried sandstone. Over the great altar is an 18th-century, carved wood altar-piece; the communion rail is Louis XIV cast-iron. The organ is decorated with statues of King David and Sainte Cécile. A medallion decorating the column opposite the pulpit is a reminder of Maréchal Foch's visit to the church to pray during the Battle of Flanders. The church's elegant 18th-century Baroque façade is embellished with scrolls from the former Jesuit College chapel.

The municipal museum, **musée municipal**, is in the *hôtel de la Noble-Cour*: the walls of the *salle de la châtellenie* – wood pannelled and with Louis XIV-style decorated doors – were formerly lined with the archives of the 54 parishes over which the castle had jurisdiction. The museum's 15 rooms display paintings of the Flemish, Dutch and French schools, sculptures, ceramics, earthenware (from Lille, Saint-Omer, Strasbourg, Rouen . . .), locally-made furniture (displayed in the context of a Flemish domestic interior and inn), as well as craftsmen's tools. Notice the reconstruction of Maréchal Foch's office.

• **Musée municipal** hôtel de la Noble-Cour, 'T Landshuys. Tel: 28.40.52.55. Open 15 April to 30 October daily, except Tuesday, 10am–noon and 2–6.30pm. Out-of-season and guided tours by arrangement.

Le Casteel Meulen, the last of the parish of Arnèke's mills, was built in 1948 to replace the old town mill that burnt down in 1911. It is a reminder of the 24 windmills whose sails turned in the wind on the slopes of Mont Cassel up to the beginning of this century.

• **Casteel Meulen** Open Easter to end September daily and by arrangement for groups out of season. Tel: 28.40.52.55.

LE CATEAU-CAMBRÉSIS
59360 • G-8 • 201 km

Tourist information
place Général-de-Gaulle
Tel: 27.84.10.94

Hotel
Florida **
54 rue Théophile-Gauthier
Tel: 27.84.01.07

Restaurant
Le Relais Fénelon
24 rue du Maréchal-Mortier
Tel: 27.84.25.80

If you come from Cambrai on the RN39, after the bridge over the Selle, you arrive at *place Richez* and on the left you will see the **palais Fénelon**, former residence of the archbishops of Cambrai, rebuilt in 1770. Fronting the road, the blue stone columns of the great portal have a Doric frieze and open on to the palace courtyard. The restrained lines of the building alternate rows of brick and stone, topped by a stone corniche and, in the centre, a triangular pediment to the north, a composite pediment to the south. Tall rectangular windows framed in stone give rhythm to the front of the building. The north façade overlooks the calm of a garden, fringed with 100-year-old lime trees sloping gently down to a stretch of water.

This has been the home of the **musée Matisse** since 1982. Matisse came from Cateau and the museum opened with his donation of 35 drawings, 27 engravings, 2 large paintings, 5 sculptures, 1 tapestry, 2 linen hangings and 10 illustrated books. Matisse's donation was followed by one from the painter Herbin (born in a neighbouring village, in 1882) who gave the museum 22 paintings and 7 drawings. In 1982 the Matisse family made significant further contributions, making the museum the third largest Matisse collection in France.

• **Musée Matisse** palais Fénelon, place Richez. Open daily, except Tuesday, 10am–noon and 2–6pm; Sundays 10am–12.30pm and 2.30–6pm. Tel: 27.84.13.15.

As you leave the palais Fénelon, you will notice the illustrious priest's bust, in the former palace garden, now a public park (access from *rue des Poilus* to the left of the palace). Close by is the **hôtel de ville**, with stepped gable-ends, constructed in 1521 by the bishop of Croÿ. The elegant belfry was built in 1705, during the time of Fénelon's episcopate. The statue in the square is of the Maréchal Mortier, Duc de Trévisse, by Bra.

From *place Carnot* you come to **Saint-Martin**, the former collegiate church built to the Jesuit, du Blocq's, design in the 17th century, with fine bell-tower and slate pinnacle and baroque stone façade: garlands, fauns, twisted batons forming the cross of Saint-André – emblem of the house of Burgundy, the abbey's benefactor. In the nave are the exuberant sculpted friezes, masks and cherubims of Marsy. The dome, lit by the high windows, is supported by four pillars, decorated with the symbols of the Four Disciples.

The oldest part of the church is the Notre-Dame chapel, restored in 1630, now the sacristy. On its ceiling are the Burgundian arms and flower garlands. To the right of the church entrance is a little room over whose door is inscribed *Porte de la Vie éternelle* (doorway to eternity). This was the entrance to the cloister, no longer standing.

CAYEUX-SUR-MER
80410 • F-1 • 125 km

Tourist information
boulevard Général-Sizaire
Tel: 22.26.61.15

Hourdel harbour and marina
Tel: 22.26.61.55

Nearby
Le parc aux Huîtres **
Le Hourdel (5km)
Tel: 22.26.61.20

'L'Oiseau à portée de la main'
('A bird in the hand')

A mile or two from Cayeux, at the Hourdel-Lanchères crossroad, is the **maison de l'Oiseau** (house of birds), a collection of 300 species of stuffed birds, the result of a joint venture between a family of taxidermists, *les Becquets*, and a local cooperative. The birds are grouped into three exhibits: birds and nature, bird and man and birds as a species. This bird journey includes the study of bird anatomy, behaviour, feeding and reproduction . . . Nearby, the reed-encircled pond of **le Hâble d'Ault** is busy with hundreds of different species of ducks and wildfowl, with as many as 200 species being recorded throughout the year.

• **Maison de l'Oiseau** carrefour Hourdel-Lanchères D204. Tel: 22.26.93.93. Open 1 February to 15 November daily 10am–6pm; in July and August, 10am–7pm. English and German headsets for hire.

LA CHAUSSÉE-TIRANCOURT
80310 • H-3 • 142 km

Nearby
Hostellerie de Belloy *
29 route nationale
Belloy-sur-Somme (3km)
Tel: 22.51.41.05

Overlooking the marshes a few miles to the west of Amiens, there once stood the fortified Celtic settlement of **Samara**. Today, the site is a classified historic monument and France's largest archaeological 'park'. Finds from extensive archaeological excavations are displayed in reconstructions. It is also the site of former valley bottom peat marshes, the first alluvial terraces and chalk hills linking the area to the Picardy plateau. A 70-acre site features the area's two important resources: its exceptionally rich natural resources – actively exploited by the peat-diggers into the 19th century – and its archaeological inheritance dating from the very earliest time of human settlement (400,000 years BC). In the exhibition centre, visitors journey through space and time, from the prehistoric period to Roman-Gallic occupation, to see reconstructions of dwelling places, artisan workshops, streets . . . Exploratory trails reveal the living conditions of Neolithic to Iron Age man, describe their methods of fortification, depict the Somme valley as it would have appeared; as well as illustrating the natural resources of the site (arboretum, botanical garden, marshland, etc).

• **Samara** Tel: 22.51.82.83. Open 13 March to 30 November daily 9.30am–8pm.

COLEMBERT
62142 • C-2 • 28 km

Hotel
Hostellerie du Château des Tourelles **
D 127
Tel: 21.33.34.78

The coastal arm of the Boulogne regional park, **parc naturel régional du Boulonnais**, has an information office in Colembert at Huisboit Le Wast Manor (tel: 21.83.38.79); responsible for more than 60 miles of coastline – cliffs, dunes, marsh and mud flat – from Authie to Oye Plage, a paradise for bird and plant life. Itineraries and waymarked routes with points of interest are available from the park information office.

CONDÉ-SUR-L'ESCAUT
59153 • E-8 • 180 km

Tourist information
at town hall
Tel: 27.40.01.62

Hotel
du Lac **
24 route de Bonsecours
Tel: 27.40.32.40

Croÿ's 18th-century **town hall** stands in the *place Delcourt*. The ground floor has fine brick-and-stone arches. A *metre etalon* standard measure is installed in the entrance.

Saint-Wasnon square is the address of the **church** of the same name, built in 1751. The tower, built in 1608, is topped with a spire curved out at the top and with bells on either side. Inside, the choir has Louis XV wood carving, and each of the stalls has its own little carved dome. A musical instrument decorates each stall end, probably in hommage to musician Josquin des Près, director of the choir, who died in Condé.

The square *place Verte* is dominated by the **château de Bailleul**, built in 1411 by Jean de la Hamaïde. Though destroyed in part during the Revolution, the main 15th-century section of the castle remains. The quadrangular building is in cut sandstone, with a ground-

Corbie: Saint-Pierre's flamboyant rose window

level tierce-point arcade and cantilevered turrets.

There are fine houses in the *rue Notre-Dame*. From *place Rombault* in the north part of the town, a pedestrian way (to the left) takes visitors to the ramparts. To the right is **lac Chabaud-Latour** and a 40-acre sports and recreation complex. The **mineshaft** on the other side of the lake is now an historic monument and the replanted area (more than 550 acres financed by the European Community) is dominated by a 170-feet-high conical slag heap. Access to this area is from the GR122, from which there are glimpses of Mons and Valenciennes.

Driving towards the Belgian frontier on the Bonsecours road, notice the lovely **château de l'Hermitage**.

COQUELLES
62231 • B-2 • 6 km

Coquelles is the site of the French Channel Tunnel terminal. The **Eurotunnel Information Centre** houses an exhibition of the Eurotunnel transport system and recounts the major phases in the 'century's biggest building project', through audiovisual displays, models and films. A viewing tower affords a panorama over the terminal and surrounding region, and there is also a cafeteria and shop.

• **Centre d'information Eurotunnel** BP46. Tel: 21.00.69.89.

CORBIE
80800 • H-4 • 163 km

Tourist information
place de la République
Tel: 22.96.95.76

Restaurant
La Table d'Agathe
6 rue Marcellin-Truquin
Tel: 22.96.96.27

Nearby
Le Val d'Ancre
Bonnay (3km)
Tel: 22.96.99.50

La ville d'or, la seconde Rome (City of gold, the second Rome), so called because of Corbie's wealth and power during the

Middle Ages. The 18th-century Gothic **Saint-Pierre collegiate church** could be mistaken for a medieval cathedral: the nave, the 180-feet-high towers and the flamboyant rose window together comprise an architectural style of grandiose simplicity. The church was erected upon the remains of the former abbey, in 657–663, by Queen Bathilde and her son Clothaire III who brought monks from the Luxeuil monastery to live here. From 771 to 826, the monastery's abbot was Adelhard, cousin of Charlemagne. In 896 Abbot Franon fortified Corbie against Norman invasion. Corbie was given town, or *commune*, status in 1180 by Philippe Auguste. In 1475 Louis XI laid siege to, and took, the town. Later Richelieu and Louis XIII liberated Corbie from Spanish occupation. In 1791, during the Revolution, the abbey was closed and its manuscripts transferred to Amiens. The Museum of the Friends of Old Corbie, **musée des Amis du vieux Corbie** includes Carolingian pottery, cloister sculptures and arcatures, manuscripts and 16th-century coins found on the abbey site, as well as a model of the Spanish siege of Corbie in 1636. There is also a display of documents relating to the town's twinning with Hoxter in Germany and Pickering in Great Britain.

• Musée des Amis du vieux Corbie 20 rue Paul-Baroux. Tel: 22.48.44.95. Visits by arrangement.

CRÉCY-EN-PONTHIEU
80150 • F-2 • 103 km

Tourist office
in the town hall
Tel: 22.23.54.43
(In season, rue Général-Leclerc. Tel: 22.23.93.84)

Hotel
La Maye **
13 rue de Saint-Riquier
Tel: 22.23.54.35

Crécy was the site of one of France's greatest and most celebrated military defeats on 26 August 1346, when Philippe VI, King of France, was vanquished

by the English under Edward III. Philippe VI lost 20,000 horsemen and was forced to take refuge in the château de Ladroye on the banks of the Authie. On the road out of Crécy north toward Walicourt and Dampierre a little **watch-tower** and viewing platform has been erected on the battle site. Going east towards Fontaine-sur-Maigne, is another monument, this time a cross, to the memory of **Jean de Luxembourg**, or Jean l'Aveugle (the blind), who fell during the battle. At Crécy itself there are lovely walks in the huge oak forest, **la forêt domaniale**.

CREUSE
80480 • H-3 • 161 km

La Ferme d'antan farm is a working memorial to past farming practices, with a collection including tractors, threshers and a 17th-century cider press, as well as farmyard animals given a considerable amount of freedom to wander. An exhibition of old posters and photographs and a video recall rural life at the turn of the century. A nature festival, *la fête de la nature*, is organised every May, the festival of Picardy days, *les Journées picardes*, in July. Picnic facilities available to visitors.

• La Ferme d'antan Open daily 9am–6pm. Tel: 22.38.98.58.

LE CROTOY
80550 • F-2 • 95 km

Tourist information
1 rue Carnot
Tel: 22.27.05.25

Somme Bay sailing club and marina
digue Mercier
Tel: 22.27.83.11

Restaurants
Chez Gérard
rue Victor Petit
Tel: 22.27.04.50
Chez Mado
6 quai Léonard
Tel: 22.27.81.22

Of the original town where **Jeanne d'Arc** was imprisoned in 1430, before she was handed over to the English (her statue is in the town square), little re-

mains. Crotoy was home to many famous artists and writers around the turn of the century: Jules Verne (1865–1871) wrote his *Twenty thousand leagues under the sea*, here, Colette lived here in 1908, as did Toulouse-Lautrec and Guerlain (perfumer to the empress) . . . The Caudron brothers carried out their first aeronautical trials nearby. The fishing port supplies the locality with fish from Somme Bay. The **water sports centre** offers a wide range of water-based activities including sailing, windsurfing, canoeing and diving.

DIEVAL
62460 • E-4 • 102 km

At Dieval, in an old, white-stone farmhouse, visitors can follow the stages of honey production from hive to honey pot. There are 19th-century straw hives, wooden hives, and glass-sided hives where you can see the bees at work; also a video on beekeeping. A flower garden displays those flowers most loved by the bees (with the most nectar). The visit ends with an opportunity to sample different blends in the honey shop.

• Musée de l'abeille 8 rue Monseigneur-Eloi. Tel: 21.41.50.11.

DOUAI
59500 • F-6 • 125 km

Tourist information
70 place d'Armes
Tel: 27.88.26.79
Guided tours of the town every Sunday 3.30pm May to October

Hotels
La Terrasse ***
36 rue Saint-Pierre
Tel: 27.88.70.04
Le Chambord **
3509 route de Tournai
Tel: 27.97.72.77
Climat de France **
Place Pierre-Brosselette
Tel: 27.88.29.97
Ibis **
Place Saint-Amé
Tel: 27.87.27.27
Volubilis **
Boulevard Vauban
Tel: 27.88.00.11

Restaurant
au Turbotin
9 rue de la Massue
Tel: 27.87.04.16

Dans les environs
Le Manoir de Fourcy ★★★
48 rue de la Gare
Tel: 27.96.44.90

Excavations carried out in the centre of the oldest part of town have revealed 6th-century wattle and daub thatched huts, precursors to a little agricultural village on the site. From the 9th century onwards, the number of houses grew to form a sizeable settlement. Douai's position meant that it was directly in the firing line during conflicts between the King of France and the Comte de Flandre during the 13th century. Part of France between 1306 to 1369, the town subsequently followed the destiny of the Comte de Flandre, belonging successively to the Dukes of Burgundy, then Charles Quint, to Philippe II and to the kings of Spain. A year after Louis XIV's siege of 1667, the town became part of France once more, remaining so except for a brief episode of Dutch domination between 1710 to 1712. The Flanders Parliament was established in Douai in 1714, and this was replaced after the Revolution by the Court of Appeal. Present-day Douai underwent a great deal of damage during both World Wars. The town is crossed by the River Scarpe and its canal. Parts of the town have fine and rather charming 18th-century houses which replaced the old fortifications at the end of the 19th century. Douai is the birthplace of painter Jean Bellegambe (c1475–1540), the 'master of colour'. You can see his masterpiece *le Polyptye* (formerly at Anchin abbey) in the museum. Sculptor Jean de Bologne was also born here in 1524.

La place d'Armes was damaged in both wars. Now pedestrianised, the square has cascades and attractive lighting and is further embellished by the **Hôtel Dauphin** (home of the tourist office) with its decorative iron-work balcony, the work of

Jean Bellegambe, The Virgin Protectress of the Cistercians *at Douai*

Cambrai blacksmith Mariette. Built in 1754, this became the home of the schools of art and music in 1860.

The **belfry** is a magnificent sandstone tower built in 1380. Around 1475, a 180-ft spire and Gothic bells were added to the existing 130-ft tower. On top, a lion keeps watch over the town. It was the subject of a painting by Corot in 1871. To the right of the belfry, the **magistrates' hall** has stone pillars supporting stone-ribbed, vaulted brick arches. The former magistrates' chapel – now serving as a lobby – was built between 1471 and 1475. It has a 21-feet-high central pillar fashioned in a spiral, the top decorated with the Burgundian heraldic emblem, the Beagle of Burgundy. The ground floor council chamber is 1463 Gothic. The rest of the Gothic-style building dates from 1840–1880. A 62-bell carillon is on the fourth floor of the belfry. Special bell concerts are arranged each week and on public holidays.

• Visits for individuals: Sunday and bank holidays at 10am, 11am, 3pm, 4pm and 5pm; for groups, all year by arrangement with the tourist office. 1 July to 31 August daily at 10am, 11am, 2pm, 4pm and 5pm for individuals. Tel: 27.88.26.79.

From the top of the belfry the view encompasses the great mass of Saint-Pierre church and a jostle of 18th-century rooftops. Through an arched passageway and the town hall courtyard, you can reach the *rue de l'université* and see the **Mont-de-Piété** (1628). This was converted into a national agricultural school; in the 19th century it became the faculty of letters and law. On the *rue de la Comédie* is the 18th-century theatre (Louis XVI façade). To the right, the **Hôtel d'Aoust** is a beautiful example of Louis XV architecture. Notice the allegories on the front.

La rue des Foulons, to the right, includes the **hôtel de la Tramerie** (1640), now the school of fine arts; at the bottom and to the right of *place Lannoy,* follow *la rue Merlin-de-Douai,* then left into *la rue Pallinchove* with the harmonious façade of the **palais de justice** law courts, former Flanders parliament building. Bound on one side by the River Scarpe, this originally served as refuge for the monks of Marchiennes Abbey in the 18th century; it was a military hospital during the War of Spanish Succession; in 1667 Louis XIV and his queen stayed here. In 1786, the main entrance was redesigned by architect Lillois Lequeux. It is occasionally open to the public , when it is possible to see the great wood-panelled chamber of the Flanders parliament, decorated with six allegorical paintings by Brenet: *la Vérité, la Science, l'Indépendance, la Prudence, la Religion* and *la Justice*. On the ceiling is the fleur de lys blazon, encircled by the collar of the Order of Saint-Esprit, refurbished at the time of the Restoration. The chamber is used for special sessions of the Court of Appeal. The banks of the River Scarpe by the law courts correspond to where the river itself flowed in medieval Douai. Warehouses that stood here were abandoned in the 14th century with the rerouting of the river. Some charming old houses grace the opposite side of the river on the *quai Bertin.*

Back at the *place d'Armes,* follow *rue de Bellain* to the **collegiate church of Saint-Pierre** whose monumental tower dates back to the 16th century, and the 18th-century church. The building's classic lines are particularly harmonious. The choir, formerly the reserve of canons and members of parliament, is longer than the nave. The organ was sumptuously decorated in the 18th century by the Valenciennes cabinet-maker, Gillis, for the Benedictine Abbot of Anchin.

Near the collegiate church, discover **rue Jean-Bellegambe**, formerly *rue Saint-Pierre*: **No 25** was the birthplace of Henri-Edouard Delacroix, the neo-Impressionist painter. **No 37** was the birthplace of Jean-Bellegambe (1470). **No 57** has giant sunflowers by Albert Pépe decorating the modern façade.

A little further along is the entrance to the **jardin des plantes** and opposite, the **bibliothèque-conservatoire.** This library has one of France's richest collections of ancient manuscripts, early printed books and illuminated manuscripts, drawn mostly from the monasteries of the Scarpe valley, from Anchin, Flines and Marchienne. In the 16th and 17th centuries Douai was the home of numerous printers who had links with the university.

• **Bibliothèque municipale** 117 rue de la Fonderie. Open daily, except Monday, 9am–noon and 1.30–6.30pm; Saturday 9.30am–noon and 1.30–5pm. Tel: 27.97.88.51.

Continue along *rues d'Arras, Samson, des Récollets* and *des Anglais* to the **church of Saint-Jacques**, built between 1706 and 1709. This was originally the old friars' chapel, founded in 1626, and is a reminder of the Engllish catholics exiled at Douai, first when they were forced to flee Henry VIII, and second to escape persecution during the reign of Elizabeth I. This became a parish church after the Revolution and was enlarged from 1825 to 1855 by the Arras-born architect, Grigny. Inside, the column capitals are decorated with radiant hosts and the wooden Gloire depicts the miraculous vision of the Abbot Piquette. Pictures of Colas decorate the ambulatory.

In *rue des Chartreux*, visit the **ancienne chartreuse Carthusian monastery** – an ensemble of 16th- and 18th-century buildings. To the left is the **hôtel d'Abancourt Montmorency** (1559–1608), the Flemish Renaissance-style home of the first Carthusian monks in the 17th century, who subsequently built the little cloister, refectory and church. The great cloister and the monks cells were destroyed during the Revolution. The convent houses the **musée de la chartreuse** with its prestigious collection of paintings (including the celebrated polyptych of Jean Bellegambe), sculptures and other pieces of art. The **Augustin Boutique Foundation**, in a little building to the right, looks after and displays the 25,000 glass plate negatives of the celebrated local photographer, Augustin-Boutique, who captured on film the life of northern France around 1900.

• **Musée de la chartreuse** 130 rue des Chartreux. Open daily, except Tuesday and public holidays, 10am–noon and 2–5pm, Sunday 10am–noon and 3–6pm. Tel: 27.87.17.82.

DOULLENS
80600 · G-4 · 118 km

Tourist information
Beffroi
rue du Bourg
Tel: 22.32.54.52

Hotel
Le Sully
45 rue d'Arras
Tel: 22.77.10.87

Doullens has some fine buildings characteristic of the Picardy region. Former frontier town to the Spanish Low Countries, Doullens once had a **citadel** built by François I in the 16th century, and reinforced in the 17th. This was later to become a prison (Albertine Sarrazin was imprisoned here). The guided tour allows visitors to see the underground military quarters: galleries, rifle room, weapons store …

• **Citadelle** Guided tours from 1 May to 30 September, Saturday, Sunday and public holidays 3–4.30pm. Tel: 22.77.34.93.

In the town is the brick-and-stone **belfry** (1363). **Notre-Dame church** has a sepulchre chapel and a *Mise au tombeau* painting. The former **church of Saint-Pierre** (13th century) was destroyed in the Revolution; only its nave remains, with fine twin pillars, capitals and triforium (upper gallery).

The **musée Lombart**, founded in 1908, is in a beautiful garden where you can also see the Marmousets' well, *puits des Marmousets*. Various rooms present a diverse collection of French and Flemish paintings, Poulbot lithographs and porcelain brought back from the East and Far East by Lombart. The Dames-de-Lorencourt chapel has antiquities from Egypt and the Far East, and a mummy.

• **Musée Lombart** 7 rue du Musée. Tel: 22.77.06.85. Open summer, Wednesday, Saturday and Sunday, 3–6pm; winter, Wednesday, Saturday and Sunday, 2.30–5pm and by arrangement.

It was at the **hôtel de ville** in Doullens that Field Marshal Foch was appointed sole commander of the Allied armies during the First World War on 26 March 1918. The occasion is immortalised in a stained glass window by Gérard Ansart, recalling the different French and English witnesses of this ceremony.

• **Salle du Commandement unique**, hôtel de ville. Open daily 8am–6pm. Tel: 22.32.40.05.

DUNKERQUE (Dunkirk)
59140 • B-4 • 45 km

Tourist office
Le Beffroi
rue de l'Amiral-Ronarc'h
Tel: 28.26.27.28 and
28.66.79.21
Guided visits of the town
Tel: 28.26.27.27

Hotels
Altea Reuze ***
2 rue Jean-Jaurès
Tel: 28.59.11.11
Europ'Hôtel ***
13 rue du Leughenaer
Tel: 28.66.29.07
Welcome Hôtel ***
37 rue Poincaré

Tel: 28.59.20.70
Inter Hôtel ***
6 rue L'Hermitte
Tel: 28.66.51.80
L'Hirondelle **
46–48 rue Faidherbe
Tel: 28.63.17.65
Le Select **
25 place de la Gare
Tel: 28.66.64.47
Le Tigre **
8 rue Clémenceau
Tel: 28.66.75.17
Le Trianon **
20 rue de la Colline
Tel: 28.63.39.15
Le XIXe Siècle **
1 place de la Gare
Tel: 28.66.79.28

Nearby
La Meunerie
D204, Téteghem (6km)
Tel: 28.26.14.30

Until the 16th century, the site of Dunkirk was probably a lagoon; an upward movement of the earth and a receding sea meant that fishermen were able to settle in a little cove formed by a bend in the River Colme. The village became a port round about the 8th century and in the 10th century it was fortified by Boudouin III, Count of Flanders. The township was then called *Saint-Gilles*, its present name not appearing until 1067, in a Charter of Boudouin de Lille. Since that time its history has

Dunkirk: carnival scene

been a catalogue of siege and destruction: 11 times besieged by the Spaniards, the English, the French and the Dutch; the siege of Turenne in 1658 lasted 28 days. In 1662, Charles II of England sold the town to Louis XIV, who immediately instructed its fortification by Vauban.

Through all its armed conflicts, the town's resilient inhabitants continued their fishing and pirating in the Straits of Dover. Dunkirk is also the city of Jean Bart and his pirates who, in the name of Louis XIV, waged a merciless war against the English and the Dutch. Following these exploits, Jean Bart was nominated head of the squadron of Louis XIV's royal fleet. After a period of prosperity the Treaty of Utrecht (1713) called for the destruction of the harbour. In order to maintain access to the sea, the Mardyck canal was dug. In 1793 the battle of Hondschoote allowed Dunkirk to remain French. But, Napoleon was unfortunately to favour Antwerp. In spite of this, the stubborness and courage of the people of Dunkirk helped it to regain some of its former importance. It was, of course, subject to considerable destruction during the two World Wars: in 1940, 80% of the town was destroyed and the harbour left unusable. Dunkirk was the last town in France to be liberated (10 May 1945), two days after German

Dunkirk: Charles de La Fosse,
God the Father supported by angels

capitulation. On 1 January 1970 the town merged with Malo-les-Bains and, on 1 January 1972, with Rosendael and Petite-Synthe. Today, the port ranks third nationally for the total amount of traffic and first for its port operations, excluding hydrocarbons. It is also the leading port in the world for computerised customs clearance of international freight. Dunkirk has a new university and plans to extend the present town centre towards the old docks (*opération Neptune*).

Jean Bart welcomes the visitor from the top of his statue, a work by the sculptor Pierre-Jean David, so-called 'David of Angers' (1788–1856, Rome prize 1811); with his noble brow and proud bearing he looks in defiance at his old enemies across the sea.

To the west of *place Jean-Bart*, at the far end of the *rue de la Marine*, stands the **porte monumentale de l'ancien arsenal**, erected in 1686 by Vauban, which gives access to the **parc de la Marine**.

On *place Jean-Bart*, the 15th-century **belfry** towers above the town. Built in brick, it is decorated on three levels with blind arcatures. The belfry houses 48 bells which play the cantata to Jean Bart on the hour, and on the half and quarter hour, other popular refrains. This tower used to be part of the church of Saint-Eloi from which it became

separated in the 18th century with the building of *rue Clémenceau*. There is a lovely view from the top, which can be reached by lift (a watch kept guard over the town from the belfry until 1940).

• Guided visits of the belfry and the bells in July and August daily, except Sunday, 9.30am, 10.30am, 11.15am, 2.30pm, 3.30pm, 4.30pm, 5.30pm. Tel: 28.26.27.89.

L'eglise Saint-Eloi was built after 1450 on the site of the chapel of Saint-Gilles; it is a five-nave *hallekerke* which was rebuilt in the 16th century after a fire in 1558. On this occasion, a new choir was built; it was made up of five bays and a many-sided apse surrounded by an ambulatory with chapels radiating off. In 1783 Louis, the Duke of Orléons' famous architect, transformed the lateral chapels, pulled down the 16th-century transept and nave and gave the building a classical façade. In 1885–1890, the architect Van Moé replaced it with a neo-Gothic façade. It is a remarkable building. The interior is lit by large, elegant windows in Flamboyant Gothic style and there are a number of important paintings including *The Last Supper* by Otto Venius, today attributed to François Pourbus, and *The Adoration of the Shepherds* by Crayer (1669); to the left of the choir, not very visible, is Jean Bart's funerary plaque and

tombstones bearing inscriptions in Flemish and Spanish.

Returning up *rue Clémenceau*, you come to *place Charles-Valentin* and the *hôtel de ville*. En route, you pass the **maison et la tour de l'Armateur** (18th-century shipowner's house) at number 15, *rue Faulconnier*. From the tower in the courtyard, they used to watch the ships returning to port.

The **town hall** was erected by Louis Cardonnier in 1901. The central pediment of the red brick eastern elevation is decorated with an equestrian statue of Louis XIV and, on either side, statues of local notaries: from left to right, Guilleminot, Count of Cassel, Emmery, Vanstabel, Baudouin and Jacobsen. Inside, a stained glass window by Felix Gaudin shows Jean Bart after the victory of Texel.

Le vieux port, old port, is dominated by the **tour du Leughenaer** (meaning 'the liar' in Flemish), the name which was given it following a notorious false alarm. This is the sole survivor of the 28 towers which once made up the 1405 fortifications. Nearby is the very lively **Minck fish market** and its numerous taverns. The *rue du Loug henaer* leads to the **colonne de la Victoire**, built to mark the 1793 victory; until 1940 this column stood in the middle of the dunes.

Notre-Dame-des-Dunes chapel was erected in 1403 on the site where a statue of the Virgin Mary had been found in the sand, and over the years received hommage and donations from many a sailor who survived the storm. Destroyed during the Revolution, it was rebuilt in 1815. The inside walls are covered with commemorative plaques, and models of ships hang from the vault. Every year on 15 August, during the celebration of the blessing of the sea, the statue of Notre-Dame-des-Dunes is borne in procession by the wives of the fishermen (known as *bazennes*).

Dunkirk has three excellent museums:

• **Musée des beaux-arts** place

du Général-de-Gaulle. Tel: 28.66.21.57. Collections of 17th- and 18th-century paintings and model ships.

• **Musée portuaire** (harbour museum), entrepôt des tabacs, 9 quai de la Citadelle. Tel: 28.63.33.39.

Built in the 1850s, this warehouse is the town's oldest and most interesting, containing the centre for science and technology which features both traditional and present-day activities of harbour life.

• **Musée d'art contemporain** (museum of contemporary art), av des Bains. Tel: 28.59.21.65.

In a sculpture garden not far from an old naval yard, this museum has contemporary paintings and stages temporary exhibitions.

The 18,000-litre *aquarium municipal* contains marine species from the seas of the world.

• **Musée d'aquariophilie** avenue du Casino. Tel: 28.59.19.18. Open daily, except Tuesday, 10am–noon and 2–6pm.

Dunkirk is also a carnival town. One of France's most famous carnivals is held on the Sunday before Shrove Tuesday; its *Vischerbend* (fishermen's band) is unique. Originally, this band was formed by the cod fishermen who celebrated before setting sail for long months off Iceland. Membership of the today's *Vischerbend* is open to all who want to have a good time: with painted faces and disguises, they form a dancing procession behind the brass band, fifes and drums, under the direction of a drum-major in the costume of the imperial guard. The procession makes its way round the town under a shower of confetti, and, on reaching the town hall, they are greeted with a shower of smoked herring! For lovers of folklore and festivals, this is an event not to be missed. A two-month programme of events surrounds the carnival, including numerous balls (*bal des Corsaires, bal des Acharnés, bal du Chat-Noir . . .*).

• Festival dates: Tourist office, Tel: 28.66.79.21.

EPERLECQUES
62910 • C-3 • 33 km

Tourist information
4 rue de la Mairie
Tel: 21.95.66.25

A huge cement **blockhaus** (the largest ever built) rises out of Eperlecques forest at a height of 72 feet. It was built in 1943/44 to launch the famous German V2 rockets on London. Bombed by nearly 200 RAF flying fortresses, the *blockhaus* was partially destroyed and converted into a liquid oxygen plant. Its walls are 16 feet thick and are topped with a stone slab 22 feet deep. Today, there are archives and a film to see (guided tour).

• **Blockhaus d'Eperlecques** Tel: 21.88.44.22. Open July and August daily 10am–7pm; in May, Mondays to Saturdays 2.15–6.00pm and Sundays 10am–7pm; in April, October and November daily 2.15–6pm; in March, Sundays 2.15–6pm.

ESCALLES
62179 • C-2 • 11 km

Hotel
Le Cap **
place de la Mairie
Tel: 21.85.25.10

Opposite the Blanc Nez headland, close to the Eurotunnel information centre at Coquelles, a panoramic restaurant offers a permanent exhibition on *La folle aventure du détroit* (The mad undertaking of the Channel link). This recalls the turbulent history of the site, the various ideas put forward for a fixed link between England and France, plus all the fanciful aspects connected with the history of the Tunnel.

• **musée international du Trans-manche** Mont d'Hubert. Tel: 21.82.32.03. Open 16 April to 14 October daily 10am–noon and 2–6pm; 15 October to 15 April, Saturdays and Sundays, the same hours as above.

FORT-MAHON-PLAGE
80970 • F-1 • 85 km

Tourist information
Tel: 22.23.36.00

Hotels
de la Terrasse ***
1461 avenue de la Plage
Tel: 22.23.37.77
La Chipaudière **
1440 avenue de la Plage
Tel: 22.27.70.36

Nearby
Auberge du Fiacre
Ronthianville (2km)
Tel: 22.23.47.30

Inspired by examples over the Channel, local initiatives have combined natural resources with a leisure complex: this beach area welcomes nearly 100,000 visitors daily during the summer. The **Aquaclub**, in the heart of a large pine forest, sheltered by a chain of dunes, offers all sorts of water sports and games; after your sporting rigours, lie back and do nothing; a sauna, solarium and Turkish baths . . . or enjoy the air-conditioning of the conservatory bistro.

• **Aquaclub** promenade du Marquenterre, tel: 22.27.48.47.

Next to the Aquaclub, the **Belle-Dune golf club** offers a high quality course against the backdrop of the Marquenterre dunes (tel: 22.23.45.50). The French school of sand-yachting (Eolia) is also based here and practical courses are organised on the beach at Fort-Mahon.

• **Eolia** centre nautique, boulevard Maritime Nord. Tel: 22.23.42.60.

FOURMIES
59610 • G-9 • 236 km

Tourist information
place Verte
Tel: 27.60.40.97

Hotel
Ibis **
Les Etangs des Moines
Tel: 27.60.21.54

In the 16th and 17th centuries, Fourmies lay on the border with the province of Hainaut, protected by a fort; in 1637, it was captured and burnt to the ground by the Governor of La Capelle. From the 18th century onwards, Fourmies became an industrial centre (glass and lace factories) and after 1810 the first woollen and cotton mills appeared.

One particular event marks both the history of Fourmies and that of the French trade union movement, the Fourmies riots. On 1 May 1891, in the face of opposition by factory managers, the workers formed a union and witheld their labour pending agreement to their demands. Troops were called in to disperse the demonstrators, who had gone to lodge a complaint at the town hall. Shots were fired; ten were left dead and numerous injured. A **monument** in the cemetery marks the painful episode in local industrial relations.

The **écomusée de la région Fourmies-Trélon** (ecological museum) is based at Fourmies and manages the nine satellite museums distributed throughout the region which each present a different aspect of the region.

• **Ecomusée de la région Fourmies-Trélon** place Maria-Blondeau, BP 65. Tel: 27.60.66.11.

The Fourmies 'satellite' is the **musée du textile et de la vie sociale** (textile and social life museum) and can be found in the premises of the old Prouvost-Masurel mill. Its display covers a century of local history and includes several reconstructions (tavern, school, shop . . .); there is also a collection of machines in working order, from fibre textile machines to domestic implements.

• **Musée du textile et de la vie sociale** place Maria-Blondeau, BP 65. Tel: 27.60.66.11. Open July to September daily 9am–6pm; March to November, Mondays to Saturdays 9am–noon and 2–6pm; Sundays and public holidays 2.30–6.30pm.

GRAVELINES
59820 • B-3 • 23 km

Tourist information
11 rue de la République
Tel: 28.65.21.28

Hotels
Le Beffroi ***
place Charles-Valentin
Tel: 28.23.24.25
Polder Hôtel
rue Rubens
Tel: 28.23.90.90

Situated on the River Aa, between Calais and Dunkerque, the old fortifications of Gravelines form a 3km ring; Gravelines and its hamlets, les Huttes to the east, and Petit-Fort-Philippe to the north, today cover an area of over 5,700 acres. Because of its geographical position, the town is able to play an important role, politically, strategically and commercially. Originally a little fishing village called *les Huttes*, it was first fortified in 1160, by Thierry of Alsace, Count of Flanders, who also wanted to create a harbour. The estuary of the Aa was developed and gave birth to the port of Gravelines.

Expansion followed in the form of sheep rearing on nearby land reclaimed from the sea, herring fishing and trade in salt, fruit and wine. In 1212, as a punishment to the Count of Flanders, who refused to join the anti-English cause, Philip Augustus ravaged the town. It suffered further attacks by Oudard of Maubuisson (1302) and the English (1383). In the 15th century it was returned to Jean of Luxemburg and once more fell victim to clashes between Charles the Bold and Louis XI. The war between Francis I and Charles V of Spain led to the rebuilding of the four bastions of the fortress and to the reinforcement of the château-arsenal; these works were financed by neighbouring towns (Ghent, Ypres, Bruges . . .) and, as a result, Gravelines was able to hold out against the siege by Maréchal Thermes, Governor of

Calais, which town had recently become French. When Louis XIV took Flanders again, Gravelines succumbed, in spite of the construction of a double fort – **Grand-Fort** and **Petit-Fort**; it was to be taken time and time again before being permanently joined to France in 1659, by the Treaty of the Pyrenees. Nominated Governor of Gravelines in 1706, Vauban carried out external defence work comprising a collection of half-moon defences, counterscarps and glacis and by building a lock on the River Aa (*see* Fortified towns route, p169). A design for a harbour fairway by Philip IV, King of Spain, was carried out under Louis XV; the draining of Hems de Saint-Pol began and between 1761 and 1852 four new dykes allowed more land to be reclaimed. **Grand-Fort-Philippe** was built on the west side of the mouth of the new harbour; while, on the other side, an earthen pentagon was a prison for English smugglers. The town ramparts helped in the resistance against the Germans in 1940 and today are a source of civic pride. The new harbour dug in the dunes at Petit-Fort provides shelter to mainly pleasure craft (*anse des Espagnols*).

In the town centre, the early 19th-century **belfry** towers above the town in the *place Charles-Valentin*, the third belfry to have stood on this spot.

The **hôtel de ville** dates from 1836 and was renovated and extended in 1989. The façade is decorated with the town's coat of arms and a sundial; in the

Fourmies: musée du textile et de la vie sociale, milliner's shop

Aerial view of Gravelines

time when trawlers set sail for Iceland, its cellars were used to stock salt.

Nearby, the **château-arsenal** (13th century) constitutes the main element of Gravelines' fortifications; begun by the architects of Philip of Alsace and Charles V of Spain, these were later extended and improved by Vauban and today include a series of military buildings: underground blockhouses, artillery room, a blockhouse converted into a bakery in 1693 (one oven cooked 40 loaves of bread each weighing 11lb), gunpowder room (built in 1742 by the engineer Feuillé, the first level housing the gunpowder reserve and the underground guns of the artillery).

In the gunpowder room of the Arsenal is the **musée du dessin et de l'estampe originale**, France's only gallery of its kind with a large collection of 19th- and 20th-century artists. It also organises temporary exhibitions and shows original contemporary works.

• **Musée du dessin et de l'estampe originale** Arsenal. Tel: 28.65.50.60.

The **church of Saint-Willibrord** is late Gothic with a Renaissance portal dating from 1598. The choir and transept have ribbed vaulting with hanging keystones. The confessionals, the pulpit and the organ case date from the 17th century. In the left aisle is the cenotaph of Berbier of Metz, Governor of Gravelines, killed in the siege of Saint-Venant in 1657. This mon-

ument is attributed to the sculptor Girardon (creator of the statue of Richelieu at the Sorbonne). Notice also a 16th-century triptych representing Philippe Lequien, another Governor of Gravelines; the marble baptismal fonts date from 1634; a statue of Notre-Dame-de-Foy from the 18th century; a painting representing the Crowning of the Virgin from the 17th century. Outside, on the right side of the church, a lowered arcade follows an ancient *citerne militaire*, a military water tank (1724) built in Boulonnais sandstone and decorated with bronze dolphins serving as taps. It used to collect rain water to supply the town in case of siege and was able to hold 1,420,000 litres.

Going towards Petit-Fort-Philippe, you will see Flanders' smallest wooden windmill, the **moulin Lebriez** (visits by arrangement with the tourist office).

On the way to the beach of Petit-Fort-Philippe is **Sportica**, the largest sports complex north of Paris. Opened in 1985, about 20 different activities are on offer: swimming, sauna, squash, basket ball, volley ball, tennis, fitness training, martial arts, bowling, roller skating . . . A multi-purpose hall accommodates up to 2,700 people; plus cafeteria, shopping mall, cinema, group accommodation facilities and a hotel, all complementing the sports and leisure facilities to make this one of the activity high-spots of the coast between Belgium and the Bay of the Somme.

• **Sportica** Espace international du sport et des loisirs, place du Polder. Tel: 28.65.35.00.

Gravelines is also home to a large nuclear power station which, in 1992, produced nearly 35 billion kWh, making it France's number one power station. It employs nearly 1,500 people and thousands of visitors (18,000 in 1992) have taken advantage of the station's three-hour conducted tours.

• **Centrale nucléaire** Tel: 28.68.42.36.

GUÎNES

62340 • C-2 • 15 km

Hotel
Le Lion d'Or *
7 place Maréchal-Foch
Tel: 21.35.20.51

Guînes still has its feudal mound (15th century) where Sifrid the Norman is said to have drawn up his first defences. Today, a tower, the **tour de l'Horloge**, is all that remains. Guînes grew in importance under the 16 Counts of Guînes until 1351, when Raoul de Brienne was executed on the order of the King of France and then, like Calais, it was occupied by the English. Later, a fortified castle was built from which a fortified town developed. The English presence lasted two centuries, during which time the town became the southern fortress of the Pole, the name given to the occupied zone round Calais. In 1520, Henry VIII built the famous

Hondschoote: town hall

crystal palace there, to receive Francis I during the discussions of the Field of the Cloth of Gold. In 1558, after taking Calais, the Duke of Guise took Guînes from the English and razed the castle to the ground. The present town centre was built on the old castle foundations, the streets following the contours of the old walls. Protestants fleeing persecution contributed to the rebuilding and development of the town before they were driven into exile following the Revocation of the Edict of Nantes. This was a hard blow for the town which was thus deprived of a large part of its elite and active merchant class.

The best way to get to know the town is perhaps by following the perimeter of the ancient fortified castle: *place Fach* contains the beautiful **hôtel de ville** (1684); in *place des Tilleuls* look at the **statue** of the Duke of Guise and the **church of Saint-Pierre-aux-Liens** (with its re-

markable original pulpit from 1706). Exhibited in the **Emile-Villez museum** are memorabilia from Blanchard and Jeffries' Channel crossing in a balloon, Roman coins, Merovingian tombs, 17th-century paintings and sculptures and memorabilia from the two World Wars.

• Musée Emile-Villez rue du Bassin. Tel: 21.35.21.13. Open Sundays 3–6pm; from 1 July to 30 September, Wednesdays 2–5pm and by arrangement.

As you leave the town, admire the little Louis XV-style **château** (1806) at La Bien-Assise, based on a design by Ledoux, architect to the King. A **forest** which is part of the castle estate has way-marked paths and bridlepaths and, at its centre, the inhabitants of Guînes have erected a **monument** commemorating the feat of balloonists, Blanchard and Jeffries, who landed here after crossing the Channel from Dover in 1785.

HARDELOT
62152 • D-1 • 46 km

Tourist information
23 avenue de la Concorde
Tel: 21.83.02.65

Golf des Pins
Tel: 21.83.73.10
Golf des Dunes
Tel: 21.91.90.90

Hotels
du Parc ***
111 avenue François-Ier
Tel: 21.33.22.11
Regina **
avenue François-Ier
Tel: 21.83.81.88

Restaurant
Restaurant du Golf
av du Golf
Tel: 21.83.71.04

This resort offers a wonderful natural environment thanks to the quality of its sandy beaches and extensive forest where pretty seaside villas nestle. Numerous sports and leisure activities are on offer as well as a couple of golf courses (18-hole).

HARNES
62440 • E-6 • 115 km

This commune situated at the heart of the coalfield has responded to pit closures with the opening of a large industrial zone. The **musée municipal** (50 rue André-Desprez, tel: 21.20.13.26) has exhibits of local archaeology and of the two World Wars which left such a deep impression on the town (open Wednesdays 10am–noon and 3–6pm; Sundays 10am–noon; and daily by appointment). The **musée de l'école et de la mine** (20 rue Montceau, tel: 21.20.46.70) shows reconstructions of a classroom in 1900 and authentic mining galleries (open Thursdays 2–6pm and by appointment). Not far away, the commune of **Noeux-les-Mines** has a **musée de la mine** (avenue Guillon, tel: 21.26.34.64) where 220 yards of tunnel have been reconstructed (open first Saturday in the month at 3pm and 4pm and by arrangement).

HAZEBROUCK
59190 • D-5 • 68 km

Tourist information
place Général-de-Gaulle
Tel: 28.49.59.89

Hotel
Auberge de la Forêt **
La Motte-au-Bois
Tel: 28.48.08.78

Restaurants
Auberge St-Eloi
60 rue de l'Eglise
Tel: 28.40.70.23
La Taverne
61 grand-place
Tel: 20.41.63.09

Hazebrouck is today an important agricultural centre with industry also in evidence.

Le musée Abbé-Lemire
From 1914 to 1928, Abbot Lemire, curate of the parish, was the mayor of Hazebrouck; this ecclesiastic was one of the great figures of social Catholicism at the beginning of the century, famous in the north, in particular, for his action in favour of workers' gardens.

The façade of the museum is in brick, decorated with a sculpture of a lion holding a coat of arms with hare, the town's coat of arms. On the ground floor are the furniture, letter and photographs of the former deputy mayor.

• **Musée Abbé-Lemire** Tel: 28.49.59.59. For visits apply to Centre culturel André-Malraux.

The **church of Saint-Eloi** is a very beautiful brick-and-stone building with three naves; its imposing tower dates from 1532.

From the north side of the church, you walk into the **îlot Saint-Eloi** district, a new quarter of town built on the site of the old college of Flanders and a great architectural success, all in traditional Flemish materials and style. Nearby is the old **Augustine convent** housing the **musée municipal**. Restored in the 19th century, this brick and stone-faced building is one of Flanders' most beautiful. The left wing dates from 1518 and is adorned with stepped gable-ends; the right wing, dating from 1616, has scrolled gables and a

remarkable lateral façade where windows, arched doors, recesses and sculptured motifs are juxtaposed harmoniously to form a coherent whole. Inside, the cloister has been restored and recaptures its original character.

• **Musée municipal** place G Degroote, tel: 28.41.83.34.

HESDIN
62140 • E-3 • 86 km

Tourist information
Tel: 21.86.84.76

Hotel
Les Flandres **
22 rue d'Arras
Tel: 21.86.80.21

Hesdin's beautiful national forest covers over 2,500 acres and offers a network of way-marked footpaths. Public picnic areas. Clumps of oak and beech.

HONDSCHOOTE
59122 • B-5 • 61 km

Tourist information
route des Moëres

This small Flemish town groups spruce houses and gardens full of flowers around its church and town hall, both of which bear testimony to the town's splendid past. The **Moëres**, north of Hondschoote, were drained by Wenceslas Coebergher. After being devastated by the Normans and set ablaze by the soldiers of Charles VI in pursuit of the English, Hondschoote acquired prosperity with the development of *sayette* or light woollen cloth manufacture. In the 16th century, there were about 3,024 workshops and the population numbered almost 20,000. The cloth was exported via the port of Bruges to the Levant, to the Baltic States and later to America. But the town's wealth gradually declined up to the end of the 18th century as a result of the wars and disruptions of the Reformation. The *sayetteurs* (cloth-makers) withdrew to Bruges in 1697 leaving only 1,800 inhabitants behind. A famous battle in 1793 brought honour back to the town; the French, under the orders of

Generals Hauchard and Vandomme, defeated the English under the command of the Duke of York. This victory of the Revolutionary armies, which saved France from invasion and liberated besieged Dunkerque, is marked by a monument in the town.

The **church of Saint-Waast** was built in the 16th century in sandstone and has a 270-ft tower, **De Witte Torre** (the White Tower). It was saved from the fire of 1582. Its spire is very characteristic of local contemporary style. The three naves of this *hallekerke* and the apses date from the 17th century. Inside, the beautiful 18th-century furnishings include the carved communion rail (1746) and the pulpit (1753). Saint Waast, patron saint of the parish, is depicted on the pulpit supporting column and in the choir a flagstone marks the spot where Marie Bart, niece of the famous pirate Jean Bart, is buried.

The **town hall**, erected in 1558, is one of the jewels of French Flanders. In Gothic style, its stone façade comprises high mullioned windows joined vertically by fine mouldings; the walls under the windows are decorated with lancets, curved and countercurved arches and heraldic shields displaying the coat of arms of the Baron of Coppens. From the rear of the adjacent inn, you can admire the back of the town hall and, in particular, the sparrow-stepped gables, the windows and the octagonal tower with onion-shaped dome tapering into a spire. For visits to the **guard-room**, with its vaults supported by impressive pillars, apply to the town hall.

Le musée municipal is in the town hall. Admire the 17th-century statues and paintings including *Neuf Pieuses* (Nine Pious Ladies) and *La Bataille d'Hondschoote* (the Battle of Hondschoote) by Bellange (1840), which is a copy of the painting in the Louvre and was presented by the Ministry of the Interior in 1852. Display cabinets contain sealed parchments and written documents relating to the history of the town.

• **Musée municipal** hôtel de ville, tel: 28.68.31.55. Open all year; apply to the tourist office.

Behind the church, the well which was a gift from the poet Lamartine, supplied the population with water. The poet stayed here on numerous occasions with his sister Eugénie, who was married to Baron Bernard Coppens. He was invited to stand for Parliament in 1831 but was beaten by the opposition candidate.

In the **square**, surrounded by steep-roofed 16th- and 17th-century houses with picturesque chimney stacks, stands a **monument** by a Lille sculptor commemorating the French victory of 8 September 1793.

Finally, Hondschoote has two windmills, the **Historique** and the **Noordmeulen windmills**; these have recently been restored by the Regional Friends of Windmills Association (ARAM). The Historique or Spinnewyn mill played an important part in the victory of the Battle of Hondschoote, and it was in order to commemorate this victory that various groups were anxious to participate in the rebuilding of the mill.

• **Moulin Historique et Noordmeulen**, tel: 28.68.31.55.

HYDREQUENT
62720 • C-2 • 25 km

In the old co-operative quarries, the **maison du marbre et de la géologie** offers an insight into quarry exploitation and quarry by-products. The fossilised remains of a huge marine reptile (pliosaur) have raised great interest, both among scientists and the general public, and can be seen at *rue Henri-Barbusse*, tel: 21.83.19.10. Open 1 June to 30 September daily 2.30–6.30pm; I March to 30 November, Sundays and public holidays 2.30–6.30pm.

LANNOY
59390 • D-7 • 126 km

The family bearing this name appeared in the 11th century and played a leading role in the history of the Netherlands; Jehan III of Lannoy, who died on 18 March 1492, was adviser to Philip the Good, Governor of Holland. After building a castle here in 1452 (later razed to the ground during the French Revolution), he obtained permission, in 1458, to build a walled town around it. He was also granted franchises for the organisation of trade fairs and markets. Lannoy is the smallest county town in France, made up of just a few streets and four squares, still encircled by its old houses. Seventeenth-century Lannoy became an important cloth manufacturing town. Like many other northern towns, it also suffered countless sieges and battles. François Rapheleng, a famous orientalist, was born here; he married the daughter of the Antwerp printer Plantin and contributed to the publication of the multi-lingual Bible. Other well-known people born in Lannoy are Charles de Lannoy, who defeated François I at Pavia, while in the service of the kings of Spain; the Viceroy of Naples and the family of President Franklin Delano (De Lannoy) Roosevelt (which emigrated during the Wars of Religion).

The **church of Saint-Philippe**, built at the beginning of the 16th century, has a Gothic choir, decorated with Louis XV panelling enhanced with gold, and paintings recounting the life of Saint-Philippe. On either side of the choir are two beautiful polychrome busts of the Saints-Philippe and Marcoul. The baptismal fonts in Tournai stone date from the founding of the church and are surrounded by a beautiful wrought-iron grid. In *rue de Tournay*, the portal of the **couvent des croisiers** (1474) has just been restored and classified as a historical monument.

The **hôtel de ville**, built in 1783 by Lille architect Gambert as a cloth market, is situated in *place Carnot*; the pediment is decorated with the town's coat of arms and those of Count Vilain of Ghent, the last owner of the fief. Some **old houses**, one dating from 1608 (*9 rue Nationale*) remain. Parts of the old ramparts and a round corner tower can be seen in the **parc des Croisiers**; opposite, in the parc des Prévôts, the provost's house (1461) awaits promised restoration. Finally, not far from the town hall, the ancient feudal mound, popularly known as the **île aux Amours** (lovers' island) rises up in the middle of a green open space. The moat was drained a few years ago.

LEWARDE
59 287 • F-1 • 135 km

Situated along the Roman roads leading to Cambrai and Bavay, Lewarde became a historic mining centre. In a wooded area, near the Sensée marshes, the *fosse* (pit) *Delloye* bears testimony to 250 years of mining activity. Until quite recently, 1,000 tonnes of coal were produced daily by 1,000 miners. A guided visit of the mine, including memorabilia and literature, is recommended.

• **Centre historique minier** Fosse Delloye, tel: 27.98.03.89. Open 1 April to 30 September 10am–5pm (for groups, from 8am); 1 October to 31 March 10am–4pm.

LILLE
59000 • D-1 • 115 km

Tourist office
place Rihour
Tel: 20.30.81.00

Hotels
Lille has 37 classified hotels. List and information from the tourist office, *see above;* alternatively book direct in Paris at the Maison du Nord/Pas-de-Calais, 1 rue de Châteaudun, 75009 Paris. Tel: 40.16.07.07

Restaurants
A l'Huitrière
3 rue des Chats-Bossus
Tel: 20.55.43.40
Le Paris
52 *bis* rue Esquernoise
Tel: 20.55.29.41
Le Hochepot
6 rue du Nouveau-Siècle
Tel: 20.54.17.59
La Fringale
141 rue Solferino
Tel: 20.42.02.80

Alcide
5 rue des Débris-Saint-Etienne
Tel: 20.12.06.95

Nearby
La Laiterie
138 avenue de l'Hippodrome
Lambersant (2km)
Tel: 20.92.79.79
Le Septentrion
parc du Vert-Bois
Marcq-en-Barroeul (5km)
Tel: 20.46.26.98

Ten centuries ago, this town was made up of numerous little islands encircled by the River Deûle. Boats coming up river met an obstruction in the waterway which obliged them to unload their goods and pick them up again further downstream. From this necessity, a trading centre was born around which a town developed. The unnavigable area extended between today's *avenue du Peuple-Belge* and the *quai de Wault*. Commercial exchange between the Low Countries and the famous trade fairs of the Champagne region developed along a north-south axis which lead to the construction of a road, the *grande chausée*, which still exists today under the same name.

The first written text on the town is the famous charter in which Baudouin, Count of Flanders, endowed the collegiate church of Saint-Pierre in 1066. At this time, the Counts of Flanders owned a castle on an island in the River Deûle (where Notre-Dame-de-la-Treille stands today) and a market (where the grand-place stands today). The town developed steadily, thanks to the cloth industry, but was subject to much disruption, because Flanders, and Lille in particular, was the subject of bitter disputes between the Counts of Flanders and the King of France. In 1205, Baudouin IX died in Constantinople leaving two daughters: Jeanne who was to marry Ferrand of Portugal, and Marguerite. In 1215, this confrontation with the King of France was resolved at Bouvines by the victory of Philip II Augustus and the imprisonment of Ferrand of Portugal. Between 1214 and 1244, the town ben-

efited from the good government of Countess Jeanne. She developed the course of the River Deûle, granted the town a charter in 1235, which allowed the judiciary, administrative and financial powers to be reorganised (this charter was to form the basis of municipal life until the Revolution); she also built solid walls around the town and founded a hospital on the site of the present-day Hospice-Comtesse. Her sister Marguerite took over from 1244 to 1280; at this time, the town was made up of four parishes: Saint-Pierre, Saint-Etienne, Saint-Sauveur and Saint-Maurice. In 1302, following the battle of Eperons d'or at Courtrai, Lille fell into the hands of Philip the Fair, King of France. After a difficult period, the town remained under the distant yet benevolent supervision of the kings of France. But in 1369, after the marriage of the daughter of Louis de Mâle, Count of Flanders, to Philip the Bold, brother of Charles V, the latter relinquished the town. In 1384, Louis de Mâle died and was succeeded by his son-in-law, Philip the Bold, Duke of Burgundy. Until the end of the 17th century, the banner of the Lion of Flanders was flown without interruption from the rooftops of Lille. Philip the Bold gave the town a chamber of finance, and thereby introduced a brilliant and prosperous period for the people of Lille. In 1419, John the Fearless extended the town, developed the Deûle, built the Wault quay and founded the famous tournament of Epinette. In 1430, Philip the Good held the first chapter of the *Toison d'Or* (Golden Fleece) at the collegiate church of Saint-Pierre and, in 1454, the famous and celebrated *repas dit voeu du Faisan* took place in the Salle Palace. On his subsequent visits, Philip the Good decided to have a much larger ducal palace built: the **Rihour Palace**; it was there that he received the future King Louis XI for diplomatic negotiations and Marie of Burgundy,

*Lille: Vieille Bourse,
detail of a caryatid*

daughter of Charles the Reckless, in 1477. From 1482 to 1515, Lille came under the control of the House of Hapsburg along with Flanders, and then came under Spanish domination until 1667. Under Charles V and Philippe II of Spain, the town continued to grow in size and wealth, in spite of religious wars and difficulties. During the reign of the Archdukes Albert and Isabelle, a town centre was laid out and numerous new buildings were begun: the Bourse (Stock Exchange) (1652), Gilles de Boë house, Jesuit convent (military hospital), the Gates of Ghent . . .

11 April 1713 At the peace of Utrecht, France surrendered Tournai and her possessions in the Low Countries, in return for Béthune, Saint-Venant, Aire-sur-la-Lys and Lille. The people of L'ille became citizens of France. The 18th century was troubled by the war of Austrian Succession, but the victory of Maurice de Saxe at Fontenoy (11 May 1745) finally removed this threat. Louix XV came to Lille at this time. During the Revolution, at the time of the creation of the Nord *département*, Douai was named the principal departmental town, Lille only receiving the status of principal town of the district. However, it was Lille that became the chief departmental town in 1804. During the 19th century, Lille's economic base was strengthened by the building of the Paris-Lille railway, the transfer of the regional university from Douai to Lille and by the creation of the Lille suburbs of Fives, Esquermes, Moulins

and Wazemmes. At the turn of the century, living and working conditions were poor and the rate of infant mortality was high. Before the war, Lille became the see of a bishop. The two World Wars were particularly difficult for Lille, both by virtue of the German occupation of the town as well as the bombing raids and combat it had to endure. Like neighbouring Roubaix, Lille was a socialist stronghold. Lille personalities have contributed both to regional history (Achille Liénart) and national destiny (Charles de Gaulle). In the postwar period, the renovation of the Saint-Sauveur quarter was

followed by the creation of an urban motorway network and the building of the new town of Villeneuve-d'Ascq.

The era of transport In the 1980s, Lille saw the installation and operation of the first completely automated public transport system, known as VAL, followed on the eve of the 90s by the *TGV*, and now, less than an hour from the Lille metropolis, comes the opening of the Channel Tunnel. The Euralille company aims, by the year 2000, to develop a business centre in the area of the town's railway stations, notably the TGV station. This business zone will extend

over a 300-acre site (once belonging to the military beneath the town's old fortifications), near *quartier Saint-Maurice*. The architect of the vast complex is Rem Koolhaas, whose previous projects include Belgium's new sea port at Zeebrugge, Paris's science park at La Villette and La Haye's town hall in the Netherlands. Lille is also home to France's third largest river port.

The cultural life of the town combines the best of Flemish and French traditions and is enriched by the activities of: the Lille National Orchestra (directed by Jean-Claude Casadesus) resident in the Nouveau Siècle

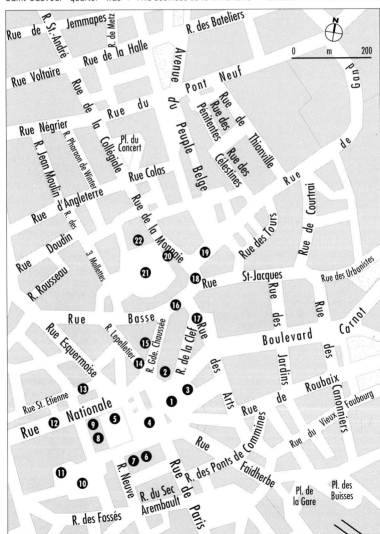

Palace; La Métaphore theatre (directed by Daniel Mesguich); the Lille Opera and the town's museums, the Hospice-Comtesse museum and the palais des Beaux-Arts gallery. Societies and interest groups abound, as everywhere in the *département* and, commercially, the town enjoys the same sort of prosperity it saw under the Dukes of Burgundy and the Counts of Flanders. At the heart of northern Europe, the town and its agglomeration number some 1.5 million inhabitants, one of France's largest towns.

Old Lille is best discovered with one's nose in the air, in order to appreciate the beautiful 17th- and 18th-century buildings which line the old streets of the centre. A characteristic feature of Lille is the rows of houses. Two influences are evident in their architecture: 17th-century Low Countries and 18th-century French. Between the years 1603 and 1620, the merchants and artisans of the town copied the styles of neighbouring and rival communities. After 1763, Lille became French; Vauban became its town planner, responsible for the layout of the new quarter (*rues Royale and Saint-André*) and the new citadel.

In the **place du Théâtre ❶**, the **new Bourse ❷**, built in 1910 to 1924, is the home of the regional chamber of commerce and industry, and the Lille-Roubaix-Tourcoing chamber. Architect Louis Cordonnier combined 18th-century Flemish inspiration with monumental proportions to reflect the region's economic and commercial prosperity. The 250-ft bell-tower has a carillon that plays popular tunes.

To the left is the **theatre ❸**, begun in 1907, completed in 1914 and inagurated by Guillaume II at the beginning of the First World War. It suffered bomb damage but was reopened following restoration work in 1923. The Louis XVI-style façade is decorated with bas-reliefs; to the right, Lemaire's *la Tragédie*, to the left, Alphonse Cordonnier's *La Musique*. The pediment is decorated with Hippolyte Lefebvre's *Apollon entouré de ses muses*.

Opposite the theatre, the **Vieille Bourse ❹** is one of the most remarkable buildings in Lille and, indeed, the Nord *département*. It was built in 1652, at the behest of the town's merchants, on the site of the pillory, the *chapelle des Ardents* and the *fontaine aux Changes*. Ghent and Antwerp already had their *bourses de commerce* or corn exchanges, so that Lille, an important textile centre, felt it, too, clearly needed one. This was built between 1652 and 1653 by Julien Destrée. A corner of the cloister on *place Général-de-Gaulle* bears the letters patent of Philippe IV of Spain, giving permission for its construction. Twenty-four identical buildings surround an interior courtyard. The ground floor constitutes the building's foundation, the two further storeys are decorated with Doric and Ionic pilasters, topped by a roof with dormer windows. All four sides of the building have an impressive portal allowing access to the interior courtyard. The façades are pilastered, with broken pediments, prominent cornices, elegant caryatids, impressively bearded old faces . . . complemented by the gracious lines of garlands of fruit and flowers. On the corner of *rue Manneliers*, notice King Midas with his ass's ears. Extravagantly decorated façades were particularly prized during the Flemish Renaissance. The portals are decorated with sculpted cornucopias (symbol of prosperity) and Flanders' lions (a reminder of Lille's earlier Flemish possession). The courtyard was a place of great animation, for this was the venue of commercial exchange. An open gallery has columns supporting a single storey. On the walls are black marble plaques (added around 1850), bearing the history of local commerce (Lille architect Benvignat) and busts of French inventors and scientists. The whole is surmounted by a campanile crowned with a statue of the god Mercury. In earlier times and during the festival of the lace-makers, little cakes called *couques,* in the form of the baby Jesus, were thrown from the bell-tower. Thanks to the efforts of local collectives and private enterprise, the Vieille Bourse is now restored to its former glory, its courtyard a venue for book and flower sellers.

On the grand-place, *place Général-de-Gaulle*, can be seen the statue of **la Déesse ❺**, which commemorates the French victory over the Austrians after the siege of 1792. The sculptor Bra gave the goddess the features of the wife of the mayor of the time, Madame Bigo-Danel. One of the sides of the square is occupied by the **Voix du Nord ❻** building, erected in 1936 by the architect Laprarde. At the top of the gable, a bronze group represents the three former provinces of the region, Flanders, Artois and Hainaut and is the work of Couvegnes (1893–1985). The façade is decorated with the coats of arms of the *département*'s towns and references to the 28 regional editions of the daily newspaper.

La Grande-Garde ❼, former guard-room, was built in 1717 by Lille architect Gombert; the rigour of this very classical, typical French façade contrasts strongly with much of Lille's other architecture. The triangular pediment is decorated with the Royal Sun and the great staircase affords a fine view over the square. The building is home to **La Métaphore** theatre.

Around the *grand-place*, **Nos 9 and 11** are reconstructions of pastiches from François Watteau paintings on view in the Hospice-Comtesse gallery. The **Fuet du Nord ❽** bookshop claims to be the biggest bookshop in the world. The **hôtel Bellevue ❾** is built on the site of the former *hôtel Bourbon* of 1765. From the square, walk into *rue du Palais-Rihour* and note the two rows of houses facing one another. The even numbers date from 1687, the work of Carpentier, master mason; above the arcaded sandstone ground floor, piers and vertical pilasters are decorated

Lille: Hospice-Comtesse, the kitchen (late 17th century)

with helmeted, plumed heads; below are sculpted medallions with garlands and bunches of fruit. The *vernicule* bays are surmounted by a curved pediment on the first floor. Restoration work has restored these details to their original glory. Opposite, the odd numbers date from 1733; these more sombre white stone façades bear witness to French influence.

A fountain in the shape of a pyramid plays over the metro station which is under the **place Rihour ❿**. The **palais Rihour ⓫** was home to the Chapter of the Golden Fleece, and welcomed Charles Quint in 1561, Henry VIII of England, and the archdukes Albert and Isabelle on their visit to Lille in 1600. In 1664 the palace was sold by Philippe IV to the magistrate of Lille. The first elected local authority had its headquarters here in 1790. From 1847 to 1859, the authority built a new Italian Renaissance-style town hall on this site; it was burnt down in 1916, and only the Duc Philippe le Bon staircase and chapel survived. The octagonal tower called the **tour de la Garde des joyaux**, is in attractive brick with a spiral staircase. The imposing *escalier d'honneur* staircase leads to the **palais Rihour**. Saved from demolition in 1857, this was relocated near the chapel. Notice the chevet wall with its diamond-shaped, glazed black bricks in the form of the cross of Saint-André (patron of

the house of Burgundy); simple decorative weather mouldings run along above the windows. While on the other side, finialled ogee arches, pinnacled buttresses and gables and tri-lobed stone-mullioned windows represent many of the decorative features of Gothic architecture. Inside, the guard-room, the former low chapel, is separated into two naves by three octagonal pillars; bevelled capitals support an arched vault. The only relief to the space is a great fireplace ornamented with a floral frieze and benches built into the window casing. The great staircase leads to the **salle du Conclave**, or former high chapel, given this name in 1664 when it was used as a counsel room for the magistrate. It was once decorated with carved wood and tapestries. The door leading to the sacristy is surmounted with a finialled arch and the letter E in Gothic script in honour of Elisabeth of Portugal, the third wife of Philippe le Bon. The liernes and tiercerons of the sacristy are reminiscent of those of the *escalier d'honneur*. The stained glass was added at the end of the 19th century and came from a Gothic church close to Lille. The wooden staircase leads to the Duchess oratory. A hagioscope allows a view of the chapel without oneself being seen.

Return to the *grand-place* where the market stood in the Middle Ages and then into: ⓬ **rue Esquernoise:** at the be-

ginning of the street, notice the **maison du Fourreur** or furrier's house, and its neighbour at the sign of the Capon. The façades of **Nos 4** and **6** are decorated with elegant figures who, depending on whether they belong to the same owner or not, kiss or turn their backs on one another. In **rue Saint-Etienne ⓭** is the beautiful Renaissance **hôtel Beaurepaire** (1572). In *rue de la Bourse*, notice the façades of **Nos 1, 3, 5, 15, 17, 19** and **23**, a row of typical 17th-century Lille dwellings. Turning into **rue Lepelletier ⓮** a lovely grouping of restored 17th-century houses has sculptures of children and grimacing masks high up on the first floor. Next is **rue Grande-Chaussée ⓯** one of Lille's oldest streets which once joined the *castrum* or Roman fortress to the commercial district of the town. Many of the houses here are 17th and 18th century. In **rue des Chats-Bossus ⓰** (Humped cats street!), the former tanners' quarter, the façade of the **Huîtrière** catches the eye with its mosaic of fish and shellfish. The little **place des Patiniers ⓱** is bordered with old houses; notice the windows of **Nos 20** and **22**, with arched drip rails and diamond-cut stones. This type of house was common in Lille during the 17th century when they replaced the wooden houses that were banned in the fight against fire. In **place du Lion-d'Or ⓲**, built on the site of the feudal mound, **No 15**, **la maison des Poissonniers** (1764), has handsome vaulted brick cellars. On the corner of **place des Bettigniers ⓳** and *avenue du Peuple-Belge* stands **la maison Gilles de Boë** (1636). This beautiful residence of a wealthy wax-chandler is an example of Low Countries second Renaissance baroque. The ground floor has restrained, flattened arches. The first floor has harmonious if liberally ornamented rectangular bays: heavily reliefed cornices (depicting the Vieille Bourse) which scarcely leave room for the additional brickwork 'tapestries'.

La rue de la Monnaie ⓴ is one of the loveliest of Lille's old streets; its name derives from the former *hôtel des monnaies*, a mint built in 1685 on the instructions of Louis XIV. Formerly *rue Saint-Pierre*, in the 11th century, it crossed the fortress from east to west; the houses on the even numbered side of the street were built before 1695. On the left, **Nos 3** to **31** form a handsome 17th-century group; **No 3** has an alambic mortar (apothicary sign); then some restored façades decorated with palms, ears of wheat, dolphins … **No 15** has beautiful interior beams; between **Nos 31** and **33**, a passage runs down towards the **de la Treille cathedral**, Bouillet's imitation-Gothic work (1880); **No 8** is decorated with ears of wheat; the brick extending wall is on the site of the Saint-Pierre mill. Notice the date, 1649, on the Flanders and Burgundy coat of arms inscribed on the door (this piece of wall is all that remains of the mill). Beneath this vault, the Cirque canal once flowed, tumbling at this point into the lower River Deûle. A statue of Achille Liénart can be seen near the hospice medical garden.

If you follow the *passage de la Treille* **20** you come to **Notre-Dame-de-la-Treille cathedral 21** this colossal, Gothic pastiche basilica-cathedral is as yet unfinished; erected in 1854 on the site of the mound *motte Madame* upon which the earlier château de Buc – legendary cradle from which Lille grew – stood. Plans for the building of this cathedral were published far and wide throughout Europe in 1854 and, of the 40 proposals submitted, those of regional architects Lercy and Martin were successful. Wanting to build the ultimate Gothic cathedral, they produced a synthesis of all the submitted designs. The first stone was laid on 9 June 1853; numerous problems impeded the project's completion, in spite of the efforts of Cardinal Liénart after the Second World War. The neo-Gothic cathedral is built as a basilica in the form of a Latin cross 145 yards long by 28 yards wide. The chevet or eastern end of the choir is crowned

Lille: Goya, les Jeunes *(palais des Beaux-Arts)*

by archangel Gabriel, the north portal is dedicated to Saint Joseph and the south portal to Saint Aubert. The height of the nave takes the breath away. The **musée d'art religieux 22** in the centre of the cathedral, has old masters, statues, and 12th–20th-century Italian relics, some brought here from ruined or deconsecrated churches, or donated by collectors.

• **Musée diocésain d'art religieux** Crypte de la cathédrale, Notre-Dame-de-la-Treille, tel: 20.72.53.61 and 20.55.28.72. Open Saturday 4–5pm and, by arrangement, the first Sunday of the month 11am–noon (the collection of liturgical ornaments can be viewed by arrangement, tel: 20.31.63.80).

On the other side of *rue de la Monnaie*, go through the entrance porch of the **Hospice-Comtesse**, one of Lille's most interesting buildings. Founded in 1237 by Jeanne de Constantinople, Countess of Flanders, it was one of Lille's biggest and best equipped hospitals up to the time of the Revolution;

becoming a hospice in the 19th century, it remained in service until 1939. The original buildings were destroyed by fire in 1468, the current building being constructed from the 15th to the 18th century. The side of the building that faces the street consists of properties that are rented out for commercial use, and these back on to the hospice. Their ground floor has ornate arches, with decorative drip stones running along under first floor windows. The building style belongs to the first 30 years of the 17th century. The 1649 portal is vast. As you walk along the passageway towards the courtyard, notice the ribbed brick vaults and white stone *pendentives*. The courtyard is lined by the long building of the **salle des Malades** or sick room (15th century); the elevation is simple, relieved by broken window arches and a moulded cornice. The community buildings are on two levels; the ground floor is of the same period as the *salle des Malades* and its façade reproduces the elements used in the *palais Rihour*. The decorative motifs are in brick; weather mouldings and other elements in stone. Braced bays are topped by flattened arches, alternately in brick and stone. After the fire of 1648, the *Hospice-Comtesse* was rebuilt and its first floor is in a later idiom. The wing running parallel to the *rue de la Monnaie* dates from 1649, and is topped by a square tower above the portal. The Hospice-Comtesse is today a museum, as interesting for its architecture and historical background as for its collections. Visitors to the **salle des Malades** find themselves in a vast space, 130 feet in length with wood-panelled vaulting. Windows with broken arches punctuate the white stone walls. Two beautiful tapestries decorate the rear wall: Baudouin IX, his wife and daughters Jeanne and Marguerite and Jeanne de Constantinople with her husbands Ferrand du Portugal and Thomas de Savoie (sketches by Arnould de Vuez, dated 1703 and interpreted by the Lille studio of Guillaume Werniers). The chapel was destroyed by fire in 1652 and rebuilt in the 18th century; a rood-screen separates it from the *salle des Malades*. Inside the chapel, there is an altar painting by Arnould de Vuez, *Présentation de la Vierge au temple*, Ghent statues (1652): Saint Joseph, Christ, Saint Anne, The Virgin. A plaque recalls that, in 1745, officers wounded at Fontenoy were cared for at the hospice. The vault was decorated by a former orphan from the hospice in 1853; the coat of arms recalls the principal benefactors of the hospice since the time of its foundations. The museum extends to the community buildings, where there is furniture, china collections, sculptures, pieces of gold and silver plate, as well as Flemish and Dutch paintings, including some by Watteau. In the part of the building leading to the second courtyard is the Hel Collection of musical instruments. The museum is currently undergoing renovation but, in the very near future, will house displays identified under the themes of Lille, the Nord *département* and the Netherlands.

• **Musée de l'Hospice-Comtesse** 32 rue de la Monnaie, tel: 20.49.50.90. Open daily, except Tuesday, 10am–12.30pm and 2–6pm.

Going north, along *rue Princesse*, you come to **No 9**, the **birthplace of General de Gaulle**, now a museum. Little has changed since the day on 22 November 1890 when the future general was born here. His mother, Jeanne Maillot, was the daughter of a tulle manufacturer who had his workshop in the same house, and his father, Henri de Gaulle, was a teacher. The building is typical of the Lille 19th-century, bourgeois home. A drawing room, diningroom, kitchen and verandah on the ground floor and, on the first floor, the bedroom where Charles de Gaulle was born. In the right-hand part of the house lived Gustave de Corbie, Charles' godfather. The museum presents a retrospective of the life of the great man, through photographs and various artefacts (including the Saint-Cyrien sword) as well as the famous car in which Charles de Gaulle and his wife escaped an attempt on their lives at Petit-Clamart.

• **Musée Charles-de-Gaulle** 9 rue Princesse, tel: 20.31.96.03. Open daily, except Monday and Tuesday, 10am–noon and 2–5pm.

Charles de Gaulle

Lille: Bourdelle, Penelope *(palais des Beaux-Arts)*

La citadelle, that 'five-pointed star come down to earth', lies beyond the bridge which spans the River Deûle. It is reached via the lovely **porte Royale** (1670) which bears a Latin inscription in praise of Louis XIV and Lille. This perfectly-preserved piece of military architecture was the work of Lille architect Simon Vollant, to a design by Vauban. Inside its walls can be seen all the elements of the contemporary military town: streets, bakery, chapel, Governor's house ... Walking round the citadel, along the line of its trenches and fortifications, you come to the **porte Dauphine**. Nearby are the fringes of Deûle Wood, which in turn extend into Boulogne Wood with its playground and little zoo. In the Vauban garden, a monument recalls the Lille poet Albert Samain.

• **Citadelle Vauban** Tours Sundays April to October, organised by the tourist office. Tel: 20.30.81.00.

In the 19th century, the town benefited from several large-scale construction projects, including the building of the main roads (1868), *Faidherbe*, the *Liberté* and *Carnot* boulevards, the station façade in 1867 (this was in fact taken from the old Paris Gare du Nord). One of

Lille's biggest 19th-century building programmes was the joint construction of the *préfecture* council offices in 1870, the central Post Office or *grande poste* and the **palais des Beaux-Arts** or art gallery (1885), by Bérard and Delmas. Built 20 years after the Second Empire, the *palais* is an expression of Napoleonic triumphalism. The *palais des Beaux-Arts* is the home of the biggest museum in the Nord and ranks as the country's second museum (after the Louvre) in terms of the wealth of its collections. It has been closed for several years, in order to upgrade its exhibition rooms, and the official re-opening is scheduled for early 1995.

• **Palais des Beaux-Arts** place de la République, tel: 20.57.01.84. Open daily (except Tuesday) 10am–6pm.

The **musée d'histoire naturelle,** or natural history museum, was established in 1921 by the Lille Society of Science, Agriculture and Arts, and has some rare and wide-ranging geological and zoological exhibits, which place it among the top French museums. A planned renovation programme will include additional exhibits.

• **Musée d'histoire naturelle et de géologie** 19 rue de Bruxelles, tel: 20.53.38.46. Open daily, except Tuesday and Saturday, 9am–noon and 2–5pm, Sunday 10am–5pm.

LUMBRES
62380 • D-3 • 58 km

Hotel
Auberge du Moulin de Mombreux ★★★★
route de Bayeughem
Tel: 21.39.13.13

Lumbres has a lovely 18-hole golf course set in undulating countryside (Aa Saint-Omer Golf Club, tel: 21.38.59.90) and facilities for pony-trekking (Ferme équestre, tel: 21.93.60.69). At nearby Longuenesse, the little flying club offers trial flights (tel: 21.38.25.42). And last but not least, at Dennebroueucq's **moulin de la Tour**, there are amusements and picnic/restaurant facilities for all the family, and dancing to the accompaniment of an organ (tel: 21.95.11.39).

MAROILLES
59550 • G-9 • 177 km

Tourist information
rue des Juifs
Tel: 27.84.74.18

"Ville ne suis, bourg ne daigne.
Suis Maroilles, reine des prés."
"Neither town nor market town
would I call myself
I am Maroilles, queen of the
meadows."

Set among mixed wood and pastureland, Maroilles is known throughout France for its cheese. Its history is closely linked to the Benedictine abbey, founded in the 7th century by the Comte Chanebert and whose first abbot was Humbert. After a propitious beginning, the abbey was to endure repeated invasion, war and destruction up to the 15th century. The abbey enjoyed renewed vigour in the 18th century, and wealth too, giving rise to countless legal disputes between the landowning monks and their neighbours. On 29 July 1789, the people of Taisnières pillaged the abbey and this was, unfortunately, the final blow and end to the abbey.

L'abbaye de Maroilles The square has a pretty garden, at the far end of which is a stone pillar recalling the creation of Maroilles cheese by the monks of the celebrated abbey. This cheese – which was highly prized by the King of France – is on sale from various village outlets, as posters here and there indicate. To the right of this little memorial, and over the other side of the road, stand the remains of the abbey. On the corner of the little street, the **Frère Potier** house has just been restored; inside, it has local archaeological artefacts and its walls are encrusted with heraldic stones from the abbey, one of these dated 1585. An alley leads to the vast 17th–18th-century, red-brick-on-stone **logis des Hôtes residence**, soberly beautiful with its roof of slate. Continuing along the path, you will see a mill down to the left side and, a little further on, the **tithe barn** where the inhabitants' tithes were stored: thick brick walls with 17th-century Baroque stone window surrounds and a restored roof making it among the finest examples of local agricultural architecture. Retracing your steps to the square, take a look at the monastery buildings: stables, dairy . . . and the (1704) **town hall** housed in the former magistrates' court. Nearby, houses still bear the abbey's coat of arms, although many others were knocked down during the Revolution.

The church was built between 1729 and 1738; the porch on either side of the tower is decorated with gracious *volutes* or scroll-like decorations. Behind the apse is a cross-and-

Lille: the arsenal inside Vauban citadel

mitre blazon (1768). The organ retains a remarkably good tone; beneath is a portrait of the last abbot of Maroilles. The great altar is decorated with glass ornaments and a pivoting marble and wood tabernacle. The two naves are decorated with busts and paintings – the latter including *Saint Catherine de Sienne*, by Philippe de Champaigne, Jansenist painter from Port-Royal.

As you leave in the direction of Avesnes-sur-Helpe, notice – as you pass under the triumphal arch – a replica of the abbey gate that was erected in 1807 to celebrate the Napoleonic victories.

MAUBEUGE
59600 · F-9 · 200 km

Tourist information
porte de Bavay
Tel: 27.62.11.93

Hotels
Grand Hôtel **
1 porte de Paris
Tel: 27.64.63.16
Resthôtel Primevère **
avenue Jean-Jaurès
Tel: 27.62.15.00
Grill Campanile **
route de Valenciennes
Tel: 27.64.00.91
Shakespeare **
3 rue du Commerce
Tel: 27.65.14.14

Restaurant
L'Abattoir
46 bd de l'Europe
Tel: 27.64.64.14

Nearby
Auberge de l'Hermitage
RN 2 Beaufort (6km)
Tel: 27.67.89.59

Following the Treaties of Nimègue in 1678, Vauban enclosed Maubeuge with fortifications including seven bastions, wide ditches and a series of outer defences. Visit the **porte de Mons**, built in 1682 and the only survivor of the town's four gates: an imposing structure. A Latin inscription celebrates the glory of the king. Beneath the vault, and on either side, are the mounted insignias of Colonel Schouller and General Fournier who defended Maubeuge in 1814 and 1914, respectively. Note the impressive mechanism of the drawbridge, restored by the Vauban Association in 1978; here and there about the gate, a few vestiges of the Vauban fortifications. Beyond and looking out towards the countryside is a mansarded guard-house; then further on, the north face of the ramparts can be seen from the glacis. The Vauban Association has been undertaking the restoration of the area around the ramparts and the *porte de Mons* since 1972.

The **béguinage des cantuaines** convent is in *rue Sculfort* (east of *place Verte* and *rue de la Croix*). Push open the convent door to see the modest, flower-decked little houses inside; the chapel that stands in the middle of the courtyard has a Gothic choir (1562). This was founded in the 16th century by Jean Gyppus, canon of Maubeuge.

The **church of Saints-Pierre-et-Paul** (1955) is the work of the architect Lurçat, a modern edifice flanked by a tall, square, concrete tower and glass flagstones. The porch is decorated with a Murano enamel mosaic by ceramist Schmidt-Chevalier, from drawings by the architect. In the tower, 28 bells, made at the foundery in Colmar, are rung in concerts every first Sunday of the month and Saints' Days at midday). The treasure of Sainte-Aldegonde is on permanent display in a chapel in the left arm of the transept. The shrine of the veil of Sainte-Aldegonde is in gilded silver (a masterpiece of French 15th-century goldsmith craft).

The **zoo** was established in 1955 and allows animals considerable freedom of movement within an environment adapted to meet their needs and habits. The zoo farm opened in 1980 and has both small and large animals.

Olhain: the castle

• **Parc zoologique** place de l'Hôtel-de-Ville. Open 15 February to 30 April and 1 September to 30 November, 1.30–5.30pm; 1 May to 30 June, 10am–6pm; 1 July to 31 August, 10am–7pm. Tel: 27.65.15.73.

MONTREUIL-SUR-MER
62170 • E-2 • 70 km

Tourist information
place Darnétal
Tel: 21.06.04.27

Canoes
4 rue du Moulin des Orphelins
Tel: 21.06.20.16

Hotels
Château de Montreuil ★★★★
4 chaussées des Capucines
Tel: 21.81.53.04
de France ★★
rue Coquempot
Tel: 21.06.05.36
des Remparts ★★
46 place Général-de-Gaulle
Tel: 21.06.08.65
Les Hauts de Montreuil ★★
21 rue P Ledent
Tel: 21.81.95.92

Nearby
Auberge de la Grenouillère
La Madeleine-sous-Montreuil
(2.5km)
Tel: 21.06.07.22

Montreuil-sur-Mer still has the look of a typical northern French town, with cobbled streets and small, lime-washed houses beneath tiled roofs. The town has plenty of interesting buildings and monuments to offer, particularly its fortifications: 13th–17th-century **ramparts** and rampart walk beneath the elms with a view over the Canche and Course valley; 12th–16th-century **citadel**, *la tour de la reine Berthe*, and *la tour Blanche* (English guided tours); the old walls of the Garenne warren, *fontaine des Clercs* (beneath the citadel walls) and the courtyard of the old cloister of Sainte-Austreberthe's Monastery.

• **Fortifications** Open all year, except October and Tuesdays, 9am–noon and 2–6pm. Tel: 21.06.10.83. Guided tours on request at the town hall.

In the square **place Général de Gaulle,** stands a statue of Field Marshal Haig on horseback. The collegiate **church of Saint-Saulve** (12th–16th century) houses precious treasures secured in a glass case high over the left lateral nave: the relics and cross of Sainte Austreberthe.

NAOURS
80260 • G-4 • 134 km

Rediscovered in 1887 by the Abbot Darnicourt, **les grottes de Naours** caves are an unusual example of the many underground hideaways tunnelled out when invasion threatened. Entirely man-made, mostly 110 feet deep, some thirty 6-ft-high galleries total a length of over one mile. The earliest of the caves date from the Barbarian invasions of the 3rd–5th centuries, others from the Norman invasions of the 9th century. Wall graffiti recall what life was like in these underground shelters. Cells with doors were used by family groups, and rings in the walls attest to the presence of animals. Even a chapel and three naves are identifiable, with dates embracing the period from 1340 to 1792. The Abbot Darnicourt retrieved many artefacts from the caves but these were sadly lost during the course of the two World Wars; the abbot gave some of the galleries the names of village streets. Open to the public since 1949, these caves are an important part of the history of Picardy, and are complemented by a small **museum** of traditional Picardian craft – basket-making, weaving, shepherding, etc. Nearby, on Guet hill, two wooden **mills** (one an oil mill, one flour) dominate the town and the valley of Naours.

• **Grotte de Naours** Tel: 22.93.71.78. Open 1 April to 30 September daily 8.30am–noon and 1.30–6.30pm; in October, November, February and March 11am–noon and 2–5pm; closed 15 November to 31 January. English spoken.

OLHAIN
62150 • E-5 • 98 km

Tourist information
62150 Houdain
Tel: 21.65.86.66

9-hole golf course
Golf du parc d'Olhain
Tel: 21.27.91.79

Restaurant
Auberge du Donjon
place du Château
Tel: 21.27.93.76

In a wooded area adjoining the national forest of the Artois hills, a **park** offers children's amusements and leisure activities (tennis, mini-golf, cross-country skiing, swimming pool, etc) as well as restaurant facilities (tel: 21.27.91.79).

The **château d'Olhain** has survived from distant medieval times, preserved in its original condition – complete with farmyard – an unviolated example of the plains castle fortress. Its towers rise up out of the water in a peaceful setting 12 miles from Arras.

• **Château d'Olhain**, tel: 21.27.94.76. Open 1 April to 30 October, Sunday and public holidays 3–6.30pm; Saturday during school holidays 3–6.30pm and by arrangement.

PÉRONNE
80200 • H-6 • 159 km

Tourist information
31 rue Saint-Fursy
Tel: 22.84.42.38

Hotels
Hostellerie des remparts ★★
23 rue Beaubois
Tel: 22.84.01.22
Le Saint-Claude ★★
42 place Louis-Daudré
Tel: 22.84.46.00

Restaurant
Auberge la Quenouille
4 avenue des Australiens
Tel: 22.84.00.62

Established on the upper Somme in the Merovingian era, Péronne has a long history as a fortress town. Of its 9th-century fortifications nothing remains but the **porte de Bretagne** gate. In the First World War, the town was occupied from 1914 onwards and experienced considerable military activity, most notably during the Battle of the Somme, before being evacuated by the Germans in 1917. In 1986, a decision was taken to create a First World War memorial museum, **l'Historial de la Grande Guerre**, in the château de Péronne, and this opened in 1992. The exhibition examines anew the first ever world-wide conflict, the First World War, not just from the standpoint of Franco-German confrontation, but from a global standpoint, the Somme was, in fact, the stage upon which 35 countries acted out their conflicts. The exhibition also illustrates the extraordinary death-blow that the war dealt to the established pattern of rural life, changed irrevocably by the mechanisation and new technology evolved by the military. The museum conveys this message via a multi-media

Rambures: the castle

approach, supplemented by exploratory trails and memorial walks to battle sites.

• **Historial de Péronne** place du Château, tel: 22.83.14.18. Open 19 January to 30 April and 1 October to 19 December daily, except Monday, 10am–5.30pm; 1 May to 30 September daily 10am–6pm.

LE QUESNOY
59530 • F-8 • 180 km

Tourist and craft information
1 rue Maréchal-Joffre
Tel: 27.49.05.28

Baudoin IV, Count of Hainaut, built a castle at Quesnoy from 1150 onwards, and went on to add fortifications that made it one of the region's premier fortress towns.

In 1477, Louis XI took possession of the town, later rebuilt by Charles Quint in 1525. Conquered by Turenne in 1659, Le Quesnoy became French fol-

lowing the Treaty of the Pyrenees. Under Vauban's direction, the fortifications were modernised in 1686. During the Revolution, General Shérer liberated the town from Austrian occupation. During the First World War, New Zealand soldiers scaled the fortifications with ladders to liberate the town. Le Quesnoy's surrounding countryside is very varied. Three miles to the east is the **Forest of Mormal**, the north's biggest forest extending over more than 22,000 acres; to the south is the mixed woodland and pastureland of the Avesnois valley, while to the west and north are the fertile soils of the Hainaut sloping down to the Escaut.

The narrow streets of the fortified town are lined with beautiful old red-brick houses, their doors and windows framed in the blue stone typical of the Avesnois region. The elegant **town hall** was built in 1700 by Jacques Nicolas, and is dominated by a 48-bell belfry (tel: 27.49.12.16, visits by arrangement). Inside, the town hall has an impressive marble and wrought-iron staircase. At the top on the first floor is a New Zealand tribal sculpture, *Teko Teko maori,* in recognition of New Zealand's part in Le Quesnoy's First World War fortunes.

Rue Thiers is home to a flamboyant little chapel, **la chapelle des Soeurs-Noires**, built in 1440 within the hospital, and now open to the public.

The Vauban fortifications
Completed between 1668 and 1673, the Vauban fortifications encircle the town in an irregular octogan 2,000 yards in length and 1,200 yards wide; these are low fortifications with bastions. Before the Revolution, the addition of water-filling ditches added to their effectiveness. A system of sluices enabled these to be easily emptied of, or filled with, water.

• **Maison du tourisme et de l'artisanat** 1 rue Maréchal-Joffre, tel: 27.49.05.28. Guided tours for groups by written arrangement with the tourist office, *see above*. In July and

August, Sunday afternoon visits for individuals on request. Tour lasts 1 hour 30 minutes on foot, 1 hour by bus.

Alternatively, visit the **jardin néo-zélandais**, the New Zealand Garden, built at the foot of the wall scaled by New Zealand soldiers on 4 November 1918. Access is via a path to the left of the **porte de Cambrai** gate. A bas-relief commemorates the heroism of the men who came from the other side of the globe to help liberate France.

RAMBURES
80140 • H-2 • 132 km

Nearby
Auberge Picarde **★★**
place de la Gare
Chepy (15km)
Tel: 22.26.20.78

The site of a town since 1058, Rambures' **castle** was built by David de Rambures in 1412. The construction of the present castle was completed in 1470 and was the first brick-and-stone castle to be built in France. In the 15th century, the Rambures were powerful lords who reigned over Ponthieu; the most illustrious member of the clan, Charles de Rambures, received Henri IV here on his way through Picardy to the Battle of Arques, and went on to save his life at Ivry in 1590. In recogition of which favour, Louis XIII saved the castle from the dismantling which Richelieu ordered for all feudal fortresses. In 1676, the configuration of the entrance was changed and other buildings added. Having survived the vicissitudes of the Revolution, the castle was accorded historic monument status in 1840. A programme of restoration was undertaken in 1971, and the castle is now open to the public. It is the most complete example of 15th-century military architecture in Picardy. Squat in appearance, it consists of four towers linked at regular intervals by rounded walls, and was designed to favour the maximum use of artillery: 10–20-feet-high walls with canon breaks; built in brick to be more resistant to

bombardment than stone; convex exterior walls.

The courtyard looks much as it must have looked five centuries ago; a second drawbridge protects the access to the main part of the fortress; wide ramps lead to vast vaulted cellars that could take an entire garrison under attack – military equipment, citizens and animals included. A series of rooms interconnect, with the exception of the north-west tower which served as a prison or dungeon. In the 16th and 17th centuries, these rooms were modified and furnished for ordinary use as a guard-room with Louis XIII ceiling and 16th- and 17th-century chests and furniture; a neo-Gothic dining-room with wood-carving and lit by two stained glass windows; the king's bedroom (known as the *chambre du Roy Henri IV*); the great salon with ornate wood carvings, painted stucco work and furnishings from several eras; the great 18th-century wooden staircase leading to the archers' and crossbow-men's parapet.

Above the great salon is the library and, above this, the alcoved, 18th-century *chambre romantique*.

The castle is set in lovely grounds which also have an arboretum: 30 different species of tree, white mulberries (the only ones in northern France), giant sequoias 200 years old), lime trees, conifers, chestnuts … Also in the grounds is a little chapel. Exhibitions, displays of local crafts, cider-making, etc complete the castle's attractions.

• **Château de Rambures** Tel: 22.25.10.93. Open 1 March to 31 October daily, except Wednesday, 10am–noon and 2–6pm; 1 November to 28 February, Sunday and public holidays 2–5pm.

ROUBAIX
59100 • D-7 • 128 km

Tourist information
Eurotéléport
78 boulevard Général-Leclerc
Tel: 20.65.31.90

Hotels
Grand Hôtel Mercure **★★★**
22 avenue Jean-Baptiste-Lebas
Tel: 20.73.40.00
Ibis **★★**
boulevard Général-Leclerc
Tel: 20.45.00.00
Campanile **★★**
avenue des Nations-Unies
Tel: 20.70.19.20.
Au Coq Hardi **★★**
1 place de la Gare
Tel: 20.70.82.06

Restaurants
Le Caribou
8 rue Mimerel
Tel: 20.70.87.08
Chez Charly
127 avenue J B Lebas
Tel: 20.70.78.58

Nearby
Auberge de la Marmotte
5 rue J B Lebas
Lys-lez-Lannoy (5 km)
Tel: 20.75.30.95

Since the 9th century, Roubaix has been much like the seat of a feudal manor, maintaining legal and fiscal jurisdiction over an otherwise disparate scattering of small farms. The lords of the manor who lived there during the 11th to 13th centuries were part of the entourage of the counts of Flanders, one of the most celebrated of these being Jean III de Roubaix (1368–1449), adviser and chamberlain to the Duke of Burgundy, Philippe Le Bon. He was one of the first Knights of the Golden Fleece and was granted leave to create a magistrates' court within his see. When Jean II's son obtained a manufacturing permit from Charles le Témeraire in 1469 (a privilege usually reserved for towns such as Lille), the inhabitants of Roubaix were able to begin to manufacture their own goods. In 1677, the victory of the French over the Spanish gave rise to unification of France and French-speaking Flanders, which included Lille and Roubaix. Fire destroyed a part of the town in 1684 and, in 1724, the land passed to the Rohan family, with whom it stayed until the Revolution. In the 19th century, the textile trade enjoyed a tremendous spurt of growth; the town's population soared from 8,000 in 1800 to 25,000 in 1850 and to 120,000 in 1913, with a total of 200 factories in the year 1914. Such intensive industrial activity inevitably changed the face of the town and the surrounding countryside, where chimneys and factory buildings still dominate. But, since 1960, the town has been hard hit by the textile crisis and the unemployment rate in Roubaix is extremely high. Nearly 20% of the population are immigrants. Roubaix and its suburbs are, however, home to the head offices of more companies than anywhere else in the region: a mail order capital with the La Redoute company producing 140,000 parcels daily, not to mention Damart. The Industrial Revolution brought factories and worker housing to the town centres. Today, the factories are built on the outskirts of the towns and, bit by bit, the town centres take on a different look . . . Meanwhile, Roubaix has become a university town with more than 8,000 students. The **Motte-Bossut mill**, an earlier flower in the crown of Roubaix's industrial base, has been converted into a data store and Eurotéléport.

Le Parc Barbieux Coming from Lille, the visitor drives alongside the magnificent Barbieux park, landscaped in 1857 by Georges Hautmont. It extends along the valley for almost a mile, covering an area of over 80 acres. The Roubaix canal should have passed through at this point in an embankment but, because of practical difficulties with the grade of the slopes, the authorities found an alternative solution in the creation of this lovely park, with its delightful string of little lakes. Roubaix can feel justly proud of its green spaces, which extend to 275 acres and make the town the eighth in the *espaces vertes* league of French towns. The *boulevard Général-de-Gaulle* leads into the town centre. Once lined with imposing and impressive houses, a few turn-of-the-century houses remain: of note are **No 84** – notice the two greyhounds at the window; **No 64**, a

house built by the Motte family and now part of the Chamber of Commerce; **the corner of rue Charles-Quint** – Drapers' Row, eclectic in style.

On *boulevard Leclerc* is the famous **Motte-Bossut**, a typical town centre factory built in 1853 with crenellated towers (1889–1891) and combining features of the British prototype (Samuel Lister's Manningham Mills at Bradford) with elements frequently found in Lille. This, the biggest mill, employed several hundred workers. It closed in 1981. Today, it houses the tourist office, an international centre for communications and the Eurotéléport. But chiefly responsible for its distinctive transformation, by the architect Sarfati, was the creation here of the *Centre régional des archives du monde du travail*, inaugurated in 1993.

• **Centre régional des archives du monde du travail** 78 bis, boulevard Leclerc. Lecture hall open Monday to Friday 9.30am–2pm; exhibition hall Monday to Friday 3–7pm (group visits by arrangement). Tel: 20.65.38.00.

Via the *rue de la Sagesse*, you come to the main square where one of Roubaix's rare early buildings can still be seen, the **church of Saint-Martin**. This Gothic church has undergone many alterations and was enlarged in the 19th century. The tower dates from 1471, which date is written in iron anchors at its summit; over the porch are the arms of the House of Roubaix; the bell-tower encloses 38 bells. Inside, a beautiful 16th-century altarpiece depicts the life of Saint-Jean-Baptiste; the baptismal fonts are 16th century and one of the tombstones is consecrated to Jacques de Luxembourg, son of Isabeau de Roubaix (in blue marble, 1472).

Opposite the church is the **hotel de ville**, or town hall, the work of the architect Laloux (1911). Six carved tablets illustrate different aspects of textile production. Inside, a monumental staircase leads to some stunning rooms: the town council

room, the marriages room, the banqueting room . . . decorated with frescoes by Jean-Jacques Weerts.

The old **bourse de la laine** or wool exchange is serving as a museum until the new one, being set up in what was the swimming pool, is ready. The more important pieces of the *musée d'art et d'industrie* are displayed here in rotation, and the majority of these deal with Roubaix's history as presented through its urban architecture and its collection of paintings and decorative art.

• **Musée d'art et d'industrie** hôtel de ville, BP 737, tel: 20.66.46.93. Open daily, except Monday, 1–6pm.

RUE

80120 · F-2 · 98 km

Tourist information
54 rue porte-de-Bécray
Tel: 22.25.69.94

Hotel
Le Lion d'Or **
5 rue de la Barrière
Tel: 22.25.74.18

This former port is now at the heart of the vast Marquenterre nature reserve and leisure park (Aquaclub, Fort-Mahon beaches . . .). The English and French fought over Rue throughout the Middle Ages. The town walls were dismantled at the end of the 17th century, but there are still several fine old buildings to see. The base of the **belfry** is 15th century; built on top of the ruins of its predecessor, it affords access to the parapet from which there is a lovely view. On the ground floor, murals by Siffait de Moncourt decorate the museum dedicated to the aviation pioneers, the Caudron brothers. (Open 1 April to 20 September, except Sunday and public holiday afternoons, 10am–noon and 3–6pm. Tel: 22.25.75.37.)

See also **la chapelle de l'hospice**, the hospice chapel built in the 16th century, with wood vaulting. This is an excellent example of Flamboyant Gothic, with delicate ornamentation. The exterior portal depicting The Passion suffered damage during the Revolution. There are 15th- and 16th-century statues and a stone altarpiece.

• **Chapelle de l'Hospice** Tel: 22.25.00.43. Open 1 July to 31 August daily 9am–noon and 2–6pm.

La chapelle du Saint-Esprit is a magnificent example of 15th- and 16th-century Flamboyant Gothic art. The crowns of the sculpted façade are exceptionally fine. A stopping point on the road to Compostella, the chapel was built with donations from wealthy French and foreign benefactors.

• **Chapelle du Saint-Esprit** hôtel de ville. Open 1 May to 30 September daily 10am–6pm; 1 July to 31 August daily, with guided tours available, 9am–noon and 2–6pm.

LES RUES-DES-VIGNES
59258 • G-7 • 159 km

Tourist information
Town hall
rue Haute
Tel: 27.78.92.16

The **archéosite archaeological exhibition** in the very heart of Rues-des-Vignes portrays the everyday life of the people who lived here many hundred years ago, with reconstructions including the workshops of the potter, the spinner, the bronze founder and the thatcher.

• **L'archéosite** 62 rue Haute. Tel: 27.78.99.42. Open daily March to November 9.30am–6.30pm (8pm in summer).

Vaucelles Abbey This belonged to the Cistercians who founded numerous religious communities both in France and in other countries. In 1131, local lord of the manor, Hugues d'Oisy, met Saint Bernard and offered him more than 6,000 acres of the forest of Ligescourt near the right bank of the River Escaut, on which to build a monastery, in return for the expiation of his sins. The name Ligescourt was changed to *Vallis Cellae* (monastery of the valley). During his time as abbot,

there were 103 monks, 13 novices and 130 converts. The church was consecrated on 21 May 1149 and is exceptional in not looking east, but north. The rapid growth of the community required the building of a second church, Europe's largest Cistercian church, measuring 150 yards in length, with a transept 70 yards wide. Villard de Honnecourt, born nearby at Honnecourt, would have directed the construction of this sumptuous abbey church. The plan of the choir appears in Villard's celebrated Album of Gothic architecture and decoration. The Revolution and the First World War damaged everything except the ground floor of a vast building that once joined the northern arm of the church transept, the walls of the abbey palace and some outbuildings, today part of a neighbouring farm.

Built in stone, as were all Cistercian monasteries, Vaucelles was a place of refuge for the poor. Up until the Revolution, the monastery undertook to feed 3,000 poor people and workers from the villages of Crèvecoeur, Lesdain, Bantouzelle and Banteux, every Easter, Pentecost, Assumption, All Saints Day and Christmas.

At the time of the Revolution, the church and the other buildings were sold off by the state for building material; the abbey church, built in 1760 and which also contained the library, was burnt by the Germans in 1917. Monk Dom Ruffin had assembled one of Europe's largest book collections here, numbering some 40,000 volumes. Now, all that remains is the still elegant stone façade of the church. Of the 18 miles of fortifications, only the 16th-century look-out turret remains, standing in splendid isolation on the plain one mile distant from the abbey site.

For nearly 20 years, the monastery underwent a rigorous restoration programme and, in 1988, was re-opened to the public. It stages various exhibitions and concerts each year. Visitors can view:

La salle des moines, the monks' room: pre-Gothic, used as a common room or scriptorium.

L'auditorium or *parloir*: the only room in which the monks and the prior could talk. Elsewhere, the rule was absolute silence. On the walls, two memorial stones are the sole survivors of Revolutionnary unrest and 1914–1918 German occupation. The choir stalls are from the Dames Bernardines chapel in Esquermes Abbey. Jewel in the monastery's crown is the **salle capitulaire**, the longest room of its sort in Europe (60 feet) with acoustics which are outstanding. Here, the monks met twice daily to hear the reading of *la Règle de Saint Benoît* and the exhortations of their abbot. Beneath its floor are buried the remains of most of the monastery's past abbots.

Passage sacré: where the various members of the community donned their different garbs as the bell sounded to call them to prayer. This is also the resting place for the monastery's first three abbots canonised by Pope Alexandre III in 1179.

L'église abbatiale, abbey church, begun in 1190, completed in 1235 by Henri de Dreux, archbishop of Reims: the biggest Cistercian church in Europe, bigger even than Notre-Dame de Paris, measuring 150 yards in length with a transept of 70 yards and a 26-yd-wide nave. Having survived the Revolution, it was demolished at the end of the 18th century to provide stone for other buildings. Recent excavations have revealed a tiled floor in good order, especially in what was the ambulatory.

• **Abbaye de Vaucelles** (12km from Cambrai, 30km from Valenciennes, 65km from Amiens; exit no 9 off A26 autoroute). Tel: 27.78.50.65 and 27.78.98.98. Open 1 March to 30 October daily, except Tuesday, 10am–noon and 2–5.30pm; Sunday and public holidays 3–6.30pm. Guided tours available or Laserphone system in English and French.

SAINT-AMAND-LES-EAUX

59230 • E-7 • 179 km

Tourist information
91 grand-place
Tel: 27.22.24.47

Hotels
Grand Hôtel de Paris **
33 grand-place
Tel: 27.48.21.00
Grand Hôtel Thermal **
1303 route de la Fontaine-Bouillon
Tel: 27.48.50.37

Restaurant
Auberge de la Forêt
92 route de Reims
Tel: 27.25.51.98

A spa since Roman times, the town owes its name to the bishop of Maestricht, Saint Amand, who founded a monastery here between 633 and 639. Monks cleared and began to cultivate the surrounding area, and established a study centre which became celebrated during the Carolingian renaissance. The first poem written in a Romance language, *la Cantilène de Sainte Eulalie*, was written here, as well as the first Germanic language poem, *le Rythmus Teutanicus*. Normans laid waste to the monastery and massacred the monks around the year 833. In the 10th century, the monk Hucbald broke new ground in the development of polyphonic music at St-Amand. In 1432, Jean de Gênes completed the *Catholica encyclopaedia* – of which the municipal library has one of only five copies.

La tour abbatiale, or abbey tower, dominates the town and is visible from a great distance. Sited in the main square, it was built between 1626 and 1640 on the orders of the Abbot du Bois. The 270-ft-high tower, flanked by two turrets, formed a sort of towered gateway to the abbey church. The ground floor foundations are in sandstone, the exterior stonework comes from Avesnes-le-Sec, while the aerial gallery is built of Tournai stone. The interior still retains parts of an old Roman tower. As the schematic cross-section illustrates, the tower up to the first floor of the vestibule consists of five parts representing the five orders: Tuscan, Doric, Ionic, Corinthian and Composite. On the second level, note the elegant perspective of the three-nave church. At the base of the third level, a frieze of interlaced letters imitating foliated scrolls spells out *sanctus*. At fourth- and fifth-floor level, columns frame "a vast circular space, supported by arches whose 10-ft midway span embraces a statue of God the Father sitting majestically on a throne of clouds with the globe of the world in his hands, in the act of benediction". In the undercroft, the abbey's weapons and those of its founder, Abbot Dubois, are stored, according to established custom. Two turrets rise from the fifth floor, together with an octagonal dome decorated with dragons to symbolise Saint Amand's domination over evil spirits. The stone vaulting of the ground floor is extremely beautiful. In the centre, a large circular opening allows for the ringing of the bells high up in the tower.

The **musée municipal**, municipal museum, occupies the first two floors of the tower; its collections include local ceramic production, as well as a selection of 16th- and 18th-century Flemish paintings and sculptures. Three hundred and sixty-five steps lead up to the clock mechanism, installed in the 17th century and currently closed for repairs. There is a half-hour daily carillon concert at noon.

• **Musée municipal** Tour abbatiale, grand-place. Open 1 April to 30 September daily, except Tuesday, 10am–12.30pm and 2–5pm; Saturday, Sunday and public holidays 10am–12.30pm and 3–6pm. Tel: 27.22.24.55.

From the town hall square, or Priory, you can walk along *rue Thiers* to the **church of Saint-Martin**, built in 1787 in Doric style. Inside, there is a *Mise au tombeau* attributed to Rubens and a painting of Madeleine washing the feet of Jesus at Veronese. The baptismal fonts date from the 16th century; the choir has oak stalls decorated with the arms of Abbot Honoré, taken from the abbey. The Saint-Benoît altar has a painting attributed to Rubens, The Flight from Egypt, while the Saint-Cyr altar is decorated with works by Jordaens: The Emmaü Pilgrims and Jesus on the Clouds. The pulpit is 18th-century rococo with a Renaissance-style group in marble to its right. The alabaster calvary in front of the pulpit also comes from the abbey. The Louis XV altar, in the right transept, was executed by Leblanc in 1766, at the request of the abbey monks. The painting of The Virgin at the Cradle is attributed to Van Dyck. The altar of the left transept comes from the Benedictine convent of Notre-Dame-de-la-Paix. The modern stations-of-the-cross is the work of artist Anzin Lucien Jonas (1943).

Saint-Amand's **thermal baths** have always enjoyed a reputation for the excellence of their waters, prized since Roman times – Roman medallions and fragments of the Roman baths have been unearthed. Many are the illustrious figures who have sought the curing properties of the spa waters here, including the Archduke Leopold of Austria in 1648, and Louis Bonaparte and his wife Hortense de Beauharnais in 1806; in 1910 eminent specialists vaunted the merits of this particular spring at the Fifth International Medical Congress and, during the First World War, the water was discovered to contain rare gases deemed beneficial in the treatment of rheumatism, cellulite, arthritis, inflammation of the joints . . . The thermal baths, hotel and casino were all rebuilt and newly opened to the public in 1966, and now employ among the most up-to-date procedures anywhere.

• **Etablissement thermal** 303 route de la Fontaine-Bouillon. Tel: 27.48.25.00.

Saint-Amand is also the headquarters of the first **regional park** created in France (1968). This 'park' includes 52 *communes* or parishes, distributed through 110,000 acres of forest and surrounded by an equal acreage of fields and lightly wooded terrain, combining together to create an exceptionally attractive tract of unspoilt countryside. The park occupies the whole of the Scarpe valley depression, embracing forest, agricultural land and the sites of now disused mines. Bridleways and footpaths have been created, together with a path to an observation point at the old Sabatier mine, from which visitors can look down on the forest and plain of the Scarpe and Escaut rivers. Various half-day guided excursions are available. At Goriaux mere, parts of a bird reserve are open to the public (exit 6, A23 motorway).

• **Parc naturel régional de Saint-Amand-les-Eaux** 357 rue Notre-Dame-d'Amour. Tel: 27.27.88.27.

SAINT-OMER
62500 • C-4 • 46 km

Tourist information
boulevard Pierre-Guillain
Tel: 21.98.08.51

Saint-Omer: St Bertin Abbey

Hotels
Le Bretagne ***
2 place Vaniquai
Tel: 21.38.25.78
Le Buffet du Rail **
place de la Gare
Tel: 21.93.59.98
Les Français **
3 rue Carnot
Tel: 21.38.59.98
Le Grand Saint-Louis **
25 rue d'arras
Tel: 21.38.35.21

Restaurant
Restaurant le Cygne
8 rue Caventon
Tel: 21.98.20.52

At the beginning of the 7th century, the Frankish king Dagobert sought to convert the northern part of his realm, hitherto largely pagan, to Christianity and, to this end, appointed Audomar (Omer) as bishop of what was then Thérouanne; this native of the Cherbourg peninsula knew no Flemish and so employed the services of Bertin and his companions, Austrasian monks who had come to settle as hermits in the region. As a consequence, two churches were soon built, one near the marshes where Saint Bertin's remains were interred, the second up on a hill on the burial site of Saint Omer.

The church on the higher ground was fortified against Norman invasion, and gave birth to *castrum Sancti Audomari* (Saint Omer castle). The town proper was founded around the year 900 when the monks withdrew to the sanctuary of Notre-Dame. Saint-Omer continued to grow rapidly into the 14th century (in 1350 it had a population of 35,000), and numbered six parishes within the city walls and a further three outside. A separate community established itself out in the marshes, where boats were an important part of life and where they grew vegetables and raised fish . . . Saint-Omer produced textiles; there were tanners, wine-pressers, dyers. Quays and canals were created and, with the canalisation of the River Aa, the town was linked to the sea. Many of its merchants were involved in international trade and this improved the economic life of the town. Saint-Omer was, nevertheless, to suffer both plague and warfare, through which it lost nearly two-thirds of its inhabitants. In the 17th century, nearly one third of the town's surface area was occupied by a religious building of some sort, including the two immense Jesuit colleges. The

English Jesuit College educated young catholic 'gentlemen of Albion' over a period of two centuries. The bastioned city walls, perfected by Vauban, were demolished in 1890 to make way for a very beautiful garden. Saint-Omer's period of prominence and economic development was followed by a more stagnant 19th century during which visitors came here to enjoy the provincial, rather old-fashioned, charm of the town – as presented in Germaine Acremant's novel, *Ces dames aux chapeaux verts*. Today, however, it is again a bustling town, with a vigorous restoration campaign set to make the most of its exceptional urban heritage.

Notre-Dame cathedral is one of northern France's finest, intact Gothic monuments. Begun in the 13th century, but not completed until the 16th, it has a fine baroque organ encased in Danish oak (1717), and a clock-astrolabe (1556). Note, too, the **Grand Dieu** sculpture which formerly ornamented the west porch of the cathedral destroyed in 1553 by Charles Quint.

The town boasts many picturesque streets and buildings (**Saint-Bertin Abbey**, the **Lycée chapel**, **Saint-Sépulcre church**) which are included in guided tours organised by the tourist office (in English, Sundays and public holidays).

Saint-Omer marshes can be visited by boat: extending to 8,500 acres, with different excursions available (information from Parc naturel régional audomarois, la grange nature de Clémarais, tel: 21.95.23.40 and 21.98.62.98).

Le musée de l'hôtel Sandelin, Sandelin museum, is housed in a beautiful 18th-century building. On the ground floor, three finely decorated, panelled rooms (dining-room, drawing room – *salon doré* – and music room) retain their original features and furnishings: a beautifully laid table, Louis XV furniture and rare, 19th-century musical instruments. Paintings include works by Nattier, Greuze, Lepicé, Boilly. Still on the ground floor, several

rooms are devoted to medieval art – the treasure room or *salle du trésor* draws the greatest number of visitors: Roman ivories sculpted at Saint-Omer (*Vieillard de l'Apocalypse*), a deposition from the cross from Saint-Bertin Abbey (by Meuse, around 1180) and a cross from a shrine at Clairmarais Abbey (northern France, 1210–1220). Note, too, the Dutch and Flemish display cabinets as well as the primitive paintings gallery which has a selection from the 15th to 17th centuries. Upstairs, Saint-Omer and Saint-Amand ceramics are on display in four rococo Louis XVI rooms. Aficionados will be pleased at finding china from the major European ceramic centres. On the mezzanine, the pipe room displays examples of the once highly esteemed pipe production of the region.

• **Musée de l'hôtel Sandelin** 14 rue Carnot. Tel: 21.38.00.94 and 21.98.08.51. Open Wednesday, Saturday, Sunday 10am–noon and 2–6pm; Thursday and Friday 10–12am and 2–5pm and by appointment. Tours in English, German or Dutch.

The **Henri-Dupuis museum** is a natural history museum housed in the former private residence of 18th-century Enlightenment collector, Henri-Joseph Dupuis. The ground floor is almost exclusively ornithological; birds from five continents are displayed in vast dioramas showing their natural habitat, with a significant part of the display devoted to little-known or threatened species. Also included is a Flemish kitchen of the sort that might have been found in a bourgeois interior of the period. Upstairs, the walls are covered by a mollusc collection (20,000 shells: gasteropods, bivalves, cephalopods) displayed in 18th-century, natural-history-collection style. Finally, a mineral collection (quartz, gems, semi-precious stones, etc).

• **Musée Henri-Dupuis** 9 rue Henri-Dupuis. Tel: 21.38.24.13. Open Wednesday, Saturday and Sunday 10am–noon and 2–6pm; Thursday and Friday

10am–noon and 2–5pm. Combined ticket with Sandelin museum. Guided tours on request.

SAINT-QUENTIN-EN-TOURMONT

80120 • F-1 • 93 km

Le parc ornithologique du Marquenterre The 625 acres of the Marquenterre bird park (a coastal conservation site) safeguard the fragile flora and fauna of the Picardy shoreline. Once under cultivation (growing flowers), the area became an ornithological park in 1973. Its particular success lies in its European position, midway between northern Europe and the Mediterranean basin, and its excellent varied terrain (marshland, dunes, meadow and forest) drawing some 300 species of birds. Twinned with the great reserves of Zwin (Belgium) and the Danube Delta (Rumania), its combined 2,500 acreage offers wide-ranging activities centred on nature exploration and sport – including horse-riding, archery, tennis . . . An observation walkway allows visitors close-up viewing of the birdlife: unseen in hides, visitors can view at their leisure parades of avocet (the park's emblem) and shelldrakes, or witness the ballet of the little waders. There are two alternatives for visitors to Marquenterre: either a 1h 30 min introductory tour with information panels; or a more in-depth visit including admittance to the hides (from 2 hours to all day).

There is a shop and self-service for refreshments/meals. Alternatively, you can stay in the Garennes apartments (up to seven people) for a weekend or whole week with free access throughout to the ornithological park.

• **Parc ornithologique du Marquenterre** domaine du Marquenterre. Tel: 22.25.03.06. Open end March to beginning November 9.30am–7pm. Best time to visit is April and May, and end August to beginning October, preferably at high tide. Visits are lead by a warden (can be booked in advance); binoculars are essential (can be hired); dogs are not permitted in the reserve.

SAINT-RIQUIER
80135 • G-3 • 120 km

Tourist information
place du Beffroi
Tel: 22.28.91.72

A few miles from Abbeville, Saint-Riquier's imposing church, monastery and belfry testify to a thousand-year prosperity now gone. The **Benedictine monastery** is thought to have been founded in the 7th century on the site of Saint Riquier's tomb, and reached its peak during the time of Charlemagne, by which time the surrounding town had grown to 15,000 inhabitants. The **church** is one of the most beautiful examples of medieval architecture in Picardy and, together with Corbie (Somme *département*), was one of the cultural and religious high points of the west in medieval times. The lover of Gothic architecture will find examples of every phase in its development here: from 13th-century transept and choir to Flamboyant Gothic naves and chapels of the ambulatory . . . to the exuberance of the far west bays of the façade, with their profusion of statuary, dominated by a Crowning of the Virgin. The classic form is also represented, particularly in the design of the choir and the chapel furnishings. Yet this splendid church is only a taste of the greater splendour to come in the great Carolingian basilica created by Angibert; a frequent visitor to Charlemagne's court, he was charged, at Saint-Riquier, with the creation of a model that would serve for all the great monastic centres of Europe. The history of the monastery is peppered with accounts of fire, destruction and pillaging. Destroyed in 881, rebuilt in the 11th century, it was again destroyed in 1131. Earlier, in 1126, the King of France, Louis le Gros, had asked the abbot to grant the *bourgeoisie* of Saint-Riquier a charter of independance that would allow the

Flora of le Marquenterre

town to become one of the premier *communes*, or parishes, of France – as the impressive belfry indicates. Sadly, in the event, Saint-Riquier's influence diminished as Abbeville's grew. During the Revolutionary period, the abbey church was converted into a parish church and in the 19th century became a secondary school for Amiens.

Owned by the Somme *département*, the **church** is now an arts and entertainment centre, and a principal focus for tourism in the region. The abbey church (105 yards long, 30 yards wide, 80-ft-high vaults) boasts nearly 165-ft-high towers. Its stunning Gothic façade, heavily ornamented with statues and pinnacles of every kind, provides a marked contrast to the majestic serenity of the nave. Thirteenth-to 15th-century elements blend harmoniously in this exceptional interior. The *salle du Trésor* is particularly noteworthy, with its mural painting (1528) and the

Assumption of the Virgin painted panel (1480), with a Madeleine tint drawing of particular virtuosity on the reverse. The monastery has a particularly fine *évangeliaire* (book of the Gospels), thought to be Carolingian, a manuscript on purple vellum depicting the four evangelists, but this is kept at the Boucher-de-Perthes museum in Abbeville.

Adjoining the abbey, other attractions include:

• **le musée départemental de la vie rurale**, departmental museum of rural life: exhibits depicting the farming and rural life of Picardy (ploughing, sewing, harvesting, cider-making);

• **le musée national des arts et traditions populaires**, vine-growing and winemaking exhibits (an activity which took place in the Somme up to the 16th century) and agricultural instruments (ploughs and harrows);

• **le centre culturel**: temporary exhibitions of art, ethnography, history;

• **Classic music festival** (information, tel: 22.28.82.82);

• **Abbaye de Saint-Riquier** Tel: 22.28.81.51. Open 10 February to 30 May weekdays 2–6pm; weekends 9.30am–noon and 2–6pm; 1 June to 30 September daily 9.30am–noon and 2–6pm; 1 October to 11 November weekdays 2–6pm; weekends 9.30am–noon and 2–6pm.

SAINT-VALERY-SUR-SOMME
80230 • F-2 • 110 km

Tourist office
2 place Guillaume-le-Conquérant
Tel: 22.60.93.50

Sailing club
Maison des plaisanciers
Tel: 22.26.91.64

It was from the port of Saint-Valery that William the Conqueror set out for England in 1066. In 1475, Louis XI set fire to the town rather than allow the

*Saint-Riquier:
the church façade*

English to take it. Present-day Saint-Valery retains something of its medieval aura, partly, of course, due to the ramparts which enclose the upper town, accessed via the Nevers gate. The Gothic **church of Saint-Martin**, constructed in chequered stone and napped flint, still retains 13th-century features, while in the left nave is a Renaissance triptych. As you walk towards the *porte Guillaume*, notice the beautiful timbered houses. The view across the bay from Saint-Valery is marvellous. There is a yachting basin, for those who would perfect their sailing skills, either across the Somme Bay or indeed across the Channel – tides and winds permitting. North of Saint-Valery, the stone and napped flint **chapel of Saint-Valery** stands on a rise; from the furthest point of the cliff, **cap Hornu**, you can enjoy a vast panorama. Across the mussel beds, with their little huts and wildfowl pools, you come to Le Hourdel. **L'ecomusée Picardie**

displays nearly 6,000 tools in contemporary contexts of workshops, schools, market stalls, farms, inns . . . to create a picture of 'pre-motorcar Picardy'. The first floor of the museum has exhibits relating to the production of linen, Jacquard weaving, cloth-cutting and dressmaking.

• **Ecomusée Picardie** 5 quai de Romerel. Tel: 22.26.94.90. Open daily, except Tuesday, May to September 2–7pm and by arrangement.

Saint-Valery is the terminus for the **Somme Bay Railway** which operates around the bay at 12 miles per hour, from Cayeux to Le Crotoy.

• **Chemin de fer de la baie de Somme** Tel: 22.26.96.96. Regular services from Le Crotoy, Saint-Valery and Cayeux. Trips last 1–3 hours. Open 11 April to 19 September, Sunday and public holidays; 3 July to 4 September, Wednesday, Saturday, Sunday and public holidays; 8 July to 2 September daily, except Monday and Friday; special service 21 and 22 May.

SANGATTE
62231 • C-2 • 7 km
Tourist information
Blériot-Plage
Mairie annexe
Tel: 21.34.97.98

It was from the hamlet of Baraques (renamed Blériot-Plage) that the aviator **Blériot** set off on his successful airborne crossing of the Straits of Dover; a stone pillar marks his point of departure. Sangatte was also the site of the first drilling, in 1877, of an intended French-British tunnel link. In 1851, the first telephone cable to connect Britain and France came ashore at Sangatte. On the summit of *cap Blanc-Nez*, a **monument** commemorates the French sailors of the Dover patrol for their work in guaranteeing safety in the Straits of Dover during the 1914–1918 war. Today, a large part of Sangatte is occupied by the Eurotunnel terminal.

SARS-POTERIES

59216 • G-9 • 217 km

Tourist information
20 rue Général-de-Gaulle
Tel: 27.59.35.49

Hotel
Le Fleuri ★
65 rue Général-de-Gaulle
Tel: 27.61.61.44

During the 15th century, the village derived its livelihood from pot-making, the clay earth of Sars and its hamlet Offies being particularly easy to work. The pot-making tradition is thought to have been imported from Belgum (Bouffioulx) and gave rise to three different products: yellow clay pottery; sandstone pottery (with blue cobalt floral design) and pottery characterised by a white glazed interior. A few potters keep these traditions alive and welcome visits from the public.

• **Poterie Leclerc** Tel: 27.59.31.89; and **Poterie Maine** Tel: 27.61.68.11.

Le musée du verre or glass museum After contributing so significantly to the region's prosperity (between 1802 and 1937), all its past glass-makers have now disappeared, the only trace of their past activity being visible atop some of the houses which have decorative glass roof ridges. The imposing **Château Imbert**, however, houses a glass museum. Inside is a collection of *bousillés*, the name given to pieces made by the glass-workers outside their working day. With the support and participation of former glass-makers, a workshop has been set up and here, young French glass-workers are at work. This new dimension to Sars-Poterie, added to the existing fine glass collection, has made the town a reference point in glass experimentation, on a level with Paris and Aix-en-Provence.

• **Le musée du verre** 1 rue Générale-de-Gaulle. Open daily, except Tuesday and Saturday, 3–6pm. Tel: 27.61.61.44.

You may also like to visit the **water mill**, the only one in the Avesnois region to have its entire working mechanism still intact. Demonstrations are accompanied by a commentary given by the former miller (organised under the auspices of the Fourmies-Trélon region ecomuseum of which the Sars-Poteries mill is a part.

• **Moulin de Sars-Poteries** Tel: 27.61.60.01. Open 15 July to 31 August daily, except Tuesday, 3–7pm; 1 May to 30 October, Sunday and public holidays 3–7pm. Other times of year by arrangement.

As you leave the village, you will see a sandstone **megalith**, once used as a flag mount. Custom has it that this standing stone served as a pillory in the Middle Ages.

SECLIN

59113 • D-6 • 126 km

Tourist information
9 boulevard Hentgès
Tel: 20.90.00.02

Hotels
Auberge du Forgeron ★★★
rue Roger-Bouvry
Tel: 20.90.09.52
Tournebride ★★★
rue Max-Dormoy
Tel: 20.90.09.59

The collegiate church of Saint-Piat, known as the **cathédrale du Mélantois**, is among northern France's most interesting medieval monuments. Built in 1531, it was partly reconstructed in 1927; tall, relief work capitals support the nave and the crypt where the body of Saint Piat is interred. His tomb is among the oldest sarcophagi in former Belgian Gaul; covered by a 12th-century memorial tablet in Tournai blue stone it bears a picture of the saint. The unusual baptismal basin pre-dates the 13th century. Around the time of the 13th century, a Gothic church was erected on earlier Roman foundations; the ambulatory, divided into 13 chapels, and 14th-century *salle capitulaire* (meeting room, between the sacristy and the south transept) are the only surviving Gothic parts. The impressive bell-tower has a 42-bell carillon, one of Europe's finest and truest in tone.

• **Carillon de la collégiale Saint-Piat** Tel: 20.90.00.02. Concert: Monday 11am–noon (as well as certain religious and secular holidays).

L'hospice de Seclin This Flemish-baroque masterpiece lies to the south-west of the town. Of the original construction (1246), nothing remains, since this was replaced in 1614, except for the left aisle which was built later on between 1856 and 1910. The wall of the façade is brick on a sandstone foundation, with relief work and decorative stone elements. Notice the semi-circular arch of the portal with the Flanders rampant lion surmounted by the 1634 count's crown. The 17th-century wooden door is decorated with statues of Saint Roch, Saint Joseph and the Guardian Angel, protector of the afflicted. The 18th-century turret serves to break the horizontal line of the

Saint-Valery-sur-Somme: the harbour

Le Touquet: the beach

façade and separate the two different styles: vertical (to the right, medieval) and horizontal (left, classic). The cloister was built between 1634 and 1701; the semi-circular arches are supported by monolithic columns in Ecaussines stone, 6 feet high; the three sides are identical, only the decoration varies. Admire the fine balance achieved through a combination of brick, stone and sculptures. The 16th-century chapel is reminiscent of Lille's Hospice-Comtesse chapel. Consisting of a choir, transept and nave – divided by a wall that was a later addition – this was once a sick-room, restored early in the 17th century. The nearby hospital farm grouping in brick includes a dovecote and huge barn.

• **Hospice de Seclin** avenue des Marronniers. Visits can be arranged through the tourist information office.

THÉROUANNE
62129 · D-4 · 60 km

15km from Saint-Omer, nestling in the valley of the Lys is Thérouanne, a market town with a surprisingly colourful past. Capital of the ancient province of Morinie, it was conquered with difficulty by Caesar's legions; the Romans made it the chief town of the region known as *Morinie intérieur*, because it stood at the junction of several roads. After the barbarous invasions, the town prospered anew under the episcopacy of Saint Omer, its first bishop (636–670).

In the Middle Ages, Thérouanne was the seat of one of the richest bishoprics in northern France (stretching from the Canche to the Yser). Its bishops were notable ecclesiastics who wielded considerable power over the running of the town. One of these even became pope, bearing the name Clément VII, and resided in Avignon at the time of the great schism. Some magnificent buildings were erected on the southern slopes of the valley, where the town had stood in ancient times. Today, Saint-Omer cathedral still retains features of the earlier 12th-century cathedral, *le Christ Juge*. Two monasteries were established in Thérouanne: Saint-Jean-au-Mont (Benedictine) and Saint-Augustin (Prémontrés order). Then followed a series of sieges and sackings up to 1553, when Charles Quint ordered that the town walls be levelled to their foundations. Only the original fortified enclosure remains; since 1961 a permanent archaeological base has been set up on the site of the former cathedral. A museum of archaeology has varied exhibits on the ground floor: plans, old engravings, seals of the bishops of Thérouanne, excavated objects and various audiovisual exhibits.

• **Musée archéologique** Tel: 21.95.54.25. Open Monday to Friday 1.30–5.30pm. Guided tours from 1 April to 31 October 9am–6.30pm. Tel. 21.95.54.25.

LE TOUQUET
62630 · E-2 · 63 km

Tourist information
palais de l'Europe
place de l'Hermitage
Tel: 21.05.21.65

Airport
(Lydd-Folkestone and Le Touquet connections daily)
Tel: 21.05.00.66

Sailing
Centre nauitique de la Canche
boulevard Bigot-Descelers
Tel: 21.94.74.26

Casino des Quatre-Saisons
Tel: 21.05.16.99

Casino du Palais
Tel: 21.05.01.05

Golf du Touquet (18-hole)
Manoir Hôtel
Tel: 21.05.68.47

Horseriding
Centre équestre du Touquet
avenue de la Dune-aux-Loups
Tel: 21.05.15.25

Swimming/water sports
Aqualud
boulevard de la Mer
Tel: 21.05.63.59
Base nautique Nord
Tel: 21.05.12.77
Base nautique Sud
Tel: 21.05.33.51

Hotels
Le Grand Hôtel ★★★★
4 boulevard de la Cauche
Tel: 21.06.88.88
Le Picardy
avenue du Maréchal-Foch
Tel: 21.06.85.85
Westminster Hôtel ★★★★
5 avenue du Verger
Tel: 21.05.48.48
Bristol ★★★
17 rue Jean-Monnet
Tel: 212.05.49.95
Manoir Hôtel ★★★
avenue du Golf
Tel: 21.05.20.22
Novotel Thalassa ★★★
front de mer
Tel: 21.09.85.00
de la Forêt ★★
73 rue de Moscou
Tel: 21.05.09.88
Nouvel H ★★
89 rue de Paris
Tel: 21.05.87.61

Restaurants
Flavio
1 avenue du Verger

Tel: 21.05.91.55
Café des Arts
80 rue de Paris
Tel: 21.05.21.55
L'Escale, à l'aéroport
Tel: 21.05.23.22

Nearby
Dell'Hôtel *
boulevard E Labrasse
Stella-Plage (7km)

This resort is one of the most highly prized among British visitors. For a long time known as Paris-Plage, it boasts some impressive hotels and a sea-water therapy centre as well as many recreational and sports activities. The beach is one of the loveliest of the Pas-de-Calais *département,* with a yacht basin on the headland. To the east is a 175-ft-high **lighthouse** erected in 1953 in pink brick, from which visitors can enjoy a lovely view over the Canche valley, the Channel and the town. Le Touquet's natural features include a 20,000-acre forest of pines, birches and poplars . . . a hideaway for nearly 2,000 villas. Nearby is Etaples (tourist information at: clos Saint-Victor, boulevard Bigot-Descelers, tel: 21.09.56.94 and information point at la Canche car park, tel: 21.94.64.51). The **musée Quentovic**, created in 1967, has mineral and rock exhibits found in the *département* (carbonates and fossils extracted from the Ferques massif), as well as a few exceptional items from elsewhere in France and from other countries. Local archaeology is also well represented, from prehistoric times up to the Carolingian era, with artefacts found at Les Sablins and La Coloterie, including a beautiful collection of decorative buckles and ceramics.

• **Musée Quentovic** 8 bis place Général-de-Gaulle, 62630 Etaples. Tel: 21.94.02.47. Open daily, except Tuesday, 10am–noon and 2–6pm.

At **clos Saint-Victor**, near Canche bay, is the **maison de la faune et de la flore**, which reflects the natural wealth of the estuary. Guided nature walks can be organised, on request.

• **Maison de la faune et de la flore** boulevard Bigot-Descelers. Tel: 21.09.56.94. Open daily 9am–noon and 2–6pm (until 8pm July and August); from September to May: closed Saturday and Sunday.

Etaples is also the home of a **maritime museum** with exhibits and models relating to various maritime activities and subjects: whale bones, a rescue raft . . .

• **Musée de la marine** boulevard de l'Impératrice. Tel: 21.09.77.21. Open Easter to end October daily, except Sunday morning and all day Monday, 10am–noon and 3–7pm.

TOURCOING
59200 • D-7 • 124 km

Tourist information
parvis Saint-Christophe
Tel: 20.26.89.03

Hotels
Fimotel **
320 rue Gambetta
Tel: 20.70.38.00
Ibis **
Centre Général-de-Gaulle
Tel: 20.24.84.58
Resthotel Primevère **
avenue Henri-Becquerel
Tel: 20.36.01.96

The 15th-century **church of Saint-Christophe** stands on the *place de la Résistance*. It underwent a major restoration programme in 1865 and this, plus recent renovation work, has restored it to its former glory. The bell-tower consists of a 17th-century spire (restored in 1957) and a splendid 61-bell carillon.

Etaples: fishing boat

The bellringer, Jacques Lannoy, is descended from a long line of *carilloneurs.* The porch (1550) is interesting for its lateral arcades. Beneath the north arcade is a cross (early 17th century) and a statue of Saint Christophe in coloured stone (17th century). In the left nave, notice the 18th-century confessionals, with bas-reliefs ornamentation, and in the right nave, late 19th-century confessionals. The choir has an 18th-century carved wood, painted and gilded altar. The stalls date from 1723. Admire the limewood statues of Saint Charles and Saint Hilaire, the B J Wamps *Sainte Trinité* painted for the church choir in 1724 and the strange *Christ noir* of the centre stained glass window (19th century). See also, in the side choir stalls, the painting of Saint Dominique receiving the rosary, from Rubens' studio, and the Glorification of the name of Jesus (both painted in 1630). Finally, the organ and balustrade are the work of Lille cabinet-maker, Labre (1750).

• **Saint-Christophe church carillon** (visits by arrangement with local history centre, tel: 20.27.55.24).

The local history centre, *le centre d'histoire locale*, displays objects found during town centre excavations, as well as models and documents relating to the architecture and activities of the Middle Ages.

• **Centre d'histoire locale** 11 bis, place Roussel. Open daily, except Tuesday, 9.30–11.30am and 2–5pm; Saturday and Sunday 2–6pm. Tel: 20.27.55.24.

Le **musée des beaux-arts** art gallery is housed in a thirties-style house designed by Maillard. Composer Albert Roussel once lodged here. A rich variety of collections span the 16th to 20th century, with more than a thousand works of art, from Rembrandt to Picasso. Recent alterations should enable this gallery to achieve its ambition of a dialogue between different periods of art and between different art forms – from the plastic arts to the performing arts (music, theatre, dance . . .).

• **Musée des beaux-arts** 2 rue Paul-Doumer. Tel: 20.25.38.92. Open daily, except Tuesday, 10am–7pm.

TOURNEHEM
62890 · C-3 · 24 km

Hotel
Bal Park Hotel
5000 rue du Vieux-Château
Tel: 21.35.65.90

An important road junction during the Romano-Gallic period, Tournehem was endowed with a fortress during the Middle Ages. In the 15th century, Antoine de Bourgogne's richly-adorned château became a meeting place for princes and artists. In the 18th century, the wife of Tournehem's *seigneur* (who held the position of farmer-general to Louis XIV) became famous under the name of the Marquise de Pompadour. A magnificent forest today encircles the town, watered by the River Hem. The **church of Saint-Médard** has a collegiate chapel rebuilt at the end of the 17th century. Its furnishings come from the monasteries and abbeys of the surrounding region: an 18th-century altar from Chartreux Abbey at Longuenesse; stalls from Sainte-Colombe Abbey at Blendecques, a beautiful organ case from Saint-André Priory near Aire-sur-la-Lys. The **Saint-Louis chapel**, built in the 15th century, stands on a mound overlooking the surrounding countryside (with viewing platform). **Tournehem forest** (1,700 acres) is criss-crossed by numerous footpaths; in the middle of the forest stands the chapel of Notre-Dame-de-la-Forêt, built in 1713. The **maison Bal** offers various lake-side activities and refreshments (tel: 21.35.61.00).

VALENCIENNES
59300 · F-8 · 165 km

Tourist information
1 rue Askièvre
Tel: 27.46.22.99

Hotels
Auberge du Bon Fermier ★★★★

Valenciennes: Carpeaux,
The Negress

64–66 rue de Famars
Tel: 27.46.68.25
Grand Hôtel ★★★
8 place de la Gare
Tel: 27.46.32.01
Les Arcades ★★
19 rue Saint-Jacques
Tel: 27.30.16.58
Bristol ★★
2 avenue Maréchal-de-Lattre-de-Tassigny
Tel: 27.56.58.88
La Coupole ★★
25 rue Tholozé
Tel: 27.46.37.12
Hôtel de France ★★
8 place d'Armes
Tel: 27.29.36.98
Notre-Dame ★★
1 place Abbé-Thellier
Tel: 27.42.30.00

Restaurant
L'Alberoi Buffet de la Gare
place de la Gare
Tel: 27.46.86.30

The **hôtel de ville**, rebuilt in 1867, stands in the *place d'Armes*. It has a Flemish façade (1616) with elements of Napoleon II style. Following significant damage sustained between 1940 and 1944, it had to be rebuilt and only the façade of the original was retained; notice at the top the group by Carpeaux, The People of Valenciennes Defending their Ramparts in 1793, and beneath, the work of Valenciennes sculptor Henri Lemaire, depicting the Rhonelle and Escaut rivers.

North-west of the square, the *rue de Paris* leads to the *place du Marché-aux-Herbes* and the *place du Hainaut*; a little further on, *square Watteau* is a reminder that the famous painter was born in Valenciennes at 39 rue de Paris; a statue of Watteau by Carpeaux celebrates the great artist.

Nearby stands the **church of Saint-Géry** (13th and 19th century) built by Jeanne de Flandre for the Franciscans. The façade and tower date from the 19th century. Inside, notice the cylindrical pillars with relief-work decorated capitals and the 13th-century blue stone arcades. In the choir are three 13th-century chapels, now ornamented with beautiful modern stained glass.

Valenciennes: Rubens, The Martyrdom of St Stephen *(detail)*

Near the **church of Saint-Nicolas**, the façade of the **bibliothèque municipale** or municipal library is in brick dressed with stone. This was rebuilt in 1614 following war damage inflicted by the Spanish, and has beautiful first floor windows and circular windows with Louis XVI garlands on the ground floor. The great hall on the first floor dates from 1735 and has a fine ceiling, a barrel vault divided into six voussoirs or sections. Wood panelling surrounds paintings by Joseph Wamps (1689–1750). The library houses one of the finest manuscript collections of the region, gathered from its

monasteries (notably Saint-Amand); 1,100 manuscripts, 304 early printed books, the earliest being 9th century and including the *cantilena of Sainte Eulalie*, the oldest known Romance language document. Next to the library is the **école des beaux-arts** or fine arts college.

• **Bibliothèque municipal** rue Ferrand. Tel: 27.46.19.28. Open daily, except Monday and Thursday, 9–12am and 2–6pm.

Returning to *rue de Paris*, notice the **maison du Prévost** at No 13 on the corner with *rue Notre-Dame* (15th century) with its flying turrets and stepped gables. Continue along *rue Notre-Dame* and you come to the 18th-century building which houses the local government

offices. At **No 46**, *rue Famars*, notice the door panels, at **No 70** the façade, and at **No 84**, the façade, the door panels of the main entrance and the French window that opens on to the first floor balcony. From the *place d'Armes*, behind the **hôtel de ville** to the right, is the *rue Askière* and the **maison dite Espagnole**, the 16th-century half-timbered home of the tourist office. Then, *rue des Ursulines* and the **church of Notre-Dame-du-Saint-Cordon**. Built in 1852 in 13th-century style, it replaces an earlier church built on the same site. The 240-ft bell-tower houses the famous Jeanne de Flandre bell (15th century) rescued from the former belfry. Inside is a silver-plated, carved Sainte Véronique and two angels (1704). The statue of Notre-Dame-du-Saint-Cordon in the apsidal chapel is carried in the annual procession.

The **musée des beaux-arts** art gallery includes several important works, including a tapestry attributed to Brussels weavers (15th century) and paintings by Jean Provost, Cornelis Van Haarlem, Jos van Cleve and le Maître de Francfort. There are Flemish baroque pieces (Janssens, Crayer, Rubens, Van Dyck . . .), paintings by Valenciennes artists (Antoine Watteau, Jean-Baptiste Pater and Olivier le May, Abel de Pujol, Auray, Harpignies . . .) and a final complement of 18th-century French painters. An important Carpeaux bequest is particularly noteworthy, as well as a bequest of 19th-century sculptures and 20th-century Valenciennes artists.

• **Musée des beaux-arts** boulevard Watteau. Open daily, except Tuesday, 10am–noon and 2–5pm. Tel: 27.46.21.09.

VILLENEUVE-D'ASCQ
59600 • D-6 • 122 km

Tourist information
chemin du Chat-Botté
Tel: 20.43.55.75

Hotels
Le Relais d'Hermès ★★★
11 avenue de la Créativité
Tel: 20.47.46.46

Grill Campanile **
48 avenue de Cauteleu
Tel: 20.91.83.10
Ascotel **
boulevard Paul-Langevin
Tel: 20.43.82.82
Les Hauts de France **
rue Trudain
Tel: 20.05.04.03

Restaurants
Le Clos de la meunerie
204 rue des Fusillés
Tel: 20.79.00.09
La Diligence
250 rue J Jaurès
Tel: 20.72.22.51
La Planche Epinoy
95 av des Flandres
Tel: 20.72.15.01

A fragment of polished axe testifies to the presence of man here as long ago as 4,000 years before Christ. Approximately 6,000 years later – at the end of the 1960s – three former 'villages', Fler, Ascq and Annappes, were formally amalgamated into the new French town of Villeneuve-d'Ascq. The following account details some of the stages in the development of the town, now one of the biggest in the region.

In 800 AD, a text attests to the presence of a royal household at Annappes during the reign of Charlemagne, where horses were reared for the Imperial cavalry. In 1066, the Count of Flanders gave his vassals a farm at Flers. In the 14th century, during the time of the Hundred Years' War, the region was devastated by the Black Death; then, following wars during the reign of Louis XI and Charles le Téméraire, churches were built. In 1505, the population was on the increase and documents reveal: a village at Flers with 640 inhabitants, a village called Ascq with 650 inhabitants and a village at Annappes with 550 inhabitants. The land was divided up into the domains of numerous great houses: at Flers, the Enbas château (rebuilt in 1661), Celle des Prés, Quiquempois du Sar. As time went on, land passed into the ownership of rich Lille families. In 1668, Annappes and Flers became French. At the time of the Revolution, the three villages made up the canton of Lannoy but were then occupied by the Austrians in August 1792. In the 19th century, the fertile land of the area was well suited to the rigours of the intensive farming practised on it. The industrial boom that came to the towns of Roubaix, Lille and Tourcoing stimulated industrial investment at Flers, together with extensive residential development. Slowly, Flers merged with Roubaix, joined in time by Ascq and Annappes, and culminating in the eventual creation of Villeneuve-d'Ascq.

The church of **Saint-Pierre d'Ascq** has two components: the (much lower) choir and the rest of the church. In the 18th century, Louis XVI-style decorative pilasters were added; the nave and transept are 17th-century, the communion rail is Louis XV rococo, the confessionals date from 1683. The church has a pretty Flemish tapestry, les Noces de Cana (1735), executed from a sketch by Arnould de Vuez, by Lille tapestry maker, Guillaume Wernier.

The church of **Saint Pierre de Flers** was built in the 16th century (transept, nave and massive tower) with 17th-century side aisles. A turret has stairs leading up to the old lookout post. Notice the Gothic-style portal with flattened arch standing on sandstone suppports. The 16th-century nailed oak door has a pier decorated with a two-headed eagle surmounted by the Imperial crown and encircled by the collar of the Golden Fleece. The arms of Philippe de Noyelles, seigneur of Flers, are carved beneath the tower. Inside are handsome sandstone columns; the windows of the choir are decorated with 17th-century pillars and stained glass. In the right aisle is a 17th-century painted wood Virgin and Child and, in the left aisle, a 16th-century Saint Roch; and, above the altar, a 17th-century carved wood Christ. In the choir, to the right, there is a painting of Saint Druon (born at Epinoy around 1118, he lived as a hermit and died in 1186 at Sebourg); to his left, La Mort de Saphire, femme d'Ananie (1705), by the Arras painter Bergaigne. Notice, too, the Gothic baptismal fonts (1450).

The **château de Flers**, also known as the château Rouge, stands near Saint-Pierre church, and was built in 1661. On the eve of the Revolution, it belonged to the Count of Diesbash, officer of the Swiss Guard, in the service of the King of France. Exceptionally well restored since its repurchase by the town, this moated building houses various municipal offices, the archaeological museum and the tourist office.

• **Musée archéologique** Château de Flers. Open Tuesday to Friday 9am–noon and 2–5.30pm; Saturday 9am–noon. Tel: 20.43.55.55.

Within the limits of the former parish of Flers stands the **château de Sart** and adjoining golf course; the castle is ringed by water. It was built in 1760. To the right is an octagonal dovecote (1761) and an old chapel with beautiful eliptical portal.

Not far away from Annappes' Saint-Sébastien church, at the ferme Delporte, is the **musée du terroir local**, a museum run by the Villeneuve-d'Ascq and Mélantois historic society, housed in buildings set around an enclosed courtyard (18th–19th century). Inside, the rooms of this former hostelry are arranged with turn-of-the-century furniture, ornaments and games. In the barn are agricultural tools and a farrier's workshop.

• **Musée du terroir** 12 carrière Delporte. Open Sunday 9.30am –1.30pm and by arrangement. Tel: 20.91.87.57.

Return to the rue du 8 mai 1945 and, on your left, you will see the new **parc archéologique**, set in 15 acres to the north of the parc du Héron. When completed, this archaeological park will describe the northern French habitat as it evolved from the Neolithic period through to the Middle Ages. One of the phases in this development, the Iron Age, is depicted by a reconstruction of an artisan's workshop, made in the materials and manner that would have applied in the Gallic era: not a window, not a chimney, only ventilation holes up in the gables. A Neolithic house is in the process of completion.

• **Parc archéologique** Tel: 20.47.18.85. Open 1 April to 30 October on the first and third Sunday of every month from 3pm.

From the archaeological park, you come to the **musée d'art moderne**. The gallery houses one of the biggest modern art collections in the north and is also a working illustration of environment-integrated building. Originally set up with an endowment from local industrialist and art patron Jean Masurel, the collection is predominantly modern, comprising both sculptures (in the grounds) and paintings. Art through the 20th century is traced via the works of some of its greatest artists: Picasso, Braque, Miró, Modigliani, Léger. Its temporary exhibitions, audiovisual gallery, library – and cafeteria – put it on a par with the great French and foreign modern art galleries.

• **Musée d'art moderne** 1 allée du Musée, La Cousinerie. Tel: 20.05.42.46. Open daily, except Tuesday, 10am–6pm.

Three windmills stand beside the *boulevard de Breucq* (Paris–Gand motorway), saved from demolition by the Regional Friends of Windmills Association, *Association régionale des amis des moulins*, who undertook their restoration. The **moulin des Olieux** pivot oil mill (1743) originally stood in the village of Offekerque and the **moulin à Farine** pivot flour mill came from Rumingham (further details in Windmills route, p194). A water mill, *moulin à eau,* built in 1902 in Bers-sur-Selles, completes this unusual trio in the middle of the new town and the greater Lille metropolis.

• **Association régionale des amis des moulins** rue Albert-Samain. Tel: 20.05.49.34. Open 1 April–November, Sundays and by arrangement.

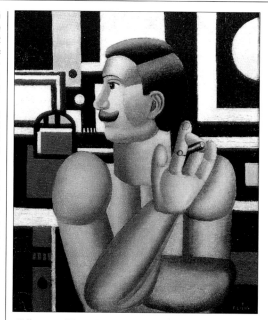

Villeneuve-d'Ascq: Fernand Léger, The Mechanic *(musée d'art moderne)*

WATTEN
59143 • C-4 • 40 km

Tourist information
place du Cimetière
Tel: 21.88.26.04

Until the 6th century, this region around the River Aa was a swamp crossed at its highest point by the Roman road linking Cassel to Boulogne. Thus travellers from Flanders, from the Artois region, from the coast and from the Audomarois had to pass through this township strategically placed on the approach road to Saint-Omer. A monastery was founded here in 1072 and subsequently became an Augustinian monastery. Around 1608, the bishop of Saint-Omer brought English Jesuits here. Later, in 1762, with the disappearance of the Order of Jesus, the buildings were demolished, with the exception of the tower, used by travellers as a point of reference.

The tower of the **church of Saint-Gilles** is in yellow brick decorated with geometric designs in red brick. The lower part of the tower dates from 1498, the upper part from 1515. The octagonal turret to the right houses a spiral staircase.

The 236-ft-high, so-called **montagne de Watten**, dominates the surrounding region. The mill also enjoys an exceptional position, built on a triangular spur dominating the Aa valley. This 18th-century replacement of an earlier, wooden, pivot mill, has served as an important observation post.

• **Moulin de la Montagne** Tel: 21.88.26.04. Visits can be arranged at the town hall.

INFORMATION
on the *départements* of Nord, Pas-de-Calais and Somme from:

• **Comité départemental de tourisme du Nord**
15–17 rue du Nouveau-Siècle, 59027 Lille Cedex. Tel: 20.57.00.61.

• **Comité départemental de tourisme du Pas-de-Calais**
24 rue Desille BP 279, 62204 Boulogne. Tel: 21.83.32.59.

• **Comité départemental de tourisme de la Somme**
21 rue Ernest-Cauvin, 8000 Amiens. Tel: 22.92.26.39.

Cap Gris-Nez and Cap Blanc-Nez

About 4 miles from the Tunnel is the exceptional natural area of Cap Gris-Nez and Cap Blanc-Nez, at the point where the North Sea meets the Channel. North of the Côte d'Opal – called the opal coast because of the milky sea that laps its shore – these capes are on the cliff bordering the Boulogne hills between Calais and Boulogne. A series of promontaries separate dry valleys, similar to the *pays de Caux* or the cliffs of Ault-Onival. Violent sea currents undercut the base of these promontaries provoking landslides which are eroding the cliffs at the rate of 27 yards per century. This stretch of shoreline – visible from Dover on a clear day – is classified as a site of national importance, the *Site des deux caps*.

At the end of Cap Gris-Nez stands a lighthouse with a range of 30 miles; a regional marine operations and life-saving centre is located at the bottom of the cape, from which point it surveys the traffic of the Channel, one of the most densely populated stretches of water anywhere in the world (about 500 ships per day including cargo boats, tankers and container carriers). The road down to the beach between Gris-Nez and Courte-Dune point (parking) takes you to the cliff bottom. Gris-Nez (164 feet high) dates from the Jurassic period and, as its name would suggest, is grey-coloured. From the beach, a section through the cliff offers a good view of the cliff's strata. Ammonites and other fossils dating from 150 million years ago are found here. The cape provides an ideal halt for migratory birds and plays host throughout the year to a rich variety of birdlife including gulls, eiderducks, scoters, gannets, sandmartins, kestrels . . .

The beach at Wissant

The 443-feet-high cliff of the Cap Blanc-Nez provides an exceptional look-out post. It is accessed from the beach either by the Cran d'Escalles or by the Les Douaniers path; by road, take the D940 to the Dover Patrol Monument car park. Blanc Nez (like the upland hills of the Boulogne region) was formed by chalk deposited by the sea 100 million years ago (chalk being the accumulated remains of sea creatures). As at Gris-Nez, here too the sea undercuts and erodes the cliff, evidenced by the tips of fallen rocks now covered by the sea except at low tide. Beneath the cape stands a monument to the aviator Latham, who attempted an airborne Channel crossing at the same time as Blériot (whose monument at Blériot-Plage celebrates the first successful airborne crossing from Calais on 25 July 1909).

PLACES OF INTEREST IN THE

GOING FROM BOULOGNE TO CALAIS

Wimereux
Tourist information
Tel: 21.83.27.17
Sailing (club nautique)
Tel: 21.83.18.54
Golf (18-hole)
Tel: 21.32.43.20
Horseriding (équitation)
Tel: 21.83.30.37
• sea wall/promenade
• Croÿ fort (visible at low tide)

• Grande Armée memorial column
• Christ ressuscité church (fine Chapuis stained glass)
• Pilâtre de Rozier monument.

Ambleteuse
Tourist information
Tel: 27.32.64.79
• 500-acre dunes south of town
• Saint-Pierre chapel (Pierre d'Ambleteuse was companion to Augustine of Canterbury)

• Second World War museum
• Vauban fort with museum of geology, archaeology, history and natural history of the coastline.

Audinghen
• modern church and belltower (stained glass windows and frescoes)
• Museum of the Atlantic Front (housed in blockhouse used by Germans for shelling England).

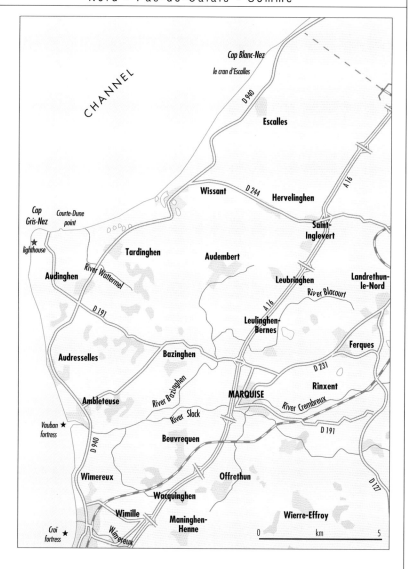

GRIS-NEZ AND BLANC-NEZ REGION

Wissant
Two Capes (Deux Caps)
Tourist information
    Tel: 21.85.15.62
• picturesque fishing village
• Saint-Nicolas church (12th-century choir)
• mill museum (former industrial flour mill with water turbines, archive documents and photographs).

Escalles
• International cross-Channel

Museum (*La folle aventure du détroit*) depicting the range of past Channel-link projects.

FURTHER INFORMATION

Parc naturel régional du Boulonnais (Boulogne Regional Park)
    Manoir du Huisbois-le-Wast
    62142 Colembert
    Tel: 21.33.38.79
Eden 62
    28 avenue Foch

62930 Wimereux
Tel: 21.32.13.74

RECOMMENDED READING

Guy and Nadine Houvenagel, *Guide naturel de la mer: Manche-mer du Nord; de la côte d'Opale aux îles Frisonnes*, ed Duculot 1978.

Brochures (*Découverte des milieux naturels*) published by Boulogne Regional Park.

The Picardy coastline

The 38-mile Picardy coastline embraces a variety of scenery arranged around the deep indentation that is *la Baie de la Somme*. From the north, and sweeping from the valley of the Authie, are a number of sandy beaches and attractions (including an aquaclub).

Then, south of this, the Domaine de Marquenterre is an ornithological reserve sure to delight any lover of nature and birdlife (birds, ducks, waders, etc), with a range of trails and guided tours.

Somme Bay is one of the *département*'s chief tourist attractions offering a network of little communities and activities (fishing, watersports and walking) through which the visitor can get to know a region where water, sky and earth join together. Places like Le Crotoy, Abbeville, Saint-Valery and Le Hourdel are all worthy of a visit or longer stay.

Fishermen have lived at Cayeux since the 7th century and, from that time through to the 17th century, the population, including the local feudal lords, have enjoyed beach-combing rights over the flotsam and jetsam thrown up by the sea. With its famous wooden promenade (one of Europe's longest) and 600 white beach huts, Cayeux has the look and air of many Normandy beaches. Cayeux is also known for the purity and hardness of the pebbles on its beach, tossed and turned by the sea over thousands of years into something exceptional.

The seaside resort of Ault enjoys a privileged position at the start of the Ault-Onival chalk cliffs and the Caux region. From the Ault cliffs, paths lead to the *hâble d'Ault*, home to some 400 species of migratory bird.

At Mer-les-Bains, turn-of-the-century villas (around 500 of them) with wooden balconies and elaborate wrought-iron ornamentation, lend an air of style and nostalgia.

SOMME BAY

The Somme Bay was created by the Somme River, widening and branching out as it approached the sea. It is the ideal spot for fishing, wildfowling and sailing. But it can be a dangerous place too. At low tide, the sea can go out nearly 9 miles. It completes the return journey in five hours, and sometimes with such devastating violence that it can catch the imprudent clam or cockle gatherer unawares. (Information from nearby tourist offices.)

THE SOMME BAY SEAL

Small for its weight (5 to 6 feet in length for a weight of 330lbs), the seal is well known for the rounded form of its head and muzzle, concave in outline, and marked by the V of its nostrils. Its skin ranges from light grey to dark brown, with darker, irregular marbling. Favouring sandy shorelines, this species of seal has been in the Bay since 1833.

Ault cliffs

Bathing huts at Cayeux-sur-Mer

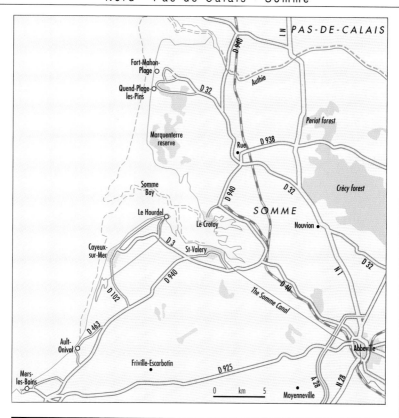

THE PICARDY COASTLINE

Fort-Mahon-Plage
Tourist information
Tel: 22.23.26.00
Aquaclub
Tel: 22.27.48.47
Sailing (Centre nautique)
Tel: 22.23.33.64
Horseriding (L'Etrier centre équestre
Tel: 22.27.45.58

Quend-Plage-les-Pins
Tourist information
Tel: 22.23.32.04
Belle-Dune Golf club
Tel: 22.23.45.50

Marquenterre
Ornithological park
Tel: 22.25.03.06
Horseriding (Centre équestre)
Henson-Marquenterre
Tel: 22.25.03.06

Le Hourdel
Bird zoo (Maison de l'oiseau)
Tel: 22.26.93.93
Lighthouse (Feu du port)
Tel: 22.26.92.07

Le Crotoy
Tourist information
Tel: 22.27.05.25

Watersports
Club nautique de la baie de Somme
Tel: 22.27.83.11
Base nautique de loisirs
Tel: 22.27.04.39
Le Nautilude
Tel: 22.27.05.57
Horseriding (Société hippique du Crotoy)
Tel: 22.27.04.67

Saint-Valery-sur-Somme
Tourist information
Tel: 22.60.93.50
Somme Bay Wildfowlers Association
Tel: 22.26.92.30
Watersports (Sports nautiques)
Tel: 22.26.91.64

Cayeux
Tourist information
Tel: 22.2661.15
Leisure centre (Centre de loisirs)
Tel: 22.26.62.36
Marina (Port de plaisance)
Tel: 22.26.61.15
Lighthouse (phare)
Tel: 22.60.60.30
Benoît-Champy Sea Rescue
Tel: 22.26.60.52

Ault-Onival
Tourist information
Tel: 22.60.57.15 and 22.60.40.06

Mers-les-Bains
Tourist information
Tel: 35.86.06.14
Sports hall (Salle des sports)
Tel: 35.86.33.58
Aero-club
Tel: 35.86.56.34
Horseriding (Centre équestre)
Tel: 35.50.71.16

OTHER ADDRESSES:

Abbeville meteorological office
Tel: 30.68.08.80
Tourist information
1 place de l'Amiral-Courbet, 80100 Abbeville
Tel: 22.24.27.92
Fax: 22.31.08.26
Departmental Tourist information
21 rue Ernest-Cauvin 80000 Amiens
Tel: 22.9226.39
Fax: 22.92.77.47

The Memorial route

The First World War laid waste to the Pas-de-Calais over a four-year period, the Front being fixed here in September 1914 until October 1918. Arrras, the pivot of the northern offensive during the push to the sea of 1914, suffered terribly during the 1914–1915 combat of Artois, yet did not succumb to German assault; her bombed belfry became the symbol of French resistance – much like the burnt-out ruins of Reims cathedral – until, in turn, the heroic defence of Verdun became the new focus of attention. Arras remembers General Barbot and his Alpine troops who defended her in 1914; the future Marshals Pétain, Fayolle and Foch played decisive roles in the battles of Artois. In the surrounding countryside numerous memorials and cemeteries recall the ultimate sacrifice made by hundreds of thousands of soldiers in the yard by yard fight for ground. To fill the vacuum left by war, 150,000 Poles, Belgians and Italians came to work here in the mines. A series of mayors initiated bold rebuilding program-mes, in Lens (Emile Basly), Arras (Gustave Lemelle) and Béthune (Jules Senis); in Arras, the architect Pacquet worked a near miracle in restoring the original character of the town, ably assisted by the entrepreneur Peulabeuf who used reinforced concrete to considerable advantage in the reconstruction of the belfry.

In 1939 war broke out in Europe for the second time in 25 years. British HQ was established in Arras – as had been the case in 1914 – and the town fell on 24 May. The Pas-de-Calais came under the control of the Oberfeldkommandantur of Brussels and endured crippling requisitioning from the Germans. Shelling brought renewed wide-scale destruction of buildings, while Resistance workers organised a network of escape

Vimy: Canadian Memorial

CEMETERIES AND OTHER

ARRAS

The citadel to the south-west of the town today serves as a monument to the 7e *Régiment de Chasseurs*. Built during Vauban's time, the citadel walls still encircle a defensive trench, which became a sanctuary for the Resistance in the Pas-de-Calais following the execution of 218 patriots on 21 August 1941 and 24 July 1944. The names of the executed are engraved on plaques fixed along the length of the walls encircling the trench, and a stake planted at the end of the axis of the ditch symbolises their great sacrifice. The whole site is enclosed by an attractive iron grill (access from avenue du Mémorial-des-Fusillés).

VIMY: a part of Canada

Because of its position domin-ating Arras, the *crête de Vimy* ridge was a strategic point on the western front and the theatre of continued warfare throughout the 1914–1918 war. A wood of Austrian and Scots pines covers the mount at the point where the front was fixed: 11,285 trees rep-resenting 11,285 Canadian soldiers who lost their lives during the terrible attack of 9 April 1917 during which the Canadian corp took the ridge and held on to it until the very last. This land is Canadian, nearly 300 acres of it, where the wounds of war remain: the trenches and the craters are still there. Canadian students explain to visitors the com-plexities of the ingenious and extensive network of trenches.

• **Mémorial et parc canadien**, 62580 Vimy. Tel: 21.48.72.29. April to 15 November, 10am–6pm.

LA TARGETTE

In the hamlet of la Targette, opposite the *monument du Flambeau*, a museum recalls the combats of the two World

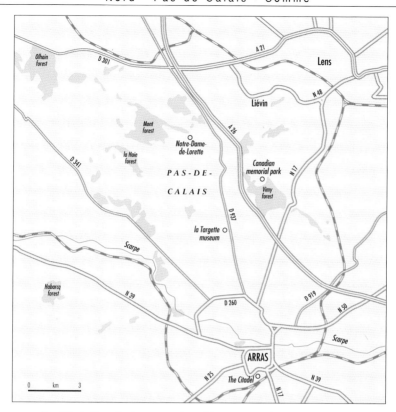

routes for Allied pilots. In the mines, the Communists provoked the great strike of 1941, and its suppression caused the death of 220 people who fell in the trenches of the Arras stronghold. At the end of 1944, Montgomery's offensive strike brought liberation to the town on 1 September. Arras embarked upon a new period of rebuilding, this time under the leadership of mayors August Lecoeur (Lens), Guy Mollet (Arras) and Jacques Vendroux (Calais).

MEMORIALS TO THE FALLEN

Wars and displays more than 5,000 objects . . . things made by the soldiers, documents, notices, uniforms, canons, machine guns . . .

• Musée de la Targette
route départmentale 937
62580 Neuville-Saint-Vaast
Tel: 21.59.17.76
Daily 9am–8pm; in January, only Saturday and Sunday.

NOTRE-DAME-DE-LORETTE

The *Blanche Voie* passes through the entrance into Lorette national cemetery where visitors can see the memorial plaque presented by Loos train escapees (Second World War). The cemetery recognises the gift of so many lives given in defence of France: 19,000 graves, a 170-feet lantern tower (Lille architect Cordonnier) and ossuary to the 6,000 unknown soliders of two wars, consecrated on 26 May 1927 (Lorin and Payne stained glass, Gaudin mosaics, Monseigneur Julien's mausoleum . . .).

• Notre-Dame-de-Lorette
62153 Ablain-Saint-Nazaire
Tel: 21.45.15.80
Summer 9am–noon and 2–6.30pm; the rest of the year 9am–noon and 2–5pm.

Also visit the 1914–1918 museum with reconstructions of daily life in the trenches and examples of equipment used.

• Musée vivant 1914-1918
1 March to 30 November, daily 9am–8pm; 1 December to 28 February, Saturday and Sunday 9am–8pm.

FURTHER INFORMATION

Tourist information
hôtel de ville
place des Héros
62000 Arras
Tel: 21.51.26.95

The First World War in the Somme
A tour of the Historial de la Grande Guerre (Péronne)

"The Somme battle field looks like nothing else on earth . . ." (Pierre Loti)

The *département* of the Somme was deeply marked by the First World War. The impact of the1916 Battle of the Somme was considerable, both because of the number of nationalities involved (more than thirty countries as we know them today), because of a death toll amounting to one million, and because of the scars and traces of battle that the Somme countryside bore after the guns had stopped: the trenches, the holes created by mines, wasted pasture and arable land . . . and of course the burnt-out towns and villages.

The Historial de la Grande Guerre at Péronne depicts the daily life of war-torn Somme through a collection of writings and artefacts, everyday objects and photographs, and personal testimonies of both the famous and the unknown.

One of the war's bloodiest battles which took place near Albert, with the French front fighting south of the River Somme and the British front to its north, ended in the laying waste of one third of the *département*. The 'memorial route', liberally strewn with

Caribou memorial in parc Terreneuvien

cemeteries and monuments to the fallen, recalls this appalling episode. (Coming out of Péronne going towards Bapaume, note the handsome monument to the Second Australian Division.)

Bouchavesne-Bergen was the furthest point reached by French trooops. Rebuilt with the help of a Norwegian industrialist, it is now called Bergen after his home town. A statue of Foch stands in the town.

At Rancourt, a private chapel adjoins the cemetery where 8,566 French soldiers are buried. Here, too, are the British and the German cemeteries.

Combles was fortified by the Germans, who held out for a considerable length of time against British and French offensives (26 September 1916).

At Guillemont, a French monument commemorates the bloody combat of August 1914.

Longueval was vital to the push east. Derville Wood was taken by South African soldiers. The struggle that took place here is marked by a monument that stands amid oak trees grown from acorns brought from South Africa. The monument itself consists of a flint wall around a triumphal arch surmounted by a bronze of Castor and Pollux, the reconciled enemy brothers (a reference to the Boer War 1899–1902). There is also a monument to fallen New Zealanders.

Canadians fought at Courcelette, and they are rememembered in an inscription in the granite memorial on the D929.

Pozières is etched into the collective Australian conscience; its name was given to a town in Queensland in memory of the Australian engagement on the Somme front. The first tanks of the war were seen on this battlefield.

Thiepval was one of the pillars of the German defence; the British army lost 20,000 men in battle here, recalled by the Ulster Tower (a replica of one in Belfast) in recognition of the losses suffered by the Irish troops.

Leaving Beaumont-Hamel, note the Scottish monument to the Eighth Argyll and Sutherland Highlanders.

Newfoundland (or in French *Terre Neuve*) played its part in the Great War as a British colony. The Newfoundland losses were particularly heavy here (*Mémorial terre-*

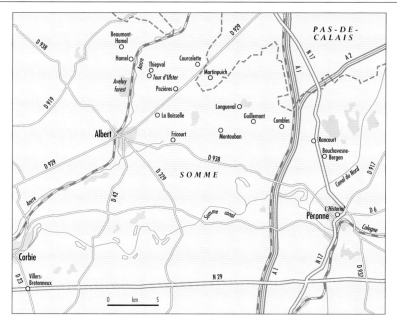

neuvien). On top of the Caribou knoll a viewing platform explains the distribution of the trenches.

A fine war memorial stands at the exit to the town of Hamel (Pietà).

Aveluy Wood Cemetery is very pretty.

At Boisselle, there is a memorial to the men of the Irish and Scottish Tyneside brigades who fell during the 1 July 1916 offensive. Near the village is the gigantic Lochnagar Crater.

In 1919, only 120 of the original 7,343 inhabitants of Albert remained, subjected to incessant shelling. One such attack knocked over the statue of the Virgin, called thereafter the leaning Virgin, or *Vierge penchée*. The town saw intensive military action after July 1915. The French war graves in the civil cemetery (monument to the soldiers of Britanny) bear witness to further sacrifices. In former dugouts, a diorama displays realistic scenes of the trenches in 1916 (further information from tourist office).

Fricourt: le Tambour (west of the village) and Point 110. (Other sites involved in the Battle of the Somme are Doullens, Noyelles-sur-Mer, Villiers-Bretonneux . . .)

THE FIRST WORLD WAR IN THE SOMME

PRACTICAL INFORMATION

British military cemeteries
Commonwealth War Graves Commission
    rue Angèle-Richard
    62217 Beaurains
    Tel: 21.71.03.24

French military cemeteries
Direction interdépartmentale des anciens combattants
    Cité administrative
    175 rue Gustave-Delory
    59084 Lille Cedex.
    Tel: 20.52.00.25 .

German military cemeteries
    SESMA
    41 rue Jules-Dumez
    59840 Pérenchies
    Tel: 20.08.73.61

Historial de la Grande Guerre
    place du Château
    80200 Péronne
    Tel: 22.83.14.18

Tourist information
    80300 Albert
    Tel: 22.75.16.42

SPECIAL EVENT

11 November:
    1914–1918 Armistice Commemoration

RECOMMENDED READING

Rose E Coombs, *Before endeavours fade: a guide to the battlefields of the First World War* (Battle of Britain Prints International, 1990).

Fortified towns

The absence of any natural frontier and its unique geographic situation have meant northern France has always been a militarily fragile region, constantly subjected to invasion.

To counteract this vulnerability, fortresses have been built here over the centuries, which today constitute a veritable museum of military architecture. The finest of these are fortifications constructed or improved under Louis XIV by the engineering genius, Vauban, whose designs were admired and copied into the 19th century.

Today, the fortifications of the Nord and Pas-de-Calais *départements* constitute both an historic inheritance and important tourist attractions. Of recent years, the relevant *communes* have become sensitized to the importance of these sites and have set about both preserving and promoting them.

Whenever Vauban worked on fortifications, an individual relief model would be made of the town in question, illustrating the strategic requirements of the site. Most of these models of northern French towns are on display at the *palais des Beaux-Arts* in Lille, with the exception of Douai and Maubeuge, which can be seen locally.

VAUBAN

Celebrated military architect and siege strategist (most notably, Lille 1678), Vauban perhaps enjoys the best reputation of any French Marshal.

He masterminded more than 50 sieges and built or improved 333 fortified towns, thus creating a barrier around Louis XIV's kingdom reputed to be unbreachable, and bequeathing a stock of military architecture which still delights today.

Sébastien le Prestre de Vauban came from the Morvan (1633–1707), and was also an economist, statistician, agronomist, forester, inventor . . . and talented writer.

The last part of his life was sadly marred by a partial fall from grace following a publication which displeased Louis XIV for criticising the plight of France and recommending a single tax from which none would be exempt. (Michel Parent, *Vauban*, ed Berger-Levrault, 1982)

Le Quesnoy:
Aerial view of fortifications

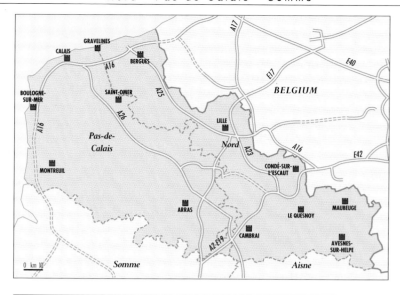

FORTIFIED TOWNS

Arras
Tel: 21.51.26.95
Vauban citadel (17th century).

Avesnes-sur-Helpe
Tel: 27.61.11.22
Romano-Gallic excavations;
Vauban fortifications;
Pont des Dames (flood sluice
for moat).

Bergues
Tel: 28.68.60.44
Medieval towers;
Vauban fortifications;
Water supply system.

Boulogne-sur-Mer
Tel: 21.31.68.38
13th-century castle with
weaponry;
Comtal château belfry (12th
century).

Cambrai
Tel: 27.78.36.15
Medieval towers and gates;
13th-century château de
Selles;
Underground passages with
14th–late 17th-century graffiti;
Passage de Selles (16th
century);
16th-century citadel modified
by Vauban.

Condé-sur-l'Escaut
Tel: 27.40.28.92
Medieval ramparts (12th
century);
Bailleul house;

Château (1184);
Vauban fortifications.

Gravelines
Tel: 28.23.39.16
Vauban fortifications;
Stronghold (arsenal) with
powder magazines and
artillery embrasures;
Water supply system.

Lille
Tel: 20.31.81.00
Vauban citadel.

Maubeuge
Tel: 27.62.11.93
Vauban fortifications;
Mons gate, guardhouse
(museum) and relief map.

Le Quesnoy
Tel: 27.49.05.28
Vauban's star-shaped
fortifications with lakes and
moat.

*Guided tours available at all
of the above. Details from
telephone numbers shown.*

SPECIAL EVENTS

Last Sunday in April: fortified
towns day, including free
guided tours and special
events including the military.

Third Sunday in September:
national historic monuments
open day.

FURTHER INFORMATION

Nord • Pas-de-Calais
Fortifications Promotions
Office
hôtel de ville
59300 Le Quesnoy
Tel: 27.49.50.05
(Monsieur F Dolphin)

RECOMMENDED READING

Anne Blanchard, *les
Ingénieurs 'du Roy', de Louise
XIV à Louis XVI, études du
corps des fortifications*,
université Paul-Valéry
Montpellier, 1979.

Nicolas Faucherre, *Places
fortes, bastion du pouvoir*, ed
Remparts, 1991.

Gaston Zeller, *l'Organisation
défensive des frontières du
nord et de l'est au XVIIe
siècle*, ed Berger-Levrault,
1928.

Windmills route

Of earlier invention than the water mill, windmills were used in the East as early as the 7th century. There are records of them in Flanders as far back as the 12th century; these were post-mills (pivot mills), the fixed tower windmill arriving some time later.

Depending on their use, the mills used the wind to power a rotating mechanism for the grinding of corn or the raising and drainage of water. Subsequent mills were geared to produce a reciprocating movement for the pounding of seed to make oil.

Today, there are more than twenty windmills in the Nord and Pas-de-Calais *départements* but, in the 19th century, these numbered more than 2,000. The vast majority of these are post-mills, sited in Flanders – the better to capture the North Sea winds.

As its name suggests, the post-mill consists of a movable part which the miller could turn to the wind by means of a winch.

The regional Friends of Windmills Association has undertaken a large campaign to raise public awareness of the mills and to protect them through renovation and, occasionally, even moving them, as in the case of Villeneuve-d'Ascq. In the inter-war period, a movement was created to protect

Coquelles: windmill

the interests of millers in the face of competition from the industrial mills.

These windmills provided ideal look-out posts during the two World Wars, given their elevated situation; though equally they made easy targets for enemy fire.

Villeneuve-d'Ascq: Flour mill illuminated for 14 July celebrations

Hondschoote: Noordmeulen

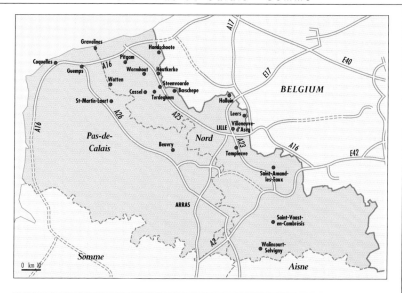

WINDMILLS TO VISIT

Béthune region

Beuvry
Beuvry windmill

Calais region

Coquelles
Coquelle windmill

Guemste Tel: 21.82.13.64
Pont de Guemste windmill

Cambrai region

Saint-Vaast-en-Cambrésis
Tel: 20.05.49.34
Oil windmill

Dunkirk region

Boeschepe Tel: 28.42.50.24
Ondankmeulen windmill

Cassel Tel: 28.42.43.22
Cassel windmill

Gravelines Tel: 28.65.21.28
Lebriez windmill

Hondschoote
Tel: 28.62.53.00
Nordmeulen windmill

Houtkerque Tel: 28.40.90.79
Hofland windmill

Pitgam Tel: 28.62.10.90
Den Leeuw windmill

Steenvoorde
Tel: 28.49.77.77
Noordmeulen and
Drievenmeulen windmills

Terdeghem
Tel: 28.48.16.10
Steen windmill

Watten Tel: 21.88.26.04
De la Montagne windmill

Wormhout Tel: 28.62.81.23
Deschodt windmill

Lille region

Halluin Tel: 20.23.89.72
Hollebeke windmill

Leers Tel: 20.75.32.06
Moulin Blanc

Templeuve Tel: 20.59.31.33
Vertain windmill

Villeneuve-d'Ascq
Tel: 20.05.49.34
Oil and flour windmills

***Other windmills undergoing
restoration are:***

Saint-Amand-les-Eaux
Tel: 27.27.85.00
Le Blanc windmill

Achicourt
Hacart windmill

Walincourt-Selvigny
Tel: 27.82.70.37
Brunet windmill

SPECIAL EVENTS

Third Sunday in June is
national windmills open day
with special events at most
windmills.

FURTHER INFORMATION

ARAM/Nord • Pas-de-Calais
(Regional Friends of
Windmills Association)
            rue Albert-Samain
            59650 Villeneuve-d'Ascq
            Tel: 20.05.49.34

RECOMMENDED READING

Jean Bruggeman, *Toujours
vivant les moulins*, ed ARAM
1986;
*Nos moulins . . . vingt ans
déjà*, ed ARAM 1993.

Claude Rivals, *Le Moulin à
vent et le meunier*, ed Serg
1976.

Cultural highways to major North-European towns

A series of suggested itineraries (encompassing museums, important monuments, sites of cultural and historical interest, outstanding countryside . . . as well as hotel and restaurant addresses) aimed at enriching your journey from Calais and the Tunnel exit to the important towns and colourful regions of northern France, Belgium and the south-west Netherlands.

(An in-depth description of the three French départements most immediately adjacent to the Tunnel — Nord, Pas-de-Calais and Somme — can be found on p115).

I
Calais–Rouen

II
Calais–Paris

Opposite:
Waterloo,
Belgium, a piper
commemorates
the battle at the
foot of the famous
lion

III
Calais–Reims

IV
Calais–Rotterdam

Whosoever sets foot on French soil resists only with the greatest of difficulty the lure of the capital. All road and rail routes converge on Paris. One third of the country's students, more than half of her research workers, and most of her writers live and work here. A centuries-long policy of centralisation has resulted in a concentration of political and administrative decision-making bodies in and around Paris, in an agglomeration of corporate head offices, and a concentration both of France's most prestigious laboratories and artistic and cultural institutions. While the whole country may benefit from this pivotal role in international affairs, more and more voices have been raised in protest at its unbridled demographic and territorial expansion. This disquiet has recently been expressed with increasing vehemence on the heels of new decentralising legislation, occasioning a revival of the great debate on national restructuring aimed at harmonious and balanced development of the French regions. Contemporary Paris wields a seductive influence upon the foreign visitor, especially on tourists arriving from Great Britain via the Tunnel and upon visitors from northern Europe (northern France, Belgium, the Netherlands, Denmark . . .), understandably drawn to the perceived epicentre of France via the Lille–Paris motorway.

This magnetic effect is readily explained: beautiful architecture, famous urban axes (from La Défense to Le Marais, from the great boulevards to the banks of the Seine and the Saint-Martin canal), and a profusion of unique museums and galleries (the Louvre, the Picasso museum, the musée d'Orsay, Beaubourg, the museum of modern art . . .).

Yet Paris is also a turntable, the pivotal point from which to access the rest of France and continental Europe. Beyond the French capital, the Parisian motorway network links the motorist with the prodigious diversity of Europe: south to the Netherlands and Belgium, east to eastern France, to baroque Bavaria, to neighbouring Switzerland, to Spain and Italy, to towns ancient and wonderful, and to all the shores of the Mediterranean.

Or for those who prefer the example of Stevenson and his mule, the Cévennes route beckons, or one of the Provence villages that Vuillard, Bonnard and Matisse so loved to paint . . . or fish by lamplight one night on the motionless waters off Sète, or at Italian Camogli.

I. From Calais to Rouen

Beyond the Côte d'Opale and the Picardy coast (see page 115), westwards towards Rouen and Upper Normandy, the cliffs of the pays de Caux, akin to the cliffs of the English south coast, extend towards Le Havre, before sweeping down to the lovely Seine valley and the delights of Rouen. The charms of this valley, frequently alluded to in the works of Maupassant, recall the paintings of the Impressionists – and, in particular, the work of Boudin and Jongkind (19th-century Dutch) – which can be seen in the galleries of Rouen and Honfleur. Further still along the Normandy coast, at Calvados, the Second World War Memorial commemorates the Allied Landing of 6 June 1944.

• **Seine-Maritime departmental tourist information** 2 *bis* rue du Petit-Salut, 76000 Rouen. Tel: 35.88.61.32

DIEPPE
76200 • E-2

Tourist information
boulevard Général-de-Gaulle
Tel: 35.84.11.77

Hotels
La Présidence ***
2 boulevard de Verdun
Tel: 35.84.31.31
Aguado ***
3 boulevard de Verdun
Tel: 35.84.27.00
L'Univers ***
10 boulevard de Verdun
Tel: 35.84.12.55
Hôtel de la Plage **
20 boulevard de Verdun
Tel: 35.84.12.28
Hôtel Epsom **
11 boulevard de Verdun
Tel: 35.84.10.18

Restaurants
La Mélie
2 Grande-rue-du-Pollet
Tel: 35.84.21.19
Marmite dieppoise
8 rue Saint-Jean
Tel: 35.84.24.26

Nearby
Hôtel de la Terrasse *
Varengeville-sur-Mer (11km)
Tel: 35.85.12.54
Auberge du Clos-Normand ®
Martin-Eglise (7km)
Tel: 35.04.40.34

With cliffs on all sides, the Dieppe of bygone days was a strategically appointed port, home to both sailors and pirates. Indeed, in retaliation for pillaging Southampton in 1339, the English seized the town and not until 1435 did French troops win it back. The port was fortified and equipped under François I. Local ship-owner Jean Ango (1480–1551) undertook expeditions to the four corners of the globe, one such expedition being responsible for the discovery of New York. Dieppe crews were involved in the struggle for French independance from the British in Quebec. Following the ravages of the plague and Revocation of the Edict of Nantes (1685), the town fell into decline, though its international links gave rise to ivory trading (elephant tusks, sperm whale teeth). More than 1,000 pieces of ivory are on show in the **musée-château**, castle museum. Dieppe suffered heavy damages during the Second World War. Today, it is largely dependent on fishing, tourism and its shops (especially those in the pedestrian streets).

Start your exploration of the town either from the vantage point of the **Notre-Dame-de-Bonsecours chapel** or alternatively the belvedere on top of the *château*. This castle museum, formerly the site of a 12th-century fortress destroyed in a battle against Richard Coeur de Lion in 1195, was replaced in the 15th century by Captain Desmaret's sandstone and knapped flint edifice, though retaining the medieval aspect of its predecessor. Since the turn of the century, it has housed a collection begun in the middle of the 19th century: on the ground floor are beautiful model sailing boats, naval furniture and navigational instruments. The first floor collection of paintings includes the works of several artists who spent time in *Haute Normandie*, or Upper Normandy: Isabey, Sisley, Pissarro, Boudin, Van Dongen . . . as well as nearly 1,000 ivory pieces. See, too, sculptures by Carpeaux, engravings by Braque and objects once belonging to the musician Saint-Saëns.

• **Musée-château** Open daily, except Tuesday, 10am–noon and 2–6pm; from 1 October to 31 May daily, except Tuesday, until 5pm. Tel: 35.84.19.76.

Also of interest are the **church of Saint-Remi** (1552–1645) where Saint-Saëns was organist, and the **church of Saint-Jacques** (13th century), with its 15th-century square tower. See, too, the port and harbour.

Close to Dieppe (11km away), the resort of **Varengeville** has beautiful gardens and an exceptional dovecote. Its church has windows by Ubac and Georges Braque (the latter is buried in the adjacent cemetery). From Varengeville, there is an excellent view over Dieppe.

SAINT-VALERY-EN-CAUX
76460 · E-2

Tourist information
Maison-Henri-IV
Tel: 35.97.00.63

Hotels
Mercure-Altéa **
14 avenue Clemenceau
Tel: 35.97.35.48
Hôtel des Terrasses *
Bord de mer
Tel: 35.97.11.12

Nearby
Les Galets
Bord de mer
Veules-les-Roses (8km)
Tel: 35.97.61.33
Les Hêtres
riyte de Fécamp (D925)
Le Bourg-Ingouville (8km)
Tel: 35.57.09.30

On the road between Dieppe and Fécamp, the interesting harbour town of Saint-Valery competed for many years with her two neighbouring parishes for Newfoundland and Iceland herring and cod. Victor Hugo composed his lament to lost mariners here, *Oh combien de marins, combien de capitaines.* After a period of decline, tourism and the Paleul nuclear power station brought new vigour to the area. The harbour, with moorings for 600 boats, is not lacking in charm; the pebble and rock beaches are well suited to fishing. The town has a few handsome buildings: the **Henri-IV house**, opposite the harbour, in Renaissance style with beautiful moulded ceilings and octagonal stair tower; also the Penitents Cloister, **cloître des Pénitents** (in the hospital) and **Notre-Dame-du-Bon-Port chapel** (1953) in the main square, with modern stained glass windows by André-Louis Pierre.

FÉCAMP
76400 · F-1

Tourist information
113 rue Alexandre-le-Grand
Tel: 35.28.51.01

Hotels
Hôtel de la Plage **
87 rue de la Plage
Tel: 35.29.76.51

Hôtel de la Poste *
4 avenue Gambetta
Tel: 35.29.55.11
Hôtel de la Mer *
89 boulevard Albert[1er]
Tel: 35.28.24.64

Restaurants
Le Viking
63 boulevard Albert 1er
Tel: 35.29.22.92
Le Maritime
2 place Selles
Tel: 35.28.21.71

Nearby
Manoir de Barville
Cany-Barville (21km)
Tel: 35.97.79.30
Auberge de la Rouge ®
Fécamp (2km from town centre)
Tel: 35.28.07.59

There has been some kind of settlement at Fécamp since ancient times, but its history as a port did not begin until the Romans arrived. This is where they built their galleys in preparation for Julius Caesar's conquest of England. Following destruction and pillage by the Normans in 841, another Norman, Guillaume Longue-Epée, undertook to rebuild the town, the abbey and the fortress. In the 11th century, the whole town came under the jurisdiction of the abbey. The monks played an essential role in the town's management and that of the surrounding region: land clearance, harbour management, organisation of herring fishing. At this time, Fécamp was a popular place of pilgrimage, thanks to the presence of a holy relic, *le Précieux Sang du Christ* (Christ's Precious Blood). Early in the 16th century, the already very busy port won a reputation for its herring, cod and mackerel processing, as well as for its trade in wood, salt, wine, coffee . . . In the 19th century, the fishermen of Fécamp were among the most successful catchers of fish off the shores of Iceland and Newfoundland. In 1900, nearly 2,000 fishermen a year departed from Fécamp. With increased competition and diminishing stocks, this fishing epic came to a halt in the 1960s with the return of the last Newfoundland trawler, the *Dauphin.* Today, only off-shore fishing

persists and, since 1989, the catches have been sold by auction on the **quai Sadi-Carnot.** Come here in the morning (7am onward, except Monday 6am) to sample the unique atmosphere as restaurateurs, fish merchants and curious onlookers seek out the best of the catch. A winding road leads to the cliff top (350 feet) and the **Notre-Dame-du-Salut chapel**, where there is a good view of the town and the sea.

The **église de la Sainte-Trinité** is one of the crowning glories of Norman Gothic architecture. Modern statues of Richard I and Richard II – descendants of Rollon and benefactors of the monastery – frame the entrance. The church, constructed on the foundations of an earlier Roman building (late 12th century), has a 210-ft-high lantern tower. The interior is a richly decorated marvel of luminosity, with a white marble Renaissance altar (behind the main altar), a stone group sculpture, *La Mort de la Vierge* (1945) and 1420 stone tabernacle; 12th- and 13th-century stained glass windows light the great apsidal chapel (guided tour, weekdays 11am–3pm, Sunday until 5pm. The **church of Saint-Etienne**, situated in the square of the same name in the town centre, is in Flamboyant style, dating from 1500.

The **musée municipal** has exhibits of Rouen and Delft pottery, porcelain, locally-made furniture and, particularly interesting, the Doctor Dufour collection – including baby bottles, toys and cradles from all over the world. There is also a section on the Fécamp seascape, and a model collection.

• **Musée municipal** 21 rue Alexandre-Legros. Open daily, except Tuesday, 10am–noon and 2–5.30pm. Tel: 35.28.31.99.

In 1862, an engineer by the name of Legrand worked out the recipe for the 27-herb liqueur known as Benedictine. He built a factory on an exceptional site that would have done justice to a palace, assisted by the architect Viollet-le-Duc. The building combines Gothic and Renaissance elements and its extravagance is reminiscent of the châteaux of Louis II of Bavaria. Inside, both décor and furnishings are of local origin, as is the collection of Roman lamps, ironmongery and religious artefacts. More than 100,000 people visit this factory museum every year (tour includes liqueur tasting).

• **Musée de la bénédictine** 110 rue Alexandre-Legrand. Open 2 January to 18 March and 14 November to 31 December, 10.30am– 3.30pm; 19 March to 27 May and 12 September to 13 November 10am–noon and 2– 5.30pm; 28 May to 11 September 10am–6pm. Tel: 35.10.26.00.

Finally, the **musée terre-neuvas,** Newfoundland trawler museum, gives an insight into the long and prestigious history of the capital of the Newfoundland fishing vessel. Alternative fishing techniques, including audiovisual presentation and commentary. Also an impressive model of the French Navy training ship, the *Etoile.*

• **Musée des terre-neuvas** 27 boulevard Albert 1er. Open daily, except Tuesday, 10am–noon and 2–5.30pm; until 6.30pm July/August including Tuesdays. Tel: 35.28.31.99.

Etretat: the Needle

ÉTRETAT
76790 · F-1

Tourist information
place Maurice-Guillard
Tel: 35.27.05.21

Festival
Bénédiction de la mer à l'Acension

Hotels
Dormy House **
route du Havre
Tel: 35.27.07.88
Hôtel des Falaises *
boulevard René-Coty
Tel: 35.27.02.77

Restaurant
Le Galion
boulevard René-Coty
Tel: 35.29.48.74

"I was impressed with what I saw of Etretat. The cliffs are pierced at intervals with huge natural archways through which the surf thunders at high tide."
(Victor Hugo, letter to Adèle, 1835)

Before tourists came to Etretat, this was largely a town of fishermen. Napoleon's earlier plans for a military port were thwarted when problems arose over the building of sea walls. From 1839, the year of the resort's 'discovery' by writer and humourist Alphonese Karr, road and rail improvements afforded easy access to Parisians, and Etretat became the fashionable haunt of artists and writers: Courbet, Isabey, Corot, Monet, Matisse, Flaubert, Degas. During the First World War, the town became a vast hospital ward for some 600 wounded British soldiers. Tourism came to the fore again after the Second World War, firmly establishing Etretat as a desirable resort in an imposing natural setting. Today, visitors can stride out along the jetty that protects the vale from the sea's fury; on one side are walks beneath the cliffs, on the other, the little town itself, with its pretty gardens and villas, and *caloges*, the upturned boats which, in traditional style, serve as stalls for produce, drinks and shellfish. At low tide, visitors can see the **chambre des Demoiselles** and the famous needle (260 ft); up on the cliff, between the cliff edge and golf course, enjoy some superb views. The **musée Nungesser-et-Coli** recounts the adventure of the *Oiseau blanc,* which attempted an Atlantic crossing on 8 May 1927. (Open weekends and public holidays 3–7pm; 15 June to 31 August 10am–noon and 3–7pm. Tel: 35.27.07.47.)

Driving on towards the delights of Rouen, discover monasteries tucked away beside the meandering Seine, but only after first detouring to Honfleur, the artists' town.

Parc naturel régional de Brotonne, including the **Forest of Brotonne** and the Lower Seine: this regional park extends over some 10,500 acres to include 50 *communes* or par-

ishes. As well as safeguarding the local environment, the park's considerable funds finance various collections exhibited throughout the park:

• **Bourneville:** *musée des métiers et industries des hommes de la basse Seine* (exhibit of crafts and industries of the Lower Seine): glassblowers, potters, ironmongers, thatchers. Open July/August daily, except Tuesday, 2–6.30pm. Tel: 32.57.40.41.

• **La Haye-de-Routot:** village baker and shoemaker.

• **Hautville:** windmill.

• **Saint-Opportune-la-Mare:** *maison de la pomme* or apple house. Tel: 32.57.16.48. Open March, Saturday, Sunday and bank holidays, 2.30–6.30pm.

• **Caudebec-en-Caux:** *musée de la marine,* museum of the sea. Open July/August daily 2–6.30pm; 15 March to 31 December daily, except Tuesday, 2–6.30pm. Tel: 35.96.27.30.

The park is also involved in: reclamation of the Vernier marshes near Quillebeuf; in replanting orchards, cider-making and

---

Cruises on the River Seine

Several companies operate cruises on the Seine between Paris and Honfleur.

• *La Salamandre*
76200 Le Havre
Tel: 35.42.01.31

A small 120-seat boat takes passengers from the port of Le Havre, across the baie de Seine to either Honfleur or Deauville, or from Honfleur down the Seine to Rouen (day trip).

• *Le Guillaume-le-Conquérant*
Rives de Seine-Croisières
quai de l'Hôtel-de-Ville
76500 Elbeuf
Tel: 35.78.14.08 and
35.78.31.70

An 126-seater cruiser takes passengers from Rouen to Paris, Deauville or Villequier.

• *Le Normandie*
Aqua Vivaport de Grenelle
75015 Paris
Tel: 45.75.52.60

One-week cruises between Paris and Honfleur (53 cabins).

---

the organisation of regular fruit and produce markets (**Sainte-Opportune-la-Mare** market hall).

Last but not least, 230 miles of footpaths have been created within the Forest of Brotonne.

• **Parc naturel régional de Brotonne** 76940 Notre-Dame-de-Bliquetuit. Tel: 35.37.23.16.

HONFLEUR
14600 • F-1

Tourist information
place Arthur-Boudin
Tel: 31.89.23.30

Hotels
Ferme Saint-Simeon ★★★★
rue Maris
Tel: 31.89.23.61
L'Ecrin ★★★
19 rue Eugène-Boudin
Tel: 31.89.32.39
Castel Albertine ★★
19 cours Albert-Manuel
Tel: 31.98.85.56
Hostellerie Lechat ★★
place Sainte-Catherine
Tel: 31.89.23.85

Restaurants
L'Assiette gourmande
quai des Passagers
Tel: 31.89.24.88
L'Absinthe
10 quai Quarantaine
Tel: 31.89.39.00

Nearby
La Chaumière ★★
route du Littoral, Vasouy (3km)
Tel: 31.81.63.20

This charming little town, which comes under the jurisdiction of the self-governing port of Rouen, marks the divide between Upper and Lower Normandy. It is dependent on fishing (sole, shellfish, etc) and tourism. Much of 17th- and 18th-century Honfleur remains today. Sixteenth-century Honfleur was home to sailors and pirates alike. The old 17th-century harbour is charming with its tall narrow houses (**quai Sainte-Catherine**); see also the beautiful 18th-century ship-owner's house on **quai Saint-Etienne.** Numerous galleries testify to Honfleur's popularity with painters since the 19th century: Corot, Daubigny . . . The **Musée de la marine,** sea museum, has beautiful models,

---

with documents relating to the region's maritime history; the **musée d'ethnographie et d'art populaire du vieux Honfleur** has 17th- and 18th-century Normandy interiors.

• **Musée de la marine et musée d'ethnographie** quai Saint-Etienne. Open 13 February to 15 April daily 2–6pm; Saturday/Sunday 10.30am–12.30pm and 2–6pm; the rest of the year daily 10.30am–12.30pm and 2–6pm; closed 31 December to 12 February. Tel: 31.89.14.12.

The **musée Boudin** is housed in the former Saint-Augustin convent and exhibits the work of Honfleur's native painter as well as of his contemporaries (Huet, Jongkind, Courbet, Dubourg . . .). The contributions of Parisian gallery owner Katia Granoff have significantly added to the interest of the collection.

• **Musée Boudin** place Erik-Satie. Tel: 31.89.54.00. Open 15 March to 30 September daily, except Tuesday, 10am–noon and 2–6pm.

Between Honfleur and Rouen, three monasteries, all close to the River Seine, are open to the public. **Jumièges** (F-2) was founded in 654 by Saint Philbert; archive material includes illustrations of an extensive complex of buildings, set around cloisters and courtyards, which was demolished during the Revolution, its stone used for new buildings. Only the skeletons of two churches remain today, open-air exhibits of old stone: one was dedicated to **Notre-Dame**, the second, built before 1000 AD, to **Saint Pierre,** with an impressive, two-towered western elevation (for information on visits, tel: 35.37.24.02). **Saint-Wandrille** was founded in 649 and the abbey grew in influence between the 10th and 14th centuries. Its great Gothic church was demolished during the Revolution (only a part of the arm of the transept remains). Benedictine monks came back to live in part of the abbey in 1930; in 1968, an old tithe barn was transported here and reconstructed to serve as a place of assembly for worship (which includes Gregorian chanting). Close by, in the woods around the abbey, a little Roman building (3-apse floor plan) can be visited on Sundays and public holidays at 11.30am, 3pm and 4pm. Tel: 35.96.23.11.

In nearby Villequier, the **musée Victor Hugo** is open to visitors from 1 November to 28 February daily, except Tuesday, 10am–12.30pm and 2–6.30pm. Tel: 35.56.91.86. The **church of Saint-Martin-de-Boscherville** was originally a college for the instruction of canons, built around 1066 by Raoul de Tancarville. Construction of the great church itself began in the 12th century: notice the great vaulted ceiling.

Rouen: Martyrdom of Joan of Arc

ROUEN
76000 • F-2

Tourist information
25 place de la Cathédrale
Tel: 35.71.41.77

Hotels
Le Quatre Saisons ***
place Tissot
Tel: 35.71.96.00
Col's ***
15 rue Saint-Pic
Tel: 35.71.00.88

Restaurants
Auberge de la Couronne
place du Vieux-Marché
(established 1354)
Tel: 35.71.40.90
Les Nymphéas
9 rue Pie
Tel: 35.89.26.69

Nearby
Pascal Saunier (R)
12 rue du Belvédère
Mont-Saint-Aignan (3km)
Tel: 35.71.61.06
La Butte (R)
69 route de Paris
Bonsecours (3.5km)
Tel: 35.80.43.11
Auberge des Deux Couronnes
Saint-Wandrille-Rançon (31km)
Tel: 35.96.11.44
Grand Sapin (R)
Villequier (39km)
Tel: 35.56.78.73

Historic Rouen, France's fifth port, takes great pride in its many museums and historic buildings. Coveted by kings of both England and France, the town was taken by Philippe Auguste in 1204; then, in 1419, taken by the English. Above all else Rouen is etched in the collective French conscience as the place of Joan of Arc's torment: following an iniquitous trial and detention, she was burnt at the stake in the marketplace on 30 May 1431. Much later, Rouen suffered heavy losses from German bombing raids during the Second World War, when 5,000 homes and 5,500 yards of quayside were destroyed. In spite of this, the centre of the old town retains its charm, in large part due to the surviving half-timbered houses. The **église Jeanne-d'Arc** stands in the *place du Vieux-Marché*, with 16th-century stained glass windows taken from the former church of Saint-Vincent. The building extends into a crypt containing documents detailing the illustrious role played by the square in Rouen's history. The spot where Joan of Arc was burnt at the stake is marked by a **cross** and a little **museum** (35 place du Marché. Open 1 May to 15 September daily 9.30am–6.30pm; the rest of the year daily, except Monday, 10am–noon and 2–6.30pm).

On the south-west corner of the square stands the **maison natale de Pierre Corneille**, the house in which 'the father of French classical tragedy' was born, and where he lived for over 50 years (4 rue de la Pie. Open daily, except Tuesdays and Wednesday mornings, 10am–noon and 2–6pm. Tel: 35.71.63.92). Corneille's country house can be visited at Petit-Couronne on the outskirts of Rouen (502 rue Pierre-Corneille, tel: 35.68.13.89). Considered as Rouen's equivalent to Shakespeare, Corneille (1606–1684) became a lawyer at the age of 18. From an early age, he began writing verse and tragedies: *le Cid, Cinna, Horace, Polyeucte* . . . From 1650 onwards, he concentrated entirely on his writing, in particular – over a period of seven years – the translation of the Imitation of Jesus Christ. Elected to the French Academy in 1647, he was to spend the last 20 years of his life in Paris, where he died on 1 October 1684.

Going west from the square, Rouen's literary pedigree is further confirmed by the **musée de souvenirs de Flaubert et d'histoire de la médecine** (Hôtel-Die, 51 rue Lecat, tel: 35.15.59.95. Open daily, except Sunday and Monday, 10am–nooon and 2–6pm). Flaubert was born in the first floor bedroom of this house where his father practised surgery. From the age of 11, he wrote historical and philosophical tales; following a few years of travel and adventure, he published *Madame Bovary* in 1857 and it was an immediate success. In his Croisset residence (**pavillon de Gustave Flaubert**, open daily, except Tuesday and Wednesday morning, 10am–noon and 2–6pm, tel: 35.36.43.91), he wrote *Salammbô* (1862), *l'Education sentimentale* (1869) and *la Tentation de saint Antoine* (1874), before dying in 1880 while putting the finishing touches to *Bouvard et Pécuchet*.

North-west of *place du Vieux-Marché* is the **church of Saint-Gervais** (19th century). In its crypt is the 4th-century sepulchre of Saint Mellon, Rouen's first bishop. Strolling through Rouen's streets, visitors delight at its lovely buildings, both public and private: the 16th-century **hôtel de bourg Théroulde**, *place de la Pucelle* with its frieze representing the Field of the Cloth of Gold, where François I and Henry VIII of Engand met on 7 June 1520; the Renaissance **Gros-Horloge** pavillon and its Gothic belfry, home to one of the oldest clocks in the world; the **ancien hôtel de ville** (1607) and the **ancien bureau des finances**, today pressed into service as the town's tourist office.

The **cathédrale Notre-Dame** (1250) is one of France's major religious edifices, (150 yards in length, 90 feet high, a four-level nave and, at 495 feet, the country's tallest spire. Its heavily sculpted façade inspired Claude Monet's celebrated *Portail de la cathédrale de Rouen, temps gris* (1892), and is flanked by two towers, the 13th-century Saint-Roman tower (270 feet and containing a 9,500kg bell) and the late 15th-century Butter Tower with its 52-bell carillon). Its richly ornamented interior includes a modern wrought-work pulpit, a 17th–18th-century organ, bas reliefs and Renaissance windows (1521), a late 13th-century stone *ecce homo*, Christ crowned with thorns, a late 16th-century *Pièta* (Mary mourning the body of Christ), a Flamboyant Gothic stone staircase, 13th- and 15th-century stained glass, a tomb containing the remains of Richard Coeur de Lion and a recumbent figure of Guillaume Longue-Epée (14th century) . . .

The **church of Saint-Maclou**, which stands in the square of the same name, is a lovely example of Flamboyant style. It has a five-bay porch and, in spite of damage suffered during 1940–45, the doors of its front elevation still boast Renaissance sculpted panels; inside, a 16th-century organ, Renaissance windows and a lantern tower. Complete your tour of Rouen's religious edifices with a visit to the **church of Saint-Ouen**, situated next to the town hall: 14th century Gothic with 270-ft central tower, Saint-Ouen's is a masterpiece of the Flamboyant style.

The **musée des beaux-arts** has a collection of paintings spanning the last six centuries. The Northern French School is represented by painters like Gérard David (*la Vierge et les Saints*), Martin de Vos, Rubens, Tenirs; from the Italian Veronese School are Caravaggio (*Flagellation*), Guerchin, and from Spain, Velasquez (*l'Homme à la mappemonde*). Further French paintings include works by Clouet, Poussin (*Vénus armant Enée*), Philippe de Champaigne, Fragonnard (*Les Lavandières*), Hubert Robert, Ingres (*La Belle Zélie*), Géricault, Corot, Delacroix (*Justice de Trajan*) . . . Neither are the Impressionists overlooked, with Caillebotte, Monet (*La Rue Lavoisée*), Sisley (*Inondation à Port-Marly*), Renoir, Dufy . . . and last, but not least, contemporary painters, Duchamp, Ubac, Vieira da Silva.

• **Musée des beaux-arts** 26 rue Jean-Lecanuet. Open daily, except Tuesday and Wednesday morning, 10am–noon and 2–6pm. Tel: 35.71.28.40 (combined ticket with, and same opening hours as, *Le Secq des Tournelles Museum* and *Great Clock Belfry*).

Le musée Le Secq des Tournelles has one of the finest exhibitions of forged iron: a 13th-century grill from Ourscamps Abbey, a ramp from Bellevue Château, a 12-lamp wrought-iron candelabra, a collection of 18th-century medieval and English keys, locks, padlocks, metal signs, surgical instruments and dental implements. Open Palm Sunday to 1 October daily, except Tuesday and Wednesday morning, 10am–noon and 2–6pm.

Le musée départemental des antiquités, with its Egyptian and medieval rooms (Lillebonne mosaic depicting Daphne pursued by Apollon), is in a former 18th-century convent (198 rue Beauvoisine. Open 10am–12.30pm and 1.30–5.30pm; Sunday 2–6pm. Tel: 35.98.55.10). The **musée d'histoire naturelle, de préhistoire et d'ethnographie** (prehistoric, natural history and ethnographic museum) has one room devoted to mammals, others to botany, paleontology and mineralogy; an audiovisual exhibit on the natural inheritance of Normandy, plus ethnographic collections from Australia, the South Sea Islands, Lapland and North America (tel: 35.71.41.50).

Fifteen kilometres from the principal town of Normandy stands the **château de Martainville**, once the feoff of the wealthy *vicomte de l'eau*, literally 'the viscount of the water', who was responsible for the control of traffic on the Seine. In 1485, the *vicomte* decided to build his country mansion here upon the foundations of an earlier castle fortress, in white stone. The ground plan consisted of a rectangle flanked at each corner by round towers in stone, sandstone and Flemish brick . In 1961, the government converted this into the **musée des traditions et arts normands**: 15th–19th-century Normandy furniture, ornaments, ceramics and glassware, and displays illustrating the different characters of Upper Normandy's several regions or *pays*.

• **Musée des traditions et arts normands** château de Martainville. Tel: 35.23.44.70. Open daily, except Tuesday, 10am–12.30pm and 2–6pm (5pm in winter).

II. From Calais to Paris

Driving through the **départements** *of Pas-de-Calais and Somme (see page 115), you cross into the* **département** *of the Oise, the last lap on the journey to the great metropolis. The Oise combines with the* **départements** *of Aisne and Somme to form the region known as Picardy; but, unlike the other two* **départements,** *it is very urbanised, a vast residential area and leisure facility for Parisians.*

• **Comité départemental de tourisme de l'Oise** 1 rue Villiers-de-l'Isle-Adam, 60000 Beauvais. Tel: 44.45.82.12

BEAUVAIS

60000 • G-3

Tourist information
1 rue Beauregard
Tel: 44.45.08.18

Hotels
Hôtel Chenal **
63 boulevard Général-de-Gaulle
Tel: 44.45.03.55
Hôtel du Palais *
9 rue Saint-Nicolas
Tel: 44.45.12.58
La Résidence *
24 rue de Borel
Tel: 44.48.30.98
Hôtel Bristol *
60 rue de la Madeleine
Tel: 44.45.01.31

Restaurants
A la Côtelette
8 rue des Jacobins
Tel: 44.45.04.42
La Coquerie
1 rue de Saint-Quentin
Tel: 44.48.58.45

The town has been the see of a bishop since the Middle Ages. During the 11th century, its bishop combined spiritual and secular offices to become one of the most important figures of feudal hierarchy of the medieval period. From the time of Philippe Auguste (late 12th to early 13th century), the town was protected by substantial walls fringed by the waters of the Thérain and its tributaries. Wood and cob buildings lined winding, narrow streets; canals turned the wheels of numerous mills used in the processing of wool and leather. And as it prospered, the town became a centre for art. When Charles le Témeraire and the Burgundians laid siege to the town in 1472, its inhabitants resisted and were ultimately victorious under the leadership of Jeanne Hachette. Whereafter Beauvais again became a favourite with the leading artists of the time: painter Antoine Caron, sculptor Jean Le Pot, architect Martin Chambiges and the master glass-makers of the Le Prince family. Textiles became important again under Louis XIV and during the 18th century; in 1644, Colbert established the famous royal carpet manufacturer here, which enjoyed particular success between 1734 and 1753 under Jean-Baptiste Oudry. Beauvais became the principal town of the *département* during the Revolution; but, with no raw materials of its own, it witnessed decline in the 19th century to became a county town of civil servants. The destruction of nearly 80 per cent of Beauvais in 1940 by German incendiary bombs (60 classified buildings were destroyed) required a rebuilding programme that continued up to 1960. Thanks to decentralisation policies and Beauvais' proximity to Paris, the town has welcomed many new companies, whose employees have swelled its population to 60,000.

La cathédrale Saint-Pierre is Beauvais' best known building. It took four centuries to amass the wealth necessary for its construction. Of the smaller cathedral, built during the Carolingian era ,only three bays of the nave survive intact. Following two fires, the bishop decided in 1225 to build a church bigger than any other existing church, a vast edifice dedicated to Saint Pierre. The founders' ambitions demanded that the towers came to within 3 feet of the height of Notre-Dame de Paris (223 ft). Problems in the course of construction threatened its eventual completion; in 1500, the bishop charged Martin Chambiges (assisted by Jean Vaast) with the task of finishing what had begun three centuries earlier. The transept was completed in 1550 and, at its crossing, an open-work tower created, surmounted by a spire whose 490-ft-high cross dominates the surrounding streets. Degradation of the supporting pillars of the spire was to cause it to crash into the nave and the cathedral remained unfinished. Inside the cathedral, one is struck by the great height of the arches (157 ft) and the technical prowess of its Gothic architecture. Sixteenth-century stained glass decorates the transept; the rose window is the work of Nicolas Le Prince (1551) and in the **Sacré-Coeur chapel** is the fine Renaissance 'de Roncherolles' stained glass (1552). Following damage sustained in 1940, new, contemporary stained glass decorates the ambulatory and its surrounding chapels; while the apsidal chapel retains its 13th-century stained glass. A 16th-century altarpiece is to be found in one of the side chapels. The astronomical clock, created 1865–1868 by the engineer Louis-August Vérité and modelled on one in Strasbourg, has a total of 90,000 components.

• **Cathédrale Saint-Pierre et horloge astronomique** Tel: 44.48.11.60 and 44.45.88.10 (guided tours). Open all year. Clock tour daily, except Sunday, 1 June to 1 November, 10.40am–2.40pm and 3.40–4.40pm.

A privileged witness to Beauvais' progress through the centuries, the **church of Saint-Etienne** is a harmonious blend of Norman and Flamboyant Gothic architecture. Apart from numerous sculptures and statues, the church also has some superb stained glass in the choir – like the *Arbre de Jessé* – superb Renaissance pieces executed by Engrand le Prince. (Open daily 9am–noon and 2–5pm; in winter 9.30–11.30am and 2–4pm). Close by, at the foot of the church, local archaeological finds can be seen in the **Galerie nationale de la tapisserie et d'art textile** (national tapestry and textile museum). This rich overview of French 15th–20th-century tapestry is drawn from the National collec-

tion (open daily, except Monday, 9.30am–noon and 2–6pm; in winter, 10am– noon and 2.30–5pm. Tel: 44.05.14.28). After a 40-year exile, **la Manufacture nationale de Beauvais**, has been reinstated in the town following the conversion of a former abbattoir. Weavers now work by natural daylight at ten looms to copy artists' designs. Their output is all sold to the government (24 rue Henri-Brispot. Open Tuesday, Wednesday and Thursday, 2–4pm. Tel: 44.05.14.28). Around the cathedral, beautifully restored houses encourage visitors to wander a little further, to discover streets like *rue du 27-Juin* and *rue de la Banque*.

Le musée départemental de l'Oise was opened to the public in 1981, following efforts of local groups who wanted the *département* to have its own reference museum. Its eclectic exhibits benefit from their setting in the **episcopal palace of the évêques-comtes** or bishop-counts of Beauvais. Notice the

massive entrance towers and the great Gothic arches, particularly those of the *salle aux Sirènes* with their impressive 14th-century paintings. From the museum's recently remodelled French garden, admire the medieval wing, the coachhouses of the Cardinal Etienne de Gesvres (1728–1772) and the Flamboyant façade built by Bishop Louis Villiers de l'Isle-Adam (1497–1521), flanked by the beautiful stair turret that houses a 16th-century clock named Louise. The abiding impression created by the museum is that of a private collection. Sixteenth- to 18th-century French and Italian paintings include masterpieces by Antoine Caron, celebrated painter of the Fontainebleau School who was born in Beauvais; works by Quentin Varin (also from Beauvais), paintings by the great Poussin, by Charles Lebrun and Jean Barbault. Art from the 17th century to the present also figures strongly in the collection. The most spectacular pieces are to be found in the former assizes courtroom, today the Thomas-Couture room, where the *Enrôlement des Volontaires de 1792* is hung alongside canvasses by Corot and paintings from the Louis-Philippe collection. The second floor art-nouveau collection centres on the work of the celebrated local potter, Auguste Delacherche: other pieces are by Maurice Denis, Vuillard, Vallotton, Roussea . . . There are room-sets, too, including a Bellery-Desfontaines dining-room (Henri Martin décor), an ornamented staircase (*l'Age d'or*) and a 19th-century library, reminder of the law courts' residence here for more than 100 years. Finally, the third floor has collections of European china.

• **Musée départemental de l'Oise** ancien palais épiscopal. Tel: 44.06.37.37. Open daily, except Tuesday, 10am–noon and 2–6pm.

Beauvais: Saint-Pierre Cathedral

CHANTILLY
60500 · G-4

Tourist information
23 avenue Maréchal-Joffre
Tel: 44.57.08.58

Hotels
Golf Hôtel-Domaine de Chantilly ★★★★
route d'Apremont
Tel: 44.57.00.93
Hôtel du Parc ★★★
36 avenue Maréchal-Joffre
Tel: 44.58.20.00

Restaurant
Tipperary
6 avenue Maréchal-Joffre
Tel: 44.57.00.48

Nearby
Le Château de la Tour ★★
Gouvieux (3.5km)
Tel: 44.57.07.39
Les Etangs (R)
Coye-la Forêt (8.5km)
Tel: 44.58.60.15

Literary figures and artists have come to Chantilly for centuries. From the Connétable (High Constable) Montmorency to the Grand Condé, from the Duc de Bourbon to the very last member of the Bourbon house, all have wanted to make **Chantilly château** a treasure trove of art. The town of Chantilly is blessed with a beautiful 16,000-acre forest and fine houses lining wide, shady avenues. Chantilly's equestrian centre and racecourse are well known.

Le château-musée de Condé was founded by the son of King Louis-Philippe, the Duc d'Aumale, who bequeathed it to the *Institut de France*. The museum keeps alive the memory of the ducs de Montmorency and the princes de Condé. On a par with some of the best European museums, its eclectic collections include 14th–19th-century French and foreign paintings (Poussin, Watteau, Greuze, Delacroix, Ingres, Véronese, Raphaël, Fra Angelico, Botticeli . . .), furniture, books and precious manuscripts *(Heures d'Etienne Chevalier* by Jean Fouquet, *les Très Riches Heures du duc de Berry* by the Limbourg brothers), drawings (Clouet), ceramics

Chantilly: the races

(china, Sèvres and Chantilly porcelain). Don't miss this important museum, the last port of call of its kind before you get to Paris.

• Château-musée de Condé
Tel: 44.57.08.00. Open 1 March to 31 October daily, except Tuesday, 10am–6pm; 1 November to 28 February daily, except Tuesday, 10.30am–12.45pm and 2–5pm. Guided tours, except Sunday afternoon and public holidays; foreign language tours on request. The grounds are open to the public on Tuesday, when the museum is closed.

Installed in the masterly 18th-century stables of the de Condé princes, the **musée vivant du cheval** is as lively as its inmates: horses, ponies, asses and mules which visitors can admire variously in their boxes or being trained (demonstrations daily at 2.30pm and 4pm). Different aspects of equestrian life are presented in more than 30 exhibits: horse-shoeing, racing, national breeding, horse care and management. Plus special displays and shows.

• Musée vivant du cheval Tel: 44.57.13.13 and 44.57.40.40. Open 1 April to 31 October, Monday, Wednesday, Thursday and Friday 10.30am–5.30pm; Saturday, Sunday and public holidays 10.30am–6.30pm; all day Tuesday in May and June, and 2.30–5.30pm in July and August; 1 January to 31 March daily, except Tuesday, 2–4.30pm; Saturday, Sunday and public holidays 10.30am–5.30pm.

COMPIÈGNE
60200 · G-4

Tourist information
hôtel de ville
Tel: 44.40.01.00

Hotels
Chateau de Bellinglise ★★★★
route de Lassigny
Tel: 44.76.04.76
Hôtel de Harlay ★★★
3 rue de Harlay
Tel: 44.23.01.50
Hôtel du Nord ★★★
1 place de la Gare
Tel: 44.83.22.30
Hôtel de France ★★
17 rue Eugène-Floquet
Tel: 44.40.02.74

Restaurant
Rôtisserie du Chat-qui-tourne
17 rue Eugène-Floquet
Tel: 44.40.02.74

Nearby
Auberge du Pont (R)
21 rue du Maréchal-Foch
Rethondes (10km)
Tel: 44.85.60.24
Auberge du Daguet (R)
Vieux-Moulin (9.5km)
Tel: 44.85.60.72
A la Bonne Idée (R)
Saint-Jean-au-Bois (11km)
Tel: 44.42.84.09

Compiègne's modern history started when *Charles le Chauve* (Charles the Bald) built a palace here – modelled on Charlemagne's palace at Aix-la-Chapelle – and a monastery, where the relics of Saint Corneille were kept from the beginning of the 10th century. The town grew up around the royal monastery (of which only the 14th-century cloister remains) and this was the final resting place of members of the royal family prior to Saint-Denis (in Paris). In the 14th century, Charles V built a *château* here. In 1430, Joan of Arc, whose equestrian statue stands in the *place du 54ᵉ Régiment d'infanterie*, was taken prisoner at the time of the English and Burgundian siege. Compiègne was a favourite among French kings, in spite of the 'primitive' nature of the château ("At Versailles I am lodged like a king, at Fontainebleau like a prince, at Compiègne like a peasant", declared Louis XIV – who had new apartments built facing the forest). The château was entirely remodelled under Louis XV who installed his court and ministers there in 1738. Louis XVI was to wait until 1785 before he stayed in the new royal apartment (which, in time, became Napoleon I's). All the palace furniture was sold during the Revolution. The palace became Napoleon I's imperial residence in 1806 and, in time, Napoleon III's favourite residence. Mérimée composed his famous *dictée* for the entertainment of the court here (which is still used today to test students' grammatical skills). During the First World War, the palace became the headquarters of Pétain; the two armistices of 11 November 1918 and 21 June 1940 were signed in the nearby forest, in a carriage stationed close to **Rethondes** station.

• **Wagon du maréchal Foch** Tel: 44.40.09.27. Open 1 April to 30 September daily, except Tuesday, 8am–noon and 1.30–6.30pm; the rest of the year daily, except Tuesday, 9am–noon and 2–5.30pm.

At the **musée national du château**, visitors can inspect the château's most splendid apartments (the ballroom, the bedrooms of the Emperor and Empress, the apartment of the king of Rome...), as well as visiting the museum itself (Second Empire), the Ferrand collection, the motorcar museum (road vehicles through the decades) and the park.

• **Musée national du château** Tel: 44.40.04.37. Open daily,

except Tuesday, 1 April to 30 September 9.15am–6.15pm; 1 October to 31 March, 9.15am–4.30pm.

Compiègne's **hôtel de ville** is a remarkable late Gothic town hall, built during the reign of Louis XII. The statues on the façade portray Saint Denis, Saint Louis, Charles le Chauve, Jeanne d'Arc, Cardinal Pierre d'Ailly and Charlemagne, set around a statue of Louis XII on horseback. The **belfry** is topped with a slate spire and four bells. The **church of Saint-Jacques** (15th-century tower) was the king's parish church, and this explains the 13th-century ornamentation: marble choir and wood carvings at the base of the nave pillars.

Le musée Vivenel is housed in a 19th-century *hôtel* or town house and has large exhibits of Picardian and Mediterranean archaeology (Greek vase collection, Egyptian sculptures and funerary objects). Wainscotted first floor galleries and collections contain paintings: the great *Passion de Wolgemut* altarpiece, ceramics, ivories, Limoges enamels ...

• **Musée Vivenel** hôtel de Sangeons. Tel: 44.20.26.04. Open daily, except Monday and Sunday, 9am–noon and 2–6pm (5pm in winter).

The **musée de la figurine historique** has nearly 100,000 model figures (in tin, lead, wood, plastic, paper and card ...) and, through a series of dioramas, recounts the most famous events in the history of France: the Napoleonic wars (the Battle of Waterloo diorama created between 1905 and 1923 by Charles Laurent has 12,000 models on a 25-sq-yd-display), the return of the Emperor's ashes ...

• **Musée de la figurine historique** hôtel de la Cloche (to the right of the town hall). Tel: 44.40.72.55. Open daily, except Monday and Sunday morning, 9am–noon and 2–6pm (5.30pm in winter).

Tourist information
1 rue René-de-Girardin
Tel: 44.54.01.58
Hotels
L'Ermitage ★★
4 rue de Souville
Tel: 44.54.00.25
Le Prieuré ★★
Tel: 44.54.00.44

Nearby
Auberge de la Fontaine ★★
22 grande rue Fontaine-Chaâlis
Tel: 44.54.20.22

On the outskirts of Paris, Ermenonville has something for everyone: for country lovers, the space and splendour of its forest; for those interested in the region's culture, there are art galleries, museums, historic buildings. History is on every street corner, and all corners lead to the **tombeau de Jean-Jacques Rousseau**, the tomb of the great French philosopher on the **Ile de Peupliers**, in the heart of the park which also bears his name. The park and buildings are part of a vast domain, landscaped during the 18th century by the Marquis de Girardin, and a comprehensive and unique example of contemporary garden design. Rousseau passed the last quiet years of his life in this rural setting. Interior décor includes work by Poussin and Watteau.

• **Parc Jean-Jacques Rousseau** 1 rue René-de-Girardin. Tel: 44.54.01.58. Open 1 May to 30 September daily, except Tuesday, 2–7.30pm; check with tourist information for opening at other times of the year.

Le musée Jacquemart-André is to be found in the 12th–13th-century **Chaâlis monastery** (Cistercian). Large collections of furniture, paintings, objets d'art from ancient times to the mid 19th century. Memorabilia and documents relating to the writer and his work can be seen in **la galerie Jean-Jacques Rousseau**. The park has ponds and a rose garden, one of the loveliest in the Ile-de-France *département*.

• **Domaine de l'abbaye de Chaâlis** Tel: 44.54.04.02. Open 1 March to 1 November daily, except Tuesday, 2–6.30pm; Saturday, Sunday and public holidays 10.30am–12.30pm and 2–6.30pm. Park open all year, except Tuesdays, 9am– 7pm.

PIERREFONDS
60350 · G-5

Tourist information
place de l'Hôtel-de-Ville
Tel: 44.42.81.44

Hotel
Hôtel des Etrangers **
10 rue de Baudon
Tel: 44.42.8018

The **château féodal** is a huge fortress erected at the end of the 14th century by Louis d'Orléans, brother of King Charles VI (and dismantled under Louis XIII). Old documents, paintings, drawings and photographs show the extraordinarily romantic silhouette of its ruins which were bought for 3,000F by Napoleon I. Napoleon III was reponsible for its much discussed restoration by Viollet-le-Duc, interesting both archaeologically and historically. A visit to Pierrefonds, even for those who have often seen it before, is a remarkable experience. The proximity of France's third largest forest assures the bonus of beautiful walks.

• **Château féodal** Open January, February, November and December daily, except Tuesday, 10am–noon and 2–5pm,

Senlis: the ruins of the feudal castle

Sunday 10am–5.30pm; in March, April, September and October daily, except Tuesday, 10am–12.30pm and 2–5pm, Sunday 10am–6pm; in May, June, July and August daily, except Tuesday, 10am–6pm, Sunday and public holidays in July and August 10am–7pm.

SENLIS
60300 · G-4

Tourist information
place du Parvis-Notre-Dame
Tel: 44.53.06.40

Hotels
Hostellerie de la Porte-Bellon **
51 rue Bellon
Tel: 44.53.03.05
Hôtel du Nord **
110 rue de la République
Tel: 44.53.01.16

Restaurants
Scaramouche
4 place Notre-Dame
Tel: 44.53.01.26
Les Gourmandins
3 place des Halles
Tel: 44.60.94.01
La Vieille Auberge
8 rue Longfilet
Tel: 44.60.95.50

There has been a settlement at Senlis since early in the first century. From the time of the reign of Clovis, the town was included in the royal kingdom and Hugues Capet was made king here in 907. Eleven centuries of royal residence guaranteed the development of the town: in the 12th century, active textile trading was accompanied by extensive public and private building. **La cathédrale Notre-Dame** was begun in 1150; not-

ice the spire, the central portal, the lateral portals and the Saint-Sacrement chapel. Wandering through the streets of the town, you will come to the 12th–13th-century **church of Saint-Frambourg** where the pianist Cziffra established an international music and songwriting centre; also, the **church of Saint-Pierre** (1029) with its Flamboyant façade and huge Renaissance tower. The **château royal** houses an exhibition on every aspect of the French hunt from the 15th century to the present day: traditions, folklore, works of art, trophies, costumes. There is an audiovisual introduction to the museum.

• **Musée de la vénerie** Tel: 44.53.00.80. Open 1 March to 31 October daily 10am–noon and 2–6pm (rest of the year until 5pm). Guided tours at 10am, 11am, 2pm, 3pm, 4pm and 5pm.

A new development at the entrance to the park houses the **musée des spahis** (French Algerian cavalry) for which there is joint entry with the *musée de la vénerie.*

Le musée municipal d'art et d'archéologie, in the former bishop's residence, has displays from archaeological digs (prehistoric to Renaissance) plus two rooms dedicated to paintings: Philippe de Champaigne, Thomas Couture (born in Senlis), Boudin, Sérusier, Séraphine Louis (known as *Séraphine de Senlis*).

• **Musée d'art et d'archéologie ancien évêché** Tel: 44.53.00.80. Open 1 March to 31 October daily, except Tuesday, 10am–noon and 2–6pm (until 5pm the rest of the year).

Final stop before Paris, **le parc d'Astérix** (Pailly) welcomes young and old to an animated reconstruction of the adventures of Asterix and Obelix. Also, a dolphin lake. Special displays, music, and refreshment facilities complete your visit to this most Gallic of Gallic venues. Tel: 44.62.34.34. Open all year but phone for precise opening times which change according to season.

III. From Calais to Reims

*The A26/E17 going east from Calais passes through the **département** of the Pas-de-Calais (see p115) and then through parts of the Picardy and Champagne-Ardenne regions. The principal interruptions to this wide and gently undulating country are the Gothic cathedrals that punctuate the view, at Quentin, Laon, Soissons and Reims: so much to see, wonderfully different, each equally inspirational. Famous centres of art (Laon, Soissons, Reims), regions with their own particular identity (Thiérache, Vallée de la Marne . . .) and battlefields of legendary renown to the French (les champs Catalauniques, le Chemin des Dames) – together these features of little-known northern France beckon and more than reward the adventurous.*

AISNE

This long thin *département* combines the *villes d'art* of Laon, Saint-Quentin and Soissons (towns that have long inspired and attracted artists) with a mix of rural landscapes: to the north, Thiérache, a small tract of wood and pastureland abutting the Belgian frontier and peppered with fortress churches (66 of them, complete with dungeons, chains, round towers and lookouts); to the south, the Marne valley and its Champagne vineyards, forests and *enfants célèbres*: Jean Fontaine (Château-Thierry), Jean Racine (La Ferté-Milon), Paul Claudel (Fère-en-Tardenois), Alexandre Dumas (Villers-Cotterêts). The centre and south of the *département* are particularly densely forested. Sounds of the hunt still resound through the forest of Retz; while, from Saint-Gobain, the silhouette of Tortoir Priory rises above the trees (Saint Norbert founded the nearby monastery of the Prémontré brotherhood in the 12th century); and, not far away, the sturdy features of Coucy fortress and the stacks of Saint-Gobain tell the prestigious tale of the former royal glassworks; last of the Aisne's forests are Saint-Michel-en-Thiérache (site of the abbey church), Vauclair (Cistercian monastery and medicinal plants garden) and Samoussy.

• **Comité départemental de tourisme de l'Aisne** 1 rue Saint-Martin, 02000 Laon. Tel: 23.26.70.00.

CHÂTEAU-THIERRY

02400 • H-5

Tourist information
11 rue Vallée
Tel: 23.83.10.14

Retz forest

Hotels
Ile-de-France ★★★
route de Soissons
Tel: 23.69.10.12
Auberge Jean-de-la-Fontaine (R)
10 rue des Filoirs
Tel: 23.83.63.89

Nearby
Auberge Le Relais ★★
Reuilly-Sauvigny (10km)
Tel: 23.70.35.36
Le Cygne d'Argent
Domptin (15km)
Tel: 23.70.43.11
Auberge de l'Omais
Baulne-en-Brie (15km)
Tel: 23.82.08.13

Prettily perched above the River Marne, the birthplace of Jean de la Fontaine (1621–1695) is, first and last, Champagne country. The Roman road from Troyes to Soissons once forded the Marne at this site, the scene of frequent skirmishes due to its coveted position close to the capital and straddling the Ile-de-France/Champagne regions. Close by are many castle fortresses: La Ferté-Milon, Fère-en-Tardenois, Seringes, Nesles, **Condé-en-Brie** (famous for its collection of 17th- and 18th-century paintings. Tel: 23.82.42.25. Open daily June to August, guided tours at 2.30, 3.30 and 4.30pm; May and September, Sundays and public holidays). With the extension of the *appellation champagne* label, this area now competes with the champagne production of Reims and Epernay. For information on visits to champagne cellars, contact **Champagne Panier**, 23 rue Roger-Catillon, tel: 23.69.13.10. The town's ancient monuments include an 11th-century castle, rampart walk, two fortified gates, the 106-ft-high Balham tower, part of a 12th-century fort built by the counts of Champagne and *la Côte 204* (Hill 204), a monument sited at an altitude of 204 metres to celebrate Franco-American co-operation, from which impressive, 25-ft-tall statues keep watch over the town and the valley of the Marne.

A particular point of interest at Château-Thierry is the **musée Jean-de-La-Fontaine** in the house where the writer was born (18th century). It contains mementoes and documents relating to the writer and the numerous (2,000) different editions of his famous *Fables* (most of them illustrated: Chauveau, the first-illustrator, Oudry, Doré, Grandville, Rabier, Chagall . . .). Furniture and paintings complement this journey into the world – as pertinent as ever – of La Fontaine.

• **Musée Jean-de-La-Fontaine** 12 rue Jean-de-La-Fontaine. Tel: 23.69.05.60. Open daily 1 April to 30 June, except Tuesday, 10am–noon and 2–6pm; 1 July to 30 September daily 10am–noon and 2.30–6.30pm; 1 October to 31 March daily, except Tuesday, 2–5pm; Sunday 10am–noon and 2–5pm.

LE CHEMIN DES DAMES
(Craonne) · G-5

Le Chemin des Dames ('Ladies Way') is so called after the daughters of Louis XIV who took this route when visiting their former governess, the countess of Narbonne, Lara, at the *château de la Bove*. This ridgeway was fiercely fought over during 1917 and 1918. The northern plateau of the Soisson region, rising some 300 feet above the Ailette valley to the north and the Aisne valley to the south, was the front line during the four years of the Great War. When

First edition of La Fontaine Fables *(musée Jean-de-La-Fontaine)*

the Germans were forced to retreat, following the Battle of the Marne, they established a stronghold between Laffaux and Craonne. The French forces fought tirelessly to regain control of this line, notably in 1917 when General Nivelle's offensive incurred awful losses: 270,000 allied soldiers died and 163,000 German soldiers. **La caverne du Dragon** tells the story of the aftermath of that battle. At the heart of this once tormented landscape, the **abbaye de Vauclair** is a haven of quiet tranquillity, open all year. Tel: 23.26.70.00.

• **Musée de la caverne du Dragon** Tel: 23.22.44.90. Open daily, except Tuesday, 10.30–11.30am and 2.30–5.30pm.

Closed during Christmas and February holidays. Multi-lingual audiovisual presentations.

LAON
02000 · G-5

Tourist information
hôtel-Dieu, place du Parvis
Tel: 23.20.28.62

Hotel
La Bannière de France ★★★
11 rue Roosevelt
Tel: 23.23.21.44

Restaurant
La Petite Auberge
45 boulevard Brossolette
Tel: 23.23.02.38

Nearby
Auberge du Lac ★★
Monampteuil (15km)
Tel: 23.21.63.87
Mercure Holifolt ★★
Chamouille (15km)
Tel: 23.2484.85

The artistic and historical legacy of Laon derives in part from its situation. Standing on a hill known as the *montagne couronnée* (crowned mountain), it was the site of first a Gallic and then Roman settlement. Saint Remi created the bishopric of Laon in the year 500, when he split up the vast diocese of Reims. From the 8th to the 19th century, Laon was the privileged residence of Carolingian kings. The Middle Ages were an auspicious period for the town with extensive building being undertaken (80 historic monuments). During the 12th century, Laon became one of Christendom's great centres of learning and the Laon School flourished under the auspices of Irish monks and

Condé-en-Brie: castle

Laon: Notre Dame Cathedral

the great scholars Anselme and Raoul. The first system of musical notation was invented here and the fair youth of European aristocracy came here to be taught. The vast five-towered cathedral, the bishop-dukes palace, Saint-Martin monastery and its collection of ancient manuscripts, the chapel and museum of the Knights Templar . . . all are important historical monuments and milestones. Highly recommended is a walk along the old city walls which afford some fine views across the plain.

La cathédrale Notre-Dame (120 yards long and 33 yards wide) was built between 1155 and 1235. This building, unmistakable with its five towers, is one of the high points of primitive Gothic art; in particular, its stained glass windows and its towers decorated with magnificent oxen scanning the skies at a height of more than 180

feet. Beneath the six-part vaulted ceiling, the nave is on four levels: magnificent arcades, gallery, triforium and high windows. The choir is wide and spacious. The 250-ft towers are most impressive, silhouetted in the setting sun (open daily 9am–7pm; guided tours on request at tourist information office). Le palais épiscopal retains its original 12th-century appearance, an extension of the cathedral apse, with gargoyles depicting the seven deadly sins. The palace includes two lovely chapels added at a later date.

Le musée archéologique municipal (see the famous recumbant figure of Guillaume d'Horcigny, doctor to mad king Charles VI, in the courtyard) has one of France's finest collections of ancient Greek and Egyptian artefacts after the Louvre. Neither are paintings poorly represented, with original works like Mathieu Le Nain's *le Concert*.

• Musé archéologique municipal 32 rue Georges-Ermant. Tel: 23.20.19.87. Open daily, except

Tuesday, 1 October to 31 March 10am–noon and 2–5pm; rest of the year until 6pm.

SAINT-MICHEL-EN-THIÉRACHE

02830 • F-6

Tourist information
Maison de la Thiérache
02260 La Capelle
Tel: 23.97.84.75

Founded on a site of pilgrimage by Irish monks in 945, the **ancienne abbaye** underwent countless fires between the 10th and 15th centuries. Very little of the original building remains; the choir, transept and parts of the cloister recall the fine Gothic monastery built at the end of the 12th century; the nave collapsed in the 16th century and was rebuilt in 1700, under the direction of Jean-Baptiste de Mornot, responsible for the fine Italian façade. A further fire was followed by extensive restoration work; Boizard's great organs, delivered in 1714, escaped damage and are an example of contemporary French workmanship at its very best. Concerts in June and July.

• **Abbaye de Saint-Michel-en-Thiérache** 4 rue du Chamiteau. Tel: 23.98.79.10. Open 1 May to 30 October 2–6.30pm; Saturday, Sunday and public holidays 2.30–6.30pm (rest of the year on request).

The **musée de la vie rurale** offers an insight into countryside, grassland, forest and agricultural management . . . 34 boulevard Savart. Open 1 May to 30 October 2–6.30pm; Saturday, Sunday and public holidays, 2.30–6.30pm (rest of year on request). Tel: 23.58.27.77 and 23.98.79.10.

SAINT-QUENTIN

02100 • F-5

Tourist information
14 rue de la Sellerie
Tel: 23.67.05.00

Hotels
Le Grand Hôtel ★★★
6 rue Dachery
Tel: 23.62.69.77

Hôtel de la Paix **
3 place du 8-Octobre
Tel: 23.62.77.62

Restaurant
Auberge de l'Ermitage
4 place de la Basilique
Tel: 23.6242.80

Nearby
Hostellerie du Château *
Neuville-Saint-Amand (3km)
Tel: 23.68.41.82
Le Pot d'Etain ***
Holnon (5km)
Tel: 23.09.61.46
La Ferme du Vermandois (R)
Caulaincourt (15km)
Tel: 23.66.51.84
Auberge de Vendeuil **
Vendeuil (15km)
Tel: 23.07.85.85

Built on a chalk hill bordered by a loop of the River Somme, Saint-Quentin is dominated by the impressive silhouette of its basilica rising from the *colline du Vermandois*. In spite of damage sustained during the wars, the town has retained a few beautiful buildings: the Flemish Flamboyant Gothic **hôtel de ville**, the **basilica** masquerading as a Gothic cathedral, and the **Lecuyer Museum** containing the prestigious pastel collection of Saint-Quentin's native artist Quentin de La Tour. Rebuilding in the town has given rise to some lovely art-deco façades. Saint-Quentin replaced the Gallic city of Vermand in the first century AD. In 287, a certain Quintus was martyred here (responsible for pilgrimages to the town up to the 20th century). In the nearby valley of the Omignon is the interesting **Riqueval-Bellicourt tunnel,** where boats are pulled along by means of an underwater chain tow, while the **Saint-Quentin scenic railway** (Sunday and public holidays in June and September) affords an excellent way of seeing the region. The town has produced several prominent Frenchmen, among them Gabriel Hanotaux, brilliant Foreign Office minister between 1895 and 1898, Henri Martin, historian, the revolutionary Gracchus Babeuf who fought for the suppression of private property ownership, Fouquier-Tinville,

public prosecutor during the Revolutionary 'Terror', pastelist Maurice Quentin de La Tour and Condorcet, last of the great Englightenment philosophers.

La basilique was built between the 13th and 15th centuries. This place of pilgrimage is a showpiece of Gothic art through the various stages of its development. It has an exceptional radiocentric choir, a 285-yard-long double transept (the only one in France) and an 18th-century organ (open daily except between noon and 1pm and during *son et lumières* June to September).

Le musée Antoine-Lecuyer has an exceptionall collection of more than 80 pastels by Maurice Quentin de La Tour – the artist featured on French bank notes (28 rue Antoine-Leucyer. Tel: 23.64.06.66. Open daily, except Tuesday, 10am– noon and 2–5pm (6pm Saturday; Sunday 2–6pm). **Le musée d'entomologie** in **Saint-Jacques church** exhibits more than 600,000 insects (500,000 of which are butterflies), the largest collection of its sort in Europe (daily, except Tuesday, 2–6pm; details from tourist information office). Last but not least, the **municipal library** (9 rue des Canonniers. Tel: 23.06.30.88) has an impressive archive collection (15,000 16th–19th-century documents).

SOISSONS
02200 · G-5

Tourist information
1 avenue Général-Leclerc
Tel: 23.53.08.27

Hotel
La Pyramide **
route de Reims
Tel: 23.73.29.83

Restaurant
L'Avenue
35 avenue Général-de-Gaulle
Tel: 23.53.10.76

Nearby
Le Sermoise (R)
Sermoise (10km)
Tel: 23.72.41.71
Auberge de la Couronne
Coeuvres et Valséry (15km)
Tel: 23.55.83.83

Touring the Oise to Aisne canals
Tourisme fluvial sur les canaux de l'Oise à l'Aisne
Tel: 23.59.15.45

A hundred kilometres from Paris, the town of Soissons has a history spanning 200 years. The former capital of the Gallic region Suessions became one of northern France's strategically important towns under Roman rule. Another of the so-called *villes d'art et d'histoire*, Soisson's masterly Gothic **cathedral** and the remains of the **Saint-Jean-des-Vignes**, **Saint-Médard** and **Saint-Léger monasteries** together recall the town's one hundred bishops from the 3rd to the 20th century. The local stone, particularly easy to work, can be seen in numerous buildings: **le pavillon de l'Arquebus** (Louis XIII style) and the beautiful classic-style **town hall**, formerly the law court.

L'abbaye Saint-Jean-des-Vignes (which houses the tourist information office, tel: 23.53.17.37) has a part 13th-, part 16th-century façade with 245–260-ft spires. This is the only surviving part of the monastery, with refectory and wine store. A Merovingian house has been reconstructed on the monastery site (open daily 9am– noon and 2–6pm; Sunday and public holidays from 10am). **La cathédrale Saint-Gervais-et-Saint-Prothais** is one of the loveliest of France's Gothic buildings. Partly rebuilt after 1918, it is home to Rubens' Adoration of the Shepherds (open afternoons 2.30–-5.30pm). In the centre of Soissons, the **hôtel Barral** is a beautiful Regency building with courtyard and grand staircase, ornamental pond, sun dial and statue and, in the little stable yard, a well and old stone drinking troughs (open by arrangement, tel: 23.53.46.27).

Le musée municipal public library has archaeological displays (prehistoric to late medieval) on the ground floor; on the first floor are 17th-century to 19th-century paintings by Largillière, Daumier, Courbet,

Boudin, Renoir . . . as well as historic records of the town; the second floor has contemporary paintings.

- **Musée municipal** 2 rue de la Congrégation. Tel: 23.59.15.90. Open daily, except Tuesday, 10am–noon and 2–5pm; from Wednesday to Sunday in the summer 10am–6pm.

VERVINS
02140 · F-6

Tourist information
place Général-de-Gaulle
Tel: 23.98.11.98

Restaurant
La Tour du Roy
45 rue Général-Leclerc
Tel: 23.90.00.11

Nearby
Le Clos du Montvinage **
Etreaupont (10km)
Tel: 23.97.40.18
Domaine du Tilleul ***
Landouzy-la-Ville (15km)
Tel: 23.98.48.00
Le Huteau (R)
Plomion (15km)
Tel: 23.98.81.21

Burelles: one of 60 fortified churches in the Thiérache region

Pillaged by Barbarians in the 5th century, the Vervins region then became Christian before suffering Norman invasion in the 9th century. The town in time became the seat of the powerful house of Coucy, responsible for its 12th-century sandstone ramparts and 22 towers (11 towers remain today).

Vervins is at the heart of a region (la Thiérache) studded with some 60 fortified churches, which once served as places of refuge for the inhabitants and their animals during countless battles suffered by this part of northern France, at the time of François 1, Louis XIII and Louis XIV. Some of the best of these churches are Beaurains, Englancourt, Vervins, Prisces, Jeantes, Aubenton, Wimy . . . (guided tours arranged by the tourist information office).

The countryside is attractive, with its old brick-and-stone buildings, orchards (cider production) and flocks of sheep. Visit the **hippodrome de La Capelle racecourse**, one of the most modern circuits in France; or **Hirson** with its necklace of ponds and the **Alfred-Demasure Museum of the Second World War**; or **Saint-Michel-en-Thiérache** and its interesting 10th-century monastery.

Some other places to stay in or eat at in the Aisne region:

- **Forêt de Saint-Gobain**
  Restaurant du Parc, Saint-Gobain. Tel: 23.52.80.58
- **Auberge du Ron d'Orléans** **
  Tel: 23.52.26.51
- **La Toque Blanche** ***
  Chauny. Tel: 23.39.98.98
- **Forêt de Retz**
- **La Régent** *** Villers-Cotterêts. Tel: 23.96.01.46
- **Hôtel de l'Abbaye** **
  Longpont. Tel: 23.96.02.44
- **Hôtel Racine** ** La Ferté-Milon. Tel: 23.96.72.02

MARNE

The visitor travelling from the Aisne region, and approaching the Marne *département* from the north-west, will quickly see Reims cathedral coming into view on the horizon. Though taking its name from the river, the Marne is, of course, best known throughout the world for its Champagne. Champagne was 'discovered' around 1700 by the monk Pérignon, at Hautvillers monastery, who was also responsible for the method of corking champagne, still used today. Previously, wine had been 'corked' using hemp steeped in oil.

The Marne has witnessed great historical changes – from the defeat of the Barbars in the plains of Châlon to the crowning of the kings of France, to the German surrender at Reims on 8 May 1945. From a financial point of view, champagne production (though occupying only 3% of the *département's* acreage) overshadows other nationally prized agricultural output, namely the growing of excellent alfalfa, wheat, beetroot and rape.

The **route touristique du champagne** (follow the blue and gold signs) includes:

- **la montagne de Reims**: some of France's loveliest vineyards, as well as Hautvillers monastery (home of *dom Pérignon*), the strange dwarf beeches of Verzy forest, local heritage museums (**musée du bois at Germaine**)

and the futuristic office of the Montagne de Reims regional park at Pourcy (tel: 26.59.44.44);

• **la vallée de la Marne**, from Epernay to Dorman and at Château-Thierry: "the serene countryside that gave birth to Jean de La Fontaine and the paintings of Corot" (François Bonal);

• **la côte des Blancs et les coteaux de Sézannais**, from Epernay to Villenaux-la-Grande, the very heart of the district producing France's most prestigious of wines.

Other points of interest for the visitor: to the north, the **forest of Argonne** and historic **Sainte-Menehoud** (famous for *le pied de cochon pané*, breaded pigs' trotters), **Varennes-en-Argonne** (where Louis XVI was caught as he fled the Revolutionary forces) and **Valmy** (site of the famous battle of 20 September 1792, when the armies of the Republic confronted the Prussian army); and to the south-east, **Chantecoq lake**.

• **Comité départemental de tourisme de la Marne** Tel: 26.68.37.52. 2 *bis* boulevard Vaubécourt, 51000 Châlons-sur-Marne.

CHÂLONS-SUR-MARNE
51000 · H-6

Tourist information
3 quai des Arts
Tel: 26.65.17.89
Hotels
Hôtel d'Angleterre ★★★
19 place Monseigneur-Tissier
Tel: 26.6821.51
Hôtel Bristol ★★
77 avenue Paul-Sémard
Tel: 26.68.24.63

Nearby
Aux armes de Champagne ★★★
L'Epine (8.5km)
Tel: 26.69.30.30

Although a cathedral city whose economy is closely linked to champagne production, Châlons-sur-Marne has remained modest in size. The fabric of the town has undergone extensive renovation, giving new prominence to much of its half-timbered architecture. The

wealth of 12th-century Châlons was entirely due to its textiles. In the 16th century, Henri IV confirmed its status as capital of the Champagne region, with the first provincial administrator responsible for tax collection being appointed in 1637. The town's population never exceeded 10,000, even in the most auspicious periods. In 1872, the town became a garrison town, the headquarters of the *VI région militaire* (in 1914, out of a population of 30,000 inhabitants, there were 6,000 soldiers and 275 officers). The two wars caused substantial damage and a large-scale rebuilding programme began in 1945. Recent changes to regional planning policy have made it the regional administrative centre, employing a large civil service force and giving rise to new town planning initiatives.

La cathédrale Saint-Etienne, founded at the end of the 13th century, has a beautiful Norman tower and impressive triple nave, with 13th–16th-century stained glass windows and 12th-century baptismal font. On the opposite bank of the canal stands **l'église Notre-Dame-de-Vaux**, one of 12th-century Champagne's most remarkable buildings; its two spires mark the town centre. The galleried side-aisles have beautiful 16th-century stained glass. The **musée du cloître**, in the north of the church, contains 50 very fine column-statues, found during excavations made in 1960 and displayed as they would have been in the cloister.

• **Musée du cloître Notre-Dame** 1 rue Nicolas-Durant. Tel: 26.64.03.87. Open 1 April to 30 September daily, except Tuesday, 10am–noon and 2–6pm (until 5pm the rest of the year).

Le musée municipal has a typical Champagne region interior, a collection from southern India, Egyptian statuettes, the tombstone of Blanche de Navarre (1252), mother of Thibaut IV, the Count of Champagne and King of Navarre, and two altarpieces of the Passion (1450 and 1500). On the first floor are prehistoric and Gallo-Roman

collections; also paintings, including a *Vénus* attributed to Cranach, works by Courbet, Thomas Couture (sketch for the painting *Soldate et femme*).

• **Musée municipal** place Godart. Tel: 26.68.54.44. Open daily, except Tuesday, 2–6pm.

Complete your visit to Châlons with a visit to the old part of the **cimitière de l'ouest** with its 1780–1840 tombs. Many important names from the Napoleonic period can be read here, often on unusually ornamented tombs: masonic symbols, a pyramid, an allegory of Consolation, a statue of Chronos . . . Twelve times minister, prime minister and Nobel Prize winner (1920), Léon Bourgeois' ashes were scattered in this part of the cemetery.

DER-CHANTECOQ (LAC)
51290 · I-7

Tourist information
51290 Giffaumont-Champaubert
Tel: 26.72.62.80

Der-Chantecoq is Europe's largest manmade lake, with 48 miles of lakeshore offering a wonderful habitat to thousands upon thousands of birds: for information visit the **maison de l'Oiseau et du Poisson** (tel: 26.74.00.00). The lake is France's premier site for grey geese and other rare species and boasts some 300 different species. In addition, the lake offers wide-ranging watersports facilities.

Foot-, horse- and mountain-bike trails from the lake allow visitors to discover the local architecture and countryside . . . The **Sainte-Marie village museum** has examples of typical regional architecture, including a church brought from the village of Nuisement-aux-Bois which was submerged when the lake was created in 1974. See also the timbered churches of the **circuit des églises à pans de bois et des vitraux**.

Epernay: champagne cellar

ÉPERNAY

51200 · H-6

Tourist information
7 avenue de Champagne
Tel: 26.55.33.00

Hotels
Hôtel Berceaux *
Tel: 26.55.28.84
Hôtel Champagne *
30 rue Mercier
Tel: 26.55.30.22

Nearby
Royal Champagne ***
Champillon (6km)
Tel: 26.52.87.11
La Birqueterie ***
route de Sézanne
Vinay (6km)
Tel: 26.59.99.99

Maturing in cellars, wine stores and tunnels beneath the town of Epernay lie millions of bottles of Champagne. **Le musée du champagne** has collections of labels, glasses, bottles and wine-storing equipment. Also, a large display of pottery, some of it local. The second floor has one of France's finest archaeological collections, prehistoric and ancient).

• **Musée du champagne** 13 avenue de Champagne. Tel: 26.51.90.31. Open daily, except Tuesday, 1 March to 30 November, 10am–noon and 2–6pm.

Other viticultural museums in Epernay and the surrounding district are:

• **musée des pressoirs** (wine-presses) at the *caves Mercier* and **musée de la tonnellerie** (casks) at the *caves de Castellane* in Epernay;

• **musée de la vigne et du vin** (*caves Lannois*) at Mesnil-sur-Oger;

• **musée champenois** at Aÿ;

• **abbaye d'Hautvillers**, medieval manuscripts, illuminations and a reconstruction of Dom Pérignon's place of work.

Epernay retains many old buildings: the residence of Louise de Savoie (mother of François I), the Moët et Chandon orangery in *avenue de Champagne*.

REIMS

G-6

Tourist information
2 rue Guillaume-de-Machault
Tel: 26.47.25.69

Hotels
Les Crayères ****
64 boulevard Vasnier
Tel: 26.82.80.80
Hotel Liberté ***
55 rue Boulard
Tel: 26.40.04.08
Hôtel de la Paix ***
9 rue Buirette
Tel: 26.40.04.08

Restaurants
Le Vigneron
place Jamot
Tel: 26.47.00.71
Le Chardonnay
184 avenue d'Epernay
Tel: 26.06.08.60

Nearby
L'Assiette champenoise
40 avenue Paul-Vaillant-Couturier , Tinqueux (5km)
Tel: 26.04.15.56
L'Auberge du Grand-Cerf
Montchenot-Rilly-la-Montagne (11km)
Tel: 26.97.60.07

The **cathedral** is, of course, the most important building both of the town and the region (included on Unesco's 'world heritage' list together with Reims' **palais du Tau** and **la basilique** and **abbaye Saint-Jean**). Built at the beginning of the 12th century by four architects, it replaced the earlier Saint Nicaise 5th-century church, the crypt of which – where Saint Remi used to pray – can still be seen today. The structure was badly damaged by fire in 1481, and again during bombing raids in the 1914–1918 war, giving rise to an exceptional restoration programme. Some 2,300 statues decorate the cathedral (including the famous *Ange au sourire* – the smiling angel of Reims). A series of figures on the front elevation, created in Reims workshops between 1220 and 1250, have unfortunately been badly affected by the weather and are currently undergoing restoration. Roughly a half of the cathedral's 3,800 square yards of 13th-century stained glass has been patiently restored, notably the rose window of the façade (Virgin surrounded by apostles and angels); modern stained glass has been added, including work by Chagall, Jacques Simon's *le Vitrail du champagne* (1954). If you follow the cathedral with a visit to the **palais du Tau,** you can see some of the statues found in the bombed ruins of the cathedral in 1918, as well as tapestries, items from the cathedral treasury, the Charlemagne talisman and objects used during the last coronation (Charles X). The *palais* served as the coronation banqueting hall.

• **Palais du Tau** place du Cardinal-Luçon. Open 16 March to 30 June and 1 September to 14 November daily 9.30am–12.30pm and 2–6pm; 1 July to 31 August, 9.30am–6.30pm; 15 November to 15 March, 10am–noon and 2–5pm (6pm Saturday and Sunday). Tel: 26.47.81.79.

Le musée des beaux-arts can be found in the former Saint-Denis monastery built by Louis XV. The ground floor has local history and art exhibits as well as popular art and ceramics, while the first floor is particularly interesting for its drawings by Cranach l'Ancien and Cranach le Jeune, a work by Titus, as well as a major canvas by Philippe de Champaigne in the company of paintings by the Le Nain brothers, Poussin, Le Brun, Savery . . . Another room has furniture, glassware, paintings (François Boucher, Fragonnard . . .), while the Corot room has a unique collection of 28 paintings by the artist. Then follow paintings by Delacroix, Géricault, Millet, Bonington, Courbet, Daumier . . . and landscapes by Daubigny, Jongkind, Boudin. The Impressionists are respresented by Monet, Renoir, Pissaro, Sisley . . . and, finally, paintings by Van Gogh and Gauguin and a series of contemporary artists: Matisse, Dufy, Utrillo, Marquet, Foujita, Ubac.

• **Musée des beaux-arts** 8 rue Chanzy. Tel: 26.47.28.44. Open daily, except Tuesday, 10am–noon and 2–6pm.

The former abbey church **la basilique Saint-Remi** has a transept and nave dating from the 11th century, and late 12th-century primitive Gothic arches, choir and façade. Next to the basilica, the Saint-Remi monastery, founded in the 13th cen-

Reims: the cathedral

tury, includes the **musée d'histoire et d'archéologie,** with its prehistoric to late medieval collections (and particularly interesting regional military history section) and ten tapestries showing scenes from the life of Saint Remi.

• **Musée Saint-Remi** 53 rue Simon. Tel: 26.85.23.36. Open daily 2–6.30pm; Saturday and Sunday 2–7pm.

Also in Reims, the **musée de l'ancien collège des jésuites** and the **planetarium**; or, you may like to visit the **salle de la Reddition** (literally 'the room of Surrender'), the **chapelle Foujita** or the **automobile centre.** But no visit to Reims is complete wihout taking in at least one of the famous champagne cellars:

• **Charles Heidsieck** 4 boulevard Henri-Vasnier. Tel: 26.84.43.50

• **Lanson** 12 boulevard Lundy. Tel: 26.78.50.50

• **Mumm** 34 rue du Champ-de-Mars. Tel: 26.40.59.70

• **Piper Heidsieck** 51 boulevard Henri-Vasnier. Tel: 26.84.43.44

• **Pommery** 5 place Général-Gouraud. Tel: 26.61.62.55

• **Ruinart** 4 rue des Crayères. Tel: 26.85.40.29

• **Tattinger** 9 place Saint-Nicaise. Tel: 26.85.45.35

• **Veuve Clicquot-Ponsardin** 1 place des Droits-de-l'Homme. Tel: 26.40.25.42

TROIS-FONTAINES
51340 • H-7

Situated in the triangle bordered by Saint-Dizier, Bar-le-Duc and Vitry-le-François, the **abbaye de Trois-Fontaines** is one of the oldest and most famous Cistercian monasteries, founded by Saint Bernard on 10 October 1118. The imposing ruins of the soberly designed abbey church date from the same period. The three windows and rose window of the west portal are pure Romanesque, while the interior combines Romanesque with Gothic elements. In 1741, at the time of the monastery's rebuilding, a huge portal was added to the semi-circular archways of the courtyard: over the central doorway, an amazing statue of the Virgin dominates the monastery's coat of arms. Lovely grounds planted with rare species trees surround the buildings.

IV. From Calais to Rotterdam

The songs of French singer Jacques Brel capture the essence of Flanders, that part of Belgium adjoining north-eastern France . . .

A certain melancholy haunts the Flemish plain, marked at intervals by belfry and lighthouse. But nostalgic reverie soon yields to joie de vivre, *for the Flemish have great enthusiasm for celebration, for food and for drink. Heavy clouds cross the Flanders sky, sea winds constantly blow, filling the boatsails, bending the trees and bathing the countryside in tonic sea air.*

The visitor discovers a landscape punctuated by the secular monuments of the villes d'art: *medieval houses, old towns, Flamboyant Gothic architecture, museums that hold the secrets of a mysterious pagan past. A small area, some ten towns, bears traces of an exceptional artistic inheritance: the old towns of Ghent, Ypres, Bruges, Mechelen, Antwerp . . . So much to see, so many reminders of a lost golden age . . . before turning north to seek out neighbouring Holland, and from there travelling on to the great towns of the Netherlands, to Rotterdam, Delft, The Hague, Alkmaar . . .*

Leaving Calais on the A40 coastal motorway, you traverse the French *département* of Nord and northern Flanders (see page 115), crossing into Belgium at De Panne (La Panne). The 45-mile-long Belgian coastline includes beautiful sandy beaches, from La Panne to Knokke-le-Zoute, seaside resorts since the middle of the 19th century. Once the elegant watering places of princes, these are now popular holiday destinations, though future generations will likely decry the concrete, the consequence of half a century of lax planning, escaped by only a few towns: La Panne, Saint-Idesbald, Koksijde (Coxyde), De Haan, (Le Coq), Knokke-le-Zoute . . . Unlike the coastlines of Picardy, of Normandy or of the Netherlands, the Belgian coastline has few fishing ports, with two exceptions at Nieuwpoort and Zeebrugge.

• **Office de tourisme de la Flandre** 61 rue Marché-aux-Herbes, 1000 Bruxelles. Tel: 02.504.03.90.

OSTEND

8400 · C-5

Tourist information
2 Monacoplain
Tel: 059.70.11.99

Hotels
Ostende Compagnie ***
79 Koningstraa
Tel: 059.70.48.16
Thermae Palace ***
7 Koning-Astridlaan
Tel: 059.80.66.44

Restaurants
Villa Maritza
76 Albert-I-Promenade
Tel: 059.50.88.08
Adelientje
9 Bonenstraat
Tel: 059.70.13.67

One-time 'queen of beaches' and seaside home to the Belgian royal family, Ostend now boasts many art galleries and museums, including one dedicated to James Ensor (tel: 059.80.53.35). Ensor used violent colours and expressionist techniques to illustrate macabre and satirical themes. The carnival scenes that he liked so much to paint were forerunners of surrealism. What is perhaps his most typical painting, *Entrée du Christ à Bruxelles,1888* (Christ's Entry to Brussels), can be seen at Antwerp's **musée des beaux-arts**. It was Ensor who established the *bal du Rat mort* (Dead rat ball!), part of the carnival celebration that gives rise to 5 days of public carousing throughout the town.

Ostend's maritime tradition is marked throughout the year by the presence of the *Mercator* sail training ship; this old Belgian merchant marine ship has been at anchor in the harbour since 1964, excepting a few very rare expeditions, after an active life that took it on 41 world tours. A few exhibits recall some of its scientific missions, in particular one to Easter Island (whence came statues and the remains of Brother Damien). Visitors are given an insight into life on board a great sailing ship (tel: 059.70.56.54), from the crew's quarters to the officers' drawing room. At Ostend – as elsewhere along the Belgian coast – some *moules-frites* and a glass of Belgian beer will enable you to join the locals in enjoying the simple things in life!

KNOKKE-LE-ZOUTE
8300 • C-5

Tourist information
660 Lichttorenplein-Zeedijk
Tel: 050.60.16.16

Hotels
Fairway ★★★
9 Tuinfluiterspad
Tel: 050.61.14.67
Auberge Saint-Pol ★★★
23 Bronlaan
Tel: 050.60.15.21

Restaurants
Paul Gaelens
6 Elizabetlaan
Tel: 050.61.06.94
Gasthof Katlijne
166 Kustlaan
Tel: 050.60.12.16
La Sapinière
7 Oosthoekplein
Tel: 050.60.22.71

Before leaving the coast to drive into Holland via the Flemish *villes d'art*, try to visit Knokke-le-Zoute and the Zwin nature reserve. With its typical architecture (white brick houses with toothed gable ends), nestling in a vast pine forest, Knokke is perhaps the Belgian coastline's most attractive spot. Here, scrupulous attention to planning has ensured the survival of an elegant, family seaside resort. Leisure facilities (casino, tennis, golf) and its sea-water thermal baths put it on a par with French spas like Cabourg, Deauville or Le Touquet. But not till you visit the Zwin nature reserve will you have experienced the best the town has to offer. The estuary that once linked Bruges to the sea has been transformed into a haven for birds en route between Belgium and the Netherlands. In the midde of the reserve (375 acres) are vast enclosures of ducks, birds of prey, flamingoes, swans . . . and storks sitting in the trees.

Ostend: the beach

• **Réserve du Zwin** Open April to September 9am–7pm, until 5pm at other times of the year. Tel: 050.60.70.86.

The Zwin reserve introduces the tourist to the great coastal open spaces of the Low Countries, as yet unspoilt by urbanization. There are two alternative routes into Holland: either from the Belgian coast, via Knokke and then on the ferry (30 mins) over to Breskens and Vlissingen on the island of Walcheren; or, alternatively, through Flanders, inland via Bruges, Ghent and Antwerp. If you have a day or two in hand, we recommend the second route for discovering, in these three towns, the essential spirit and culture that is Flanders.

BRUGES (BRUGGE)
8000 • C-5

Tourist information
11 Burg
Tel: 050.44.86.86

Hotels
Relais Oud Huis vanamsterdam ★★★
3 Spiegelrei
Tel: 050.34.18.10
De Orangerie ★★★
10 Karhuizerlnenstraat
Tel: 050.34.16.49
Hostellerie Pannehuis ★★★
2 Zandstraat
Tel: 050.31.19.07

Restaurants
De Karmeliet
19 Langestraat
Tel: 050.33.82.59
De Witte Poorte
6 Jan Van Eyckplein
Tel: 050.33.08.83
Hermitage
18 Ezelstraat
Tel: 050.34.41.73
La Casserole (hotel school)
17 Groene Poortdreef
Tel: 050.38.38.88

Festival
Saint-Sang Ascension Procession

Celebrated by numerous artists and writers, Bruges is certainly the most captivating of Belgium's towns, in spite of the high season tourist throng. History is on every street corner, Bruges having being made the capital by Robert le Frison in 1093. It was already a flourishing town at that time, due largely to its port linked to the North Sea by the Zwin, and to its textile production. In the 12th century, it became a centre for English wool imports and lead the *Hanse de Londres* (an association of towns trading with England). Damme, which has remained largely unchanged, was once Bruges' outer harbour. Engaged in international trade with the countries of northern and southern Europe, Bruges was one of the most active members of the 13th-century Hanseatic League, with more than 150 boat movements daily from its port.

This intense commercial activity attracted both artists and art patrons as well as underpinning considerable private and public building programmes: the Saint-Jean hospital, the covered market, the clock tower of Notre-Dame church, the town fortifications (of which four gates have survived), the town hall (15th century) . . . Unsurprisingly, Bruges became a centre for Flemish painting: this is where Van Eyck painted his *Adoration de l'Agneau mystique* (which has graced Ghent's Saint-Bavon church since 1432); Memling (between 1435 and 1494) produced – like Rubens at Ghent – numerous paintings commissioned by the town councillors, the best of which are still in the town; Gérard David (1460–1523), Adrien Isembrant,

Ambrosius Benson, Jean Provost and Pierre Pourbus are some of the other talents in the long tradition of Bruges painters. With the 15th-century silting up of the Zwin came a period of decline and a crisis in the textile industry. Charles Quint's visit in 1520 was one of the last high points in Bruges' history before its relative demise – at the end of the 19th century – caused by the construction of a sea port at Zeebrugge, linked to Bruges by a 7-mile canal.

Different possibilities present themselves to the Bruges visitor: a stroll through its streets on foot; or in a carriage, as 19th-century visitors might have done, or by boat, in the company of a guide (commentary in Dutch, English and French). This last option is probably the best way to enjoy both the architecture and shady gardens that fringe the canals. The title 'Venice of the north', though in part devalued by fierce rival claims to the appellation by Delft and Amsterdam, is surely deserved here by the dense network of canals perfectly integrated with the town layout. The whole town is a museum: the **basilique du Saint-Sang**, the **hôtel de ville** and the impressive **clock tower**, the **béguinages** or convents (1245) – quiet places of meditation and retreat, where the holy sisters

can still be seen in habits trimmed with Bruges lace – as well, of course, as the art galleries and museums.

Le musée Groeninge (*Stedelijk Museum voor Schone Kunsten*) has two galleries devoted to a series of masterpieces from the famous Van Eyck School *(la Vierge du chanoine Van der Paela, Marguerite van Eyck, Saint Luc peignant la Vierge)*, Van der Goes (*Mort de la Vierge*), Memling (*Moreel* triptych). See also the works of Gérard David: *le Jugement de Cambyse* and the *Baptême du Christ* triptych. A further three rooms contain the paintings of Jérôme Bosch (*Jugement dernier*), Jean Provost and Pierre Pourbus. The gallery tour finishes with Flemish expressionists, Permeke, Van den Berghe, De Smet) and with contemporary Belgian artists, Magritte, Delvaux, Peire).

• **Musée Groeninge** Open daily, except Tuesday, 9.30am–6pm;1 October to 31 March, closed between noon and 2pm. Tel: 050.33.99.11.

Le musée Memling is housed in the former Saint-Jean hospital (17th century); to the right, in the cloister, is the 17th-century pharmacy; while in the old wards the life of the former hospital is depicted. Memling paintings are exhibited in the church: *la châsse de Sainte-*

Knokke-le-Zoute: Zwin nature reserve in spring

Bruges convent

Ursule is an illuminated illustration of the life and martyrdom of Saint Ursule and her companions, the 11,000 Virgins; see also *Le mariage mystique de sainte Catherine, l'Adoration des mages* (1479), showing a Virgin with lowered eyes and Balthazar as a black king; the *Déploration* triptych (1480), also called *Déposition de la croix*. Worth seeing in the chapel are the Martin van Nieuwenhove diptych and the *Vierge à la pomme*.

• **Musée Memling** Open 1 April to 30 September daily, except Wednesday, 9.30am–5pm; rest of the year, 9.30am–12.30pm and 2–5pm. Tel: 050.33.99.11.

The streets of Bruges are a delight to meander through . . . But, if you've time and energy, see the **Gruuthuse museum**, **Notre-Dame church**, **Saint-Sauveur cathedral** and the **folklore museum**.

Seven kilometres to the north-east lies **Damme** which can be reached by boat along the Bruges–Damme canal (which once joined Bruges to its outer sea port). Visit also the **Boudewijn park**, and the neo-Gothic **De Loppem castle** (7km

to the south) to see china, porcelain and religious sculptures.

GHENT (GENT)
9000 · C-6

Tourist information
Crypte de l'Hôtel-de-Ville
Tel: 09.224.15.55

Hotels
Alfa Flanders ★★★
121 Koning Albertlaan
Tel: 09.222.60.65
Gravensteen ★★
35 Jan Breydelstraat
Tel: 09.225.11.50
Astoria ★★
39 Achilles Musschestraat
Tel: 09.222.84.13

Restaurants
Apicius
8 Maurice Maeterlinckstraat
Tel: 09.222.46.00
Ter Toren
626 Sint-Bernadettestraat
Tel: 09.251.11.29
Pakhuis
Tel: 09.223.55.55

Specialty shop
Tierentijn (Ghent mustard and spices, *place du Marché*)

Standing at the confluence of the Rivers Lys and Escaut, Ghent is criss-crossed with canals. Birthplace of Charles Quint, it has always been of strategic importance. Its massive crenellated towers, majestic monasteries and churches recall a long and prestigious history: the counts' *château*, clock tower, *hôtel de ville* (mix of Gothic and Renaissance), the towers of Saint-Nicolas and Saint-Michel, the *quai aux Herbes* . . . There is a particularly evocative view from the Saint-Michel bridge. Some of the former merchants' houses (cloth manufacturers, brewers, grain measurers, coachmen) are superb examples of Gothic and Flemish architecture. The heart of the town reveals itself to the pedestrian or boat passenger, especially on summer evenings when the lights add an extra magic. The **cathédrale Saint-Bavon** (tel: 09.225.95.24), one of Belgium's most sumptuous buildings, gives shelter to the famous Van Eyck brothers' altarpiece *l'Agneau mystique*. The town is picturesquely punctuated with tiny flower and vegetable markets.

Le musée des beaux arts, sited at the edge of the old town park, exhibits numerous old paintings: Roger Van der Weyden, *Vierge à l'oeillet*, Jérôme Bosch, *Saint Jean en prière, le Portement de Croix*, Isembrant, *la Vierge et l'enfant*, Pierre Bruegel le Jeune, Roland Savery, Pourbus le Vieux, *Portrait de femme*, Rubens, Jordaens, Gaspard de Crayer, *une Etude de tête d'un jeune Maure*, as well as market scenes painted by Antwerp artist Joachim Beuckelaer. Among the largely Belgian modern exhibits are Spilliaert, Evenepoel, Claus, Ensor, painters from la Lys and expressionists like Kirchner, Kokoschka . . . and some French School 19th-century pieces including Courbet, Corot, Fantin-Latour, Géricault (*Portrait d'un cleptomane*). The museum also has Brussels tapestries and sculptures. In the same building is **le musée d'art contemporain** which traces current developments in art through temporary exhibitions: Cobra, minimalist art, hyper-realism, Pop Art . . .

• **Musée des beaux-arts** Open daily, except Monday, 9.30am–5pm. Tel: 09.222.17.03.

You may also like to visit **le musée de la Byloke**, housed in the former monastery of the same name (13th century), which has archaeological and historical exhibits: iron forgery, copper work, bronzes, pottery, ceramics . . . The first floor 14th-century refectory has a wood-panelled vaulted ceiling and frescoes. Other rooms tell something of the life of the monks who used to live here (tel: 09.225.11.06).

South of Ghent, give in to the temptation of a walk along the Lys, the river which gives vigour to the region and whose pure water was particularly favoured for flax retting. This valley, lying between Ghent and Deinze, is one of Flanders' loveliest, with handsome villas and country gardens giving down to the gentle waters of the Lys. A colony of artists once established itself here, the 'La Lys Painters' or, alternatively, the Laethem Saint-Martin School, from the name of the biggest parish in the area. Gathered together around 1900 in this little corner of Flanders, artists like Georges Minne, Fritz Van den Berghe, Saverijs, Valerius de Saedeleer, Van de Abeele, Gust De Smet, Albert Servaes, Emile Claus and Constant Permeke constituted the equivalent to the Pont-Aven movement of Gauguin and Emile Bernard. These artists marked the transition from late 19th-century impressionism to early 20th-century expressionism. To walk here is to go back to the turn-of-the-century. And to complete the experience, visit the **musée de Deinze** where vast, brightly lit rooms pay (justified) hommage to the School of Lys painters.

• **Musée de Deinze et des peintres de la Lys** Open Monday, Wednesday, Thursday, Friday, 2–5.30pm; Saturday, Sunday and public holidays,

10am–noon and 2–5pm. Tel: 09.286.00.11.

Those who feel inclined to visit the capital before visiting Antwerp and Holland will find all the information they need regarding accommodation and things to do and see in Brussels, at the town's tourist information office, the *syndicat d'initiative*.

• **Syndicat d'initiative** Grand-Place, Maison communale, 1000 Bruxelles. Tel: 02.513.89.40.

ANTWERP (ANVERS)
2000 · C-7

Tourist information
Grande-Place (Grote Markt)
Tel: 03.232.01.03

Hotels
Alfa Théâter ★★★★
30 Arenbergstraat
Tel: 03.231.17.20
De Rosier ★★★
23 Rosier
Tel: 03.225.01.40
Alfa De Keyser ★★★
66 De Keyserlei
Tel: 03.234.01.35
Villa Mozart ★★
3 Handschoenmarkt
Tel: 03.231.30.31

Restaurants
La Pérouse
Steenplein
Tel: 03.231.31.51
t'Fornuis
24 Reyndersstraat
Tel: 03.233.62.70
De Matelote
9 Haarstraat
Tel: 03.231.32.07
Den Gulden Greffoen
37 Hoogstraat
Tel: 03.231.50.46

Leaving Ghent, going towards Holland, you come to the Flemish city of Antwerp, which is also one of Europe's biggests ports: Anvers-sur-Escaut, whose river, the Escaut, widens once out of the city into the great delta that washes the islands of Zeeland province (Holland). Antwerp, Belgium's second largest town, has all the characteristics of a great metropolis, combining architecture both ancient and audaciously modern.

The city's origins are uncertain, but it is known that the 11th

century heralded a phase of new buildings and fortifications. The fortunes of the city rose dramatically in the 13th century thanks to trade in fish, salt and English wool. When the silting up of the Zwin brought economic decline to Bruges, the Hanseatic League established a trading base here, later used by the Portuguese in the 16th century, to sell spices and precious objects brought from the Indies. The year 1515 marked the establishment of the first stock exchange, concurrent with the introduction of new banking procedures (letters of exchange and letters of credit). During this period, nearly a thousand international traders were based in Antwerp, making it Europe's second largest commercial centre after Paris. This economic expansion was accompanied by extensive building and improvement programmes: the town hall, the *rue des Brasseurs*, the cathedral . . . and by artistic activity, too (Bruegel). At the end of the 16th century, Antwerp suffered repression at the hands of the Spanish following Calvinist attacks; in 1648, the Treaty of Munster decreed the closure of the River Escaut for 150 years. After the French Revolution, the town remained French and the first manmade harbour was built here (*bassin Bonaparte* or Bonapartedock). Today, Antwerp is Belgium's premier trading outlet and commercial centre. Its Berendrecht lock is the biggest in the world: 763,000 cubic yards, 550 yards long and 75 yards wide.

The port (boat trips around the docks leave from Steenplein, near le Steen in the centre of town, information: Flandria, tel: 03.231.31.00) plays an important part in the transportation of goods to various European countries (France, Belgium, the Netherlands, Germany, Switzerland) and particularly in the import and export of oil-based products, minerals, coal, wood, chemicals, vehicles, etc.

The town is also a centre for diamond cutting and trading – and has been since the 16th century, thanks to a diamond cutting technique developed in

1476 by Louis de Berken. At first, diamonds were brought from the Indies by the Spanish; then, in the 19th century, supplies began to come from South Africa. Antwerp has continued to enjoy a reputation for diamond cutting expertise, thanks in large part to the skills of Jews who emigrated from Central Europe during the19th century; diamond dealing is also the province of the Jewish community, ably assisted by immigrants from the Lebanon and Zaire. A walk along the street where the diamond merchants work is fascinating, particularly at times of huge diamond transactions or deliveries.

Begin your visit of the town at the *grand-place* with its 16th- and 17th-century **maisons des Corporations**, its stained glass windows and Dutch 'toothed' gables. The **town hall** (*stadhuis*) was built in 1564 by Corneille Floris; its façade, measuring 83 yards in length, is richly decorated combining Flemish and Italian Renaissance features. The **cathedral** is the biggest building in the country (covering an area of nearly 2½ acres), begun in 1352 and not completed until 1521. The 400-ft tower and belfry has a 47-bell carillon. Inside, it is decorated with richly ornate furniture and works of art: a pulpit carved by Michel Vervoort le Vieux (1713), Rubens paintings (*l'Erection de la croix*, 1610), *Descente de croix* 1612, *l'Assomption*, 1616). In the adjoining *salle d'art* are Rubens' *la Résurrection* and De Backer's *le Jugement dernier* . . .

• **Cathédrale Notre-Dame** Open Monday to Friday 10am–6pm (5pm from September to May); Saturday 10am–3pm; Sunday and public holidays 1–4pm. Carillon concerts on Fridays at 11.30am.

Near le Steen, towards the *grand-place*, several houses together form **le musée ethnographie**; at the entrance, visitors are greeted by the famous ancestral statue of the Luba-Hemba, from Zaire (referred to by André Malraux in his '*musée*

imaginaire'), by way of introduction to the African collections (masks, statues, precious and everyday objects), to the South Sea collections (drums and sculptures), to the American collections (funeral pillars), to the Eskimo collections (kayaks), to the pre-Columbian, Buddhist, Hindu and Japanese collections (statue of Kanon Bosatsu, 16th century, in gold-lacquered wood), to the Lamaists (plan of Lhassa designed in the 19th century), the Afghans and the Turks. The diversity of the collections mirrors Antwerp's international standing over the centuries, by virtue of her port and the dynamism of her trade.

• **Musée d'ethnographie** Tel: 03.232.08.82. Open daily, except Monday, 10am–5pm.

Right next to the musée d'ethnographie, **le musée du folklore** has Flemish street scenes, games, signs, barrel-organs, giant heads (Druon and Pallas), a toy collection, a model dispensary, a puppet theatre (tel: 03.232.94.09. Open daily, except Monday,10am–5pm).

The printer Christophe Plantin (1555) of Tours had his 'Compas d'Or' workshops in Antwerp. The quality of his work and his erudition brought him the esteem of the great men of his time, and particularly that of Philippe II who made him his official printer and exclusive seller of liturgical works in Spain and in the colonies. In association with the merchant Jérôme Cook, Plantin created the greatly admired Antwerp School of Engraving, later to be directed by Rubens. His reference work *Biblia Regia*, was printed in five languages: Hebrew, Syrian, Greek, Latin and Aramaic. His house (34 rooms) is now the **musée Plantin-Moretus**: beautiful furniture, carpets, gilded leather, paintings, a beautiful library, the private collections of Plantin (drawings, engravings, manuscripts, rare editions . . .), all present a handsome view of humanism in 16th- and 17th-century Low Countries. On the first floor, see the famous *Biblia Regia* and the *Gutenberg Bible*

(13 surviving examples).

• **Musée Plantin-Moretus** Tel: 03.232.42.37 and 233.02.94. Open daily, except Monday, 10am–5pm.

Le musée Mayer-Van-der-Berghe is in a neo-Gothic house. Fritz Mayer Van der Berghe (1858–1910) assembled this collection of medieval sculptures, illuminated designs, ivories, tapestries and paintings. On the ground floor are 12th-century column-statues from the Notre-Dame-de-Vaux cloister at Châlons-sur-Marne), a painted wood altarpiece of Simeon and Machilos (13th century) from Spoleto, a triptych of Christ on the Cross by Quentin Metsys (15th century). On the first floor are Byzantine and Gothic ivories, a sculpture of Jesus and Saint Jean (around 1300) by Heinrik von Kontanz, a Dutch diptych, *Nativité et Saint Christophe* (1400) and the museum's pièce de résistance, *Margot l'enragée* by Bruegel the Elder, an apocalyptic vision of war, next to another Breugel, *les Douze Proverbes flamands*.

• **Musée Mayer Van der Bergh** Tel: 03.232.42.37. Open daily, except Monday, 10am–4.45pm.

Antwerp also boasts the **maison de Rubens**. The works of the painter (1577–1640) can be seen at various other sites in Antwerp, but the Rubens house, bought by the painter in 1610, is the best place to discover the Rubens personality and work. He came to Antwerp at the age of 12, and first studied under Verhaecht and Van Noort, before working in the studio of painter Otto Venius. After a sojourn in Italy, he returned to Antwerp in 1608 and so began an auspicious period when he associated Italian influences with Flemish traditions. He worked with or taught Jan Bruegel, called Bruegel de Velours, and the three Antwerp artists Jordaens, Van Dyck and Snyders. His body lies in the **church of Saint-Jacques** where one of his last paintings can be seen, *la Vierge et les Saints* (1634), in which the painter is seen in the armour of Saint George. Visitors to the house can see 17th-century furniture and paintings (among these a self-portrait); in the right wing, a raised area enabled visitors to watch artists at work. The house opens out on to a garden (17th century), re-modelled according to traditional garden design; busts of philosophers and depictions of mythological stories decorate the elevation of the studio overlooking the courtyard.

• **Maison de Rubens** Tel: 03.232.47.47. Open daily, except Monday, 10am–5pm.

La maison Rockox was the residence of Antwerp's first burgermeister (1560–1640), friend and collector of the work of Rubens. Now transformed into a museum, the house has remarkable furniture (ebony cabinets and display cases), ceramics, paintings (Jordaens, Van Dyck, Teniers le Jeune, Rubens, Momers, Snyders: *Marché aux poissons à Anvers*, Bruegel the Younger . . .)

• **Maison Rockox** Open daily, except Monday, 10am–5pm. Tel: 03.231.47.10.

Sited in a a large 19th-century building, **le musée royal des Beaux-Arts** has an extensive collection of Flemish paintings (including Primitives and Rubens). Most of the older paintings were collected, from 1442 onwards, by the Guild of Saint-Luc, one of whose directors was Rubens. To enumerate every painting would take far too long, so instead we mention a few: some by Jean Clouet, Lucas, Cranach *(Charité, Eve)*, Simone Martini *(l'Annonciation*, 15th century); the Flemish Primitives are represented by Van Eyck *(la Sainte-Barbe)*, Roger Van der Weyden *(Sept Sacraments* triptych), *le maître de Francfort* (portrait of the artist and his wife, 1496, the oldest painting from the Antwerp School), Memling *(Portrait d'homme, Christ entouré d'anges musiciens)*; then some 16th-century painters who combine Flemish Primitive and Italian style: Quentin Metsys, *Marie-Madeleine* and *l'ensevelissement du Christ* triptych (Christ's

entombment), Joachim Patinir's *la Fuite en Egypte*, Pourbus (portraits), copies or imitations of Brueghel de Velours, Martin de Vos . . . and ,of course, some Rubens, showing the evolution of his art: *le Baptême du Christ* (painted in Italy), *la Vénus refroidie* (inspired by the Vatican marble), *Christ à la paille* (realist style), *la Dernière Communion de Saint François* (in sorrowful mode), *l'Adoration des mages* painted in 1624 in bright colours, very expressive. Rubens' fellow artists are also here: Van Dyck (portraits, *Pietà*), Jordaens (family scenes: *le Concert de famille)* as well as animals and still lifes (Snyders) and a Rembrandt: *Portrait d'un prédicateur* (portrait of a preacher). The ground floor retraces the high points of Belgian artistic life since 1830, with James Ensor (from his earliest impressionist-inspired canvasses to his expressionist and morbid works like *Squelettes se disputant un pendu* (1891), Rik Wouters, the Laethem Saint-Martin artists (Permeke, the De Smet brothers, Van den Berghe, Servaes, Van de Woestijne . . .), the surrealists (Magritte, Delvaux) and the contemporary artists (Alechinsky).

• **Musée royal des Beaux-Arts** Tel: 03.238.78.09. Open daily, except Monday, 10am–5pm.

There is a great deal more to see in Antwerp itself, as well as the attractions of the town's outskirts. Of the town, we will limit ourselves to drawing attention to the **Bourse du commerce** (rebuilt in 1872), the **église Saint-Charles-Borromée** (beautiful baroque façade, built between 1615 and 1621, with marble ornamented choir), and the square in which it stands, **Henrick Conscience square**, the **church of Saint-Paul** (1639 in Flamboyant Gothic style, with Rubens' *Flagellation, l'Adoration des bergers* and *le Saint Sacrement*, the **musée d'art contemporain** (housed in a quayside grain silo beside the River Escaut), the open air **musée de sculpture**

Antwerp: the grand-place

Antwerp: Self-portrait *by Rubens (Maison de Rubens)*

As mentioned earlier, you can get to Holland or Zélande via the ferry crossing to Breskens. Or, alternatively, you can take the Anvers–Bergen-op-Zoom motorway. A few kilometres after crossing into the Netherlands, turn on to the motorway that links Bergen-op-Zoom to the towns of west Holland (Goes, Middelburg, Vlissingen . . .). Once thriving centres of international trade, these are now the sleepy towns of a polder region patiently won back from the sea. By contrast, to the north lie the great cities of Rotterdam, The Hague and Amsterdam, as busy and fascinating as ever. Amsterdam, the home of Rembrandt, the other 'Venice of the north' (like Bruges), is a town of both finance and culture. In the time of Louis XIV and William of Orange, this was the economic nerve centre of the world, the place for trading in coffee from Arabia, pepper from Borneo or corn from Danzig. Amsterdam may have lost some of its former splendour, but the region of European 'low country' that stretches from Dunkirk to Luxembourg and from Lille to The Hague, remains a bustling and fertile resource of economic and artistic wealth. Not forgetting, of course, the attractions of Delft, depicted in the works of its greatest painter, Vermeer; or Rotterdam where futuristic architecture and docks and cranes combine, or Holland's outlying towns, Breda, Utrecht, Bergen-op-Zoom . . .

The Netherlands' south-western province of Holland consists of five islands separated by narrow stretches of sea and joined to one another (or the mainland) by bridges and dykes that testify to the talent of the Dutch in their long and successful fight against the sea. Six further provinces to the south and north of these islands offer alternative routes to Holland.

• **Provinciale VVV Zeeland**, Postbus 123, 4330 Middelburg. Tel: 01180.33000. Contact tourist offices for hotel reservations.

en plein air (35-acre Middelheim park) with its 300 sculptures (Rodin, Calder, Henry Moore's *King and Queen*), the **musée provincial du diamant**, deep in the diamond quarter near the station (display explaining the characteristics and origins of this crystal formed 95 miles below the earth's surface at a temperature of 2,000°C).

The **jardin zoologique** is right next to the station and museum: over an area of 25 acres, various cages, enclosures and pavillions house some 5,000 species of animal, including some very rare ones like the white rhinoceros and the okapi. Shady lawns between the animal enclosures are populated by animal sculptures by Rembrandt Bugati. Nocturnal species can be viewed in the nocturama, reptiles thrive in a suitably tropical habitat. A planetarium, aquarium, dolphinarium and natural history museum complete the attractions of this zoo.

• **Jardin zoologique** Open daily 8.30am–6.30pm; 8.45am–4.45pm, winter. Tel: 03.231.16.40.

Close to Antwerp, in the shelter of a dune, lies the little village of **Doel** with its small harbour and a **windmill**; the *domaine provincial de Vrieselholf* (between Schilde and Olegem) offers both lovely walks and a **textile museum** (manufacturing techniques, traditional and contemporary textiles); the **réserve naturelle de Kalmthoutse** (nature reserve) and **arboretum Kalmthout** are 25km north of Antwerp, in the area known as the *Campine anversoise:* 1,800 acres of pine forest, bird-populated marshland, sand dunes and heathland . . . The **Kalmthout arboretum** (alongside the N111) was created in 1857 and offers particularly interesting walks (good walking shoes) for tree lovers: many rare species of trees and shrubs, conifers, magnolias, rhododendrons, roses . . .

ZEEUWSCH-VLAANDEREN
C-6

This strip of land between Belgian Flanders (from Antwerp to Knokke-le-Zoute) and the arm of the River Escaut (Westerschelde) stands between Antwerp and the North Sea. The only part of Holland province that is part of the mainland has little creeks and beaches along the length of the Escaut (Cadzand, Breskens, Braakman . . .) and fishing ports and sailing harbours at Terneuzen and Breskens. Countless little rural parishes inland offer country parks, windmills, lakes (Braakman, Oostburg, Axel . . .) and a network of cycle tracks for quietly discovering the charms of this landscape. From Zeeuwsch-Vlaanderen, you can get to Holland's northern islands via two ferry routes, from Breskens to Vlissingen or Perpolder to Kruiningen. And as you cross, enjoy watching the great steamers and tugs as they ply their way between Antwerp and the North Sea. Alternatively, take the Antwerp–Bergen-op-Zoom motorway and then the Bergen-op-Zoom–Middelburg link across Zuid-Beveland.

ZUID-BEVELAND
B-6

With the town of **Goes** (B6) at its centre, this region is the agricultural heart of Holland province where vast arable tracts alternate with extensive orchards (the apple and pear blossom in springtime is a stunning sight to behold). Zuid-Beveland is scattered with large farms and substantial farm buildings circled around with great poplars; the working buildings of the farms overshadow the much smaller proportions of the farmhouses that look like dolls' houses beside their great barns. You may see something of local traditional life: turning off the beaten track, be lucky enough to glimpse a local couple along the way, him in velvet or black cloth, wearing short trousers, heavy stockings, silver-buckled shoes, filigree-trimmed waistcoat,

brimmed felt hat up at the back and down at the front; and the woman in a little bodice top and skirt, bare-armed with a little shawl, and a lace-trimmed cap fastened at the temple with a gold clasp.

Goes itself has two pretty ports where big traditional wooden barges are moored (mostly 19th century). Visit the **Maria-Magdelena church** (15th century), the Netherlands' largest Gothic church, as well as the **town hall**.

Tourist information
3 Stationsplein
4461 Goes
Tel: 01100.20577
Hotels
Terminus ***
1 Stationsplein
Tel: 01100.30085
Bolsjoi
28 Grote-Markt
Tel: 01100.32323
Restaurant
Stadsschuur
32 Schuttersholf
Tel: 01100.13232

To the north of Goes, **Wolphaartsdijk** is perfect for watersports, riding and discovering the flora and fauna of the Veerse Meer.

Hotel
Hôtel Royal *
9 Lepelstraat
Tel: 01100.20577

A few kilometres east of Goes, the port of **Yerseke** (B6) is interesting for its boats and numerous mussel and oyster beds (some sunken, some flat), which earn Yerseke the title of world mussel capital. The village lies behind dykes beside the Oosterschelde (another branch of the River Escaut). Visitors are greeted at the entrance to the fishing port by a charming bronze fisherman carrying a basket of oysters. You can buy oysters, mussels, crabs, shrimps, etc at very reasonable prices from the fishermen's houses along the harbour. The rise and fall of the tides is particularly dramatic in this little port, a strong reminder of the ultimate power of the sea. Take time to watch the ballet of

the birds as they swoop for molluscs on the sand banks revealed by the ebb-tide. You can take a boat trip on the Oosterschelde (including half- or full-day fishing trips).

Tourist information
1 Kerkplein
4400 Yerseke
Tel: 01131.1864
Restaurant
Nolet
5 Burg-Sinkelaan
Tel: 01131.1642

WALCHEREN
(B5)

Walcheren lies to the west, off Zuid-Beveland, and has lovely beaches and wonderful 'dune mountains' overlooking the North Sea and the beaches of Domburg and Oostkapelle. Behind the town is a patchwork of arable and pasture land (sheep and cattle). Walcheren has several interesting old towns, including the sizeable military port and fishing/sailing harbour of **Vlissingen,** sited at the North Sea mouth of the Escaut. **L'Arsenal** features the area's cultural history and maritime inheritance, and makes an interesting and instructive visit for both children and adults (large shark and ray enclosure, reconstructions of shipwrecks, view over the Escaut and North Sea, play area . . .).

• **L'Arsenal** I Arsenalplein. Tel: 01184.15400. Open 1 April to 30 September daily 11am–10pm; rest of the year, except Monday, 11am–8pm.

Holland province's capital of **Middelburg** (B6) is in the centre of Walcheren and this very old town has nearly 1,100 historic monuments, including the **town hall** and the **monastery** (14th century) with audiovisual 'historama' show (9 Abdij, tel: 01180.16448. Open 1 March to 1 November daily 10am–6pm; Sunday noon–6pm). The **Miniatur Waalcheren** (miniature park) has typical old Waalcheren buildings. Close to Middelburg is the port of Arnemuiden, formerly a busy naval

Zuid-Beveland

construction yard, where ships from all over the world once moored, its streets once filled with the sounds of many languages. Silt and sand closed the port and halted its busy life; clues of its past are still visible as you walk around the old harbour.

Tourist information
65a Markt
4330 Middelburg
Tel: 01180.16851

Hotels
Arneville ★★★★
Tel: 01180.38456
Le Beau Rivage ★★★
Tel: 01180.38060

Restaurants
Bij de Abdij
Tel: 01180.35022
Valentin
Tel: 01184.16450
De Bourgondiër
Tel: 01184.13891

Don't leave Walcheren island without visiting the old town of **Veere**, north of Middelburg, former port on the Veerse Meer. This old port received the first Spanish cargoes of sugar from the Canaries; it was the residence of admirals and councillors from the Netherlands during the time of Charles Quint and Philippe II and was engaged in a commercial war with Antwerp and Amsterdam. Once a town that boasted sixty armed

ships, Veere today is a set period piece where every building is a reminder of the glory that was Holland – once the exclusive sea port and trading centre for Scottish wool and venue for the marriage of William of Orange and Charlotte of Bourbon on 21 June 1575. The pleasantest way of exploring the town is perhaps at sunset, strolling through its tiny narrow streets lined with equally tiny houses, and on to the pretty little fortified port and the central square: see **Onze Lieve Vrouwekerk** (the church), the **town hall**, the **Scottish houses**, **Campveerse Toren** beside the Veerse Meer – excellent hotel/restaurant and local café in the tower (surely the best view in Holland, as you sip '*een zeer oude jenever*').

Tourist information
28 Oudestraat
4350 Veere
Tel: 01181.1365

Hotel-restaurant-café
De Campveerse Toren ★★
Tel: 01181.1291

NOORD-BEVELAND
(B6)

From Veere it is an easy step to the next island to the north, **Noord-Beveland** (B6), via the dyke that shuts off the North Sea to the west of Veerse Meer. This

small farming island has a few small parishes offering a variety of leisure pursuits, water-based and otherwise: Kortgene, Colijnsplaats, Kamperland, Wissenkerke . . .

Noord-Beveland tourist information
37 Voorstraat
4491 Wisserkerke
Tel: 01107.1595

Hotels
De Kroon ★★
17 Voorstraat
Wissenkerke
Tel: 01107.1324
'T Veerse Meer ★★★
2 Weststraat
Kortgene
Tel: 01108.1869
Kamperduin ★★★
1 Patrijzenlaan
Kamperland
Tel: 01107.1466

SCHOUWEN-DUIVELAND
(B7)

There are two alternative itineraries to the island of Schouwen-Duiveland: via the bridge (5km) which joins Colijnsplaats to Zierikzee or, further west, along the North Sea coast via the famous Delta (10km). The Delta Plan (*see* p10) was conceived following the terrible floods of 1953 which claimed the lives of thousands (several million Dutch people live below sea level), with the intention of creating a protective barrier for the Dutch islands against the destructive forces of the North Sea (like the Ijsselmeer in the northern Netherlands). Halfway along this gigantic 'lock', going towards Schouwen-Duiveland, is the island of **Neeltje-Jans** where visitors can discover how the barrage works (boat trips from April to October) and visit the **Delta exhibition** in an old fishing boat.

• **Delta-Expo** Neeltje-Jans. Tel: 01115.2702. Open 1 April to 30 September daily 10am–5pm; the rest of the year, Wednesday and Sunday 10am–5pm. Special excursions, group visits and guided tours available by arrangement.

With its 10 miles of beaches, the island of Schouwen-Duiveland is ideal for watersports and family holidays, given, too, that the dunes and woodland behind the beaches. Some particularly well-known resorts are located on the western side of the island, facing the North Sea: Renesse, Burgh-Haamstede and Scharendijke (plenty of choice of accommodation: hotels, bungalows, campsites). The sea around the island is also ideal for windsurfing (particularly in the north at Grevelingenmeer) and for sailing at Scharendijke and Brouwershaven (formerly a brewery depot for Delft and Dordrecht, Brouwershaven was the home of the celebrated poet Jacob Cats) and at Bruinisse.

Hotels
At Burgh-Haamstede:
Hotel Haamstede ★★★
1 Hage-Zoom
Tel: 01115.1485
De Torenhoeve ★★★
38 Torenweg
Tel: 01115.3510
At Renesse:
Apollo Hôtel ★★★★
2–4 Laône
Tel: 01116.2500
Hôtel-Delta Renesse ★★★
5 Hoogenboomlaan
Tel: 01116.2510
Orangerie Hotel ★★★
5 Stoofwekken
Tel: 01116.1788

One place not to be missed on the island of Schouwen-Duiveland is **Zierikzee** (B6), with fine old fortifications, medieval gates and monuments: **Saint-Lievens Montertoren** (15th-century church with 230-ft tower), **Noorhavenpoort** (northern gate of the 16th-century port), **Zuidhavenpoort** (southern gate of the 15th-century port, flanked by four elegant towers and a drawbridge), **Nobelpoort** (ancient gate topped with elongated pepper-pot tower), the **town hall** with bell tower (combined Chinese, Japanese, Byzantine and Muscovite style, topped with a Neptune weather-vane. The town also has a little **history museum**, a **fishing harbour** and picturesque **marina**, plus lots of shops (antiques) making

it northern Holland's principal town. Also try to take in Dreishchor (5km north-east of Zierikzee), an exceptionally lovely old town with **moat-ringed medieval church**.

Tourist information
29 Havenpark
4301 Zierikzee
Tel: 01110.12450
Hotels
Mondragon ★★★
21 Havenpark
Tel: 01110.13051
Huis van Nassau
2 Lange Nobelstraat
Tel: 01110.12012
Restaurant
Auberge maritime
Tel: 01110.12156

Complete your tour of Holland with a visit to the island of **Tholen** (B7), in eastern Holland. Today, Tholen is linked to the mainland by a series of bridges and dykes. Dykes and polders form a natural mosaic where the long-established traditions of horticulture and seed production continue. There are fishing trips from the port of Tholen (day trips) on the Oosterschelde or, alternatively, fish from the dykes to the south. The island has several villages, among them **Sint-Annaland** (local history museum, fishing harbour and marina, eel smoke-house), **Stavenisse** (charming little port at the foot of the old town windmill), **Sint-**

Maartensdijk (watersports centre). But the town of **Tholen** is the most memorable; some beautiful buildings have survived (Renaissance town hall, 13th-century church, windmill), as well as the harbour, marina and shops. A **nature reserve** visited by hundreds of bird species stretches out to the south of the little village of **Speelmansplaten**.

Tourist information
10 Haven
4695 Tholen
Tel: 01666.3771
Hotel
Hof van Holland ★
1 Kaay
Tel: 016660.2590
Nearby
De Gouden Leeuw ★★★
50 Voorstraat
Sint-Annaland
Tel: 01665.2305
De Gouden Leeuw ★★
8–10 Hoge-Market
Scherpenisse
Tel: 01666.3901

Walcheren beach looking towards Domburg

EDITORIAL CREDITS

Philippe Demoulin: Touring South-East England, pages 45–99.

Monique Teneur-Van Daele provided information on northern French towns and villages.

Martine Le Blan provided historical and geographical information.

Pascaline Dron and **Marie-Hélène Lavallée** provided information on museums.

INDEX OF
PLACE NAMES

(English place names in italics)